Driving with strangers

To Martyn

Thanking you for providing valuable support in the final stages of this long venture -

May your own travels be enriching and inspiring.

Jonathan Purkis

MANCHESTER
1824

Manchester University Press

For Bar, Murray and Chayley

and in memory of Patricia and Harry Purkis

Driving with strangers

What hitchhiking tells us about humanity

Jonathan Purkis

Manchester University Press

The right of Jonathan Purkis to be identified as the author of this work has been asserted by them in accordance with the Copyright, Designs and Patents Act 1988.

The author is grateful for quotations from copyrighted musical material:
'Barstow…' lyrics, courtesy of the Harry Partch Estate, Danlee Mitchell, Executor.
The Levellers, 'Battle of the Beanfield', courtesy of Universal Music.
Czerwono-Czarni,'Jedziemy autostopem', courtesy of Mirek Wojcik.
James Bar Bowen, 'She is', courtesy of the artist.
'The hitchhiker's song', courtesy of Shelley Segal/True Music.
Gary Snyder, excerpts from 'Night Highway 99' from *Mountains and Rivers Without End*. Copyright © 1996, 2013 by Gary Snyder. Reprinted with the permission of The Permissions Company, LLC on behalf of Counterpoint Press, counterpointpress.com.

Published by Manchester University Press
Altrincham Street, Manchester M1 7JA

www.manchesteruniversitypress.co.uk

British Library Cataloguing-in-Publication Data
A catalogue record for this book is available from the British Library

ISBN 978 1 5261 6004 1 hardback

First published 2021

The publisher has no responsibility for the persistence or accuracy of URLs for any external or third-party internet websites referred to in this book, and does not guarantee that any content on such websites is, or will remain, accurate or appropriate.

Typeset in Baskerville and Avenir
by R. J. Footring Ltd, Derby, UK
Printed in Great Britain
by Bell & Bain Ltd

Contents

Figures

In June 1959 a friend and I, two impoverished student midwives in London, had a rare weekend off. How to use it? We each had £1! Barbara was an experienced hitchhiker while I was a novice, and she suggested we go to Rye. We took a bus to take us out of the City and began to hitch. We got a lift almost immediately from two young men, one smoking a pipe. They were running in the brand new Anglia, just driven out of the showroom. I was unaware of the hitchhiking code (always leave a lift when it stops) and accepted an offer for tea in a teashop much to Barbara's horror. The outcome was that I exchanged phone numbers with the pipe smoker, got engaged six weeks later and married six months later, February 1960. We had four children and now have eleven grandchildren! I never hitched again – I now had an Anglia! – but I frequently gave lifts.

Cora Brockwell – personal email, England, June 2009

There is a day not too far distant now when a few of those who first saw another country from the gutter will be sitting in the driving seat. Politics and diplomacy should take new courses when the one-time hitch-hikers accede to power … [for they have] a view of a landscape or a people which although often disjointed and random comes nearer to understanding how a country works and what its people really think.

Ian Rodger – *A hitch in time*, 1966

And you, capricious road, now smiling, now incensed, how are we to detect the moment when your mood changes? You are life, and destiny, the unique instance of all possible combinations. Right here, right now, with this person, and we know no alternative.

Irina Bogatyreva – *Off the beaten track*, 2012

Prologue: a 'romantic and gallant and even brilliant adventure'

The road from Carlisle

I was seventeen years old when I first realised that hitchhiking could change the world. It's a feeling which hasn't waned with age or nostalgia, but has intensified into the belief that hitchhiking still has a part to play in alleviating many ongoing social, economic and ecological problems in the world. It's doing all of those things right at this moment, although you'd be forgiven for thinking that it vanished decades ago and is now something people do only in horror movies.

Hitchhiking is a global phenomenon, ebbing and flowing in popularity across all seven continents (yes, even Antarctica[1]), providing solutions to simple daily local difficulties and society-wide ones alike. It is a benchmark of how we trust each other and evolve social systems based on compassion and mutual aid. For many, it offers the strongest sensation of personal freedom they will ever experience and some will be compelled to write songs, novels, poems or memoirs about it; for others, it is as mundane as getting the kids to school or themselves to work. Yet, after more than a century of hitchhiking, the motor age which has defined it (see Chapter 1) is now in need of a comprehensive rethink, as most of the political ideas and economic systems which have fuelled it are spent and have been exposed as being incapable of responding to the global ecological crisis. Now we need fresh eyes and insights, and a lot of courage and communication, to begin to imagine a transport system that truly befits a more sustainable world. In these pages I'm going to introduce you to what hitchhikers have been saying for over eleven decades, about the people whom they meet and how life could be organised a little differently on the basis of those experiences. I'm not going to ask you to pick anyone up, or hit the road yourself, but I hope that you might begin to 'think like a hitchhiker' by the end of the book. And who can tell where that might lead?

On a hot Sunday afternoon in the summer of 1982, these notions were a long way from my mind, and my failure to read the northern English rural bus timetables properly and ask the right questions to the few staff on hand in the Carlisle terminus was a little more preoccupying. When I was finally confronted with the reality of having missed the last bus, my immediate response was 'I suppose that I will have to hitchhike then', almost as if I'd foreseen doing so, rather than it being the only available way of crossing the fifty miles to Grasmere in the English Lake District before nightfall. Yet those first five lifts, secured once I had walked clear of the urban sprawl to where the rolling fields merged into the heat haze – the friendly bemused farmer, the family holidaying in their cramped Citroen 2CV, the London-bound hill walker who took me only a mile, the two left-wing teachers with whom I talked about the English Revolution, the second, more subdued farmer in the rattling Land Rover – marked a moment of personal revelation. The buzz that I felt getting out of that final lift, gazing around me as the early evening sun illuminated the rich shades of green and brown of the mountains, was incredible. I knew that I had gained something other than a free safe passage, but the feelings were impressionistic, intuitive and hard to rationalise. As I jabbered excitedly down the telephone to my fortunately understanding parents, I felt the first stirrings of the feeling that what I had done was important on some grander scale, but I didn't have the words to describe it.

At that point I didn't know how hitchhiking had already changed societies: uniting populations in many situations of wartime fuel scarcity and social need, fostering political and countercultural identities in Eastern Bloc and former Soviet Union countries such as Poland, Czechoslovakia and Russia, as much as it had in the West. And I didn't know how long it had been associated with more responsible forms of tourism. Neither did I realise that for many developing nations, hitchhiking was not a matter of lifestyle choice or youthful rebellion: it was everyday reality, which shaped mobility in myriad mundane ways. However, I had known what to do, where to stand, how to talk to people, and it had felt so straightforward, so natural even.

Hitchhiking is one aspect of a long history of transport mutual aid and each generation which has found itself perched on the asphalt edge has had different reasons for doing so than the previous one. It can sometimes be a moment of cultural inspiration – a book or a blog – but usually the reasons are linked to a wider context. I did have some small brushes with hitchhiking-related culture in those years, in the form of Douglas Adams's surreal science fiction comedy *The hitchhiker's guide to the galaxy* and later Roger Waters's odd record/poem *The pros and cons of hitchhiking*, but neither of these are usually on hitchers' lists of motivational texts for getting out there on the road. I'd watched my parents pick up a few bedraggled hitchers in the Highlands and Islands of Scotland whilst on family holidays and felt a little excited by these strangers clambering into our lives, but there was never much discussion about it. The BBC may have blitzed my generation with public information films about 'stranger danger' (as in the 'Charley Says' series) but I suspect that the wider campaigning Quaker philanthropy of my parents somehow didn't make me too inward looking. In fact, their generation was crucial for providing the continuity of the 'folk memory' of hitchhiking through the middle decades of the twentieth century: being well placed to recall growing up when hitchhiking was a practical part of life in the Second World War and the era of petrol rationing; then seeing it redefined as part of the adventurous spirit of young people wanting more connection with the 'new' more cosmopolitan Europe of the 1950s and 1960s or wanting to take the 'Hippie Trail' to India. So, when my own generation set out amidst the cultural backlashes of the 1980s and there were dwindling numbers on the slip roads, there were plenty of folks with a broader sense of history and their own roadside debts to repay.

Underpinning those feelings of personal revelation on that sleepy Sunday was the sense that I had been admitted into a secret club guarding an 'amazing truth' about humanity which precious few knew about. Hindsight, plus an academic training, may have allowed me to find a vocabulary to explain the role of hitchhiking within different societies, but I am still staggered by the disproportionate propaganda against it. What I do know is that the desire to control independent mobility is part of a narrative that is millennia old – a dialectical relationship between sedentary and migratory instincts, and invariably a matter of resources or ideology. Yet it need not be forever. In the years since that first hitchhike, I've learned to situate and understand my 'amazing truth' less in terms of good fortune and my individual skills, but as part of a vision of our own social evolution within a more cooperative reality.

I think of this book as a 'vagabond sociology'. Each chapter raises a theme relevant to the history and experience of hitchhiking, presented through the eyes of travellers by the roadside. These are woven into a conceptual tapestry which presents tough questions about humanity at a time of ecological crisis. How free are we in our lives? How much should we trust one another? Why do we exclude or, alternatively, eulogise certain groups of travellers? Where do the dangers really lie in our societies? Can we organise how we live and move around more equally, ecologically and safely? The stranger by the roadside may be an archetype and, in the motor age, one frequently filled with negative connotations, but we can choose to alter our viewpoint, to look more benignly at one another and in ways which facilitate a more positive vision of how we might live and move.

In search of our better selves

Making the decision to hitchhike takes courage. Even in hitcher-friendly parts of the world such as Lithuania, Ireland or New Zealand, it is a vulnerable moment when you first stretch your arm out into the road. You're part of a very small percentage of the travelling population, offering to exchange miles for company, in often alienating surroundings which require awareness and constant adaptability.

Few transport experiences involve being repeatedly catapulted into other people's lives with such intensity. All of those aspirations, assumptions and anxieties unfolding in a fast-moving metal box isolated from other people, based on nothing more than an informal contract of mutual trust negotiated in a matter of seconds! Doing this once, let alone several times a day, to get somewhere, is too overwhelming for many to contemplate, unless compelled to do so. Modern mobility also rarely requires such a rich combination of practical orientation and social skills: accurate but adaptable route planning and navigation, weather forecasting, personal safety awareness and an ability to listen carefully to what is being said or is left hanging in the silences. Some psychological studies of the 'personality types' of long-distance hitchhikers point to a propensity for risk taking, adventure and spontaneity, but also a strong interest in other people and high levels of interpersonal empathy of the sort often found in the counselling professions.

Can any of this be taught? If you are a member of a hitchhiking club in Russia or Lithuania there is an expectation that one will attend some training classes, and even log hours spent on the road – all valuable experience if you are planning to engage in some 'sports hitchhiking' (i.e. racing for fun) or to take part in an expedition organised by the Academy of Free Travel (generally known by its Russian acronym AVP), where one may be exposed to gruelling weather in remote places. You may be encouraged to wear the fluorescent professional hitchhiking suit designed by Alexej Vorov, the founder of the St Petersburg Autostop League, and to dip into Anton Krotov's best-selling *A practical guidebook for free travellers*, which will advise on some in-car conversational gambits. In these clubs, hitchhikers are seen as ambassadors as well as adventurers, so the pressure to present your travel 'findings' to fellow members on return from an expedition may be considerable.

The road as educator can be dated back to Lao Tzu's aphorism on the means of a journey being more important than its ends.[2] The notion of pilgrimage certainly embodied this, whether to sites of spiritual significance or through the more secular 'Grand Tour' during the Victorian era. Here, the British upper middle classes encouraged their offspring to visit sites of cultural enrichment in Paris, Venice, Rome and Athens as an educational 'rite of passage', prior to them taking their 'place' in society. Less elitist forms of travel as education, all featuring hitchhiking, can be seen throughout the twentieth century: the 'wild tourism' of 1930s Russia, the Social Autostop voucher (or coupon) system encouraged by the Polish government between 1957 and 1995, the Canadian approach to youth culture during the 1970s (Pierre) Trudeau administration. Each was a relatively successful attempt to utilise hitchhiking as a means to engender a new national mood or resolve a temporary economic problem. The Polish system – which registered both hitchhikers and the drivers – is often cited as being the most transferable model, as it offered financial incentives for the drivers to cash in vouchers handed to them by the hitchers.

Travel as community

Official endorsements of hitchhiking are rare indeed: mostly they have been confined to the role of 'civic duty' during wartime, or in fuel crises such as those which Cuba faced in 1990 with the cessation of the supplies from the Soviet Union and its need for speedy adaptations in transport and agriculture. We often mythologise these moments when it is politically expedient to do so, whilst forgetting that they depend upon a pre-existing spirit of cooperation within the society, beyond any government decree. Our 'better selves' thrive in such circumstances, so it is probably no coincidence that one of the world's largest hitchhiking clubs – Argentina Autostop – was formed shortly after the country's economic implosion in 2000, when people distributed food and medicines themselves, devised complex 'barter' systems, took over factories and held regular public assemblies. For club founder Juan Villarino, a man the *New York Times* recently dubbed 'the world's best hitchhiker', these things are all connected, and it is a question of looking to the ability of people to help one another wherever one finds it.[3] He should know: in 2006, Juan decided to hitch across the entire Islamic world to prove that people are always welcoming; that other people's wars and political games do not erode our cooperative natures; that 'the universe will take care of you', if one embraces this as a travel philosophy.

Many more of the world's best hitchhikers will echo these sentiments in the forthcoming pages; they seek to actively nurture cooperation in others as opposed to just looking for it when they are in crisis. We've all become a little too individualistic about the practicalities of mobility, revering our personal freedom until we find it stalled in a city-centre gridlock saturated with nitrogen dioxide. This is not by accident. Since the coming of the low-cost 'democratic' Model T Ford, city planners and advertisers have shaped our realities, sometimes buying out the opposition – such as street cars or trolley buses – but very clearly selling the seductive narratives of escape, speed, sexual prowess and rebellion. As the poet Heathcote Williams famously noted in his visual deconstruction of the motor age *Autogeddon*, any alien visitor to the Earth might be forgiven for thinking that 'cars were the dominant life-form and that human beings were a kind of ambulatory fuel cell injected when the car wanted to move off and ejected when they were spent'.[4]

Climate breakdown and the shift away from fossil fuels provide an opportunity to think about where we are going more generally as a species. Cities are being revisualised to revolve around people and green spaces. We have to travel less, share the road more and do it smarter and in more community-minded ways. In some countries, the proportion of sixteen- to twenty-five-year-olds taking driving tests and buying cars is falling; the generation of Greta Thunberg seems mindful of the link between looking after the planet and keeping our mental well-being in order. 'Slow travel' is now an accepted part of staying sane, as is finding innovative ways of maximising the 'dead time' of commuting to benefit those around us. According to the geographer John Adams, there is a disproportionate connection between how far one commutes and the actual investment one has in a community, a reminder perhaps that we are thinking about this the wrong way: travel has to be a form of community, one which benefits us collectively and reflects our strongest values.[5]

Consumer societies have dulled how we visualise mobility. The COVID-19 global pandemic has sharpened all of this again, underscoring the questions about why we travel and what it is we are looking to find when we get there (unless it is just the daily commute or a mundane trip to the shops). The inequities of who is most damaged by the consequences of the motor age and its ideology of 'I drive therefore I am' have been spelled out for us in the correlation between those social and ethnic groups most affected by the coronavirus and in the fact that they live in urban areas closest to heavy industry and busy traffic corridors. It's also made us a little humbler in terms of our assumptions about freedom being linked to our entitlement to go wherever we want regardless of the costs. From our lockdown isolations we have begun to reassess our notions of community as well as the value of nature, something which offers huge opportunities for remaking our world to be more about people and less about things. In less developed parts of the world, travel as community is much more obvious and not just a poor person's burden; queuing at the local hitchhiking point becomes part of one's social routine. Sometimes even where there is public transport collective needs may outweigh individual ones, as in the case of the Turkish 'Dolbus', which sets off only when full.

So, in these pages, hitchhiking offers a way in to look at these globally important issues, now that we know our own survival is at stake if we continue on the path we are currently on. Changing course starts with the simplest of actions – focusing on the act and sensations of moving in the world – and one doesn't have to be hitchhiking to do that. But the act of waiting whilst travelling is a familiar one and this reminds us of some of the social benefits of mobility. We can all recall the moments when circumstances pitched us into each other's company at a train delay, when a road was blocked, or when we were forced to spend a night in an airport or ferry terminal. It is the random sharing of conversation, the impromptu musical performance, or the pooling of food and drink which lingers far longer than the irritation of a journey delayed. When we have to slow down, pause and savour the time and space which we are passing through; the more empathic parts of our brain wake up, temporarily freed from our more cynical views of each other.

Working those hitchhiking angels

All conversations about hitchhiking dovetail with those on human nature. It is why road memoirs are stuffed full of encouraging aphorisms, such as: 'trust everyone and you will occasionally get robbed; trust no one and you will live surrounded by thieves'. Those who have experienced the disparities between the perception and realities of the roadside feel a responsibility to share their own epiphanies about human nature. Too often we seem constrained by a 'Hobbesian' view of human societies: that they are always teetering on the brink of social collapse, with any actions not sanctioned by the State doomed to failure on account of everyone's selfish and murderous intentions. Hitchhiking sits very much in this framework, allegedly more of a dangerous sport than a mode of transport – a conceit that only an economic crisis seems to ameliorate.

Let's be clear: hitchhiking is a risky activity in any era. Terrible things have happened to hitchhikers, in peacetime, in countries regarded as pretty 'safe' and to massively experienced travellers. However rare these events have been, or statistically improbable if measured against other risks, they remain disproportionately represented in the public imagination. There is a long history of portraying the road as a terrifying place for respectable travellers, occupied by the diseased, the criminal, the vagrant or gangs of lawless youths. Overly focusing on these 'stranger danger' narratives – or the victim blaming of individual hitchhikers – deflects our attention away from the real systemic violence of a society caused by inequality, misogyny and alienation.

For all of the propaganda against hitchhiking, it is comforting to know that early representations get off to a relatively good, even beautiful, start. On 19 September 1923, the American newspaper *The Nation* included a piece penned by a regular correspondent, 'The Drifter', in which he detailed the cross-country intentions of three 'New York girls' whom he met whilst out for a drive on the back roads of rural Vermont. He described them as: 'dusty Valkyries in gray knickers and sweaters and thick stockings, stout-booted, with small gay caps, knapsacks and cameras slung over shoulders shapely even under the rough, knitted stuff'.

> One of them was communicative. 'If our luck holds we'll be hitching into Montreal tonight in time to catch a ferry for Quebec. No, we don't often sleep at inns. Usually there's a Y where we can stop nights. There are thousands of us, of course. Hitch-hiking is always done by twos and threes. We know girls who have hitched all the way to California. There's little trouble and most motorists are pretty good to us. It's a great way of seeing the country.'[6]

Inspired by their exuberant initiative to see the world and meet people this way, the Drifter (whose real identity is lost to history), dubbed it a 'romantic and gallant and even brilliant adventure', contrasting it to the comfortable predictability of motoring in the modern world. It's a lovely phrase, befitting of a way of thinking of transport as always aspiring to celebrate the best of us – a glass half full of the spirit of cooperation. My aim in these pages will be to evoke that spirit, as a riposte to the Hobbesian view of humanity; to unashamedly channel that emotional pulse of the Enlightenment – Romanticism – in its engaging mix of (proto)environmentalism, political liberty and empathy. For it, too, championed a view from the margins.

The lens was a ground-breaking collection of empathetic poetry penned by Wordsworth and Coleridge after a walking tour of the Quantock Hills. The *Lyrical ballads* seems harmless enough now, just a series of observations about ordinary country folk, describing their situation and aspirations, but they were written at the time when Britain had an eye on the French Revolution across the Channel. The poems, initially published under pseudonyms, could not be regarded as political philosophy akin to that of Rousseau or Godwin, but they had a way of looking unique to the time. To varying degrees, the Romantics all explored the individual as energised by liminal spaces and believed that in these unmediated authentic experiences, a new understanding of the world could emerge.

Many hitchhiking memoirs adopt this same pattern of personal revelation (a 'road to Grasmere' moment!) as they redress their assumptions about the world. It starts with the realisation that the fears of their peers – 'don't get your throat cut'– are quickly quashed by the reality of the kindness of strangers on the road. 'If all rides are like this, I'm converted', gushes twenty-three-year-old American Sharon Stine in *Gypsy boots*, as she communicates by hand signals and smiles over a paid-for coffee during her very first lift in the Netherlands in 1958.[7] So begins one of the best accounts of international travel by an independent-minded woman, who observes how her 'amazing truth' played out across many countries still recovering from the Second World War; the freeze of East–West relations could be thawed through meeting real people from 'enemy' countries in youth hostels and cafes and heading out of town together. Ian Rodger's *A hitch in time* does the same, offering us a hopeful vision of a new world as he shares food and advice with other national 'representatives' who have gathered at the Fontainebleau Obelisk outside Paris in 1951 to thumb south to the Mediterranean or Italy and wonder about the world which they have inherited.

All of life in a grain of asphalt

What a century of hitchhiking memoirs tell us is that the roadside is as good as any other place to begin a debate about the world we inhabit. It is a living laboratory of our best and worst selves, our most empathetic and our most draconian societies. The memoirs and road blogs, all of the representations in song, film, art, photography and advertising: all primary evidence of how we regard those on the margins, how we come to judge or make policy around them, be inspired or moved by their endeavours, suffering or artistry.

My own hitchhiking may not have counted for much in terms of variety or distances (approximately 40,000 miles, all within the United Kingdom, mainly over fifteen years), but I observed tensions, conflicts, income and social disparities within my own society which I simply would have not seen otherwise. It was nothing on the scale of what Jacob Holdt – who coined the term 'vagabond sociology'– witnessed in his five years of thumbing around the poorest parts of the USA in the 1970s. His account of that journey, *American pictures*, is still shocking today, because we realise that in many of these places, similar degrees of racism, social exclusion and disenfranchise-ment continue. Most humbling is the fact that those with the least to give seem most willing to help him, something which leads him to the maxim that there is nothing more 'secure' in the world than 'being on the road with no money'.[8]

The Russians have a word for it: *halyava*. If there is such a thing as a hitchhiking philosophy, then this is it: that the kerbside offers one access to a different reality, where lifts and conversation are part of a 'gift economy' measured in the value of experience rather than monetary exchange. Anton Krotov talks about the social adventure of 'opening a country' to unearth the cooperative nature of its people, as if it were a hidden treasure beneath the formal economic and administrative strata.[9] It is an observation straight out of the early-twentieth-century writings of socialist anthropologist Marcel Mauss, who realised that what bound together the Polynesian societies he was studying were trading systems saturated with social obligations and meanings far more sophisticated than the soulless methods of capitalist use and exchange value.[10] His book *The gift* has enjoyed a renaissance amongst environmental activists rethinking the destructive logic of growth economies on a finite planet. It is something which the Russian hitchhiking community, who have internalised a less individualistic attitude towards sharing the road, instinctively embrace.

The world capital of hitchhiking today may well be one of Russia's principal cities, but folks from Lithuania, Latvia, Germany or Poland might want to rotate the award; one thing is clear, the days of London, Paris, Athens, Toronto or San Francisco being the place to be have long gone. The former communist world is now a key player in the global network of hitchhiker gatherings, races, conferences and 'outreach work', details of which are channelled through Hitchwiki.org, currently the primary portal for 'road dogs'. These digital developments now place hitchhiking at a unique juncture – where travellers of any country can access road data on their journey, whilst doing it, can guarantee themselves a degree of electronic insurance against danger, and are able to absorb something of the history of lift giving. Watching a YouTube clip of members of the Vilnius Hitchhiking Club setting off on a recent race, I was reminded of a phrase which the historian Mark Keck-Szjabel used to describe the optimism of the generation who made the Polish Auto Stop work in the 1960s and 1970s – as if it were 'a river of young people bubbling with joy'.[11] Through their eyes one witnessed a certain *Zeitgeist*, a distilling of the hopes for a more cooperative future; of seeing that how we travel is more than just a metaphor for where we are going as a species, but also of how we approach life in general. Especially if we talk to strangers a bit more.

A lift to a better future

Anonymity is a powerful social drug. Studies show that a satisfying conversation with a stranger generates more serotonin than one with someone we know. Anonymity is one of the reasons why human societies create confessional spaces in which to work through the complexities and anxieties of being alive: they are blank slates of personal liberation and collective catharsis. Anyone who has hitchhiked will remember hearing the words 'I have never told anyone this before' and probably be able to recall the circumstances in which they were uttered. When I think back over the 1,304 lifts which followed those initial five, what distinguishes the really memorable ones was when drivers had something they wanted to share. Sure, there were the quirky lifts which fulfilled other needs: the lovely guy who wanted me to join his religious commune, the midnight poachers who talked about vegetarian cooking rather than where they were going, the spiritualist with a clutch of tall tales about the supernatural who was adamant he could read my mind (though I had to tell him when I wanted to get out) or the yuppie driving my only Porsche, who stopped because he'd seen the notorious horror film *The hitcher* and 'wanted to see what you were like'! But then there were people like Pete.

He picked us up north of Birmingham with shadows lengthening and our destination hours away. It was June 1995 and my partner and I were en route from West Yorkshire to see my sister in Cardiff. It was the weekend of the Glastonbury Festival, a time of the year when the motorway slip roads and country lanes of England are once again alive with hitchhikers. We'd opted for a quiet junction of the M6 and had neither competition nor much driver interest for about half an hour. Pete was driving a minibus which on weekdays transported clients of a charity for people with a disability. Initially shy as to his motives for giving the lift, once he'd sized us up and we'd played our destination card, he announced that he would take us the whole distance (100 miles out of his way). We were humbled and a bit overwhelmed. Then the story came out, gently and without too much anger. Pete had been at a family function in a salubrious restaurant, when unexpectedly people had made upsetting comments about his own disability (a harelip). Caught off guard and shocked by what we imagined was a sense of betrayal, Pete had made an early exit.

Rather than bristling with rage down the motorway on his own, his first action had been one of mutual aid – trying to reach out of his world into someone else's with compassion. It felt such an enormous gesture that the reciprocity of our company, a few cups of tea in Cardiff and beer to take home just didn't seem enough. Yet, for those who reflect upon their hitchhiking 'careers', it is often encounters with the likes of Pete which remain, to take out into the world as we try to be true to our better selves and the projects which we might establish with them. Too often we just don't hear these stories, let alone allow them to be the basis of our understanding of the world.

So, get yourself ready, because what follows is the route into a bigger story than my own limited roadside ramblings. I am hoping that you have got a map to hand, maybe an extra layer of clothing in case it gets a little late or cold, as we head off back down those roads and rail tracks and waterways in search of that elusive historical figure – the very first hitchhiker.

Chapter 1

The intention of a tradition: definitions of hitchhiking

The Lincoln Highway

At 6.30 p.m. on 11 October 1916, a young student alighted from an automobile on Waverly Place, New York City, having completed an 800-mile odyssey by a *modus operandi* that a week before was unknown either to him or the twentieth century. Few people noticed him: just another figure in the gathering dusk hurrying home from a day's work, but there was a lightness in his gait and his mind was awhirl with ideas. That evening, and in the days to come, he would look at people more carefully than he had done when he was last in the city; and he would smile, as though he had made a discovery of the most profound importance. Eventually, he bumped into a publishing contact who worked for the *New York World Journal*, to whom he recounted an extraordinary tale.

It had begun in the freight yards of Fort Wayne, Indiana, as his university summer holiday was drawing to a close. Sitting watching the long goods trains departing, he had contemplated whether he should smuggle himself on board one of them on account of his depleted finances. Then he noticed a 'big touring car with a large and comfortable seat in the rear' on the road parallel to the tracks and a moment of 'inspiration' came: how he could 'start at any point on the Lincoln Highway and get through to New York City within a comparatively short time by riding in different automobiles', deducing that 'people would enjoy giving him rides'. The young man considered his current appearance and attire and decided to spend most of his last $4.50 on a haircut and shave, a new shirt and some shoe polish. He then asked a policeman for directions, got on to East Main Street and headed out to where he could pick up the Lincoln Highway at the city limits. Straightening his newly brushed hat, he saw his 'first chance coming down the highway' driven by 'a huge bulk of a man with tortoise-shell spectacles and coarse black whiskers'. The young man stepped into the road, locked eyes with the driver and threw up his hands 'as a signal to stop'.

'Are you going down the Lincoln Highway?'
  'Yes, down a piece' he replied, stopping his car.
  'May I ride with you until you turn off?'
  'Where are you going?'
  I moved closer to the car, which was one of those democratic Fords.
  'New York City.'
  His face registered interest as he swung open the door nearest to me. We struck out into the rural section. He was a physician, rushing to a girl patient whose condition had changed for the worse.[1]

The novelty of the young man's method of travel was so engrossing to the doctor that he overshot his destination by ten miles. Many of the twenty-seven subsequent drivers over the following week were equally fascinated, with one, a music agent, requiring a short evening lecture on the subject to help him sell his wares. At other points in the journey, he helped with navigational duties and basic car maintenance, groomed horses and husked corn. Sleeping in barns and above shops, he met teachers, priests, publishers, farmers and bakers, none of whom were in so much of a hurry that they would not stop. The scenery shifted from endless yellow cornfield plains to

the Sunday, November 12, 1916 edition
of the New York World Journal

The First American Hitch-hiker

CHARLES BROWN JR, is the originator
of automobile panhandling, the newest game for brake beam tourists.

(well, you'd look a little strange, too, after being buried 88 years!)

Figure 1.1 'People would enjoy giving him rides'. Charles Brown Jr's 800-mile journey between Fort Wayne and New York City in October 1916 might be considered the start of 'intentional hitchhiking' in the motor age.

rich autumnal woodlands and then the rolling Pennsylvanian mountains rumoured to be inhabited by lawless 'moonshiners' brewing illegal spirits. He had a moment of doubt about being mistaken for a government inspector if caught on the open road, although his caution didn't stop him nervously joking about being a 'Lincoln highwayman' to an elderly farming couple (who promptly booted him out). Once in New York, he mused that one day he may be motivated to buy and maintain sections of what is now Highway 30, to a better standard of repair.

The enterprising young student was called Charles Brown Jr, and the article largely by him which appeared in the *New York World Journal* on Sunday 12 November 1916 was entitled 'Vagabonding by motor-car', with a by-line that he was 'the originator of automobile panhandling, the newest game for brake beam tourists' (Figure 1.1).[2] Or, alternatively: our first hitchhiker!

It was a fair claim. The most detailed piece of newspaper archive work – John Schlebecker's 'An informal history of hitchhiking' (1958) – offers no concrete examples prior to 1920, but this could be a matter of search terms. The reason why the journey of Charles Brown Jr in 1916 eluded scholars for so long may simply be down to the absence of the word 'hitch' in any documentation, yet what makes a hitched lift 'hitched' remains important for our discussion.

For American road veteran Irv Thomas (Figure 1.2), who unearthed Brown's story in 2004, the journey described in 'Vagabonding by motor-car'

Figure 1.2 Sixty years a-thumbing: Irv Thomas, icon of the digihitch.com generation and discoverer of Charles Brown Jr.

was characterised by an 'intentionality' of purpose: one unique to the new urban culture of the automobile and its potential for crossing bigger distances. In his view, the transition from a world where one might ramble along in the tradition of the itinerant farm worker – accepting short rides on horse-drawn vehicles – required a different way of thinking about the organisation of the journey itself. Charles Brown Jr's moment of inspiration was to recognise that a new set of communication skills could be utilised by the roadside traveller, based on both the willingness to share something with a complete stranger and on the signalling of one's intentions from a distance.

How one pursued this – by thumb, written sign, waved hand or pointed finger – would alter over the decades and also depended on country and custom, but in Irv Thomas's mind, what came next was critical: the act of negotiating one's passage with the offer of practical help, an aspect of transport history which may have predated the wheel itself. Instead of offering to cook or clean on board a ship, or to help mind the horses or wagons on a trade or postal route, a twentieth-century hitchhiker ventures an exchange of company and conversation for highway miles. On multiple-day road trips – as with long sea voyages – other duties may be required of a traveller, something which Charles Brown Jr took so easily into his stride.

Such a longitudinal approach to a definition of hitchhiking centred on mutual aid cuts both ways: on the one hand, it is possible to embrace a more warm-hearted view of how people organise themselves outwith the formal channels of power and commerce; on the other hand, we end up with too many speculative 'first hitchhiker' claims, which might include mythical nautical figures such as Sinbad the Sailor, Odysseus or Jonah (as in the Whale), as sometimes are made![3] More realistically, if one was trying to negotiate for a ride – on a quayside or at a wayside inn – the range of people encountered may have been quite limited: one would learn pretty quickly who to go to, how to negotiate with them and to anticipate the probable social rhythms of the journey. Modernity and its mass production of the automobile alters this, with each decade placing a greater cross-section of the population on the roads, increasing the possibilities of accessing the lives of people different to oneself.

These notions were gestating in the mind of Irv Thomas as he searched through the card indexes and microfiches of public libraries for evidence of the first hitchhiker. Someone with a degree of 'intentionality' must, he reasoned, also accept the road as a social leveller, such that there could be 'a flow of exchanges between givers … grounded in the satisfaction of human interaction'. Such sociability could only lead to a 'creative urge to use the open road as grist in a larger project'.[4]

This imaginative leap from 'sharing the road' to 'wanting to change society' may not have helped Thomas uncover the actual article in the *New York World Journal*, but it did help clarify that he wasn't searching for articles on tramps or hobos. A hitchhiker, Thomas reasoned, must be much more actively engaged in society and capable of planning and preparing a journey which required conversing with strangers – a unique (and arguably political) act in its own right.

But we are getting ahead of ourselves, so let's try to visualise where these activities were taking place, and how much the automobile was transforming the face and mind of America (and people such as Charles Brown Jr).

The motor frontier

For many of us, the motor age seems impossible to *un-imagine*. It is as much a way of thinking as it is a mode of transport shaping our societies and environment – what sociologists call 'mobilities'. Whether Roman cities designed around the army chariot, canals sculpturing lowland cities the world over, to railways opening up the hinterlands of imperial Africa for mass mining and mineral export: each transport 'revolution' has radically reorganised and often erased its predecessor. The success of the motor age has been to steadily transform its principal representative into a 'natural' expression of identity for millions of people whilst reorganising the infrastructure of our societies to suit it.

It didn't start that way. The automobile began its life as a hobby for the technically minded rich who were able to afford chauffeurs, mechanics and, in the very early days in the UK, someone to walk in front of the vehicle with a red flag warning those ahead. Mass production for the American middle classes came later, first in 1901 in Lansing, Michigan, courtesy of Ransom Olds, followed by one Henry Ford of Detroit, who, after a bit of experimentation with designing three distinct choices of car settled on one – the cheap black 'Tin Lizzie' – in 1909. This revolutionised travel in America. So, in terms of transport infrastructure, the New York that Charles Brown Jr knew as a student was full of 'street cars' or omnibuses, bicycles, carts and thousands of horses. Out in the rest of America there were about three million cars driving on the (named rather than numbered) roads, many of which were without a tar seal or markings. Signposts were rare, so if Mr Brown detoured off the Lincoln Highway, he may have had to ask for directions, as national road maps had been produced only two years before (by Gulf Oil).

What was more abundant was imagination. Keen young minds in the oil and motor industries were hard at work shaping the idea of a motor frontier for the select groups of adventure-seeking motorists. 'Manifest destiny' and rugged individualism had worked in the eras of wagon trails, mountain men, gold rushes and transcontinental railroad dreams: here was something which could translate those founding myths into the status spaces envisaged by the advertising industry. One might have only been 'going out for a drive' a few miles beyond the city with the family, but it was an experience of nature shaped by the sense of independence which the automobile offered.

Such a backdrop helps us to understand the 'intentionality' which Irv Thomas identifies as having emerged in the 'teens' in America, making hitchhiking as we know it today viable. Firstly, there was an expansion of the road network itself, with local counties and states mandated to maintain a certain level of road quality for the federal postal routes, along which trucks and vans had begun to move more goods and livestock to a wider variety of destinations. People had started to think about long-distance travel as possible other than by rail; neighbouring states were no longer perceived as foreign countries. There's a second factor: a new type of tourist industry was emerging as automobile prices began to drop. Inns and 'motor camps' catering for the increasingly mobile public started to spring up along the major highways. Then there was the romance of the road itself.

The Lincoln Highway was pivotal to this. Envisaged by Carl G. Fisher and completed in 1913, it linked thirteen states between New York and San Francisco, although many sections were still mainly dirt track at the time Charles Brown Jr was travelling. A number of high-profile society adventurers such as Emily Post (*By motor to the Golden Gate*, 1916) and Effie Gladding (*Across the continent by the Lincoln Highway*, 1915) gained plenty of publicity for their drives along it, adding a new gutsy female look to the mythical frontier spirit, complete with goggles and driving bonnets. Gladding became a kind of elder stateswoman for the road as a result of this journey, writing a foreword for the first Lincoln Highway Association guidebook; etiquette writer Post became enough of a figurehead to advise women on how to hitchhike during the Second World War, when America had introduced fuel rationing.

Charles Brown Jr's journey does not appear to elicit further comment in the press, nor do we know of its influence, but hitchhiking does begin to be noticed in the early 1920s and is initially characterised as a form of adventure. At the time, motorists were being advised to carry emergency equipment, and to fill up with gasoline and provisions at every opportunity if undertaking long journeys. Those spirited souls who struck out with far less certainty as to what the miles held in store for them did cultivate some journalistic admirers, with one suggesting that hitchhikers were adventurers 'who greatly admired hard work and free-enterprise capitalism' and doing it was 'the best possible training in the ancient virtues'.[5]

Early hitchhiking celebrities included Chicago estate agent J. K. Christian, who, in October 1921, fulfilled a bet that he couldn't travel 100 miles during a day whilst 'begging lifts', by managing to string twenty-seven of them together, covering an impressive 3,023 miles in the process. A couple of years later, a Yale student, Delzie Damaree, was able to attract the attention of the *New York Times* with a tale of frugality, having made twenty-nine cents last over eighteen days and 1,000 miles between Conway, Arkansas, and New York.[6] The newspaper seemed to warm to such stories, as it also gave coverage to a hitchhiking race between Washington, DC, and New York that involved a forty-strong Scout troop in October 1926, which may raise contemporary eyebrows a little, given that it took over ten hours and left some very hungry and dehydrated.[7]

Quirky tales in the press were one way of acclimatising the general public to the changing cultures of the road, whether they owned an automobile or not. Increasingly, they did, as the price fell and sales accelerated from three million in 1916 to nine million in 1920 to twenty-six million in 1929.[8] Yet, as historian David Kyvig notes, for all the transformation that the Model T Ford made to cities, its triumph was not inevitable. The urban environment was a sociable place, built around pedestrian flow and public transport provision, so advertisers had to convince potential drivers that that sociality was worth trading for the status and independence (and loneliness?) of being a solo automobile owner.[9]

From a hitchhiker's perspective, the novelty of the method and its association with adventure continued to hold, and there were plenty of positive representations of independent-minded women (or 'flappers') in fiction and magazines such as the *Saturday Evening Post*, flocking to liberal New York to discover themselves. One candidate for first female hitchhiker may be Irv Thomas's own aunt, Edith, who spent the summer of 1920 on a west–east hitchhike with a friend, and who featured in many local papers along the way.[10] Exactly what the provincial journalists called the women's *modus operandi* is not known, but meanwhile, in the metropolis, publishers were beginning to air a few suggestions.

The *New York World Journal* had certainly coined a good phrase in 'automobile panhandling' for Charles Brown Jr's adventure, yet it was never repeated. The periodical's larger stable mate, the *New York Times*, proposed 'auto-lifts' to describe the travels of betting man J. K. Christian, although changed this to 'auto-hikers' two years later, perhaps because this was the term which 'hobos' used to describe their new counterparts on the road.[11]

'Hitchhike' itself is first used in the now much-discussed article by 'The Drifter' in *The Nation* on 19 September 1923, to describe the travels of the trio of 'dusty Valkyries' he dubbed the 'New York girls' on their route to Quebec (see Prologue). This was a week prior to the aforementioned Delzie Damaree and is assumed by most researchers to be the foundational moment of hitchhiking, although there is a similarly laconic commentary the previous year, on 23 July, entitled 'The truth about hiking is hitching'. Penned by 'A. Hiker', the article introduces us to the roadside aspirations of another female triptych – Flora, Brunhilde and Jessica (a teacher, a chemist and an investment advisor) – who are embarking on a three-week road trip around the Adirondack Mountains. Bemused by their decision to go hiking in 'business clothes' rather than 'camp fire' outfits, he accompanies them to the New York City limits, making quips about which parts of the journey are 'really hiking', to watch 'Bruna' start waving her arm and shouting 'hitch please'.

We'll get to the choice of hitchhiking signals shortly, but it seems clear that 'A. Hiker' was being deliberately obtuse here, to help his readers. For all of his protestations, that the 'hordes' of female 'hiker-hitchers' ought to 'give out something for publication', to help explain the paradoxes of their walking and riding, he did grasp the wider reality. The economy was relatively stable, new leisure experiences were emerging and women were becoming much more confident in public life (seemingly able to 'rebel' against 'working during summer', he drolly surmises). More pertinently, he understood the principles of exchange involved in 'hiker-hitching', noting that it seemed to be defined by the 'art of listening' (specifically, being able to tolerate detailed 'farm talk' about cows and corn-planting skills) and the ability to provide a bit of spirited company. He obliges us with a quote from one driver as to the reciprocity of the arrangement: 'they paid back with a good song or story and it was always worth the price of admission.... We're raising an adventurous crop for the new generation is all I've got to say.'[12]

Defining moments: of hobos and half-hitches

In the early years, hitchhikers were rarely publicly accused of being freeloaders or of wanting something for nothing. It was also normal to see children hitchhiking (not just Scouts), although this wasn't without controversy.[13] More pressing, however, in terms of the politics of the kerbside was how our 'hiker-hitchers' and 'dusty Valkyries' were perceived by the public in relation to others on the road, such as 'tramps' and 'hobos'.

America has had an ambiguous relationship with the 'hobo', who manages to embody some of the myth of the frontier – a romantic figure from Jack

London's 1907 novel *The road*, self-reliant and answerable to few – yet only if the political mood suits. Hobos were really itinerant agricultural workers (literally, 'hoe-boys'), whose livelihood had been dependent on harvests and economic stability, something which famously came undone during the 1873 downturn. That downturn led to the creation of the 'Tramp Menace' and all of its associated imaginings of wandering threats to respectable society. The interchangeable and often wilful misuse of terminology did not help, although renowned hobo historian Charles Elmer Fox (born 1913), who hitchhiked and rode the rails for many decades, suggested that there was a useful differentiation around work. Firstly, there were 'bums', who were usually incapable of working because of drink or mental illness; then there were the 'hobos', who were always willing to hold down a job as part of their wandering lifestyle; and finally there were 'tramps', who refused employment, preferring to be independent foragers with their own networks, customs and communication hieroglyphics.[14] Hobos had their own newspapers, national conventions, songs of the road and makeshift encampments called 'jungles' near to rail yards. When feeling charitable, the press nicknamed them 'knights of the road', and was keen to report on the 'honourable' hobos who were getting behind the war effort in 1917 to work in the munitions factories.

Out on the highway, the emerging motoring public were presented with a contrasting set of roadside signifiers. The principal identifier of a 'bo' was a 'bindle' (i.e. bedroll), usually strapped to the back or to a knapsack, whereas many hitchhikers of the 1920s had a suitcase, which differentiated them and signalled that they had a more specific, immediate purpose than unspecified wandering and they wouldn't be trying to board a moving freight train (impossible one-handed; it was dangerous enough with two). The importance of image intensified when the Great Depression hit in the early 1930s, with student hitchhikers upping the ante, affixing college pennants to their suitcases, displaying their caps or holding cardboard destination signs (to prove their scholarship).

Hobos who rode the rails may have also hitchhiked, bindle and all, but for the purposes of this book, boarding a freight train itself cannot be classified as hitchhiking simply because it doesn't require an act of negotiation. For all of the sense of community which existed in the box cars and around the jungle fires, much of the life of a hobo involved the role of 'stowaway', hiding from the often brutal railyard guards (or 'bulls'). Some rail companies have been more tolerant of this than others over the decades, but there is little evidence of solidarity between officialdom and those wanting a free ride.

Here we come to the crux of the matter – the relationship between the semantics of the term 'hitchhiking' and the values which have come to be associated with it. So far, we've decided that what makes a hitched lift 'hitched' are the acts of negotiation and mutual aid, but the words themselves do not suggest this in their original usage. The word 'hitch' is generally defined in terms of the act of 'fastening one object to another', usually involving a type of knot (there are several configurations, although the 'half-hitch' is a 'tie-off' designed for quick release). This fits with the cultural significance of the horse in the days of cattle ranching on the North American plains, where a 'hitching post' was in effect an equine parking space. Yet 'hitch' also means to 'jerk' or 'pull' abruptly, implying momentum in the same way that 'hike' can – as in to 'lift up' or 'hoist' one's clothes. Both 'hitch' and 'hike' are thought to be no older than the fourteenth century and unlikely to have been in regular use before the nineteenth century (the walking connotations of 'hike' come later still).[15]

Practically speaking, this leads us into some interesting territory. Early automobiles were not so fast that pedestrians could not literally attach themselves to them. So, the implied reasoning here is that the term 'hitch' is an adaptation of those more horse-related explanations, where ambling pedestrians 'hitch' themselves to a cart or carriage, after negotiating with and being offered passage by its owner. The novels of Charles Dickens and the writings of Mark Twain are often cited as including many such events, and there is even the practice of 'riding and tying', where two people cover a distance with one horse, one taking a turn to rest with the horse whilst their companion walks on, something claimed to have been done by man of letters Samuel Johnson and the actor David Garrick in 1737.

A handful of other serious candidates for the coveted title of first hitch-hiker do require our attention, as they exist on the same cusp of the motor age as Charles Brown Jr. The American poet Vachel Lindsay is frequently at the front of the pack for his acceptance of lifts whilst on a lecturing and 'tramping' tour of the mid-West in the summer of 1912. Lindsay's strongest advocate seems to be troubadour journalist Elijah Wald, who, in the opening to his book *Riding with strangers*, argues that this journey had enough going for it to qualify as hitchhiking. However, on closer inspection of the text – *Adventures whilst preaching the gospel of beauty* – the poet seems to be prepared to accept a lift only if it is *offered* by passing drivers, as he regards cars as 'a carnal institution, to be shunned by the truly spiritual'.[16] As Irv Thomas points out, there is no motivation: 'Waiting for the offer does nothing at all to challenge the status quo of alienating privacy that the automobile engenders. And it does not change the invited rider's status from a passive recipient into a hitchhiker.'[17]

In the eyes of John Schlebecker – whose essay 'An informal history of hitchhiking' is the usual source for discussion of Lindsay – it is better to regard those moments of motor assistance as 'one possible origin' of hitchhiking, but largely falling short on the grounds that the lifts are not requested.

Dictionary definitions do not always help matters. The *Oxford English Dictionary* entry for 'hitchhike' emphasises the active procurement of the ride: to 'travel by seeking free lifts in passing vehicles'. Yet in the early years of the motor age there were other examples of lift giving which test this definition, such as the practice of 'lorry hopping' by uniformed men and women during and in the aftermath of the First World War. Did this method of moving troops around really constitute a form of hitchhiking? Both Schlebecker and Mario Rinvolucri, the English author of *Hitchhiking* (published in 1974), seem to think that it does count as part of hitchhiking history, on the grounds that those people were waiting for a lift. For me, this is also 'one possible origin', marred perhaps by the fact that no real negotiation takes place, and hopping onto the back of a lorry during wartime in uniform was not likely to fail. In effect, 'lorry hopping' was a kind of patriotic taxi service.

A world away from this, before there was even a hint of the war to come, a gentler – arguably more significant – introduction to the giving of lifts was underway in the leafy lanes of southern England. Its chief protagonist, Tickner Edwardes, a forty-four-year-old writer, photographer, naturalist and vicar, was setting out in 1909, excited by what he felt was an innovative approach to the business of travelling, and posterity demands we measure him alongside the aforementioned Mr Charles Brown Jr as our first hitchhiker.

The lift luck of the beekeeper

He called it 'an unusual plan': to set out from Torquay, in Devon, where he was holidaying during October 1909, and to return home 'by means of Lifts, taken in any chance vehicle that might be faring in my direction' to Burpham near Arundel in West Sussex. By his own admission, he was 'in no sort of hurry', which was just as well, since it was a substantial undertaking (200 miles) for a traveller of that time. As with Charles Brown Jr's journey between Fort Wayne and New York City, it might have easily passed unnoticed by history, being unremarkable in normal adventuring terms, were it not for another suggestion from Elijah Wald that this be considered the first hitchhike of any description, even ahead of Vachel Lindsay's grumbling embrace of the motor age.

It is all there in the text of his account of the journey, *Lift-luck on southern roads*, even using the criterion of *intentionality* as read through the later journey of Brown. In a dedicatory epistle to a colleague in London, Edwardes excitedly outlines his proposition:

Once clear of the great fashionable watering place in far Devon that was my starting point, my plan consisted in waiting by the roadside, or strolling gently onward,
until something on wheels, it mattered not what, overtook me; and thus by fits and
starts, slow joltings in lumbering farm wagons, steady crawls in brewers' drays, an
occasional brisk mile in a doctor's or parson's gig … after many days of travel [find
myself] in drowsy Arundel.[18]

If we forget the method of propulsion for a moment, or the fact that many
a traveller rested their limbs courtesy of a passing wagon, the key ingredient
here is visualisation. Edwardes thinks ahead, breaking down the journey in
terms of likely lifts and obstacles. Flicking through the pages of *Lift-luck on
southern roads*, it is easy to picture him ambling along the lanes, the hedgerows
bustling with wildlife and birdsong, and see him pause by a gate or tree
stump deciding that is to be 'the destined waiting point for my next lift'[19]
whilst he listens for the grind of wheels behind him, ready to hail the vehicle
in question. It is definitely hitchhiking by most people's reckoning.

Edwardes was an imaginative man, well versed in history and nature, and
already the author of what is now a wildlife classic – *The lore of the honey bee*
(1908) – who was motivated by the landscape and the people who lived in it.
Written soon after his sojourn, *Lift-luck on southern roads* is a joyful and nostalgic
book, but much more in keeping with the walkers of the Romantic era than
a Charles Brown Jr reflecting on his progress along the Lincoln Highway.
Edwardes is no lover of change and actively avoids major roads, towns, the
sight of telegraph poles and any methods of transport 'conveying tourists'.
Fifty-nine 'lifts' see him across five counties of England, with one 'wild ride' a
'Juggernaut of excruciating modernity' and its driver such a 'speed monger'
that there is an immediate need for the services of the nearest tavern to
calm his nerves.[20] Elsewhere in England, the motor age had produced its
first safety campaign after a child was killed in a hit-and-run incident in
Dunstable (1905), crowds were flocking to 'speed trial' events and there was
already a driving 'look' in fashion.

It is hard not to be charmed by *Lift-luck on southern roads*, although
Edwardes's 'unusual plan' does not represent anything different from how
a similar journey might have taken place thirty years previously. Brown's
on the other hand, embraces the motor frontier, and stirs into action those
whom he meets.

So, let's put ourselves back into Charles's shoes, in October 1916, a few
days along the Lincoln Highway, in a small Pennsylvanian town (possibly
York or Lancaster) standing slightly nervously in front of an audience. I am
imagining that he has had a bite to eat somewhere nearby, maybe even a
glass of 'moonshine', and he's now got to fulfil an obligation in return for
having received a lift earlier in the day. One would think that at this point

in his journey, Charles has a notion of what makes it unusual in the eyes of others; so how might he have approached the task of presenting the subject 'cold' to a captive audience?

The hitcher's hail

Irv Thomas seems convinced that one of the most audacious and innovative aspects of the actions of a Charles Brown Jr must have been thinking that he, as a stranger, might 'invade' the private space of another. It is an intriguing argument, but probably one rooted in a more late twentieth-century perspective, shaped by suburbanisation, consumer identities and the growth of the Interstates. In 1916, the motor frontier was on the ascendant, yet for most people it was more imagined than real, creating liminal spaces in which these early hitchhiking journeys could exist. It seems far more probable that the music agent mentioned above who asked Charles to give a lecture was inspired by the sheer gumption and modernity of Charles's journey, in all likelihood introducing him as a young man with a salutary tale of initiative, whose adventure was the equivalent of blue-sky thinking.

There's a good comparison with Edwardes's 'unusual plan' here, in terms of the visualisation of distance and how one might cross it using the cooperation of others. So, as Charles stands there, telling the tale of his moment of inspiration – whom he has met, what he has learned and why America is so beautiful and generous – my guess is that audience members are thinking more in terms of how he persuaded anyone to stop (rather than what they talked about afterwards) or how dangerous the act of doing so might have been.

In his own words (quoted above), for his first lift Charles stepped out into the road as the doctor's Ford approached and 'threw up' his hands 'as a signal to stop', which sounds rather like a cross between hailing a taxi and an emergency plea (arms waved in front of the face). The cultural meaning of the gesture may have been a little academic: preserved sections of the Lincoln Highway in rural Indiana today are not very wide, with barely enough room for two vehicles to pass each other, which suggests that the doctor may have had little choice in the matter. We shouldn't forget what a primal moment this was, even if Charles looked respectable enough with his recent shave and brush-down in the town.

In 1916 the Lincoln Highway was a national road, carrying transport which did not necessarily have a connection with the locality that it passed through. Anyone contemplating 'hitchhiking' would have had to assume that they might not be hailing a person known to them from the next village, and that they would be as anonymous as if they were walking the streets of a city. Thus, any pitch for a lift would have to make sense from distance, appear unthreatening and communicate something of their personality. Potential lift-givers may have had their own concerns: as the motor infrastructure developed, so did the plethora of visual distractions and navigational obstacles – new road markings, speed signs, traffic lights – all of which added to the psychological distractions from just keeping the vehicle under control (and away from other cars, bicycles, horses, carts and pedestrians).

Charles's ambiguous hail was probably typical of what many people would have done in the circumstances. According to Schlebecker, the early years of hitchhiking in the 1920s were characterised by a variety of hand techniques, before the thumb became the ubiquitous choice of the roadside vagabond. How and why this became the recognised method of signalling is still hard to pin down. We do know that by 1925 the use of the thumb was so recognisable as to feature on the cover of the *Saturday Evening Post* on 24 October, courtesy of Edgar Franklin Wittimack's 'The hitchhiking hobo' graphic. This leaves us exploring the possibility that the hitchhiking thumb may have started use in those more 'knot-related' equine contexts: a sign amongst rural itinerants or farm workers that they wanted to 'hitch' onto the hay wagon. How it spread to the cities is unknown; suffice to say that it might have picked up some negative associations along the way.

In Schlebecker's essay, there is a suggestion that another of the methods by which students and bohemians differentiated themselves from hobos was by *not* using their thumbs, on the grounds that it was 'useless' for soliciting lifts. Accordingly, a small section of travellers opted out of thumbing and chose to concentrate instead on facial expression and stance by the roadside – perhaps because of the possible association with the image of a 'country bumpkin'. The protest against the thumb didn't last long, but its existence is a minor clue in the larger mystery about the emergence of the most famous of hitchhiking gestures.[21]

Image and technique clearly became more of an issue once the novelty of the plucky early 'adventuring' stories had worn off. By the late 1920s there were so many competing groups and identities on the road that the press didn't find it hard to amass its share of negative news items. With an estimated one in ten people having hitched by the end of the decade, it was hardly surprising that there were some cases of murder or robbery, some of which Schlebecker puts down to apocryphal tales driven by a political (or more likely economic) agenda.[22] Yet, when the Great Depression emptied hundreds of thousands onto the highways, it became unrealistic to portray the road as a perpetually dangerous place. The Depression also led Hollywood

Figure 1.3 'It's all in that ol' thumb, see?' Clark Gable and Claudette Colbert in *It happened one night* (1934), prior to the famous use of the leg.

to make popular feel-good movies with a social conscience, perhaps in an effort to reconcile the polarisation of society, and one of these provides us with the best example of hitchhiking as 'thumbing a lift' in a mainstream film (Figure 1.3).

Fawned over by connoisseurs and hitchhikers alike, the romantic comedy *It happened one night* (1934) is a road movie which brings together an on-the-run heiress, Ellie (played by Claudette Colbert), and a streetwise but unsuccessful journalist, Peter (Clark Gable). When their bus breaks down, they travel together across country and camp wild in a hay meadow. The next morning they try their luck at hitchhiking, and Peter demonstrates the art of securing a lift.

> Peter: 'It's all in that ol' thumb, see? ... that ol' thumb never fails. It's all a matter of how you do it, though. Now, you take number one, for instance. That's a short, jerky movement like this – that shows independence, you don't care whether they stop or not. You've got money in your pocket, see.'
> Ellie: 'Clever!'
> Peter: 'But number two, that's a little wider movement – a smile goes with this one, like this, that means you've got a brand-new story about the farmer's daughter.'

Ellie: 'Hmm. You figured that out all by yourself!'

Peter: 'Number three, that's the pits. Yeah, that's a pitiful one you know. When you're broke and hungry and everything looks black. It's a long sweeping movement like this, but you've got to follow through though...'

Ellie: 'Oh, that's amazing.'

Peter: 'It's no good though, if you haven't got a long face to go with it.'[23]

Peter then fails to secure a lift, leaving it to Ellie to 'give it a go', at which point she rolls up her skirt a little and the next car screeches to a halt!

The whole sequence outlines very effectively just how the early motor age was an anthropological event as well as technological one. Hitchhiking was part of that new 'mobility' and had to evolve and adapt, just as it still does in the present century. Today, the 'thumb' may appear to be a universal signifier, but this is just the conceit of some in the West, when in fact a wide range of cultural solicitations – finger pointing, thumb raising, arm waving – is available across the globe. If one raises a thumb in some parts of China, for instance, the response maybe a friendly wave back rather than a screeching of brakes: the gesture states that you are happy with the world. Less amusingly, the elevated thumb may incur agitation if delivered by the roadsides of Corsica, parts of East Africa and the Arabian Gulf: it is the cultural equivalent of 'up yours'. If you are in Ethiopia, it is best not to point your finger at the road, which works in so many countries (Russia most notably), as that is considered to be a rude gesture.

In the century since that first 'intentional hitchhike', the practice has accrued enough 'grist', as Irv Thomas puts it, to develop ways of alerting travellers to some of these cultural *faux pas* in advance, which in the days before the internet was down to word of mouth and the phenomenon of 'hitchhiker's guidebooks'.

A hitchhiker's guide to hitchhiker's guides

Emerging in the early 1970s, guides written specifically for hitchhiking played a key role in linking together the knowledge of the 'baby boomer' generation with the hopes of my own. These were lovingly assembled, often wildly idiosyncratic affairs, straight out of the underground publishing culture: a pocket encyclopaedia, crammed with every scrap of useful information of life on the roads of the developed world and further afield, in Asia, Latin America and Africa.

The most successful from a publishing perspective was Ken Welsh's *Hitchhiker's guide to Europe* (1971), which was reprinted many times, yet is equally well known for being in the backpack of one Douglas Adams, the summer he had the epiphany which led him to write *The hitchhiker's guide to the galaxy* whilst lying drunk, staring at the stars in a field outside Innsbruck. The radio series and subsequent novels summed up much of the ethos of the generation which put together the terrestrial guides – ambitious, surreal and often irreverent – but rooted in a belief in humanity's potential to overcome the stupidity of its own actions. Their editors and contributors tended to be liberal-minded, educated people who probably didn't like the American war in Vietnam, raised questions about the purpose of consumerism as an end in itself and the increasingly destructive effects of technology on the environment. Many of them believed that hitchhiking was an alternative, if not a riposte to this trajectory, encouraging dialogue and mutual respect. Philosophical quotations or aphorisms frequently peppered the guides, encouraging readers to think beyond both geographical boundaries and their own expectations.

Much of the content of the guidebooks was practical. This was a potentially diverse readership, with hitchhiker numbers at a high not seen since the 1930s and across all age groups. The provision of good guidance, with no presumptions of prior knowledge, was paramount; accordingly, the basics of road etiquette and legal advice were usually prioritised, with additional sections on staying healthy, what to wear, self-defence, where to sleep (or squat) cheaply and even how to identify roadside plants. Most of the guides were written by men (although Katie Wood co-wrote on the later editions of Ken Welsh's book) but were compiled with the assumptions that some of the readers would be female, and that some of these might be hitchhiking alone.

The philosophy of self-reliance was a key part of the culture, but so too was the art of good decision-making. Some of the guides took this to another level, supplementing tactical advice with 'hitchhiker-friendly' road maps which detailed the lift viability 'ratings' of each junction, major road or even US state. This was very timely: the West was undergoing a huge expansion of its motorway, autobahn and freeway systems within these years; unsurprisingly, any editor felt honour-bound to update subsequent editions with news of an added spur, slip road or service station. These were not trivial matters: new layouts could alter factors such as 'line of sight', the speed or flow of the traffic, and the likelihood of meeting other hitchers. The grading systems were conscientious but not without humour – ranging from the psychological bounce of a 'four star' junction (twenty- to thirty-minute wait) to a 'one star' location with a likelihood of being marooned (and a guaranteed headache, if not hypothermia). Simon Calder's 'manuals' for hitchhikers in Britain and Europe in the mid-1980s were peerless in this regard, and also proffered opinions on another much-debated matter of hitchhiking strategy: the destination sign.

Only the topic of solo female travellers divides hitchhikers more than whether or not to use signs. There are those who believe it is an indicator of amateurishness or is too tactically limiting, but it is rare to find a hitchhiker who has never wielded one. First used amongst the American college communities in the late 1930s, the cardboard sign has become so synonymous with hitching that it was even employed by the British government for the 2002 Commonwealth Games, with photographs of international athletes trying to 'hitch' to Manchester. I was always quite proud of my method: filling a twelve-inch plastic folder (a protector sleeve for a vinyl record) with my collection of destination and 'please' signs and a small road atlas for quick reference. In more recent times I have seen people deploying whiteboards, which saves time and avoids those 'soggy cardboard sign' moments!

Just as smiling has always been recommended by hitchhiking guidebooks, a touch of well-judged self-deprecation with a marker pen is usually thought to be advantageous, and probably offsets the charge that it is too much information for drivers to absorb at speed. During favourable times for hitchhiking, a special 'gesture dialogue' emerges, where drivers and hitchers exchange hand signals indicating that the driver is turning off, or can only carry one passenger and so forth. Throwing a few humorous signs into the semiotic mix – 'we have chocolate biscuits', 'just married' or 'Narnia please' – provides an extra humanising effect and is usually thought to work.

For those having a bad day on the road – when all of the clever readings of the traffic flows or the artful applications or flourishes of the thumb and marker pen don't work – there is still the chance to consult the guidebooks on how to employ a much older form of hitchhiking strategy: asking for a lift. As with the science of destination signs and communicating one's intent with digital semaphore, there is a history and art to this aspect of hitchhiking.

Haggling in the name of community

Charles Brown Jr doesn't provide enough information in his account of the journey between Fort Wayne and New York for us to know how, after that first ride, his subsequent twenty-seven lifts were attained. Did he continue to signal in the manner of his flagging down of the physician, or employ some other form of negotiation? It seems perfectly possible that the sheer novelty of Charles's adventure in the eyes of the travelling public may have facilitated all kinds of negotiated scenarios – one driver recommending another, or a host fixing up a ride for the next morning, during an overnight stop.

Reading John Schlebecker's assessment of those initial decades, it is again apparent just how much of an effect the massive swell of numbers had on hitchhiking tactics. By the end of the 1930s, not only were destination signs being used, but hitchhikers were also adopting the habit of asking for lifts at petrol stations or highway cafés. This was not without controversy, as too many people clogging up the entrances and forecourts were judged to impact on business and hitchhikers themselves could be fractious with one another for breaches of roadside 'etiquette'. Asking for a lift could be construed as a form of 'queue jumping' if there were already folks with their thumbs out, a few yards down the highway.

Approaching drivers in this manner wasn't one of my favoured options: it felt an intrusion on the lives of others, along with the nagging notion that I was somehow 'cheating' on the artistic purity of the roadside 'hitch'. Perhaps this was just my English reserve, but it did work at small rural petrol stations, when I was heading for the mountains with a climbing rope coiled around my shoulders (which perhaps assisted my credibility). Female hitchhikers have often been more regular users of this strategy, as it is far better for sizing up a person than in the adrenalin pressure of a braking vehicle and hasty exchange of questions. Some hitchhikers construct their entire mental map of a journey – what I call a 'thumb line' (Chapter 2) – on this basis, rather than through the aforementioned 'star system' of aiming for the best junctions and slip roads.

In the history of hitchhiking, it is arguably the Russians who have the most brazen attitude towards this aspect of lift negotiation, rooted in their own legacy of collectivism, and the sheer obviousness of sharing the road in remote regions where sub-zero temperatures will focus the minds of the un-assertive. These are qualities nurtured by the country's numerous hitchhiking clubs, who regard hitching as a way of life designed to make connections with others. Take the high-profile Academy of Free Travel (AVP) for instance: those who undergo training as 'free travellers' will be expected to learn the art of negotiation as a matter of club pride; they are ambassadors for a set of ideals as much as citizens of the Russian Federation. Each member is handed a letter of recommendation from their club president (at the time of writing, still Anton Krotov – Figure 1.4) which explains that the bearer is part of a scientific fact-finding expedition and is willing to assist on the journey in exchange for free passage (this usually applies when the vehicle is a train, ship or small plane). Members of the AVP are not encouraged to use money under any circumstances, which probably makes negotiating for a lift in a country where haggling is part of the culture somewhat challenging.

Any form of travel that has to be negotiated outside of the official channels requires diligence and sensitivity. The raw utopianism of the AVP, or indeed Charles Brown Jr's belief that people 'would enjoy giving him rides' all the way to New York, if he could persuade them of his plan, is beyond the self-belief of most. Fortunately, for those who prefer to negotiate travel a little less

Figure 1.4 The palms have it. In many former communist countries, one does not 'thumb' a lift. Long-time president of the Academy of Free Travel Anton Krotov shows how it is done in March 2021.

intensely, the digital age offers a range of hitchhiking and hitchhiker type of lift-sharing possibilities.

Electronic thumb prints

In *The hitchhiker's guide to the galaxy*, one of Douglas Adams's principal characters, Ford Prefect, 'thumbs' lifts from passing space vehicles using a mobile device that is able to access something called the sub-ether network, which contains travel and weather information for the galactic hitcher (plus details of hostile species and planets). Prophetic though this was for the late 1970s, the parallels with contemporary lift-sharing options are uncanny.

It is now possible to dial up a full spectrum of travel options from local 'ride-share' boards and 'dynamic journey planners' to international operators such as BlaBlaCar or long-established national schemes such as the German *Mitfahrzentralen* network; all of which allow a degree of independence from individual vehicle ownership, thanks to smart-phone technologies. Most of these initiatives have little overlap with actual hitchhiking, although some have positioned themselves as being a safer, comfortable alternative to it. A multilateral message board such as Carpoolworld shows a relaxed face to potential lift-givers or ride-seekers, striking a balance in its format between safeguards (registration process, PayPal account, a helpline) and the consolation of a filtering process as to what kind of rider/driver is preferred (gender, age, non-smoker, vegan, etc.). The behaviour instructions are not quite up to Russian free-travel guidelines, and you'll have to work out for yourselves whether or not the best driving music is Motörhead or Beyoncé, but this ride-share template is a fine synthesis of economising, being environmentally aware and indulging in a short social adventure.

Shared rides in the USA have a varied and often low-tech history, with surges in popularity during the 1973 OPEC crisis, when a number of pro-Palestine oil-exporting countries increased the price of a barrel in response to the Pentagon supplying weapons to the Israeli government during the Yon Kippur War. Neighbourhood carpooling and official car clubs became ubiquitous, along with other conservation measures, such as reduced speed limits and purchases of smaller vehicles. The ranks of hitchhikers, already at a high point, temporarily swelled with people thumbing to work, as had happened during the shortages of the Second World War. Today, if the classified advertisement listing Craigslist is to be believed, the USA boasts an average of two formal 'ride-share' schemes per individual state – with lifts arranged electronically – but the wider context is that only 10 per cent of all journeys are shared, with the numbers half of what they were in 1980.[24]

In so many cities around the world, the congestion of central business districts and attendant air pollution problems have forced the hands of government to experiment with a variety of 'cooperative' measures. Americans, as a rule, baulk at the idea of hitchhiking to work but those who opt for 'casual carpooling' or 'slugging' are definitely not catching a bus. They wait in designated pull-in areas en route into major cities such as Oakland, California, for fellow commuters to fill up their cars prior to accessing the 'high-occupancy vehicle lanes' on the way into and home from work. Here the negotiation of fares is not too demanding – some routes have a fixed price, others are free – so you doesn't have to do much haggling, except if a fellow slugger has an earlier meeting in the city than you do. The drawbacks of course are that it is limited to arterial routes and particular times of the working day, just as 'ride-share' boards tend to favour leisure-oriented intercity journeys.

Some of these difficulties could be alleviated, noted legendary hitchhiking archivist Bernd Wechner back in 1999, if a computer-assisted version of the old Polish hitchhiking voucher scheme was introduced across whole regions.[25] This much eulogised experiment ran between 1957 and 1994 and arose for very specific reasons, which we'll return to in Chapter 10, but the system of drivers cashing in tokens handed to them on the roadside by registered hitchhikers could be adapted, Wechner suggested, to help regenerate localities and give people the confidence to begin traditional hitchhiking again.

Purists may feel a bit cheated by these contrived methods, but mobile phones and specialist apps are already altering the hitchhiking experience. Some argue that it undermines trust, reduces the quality of interaction and kills curiosity in a traveller, but particularly for female hitchhikers the option to text the licence plate of a vehicle or to send a snap of 'the cool dude who I'm riding with' as a way of protecting oneself can be a life changer.

Even to talk of these arrangements and concepts such as 'twitchhiking' may seem alien compared with the world of those early twentieth-century pioneers, but many of the same ideals persist or have been embellished into life philosophies. We'll see in later chapters the importance of digital communities such as Couchsurfers and BeWelcome, which largely practise the self-organising ethos and trust economics of hitchhiking, albeit in the hospitality sector. Irv Thomas's hunch that the road – virtual or otherwise – can be the place for an exchange of ideas seems intact, however differently realised.

Perhaps less has changed in a century than we think.

On Harrison Street bridge

'Share the road' the signs suggest, on stretches of the Lincoln Highway today, as it winds through Fort Wayne. There are a number of them dotted about, towards the end of East Main Street and on the bridges which cross St Mary's River, all of which are within a braking car's distance of where Charles Brown Jr stood around noon on 4 October 1916 when he began that historic journey. They are part of the Fort Wayne 'River Greenway', a relatively recent network of cycle routes and walkways using quieter streets and paths to promote healthier mobility. It's still quite an unusual road sign, and motorists in this part of the city may sense a changed mood: that there is a greener semiotic at play here, both literally and figuratively.

I'd love to say that it was on the Harrison Street bridge that he put that moment of inspiration into action. It is the quieter of the Lincoln Highway river crossings, opened a couple of months before Charles arrived, but the narrative doesn't quite fit – he'll have walked along Washington Street, a bit further out, heading to where New Haven is today. Historians still argue about the line of the Lincoln Highway, yet Harrison Street bridge is one of the few spots where there have been commemorative engravings of any longevity celebrating the history of the road. It is a place to gather and imagine more than just the water flowing under you.

Coming across the writings of dedicated archivists of the Lincoln Highway, I found myself strangely moved. Here were people fixated with the minutiae of history as much as I was, riveted by the early motorists of this road: folks who dreamed of open-top cars and dust and the smell of leather and oil, caught by the imaginative intoxicant of the frontier; aficionados who'd put up a plaque at the drop of a hub-cap. Most modes of transport have their cult place or time – so why not mark the moment when the roadside rambler became the hitchhiker, to consolidate hitchhiking as a form of transport?

Plenty of famous people who hitched have had plaques and commemorations, but honouring hitchers for being hitchhikers is more unusual (although Irv Thomas has been in *Who's Who*). So, it would be my suggestion that when Fort Wayne next does a 'car free' day – a World Hitchhiking Day may be a way off yet – then perhaps one of the bigwigs from the local ride-share schemes could see fit to honour the very first hitchhike of any significance as having taken place on its outskirts (incidentally Hitchwiki.org reckons that Indiana is a good lift-giving state). What with all of the Lycra flowing past and a more relaxed mood to 'sharing' the urban grind, a little plaque on the Harrison Street bridge seems apposite enough (design to be decided – maybe including a thumb?).

As for Mr Charles Brown Jr himself, little more is known. We just have the one grainy portrait photograph and 1,500 words of promising prose, of the kind which he probably applied to his 'editorial appointment' in the years to come. Perhaps he continued to vagabond throughout his twenties and beyond, and conceived of equally bold ventures across the motor frontiers of North America; maybe he established an early transcontinental hitchhiking record whilst heading back from New York to his native California. It might be wishful thinking, but the concluding sentences of 'Vagabonding by motor-car' do not read as words scribed by a person who has no intention of repeating an experience; rather, they appear to be epigram for the century of hitchhiking to come.

> Great was the satisfaction of having accomplished what I had set out to do. In no other way could I have gained such a knowledge of the country and the people who have made it, and are making it. Best of all, it gave me a deeper understanding of human nature.[26]

Many would repeat remarkably similar words in countless hitchhiking documents over the next eleven decades. The motor age may have snaked its way across most of our planet and into our psyches, rendered us impatient and dependent on an armoury of glowing gadgets, but there is still a remarkable raw purity about contemplating the horizon over one's outstretched arm, and finding out that it's possible to start thinking about the world differently.

Chapter 2

How to think like a hitchhiker: an introduction to vagabond sociology

What the road reveals

The Danish human rights campaigner Jacob Holdt famously said that he'd never turn down a lift, even if there were guns lying on the front seat of the car. For him, the greatest freedom was to say 'yes' to another person and to throw himself into their lives and trust them, believing that 'every single person can teach you something'. 'As a vagabond', he argued, 'you have the freedom, energy, and time to be fully human toward every individual you meet'; each of us is a microcosm of the best values of the society we travel through.[1]

Arriving fifty-four years after Charles Brown Jr had completed that very first hitchhike from Fort Wayne to New York, Holdt was drawing some very different conclusions about the country he had chosen to negotiate by thumb. He was en route between Canada and Chile, ostensibly on a long vacation, but a few weeks of being on the kerbsides of America made him change his plans. How was it possible, he wondered, for a country with so much wealth, such noble ideals of liberty and the pursuit of happiness to be at ease with itself whilst swathes of its African American citizens were living in conditions little better than those experienced under slavery? As an educated man looking on from a well balanced progressive Scandinavian society, how had he not known about the shanty towns, ghettos, indentured labour schemes and racist attitudes in parts of the Deep South?

It was 1970 and Holdt had $40 in his pocket, which allegedly stayed there during the five years he hitchhiked around the USA, trying to document the racial and social inequality which he had been shocked by, with a simple camera, the film paid for by blood plasma donations. During this time he received many hundreds of lifts and stayed in 434 households, and was frequently overwhelmed by the incredible moments of generosity, compassion and resilience of those who had the least to give. As did Brown, he odd-jobbed and let the lifts and their providers direct his path, from which he felt able to offer the optimistic aphorism: 'security is being on the road with nothing'. But he wanted to put something back into the world and shake things up, like one of his idols, Jacob Riis, had done at the turn of the twentieth century, with his photography of the squalid housing tenements in New York and its effects on the urban poor.[2]

When Holdt used the phrase 'vagabond sociology' in the introduction to the book of these travels, *American pictures*, it seemed something of a position statement. He'd been stunned to know that there were shelves of academic papers and books on racism and economic inequality, written by people who supposedly had the ears of policy-makers. For a human rights activist, this said something about the politics of society and the ineffectual role of research in shaping it, a situation probably not helped by the absence of photographs in the journals. Holdt wasn't hiding what he saw behind words: his pictures were devastating, otherworldly. Thin harrowed families in rickety shacks, scratching a living out of the dust, standing by peeling wallpaper or perching on mattresses half clad, a naked lightbulb hanging above them. Many of these communities were up dirt tracks, miles from anywhere one could seriously hitchhike to; they were abandoned, mistreated but still compassionate enough to offer him a roof over his head.

American pictures became something of a sensation amongst liberal elites in the mid-1980s. Holdt found himself being feted by the rich and famous one day, whilst the next he could be hitchhiking with his two-year old son to reach a community hall where he would present a slideshow to the very people the book was about. Not many social scientists are that brave, but then maybe Holdt's *modus operandi* had far more in common with the campaigning photojournalism of Riis than with the publishing of scholarly articles or the gaining of peer approval.

That desire to right the wrongs of a world uncomfortably arrived upon by unexpected means is precisely why hitchhiking – through the lens provided by a Jacob Holdt – is allegorical of a way of thinking about it. Being on the kerbside allows us to by-pass the need for the gatekeepers or mediators of our travel experience and obviates our reliance on official researchers or policy-makers to interpret social problems for us. It gives us the opportunity to do it ourselves, to use the randomness of our encounters, their individual windows on the multiplicity of a society's workings, their light and shade, to benefit wider understanding. Outwith the formal economy, benefiting from mutual aid and our better natures, we build up a 'vagabond sociology' based on different ways of observing the spaces we cross and the sense of time which journeys appear to take. This allows us to think more laterally about who is

Figure 2.1 Tireless campaigning photographer and 'vagabond sociologist' Jacob Holdt, whose belief in human cooperation lay behind the inspiring maxim 'security is being on the road with nothing'.

prioritised or marginalised within a society, from the hitchhikers themselves through to the people offering lifts, even those who might leave guns on the front seat of their vehicle but still have an insightful tale to tell about their hopes and fears.

Jacob Holdt (Figure 2.1) has spent his life documenting injustices of the kind outlined in *American pictures*. His empathetic work resonates at a deep level, raising questions about who we are as individuals and societies: why we sometimes choose to exclude and persecute others because it is personally or politically expedient to do so, rather than embrace them. Yet he has seen enough of life to know that even in the most unlikely of places (he befriended members of the Ku Klux Klan) there are people who are capable of reaching out and caring for the downtrodden or needy, who might be prepared to find common association just because one happens to be hitchhiking rather than arriving in the neighbourhood in a car. Listening to him lecture forty years on from his first vagabond sociological observations offers hope to those of us who believe that the kerbside presents an opportunity for connection with others in an age of climate breakdown, renewed nationalism, economic uncertainty and now global pandemics such as COVID-19.

In the coming pages we'll be travelling in the shoes of other maverick hitchhikers, documenters and campaigners like Jacob Holdt, trying to understand how the world looks through their eyes, why they believe that it is important we adopt a vagabond sociological view of life, and why collecting the thoughts and images of those who have been there is part of that process.

But let's start with my introduction to learning to 'think like a hitchhiker'.

'Hitching time'

For many years, some of my favourite hitchhiking journeys were through the Scottish Highlands, between such places as Fort William and Stirling or Glasgow – heading back home to Yorkshire in England. It was always a long day and with cars often already jam-packed with holiday-making passengers, the early sections of the route would invariably be slow by anyone's reckoning. It was all a question of getting used to the flow of a journey. I knew that after the usual sequence of short lifts, longer ones would materialise as I hit the motorways of the Scottish Central Belt and time would be 'made up'. This was a comforting thought on the afternoon of 26 December 1985 at Glencoe in Argyll, as I skittered around on the roadside, staring at the icy mountain ramparts or the occasional vehicle, and the temperature began to resemble the chill of the mountain bothy which I had left that morning.

In four hours I had hitched less than thirty of the 400 miles required – which was alright in summer but heavy snow was on the way – and I was beginning to doubt myself and start to look at my watch (a bad omen). Fortunately, the road always throws up something: in this case Fred – a quietly spoken train driver from Cambridgeshire, who had been visiting an old friend on the Isle of Skye and was in need of company other than the melodramatic sounds of Madonna, Meat Loaf and Jennifer Rush on the tape player! Suddenly, the whole hitchhike took on a dreamlike dimension: I was in a well-heated vehicle which would provide my longest ever lift, of 320 miles, and I would be home before midnight. We settled into an easy rapport, sweeping past the shadowy outlines of peaks that were a big part of my life in those years, before the roads straightened into surreal sodium-lit carriageways through the Scottish Borders, as empty of travellers as the service stations which provided us with caffeine respite.

I averaged 34 mph for that trip, which was actually pretty good. By then I had already built up an awareness of how to assess a likely journey time, based upon factors such as likely traffic jams or potentially slow sections of road, competition hot spots, the time of the week or month of the year. This is all part of the science of hitching according to the statistical-minded folks at hitchhiking clubs in the former Soviet Union and Warsaw Pact countries, who devise equations to this effect. It turns out my journey was a pretty typical one: the average fair-weather speed in today's Russia is 35 mph (50 kph), and the maximum daily journey is around 600 miles (1,000 kilometres).[3]

Calculations such as these tell only part of the story. They are descriptions rooted in the functionality of 'clock time' rather than the ebb and flow of 'hitching time', where the passage of the hours does appear different. It is a feeling best observed when trying to hitchhike to a deadline, when it can feel as though you are swimming against an invisible tide. Most significantly, your attitude changes towards the people you are sharing time with: interactions seem more instrumental and self-serving rather than being experienced on their own terms. Frustration easily creeps in; you find yourself constantly slipping back into 'clock time': 'if only he'd go a little faster, I could pick up the rush-hour traffic from the next town'.

'Hitching time' matters! For most of us who aren't hitchhiking, our days are lived in 'organised time', filled with rituals, tasks and obligations, the accomplishment of which are more likely to be judged successful if done with speed. Ever since the Industrial Revolution, when the clock began to tyrannise the lives of factory workers, speed has underwritten the ideals of social progress, legitimated conquest and been aligned with forms of hyper-masculinity. We all unknowingly participate in what Marx called 'the destruction of space by time', where our travel infrastructure positions us in an ongoing state of cognitive dissonance (or denial). Perhaps we take holiday flights which pass over war zones and famines, or drive on a road that by-passed a shanty town or destroyed an ancient woodland to cut the commuter journey: it is all part of the same imbalance to save a bit of time.

Let's think about this counter-intuitively: how do we 'save time'? When does any transport journey actually start? In *Energy and equity*, the political philosopher Ivan Illich argued that if we factored in the real time 'spent', then the advantage of a car is an illusion, since its ownership also involves hours spent choosing, purchasing, insuring, maintaining and fuelling the vehicle. This eats into the journey time; hence the walker may set out to cover a distance of four miles in around an hour, whilst the driver is still spending time on a bit of form filling. This may be apocryphal – obviously, bikes and boots need repair too and train tickets have to be bought – but it is indicative of the kind of alternative perspective needed to rethink the assumptions of the motor age.

To the novice hitcher, this may not ring immediately true: the unfolding of a journey seems slow, uneven and frustrating, especially if viewed as though one were catching a train. 'Hitching time', by contrast, is a more sub-jective, non-linear experience, aligned to different rhythms of the road. It is where travellers 'let go' of the 'clock-driven' mode and accept the flow of lifts and waits as an organic process, not controlled by others. Here time is not an economic unit, able to be 'wasted' or declared 'dead'; rather, it provides an opportunity to reflect upon the aesthetics and politics of the journey as it unfolds. It is probably not a coincidence that a number of hitchhiking writers have drawn inspiration from the naturalistic philosophy of the Chinese classic the *Tao te ching*, likening their journeys to the passage of water finding its way across the landscape, gaining energy and meaning by easing around or deflecting obstacles as opposed to confronting them directly. According to the *Tao*, the social world is strongest when guided by the paths of least resistance, the most accepting and communicative, the least hierarchical and goal-oriented. Put like this, perhaps my waits in the December cold were just part of a pattern I was still getting used to, or nothing more than the hitchhiking equivalent of a flat tyre or a cancelled train. Usually, the temporal rhythms of a hitched journey did not preclude efficiency, and there were many occasions when I beat the time it would have taken by public transport over the same distances.

So, if our journeys take on a more organic feel and are less about charging as fast as possible across the landscape, then how might we also think about the spaces which we cross in equally lateral ways?

'Thumb lines'

If I had been an art student rather than a sociologist when observing my cold roadside vigil, I might have recalled the work of English artist Richard Long and how he had turned his own relationship with the same roads and mountains into a new mode of expression. In April 1967, Long had hitch-hiked through Glencoe, en route from London to the top of Britain's highest mountain, photographing his feet and the earth and sky every few hours, to create a visual record of the land he passed through and its effects on his body. *Ben Nevis hitch-hike*, as he called the piece, was an early example of what later became known as 'land art', a form that saw him interacting with often very desolate places, marking his passage using natural materials: rock cairns, patterns out of twigs, swirls in the sand. At the time it was an unusually intimate and ecological piece of art, a comment on his connection with, impact on and shaping by the natural world.

By contrast, I don't think I have a single photograph of the same stretches of the A82, but I did commit them to memory, so much so that I became familiar with the camber of each waiting point, the lines of sight, the shift of the gravel underfoot, that feeling of being in motion and yet stationary: waiting. More importantly, I was constantly updating the social history of the road which I had absorbed on previous hitchhikes. All of those tales told by lorry drivers about their brushes with the law, their dalliances in love, the politics of the next roadside café, the various ways that they would resist demands from the boss on their time, the international events which had occurred whilst I had been listening to them. I'd also have my own hitchhiking cartography about places to get a decent cup of coffee, to rely on at night and where not to get dropped off. I would recall people I had met on the road who might be worthy of a few minutes' discussion as we swept south down the A82 and later the A74 heading into England and use them as conversational resources to make the journey easier, perhaps reduce the gap between my companion and me in age, life experience, politics. Each fork in the road would evoke another potential marker to be engaged with, or filed for the next time.

At this point in my hitchhiking career, I hadn't heard of the Aboriginal 'songlines', but they had obviously been on Richard Long's mind. These are a complex and largely invisible map of journeys across the more inhospitable parts of Australia, which involve the actual singing of stories to mark out the length of the journeys and the physical and cultural landmarks en route. Thousands of years old, these are also of a different temporal order from 'clock time', aligned to the memories of people as they travel, with each section of a 'line' resonating with different tones or cadences, depending on the type of terrain being crossed. One 'sings' the landscape, and doing so reinforces one's own line and those of others whose songlines they may intersect with. Ever under threat from mining companies and development, the songlines have been fiercely protected by the indigenous people themselves whilst also being a source of inspiration to many Western writers and artists.

Few hitchers would actually make the comparison with their own mental topographies and the deep-time tradition of the Aboriginal 'songlines', but there are some similarities in terms of their status as persecuted migratory peoples, often at the bottom of their respective social hierarchies. Should we choose to examine the social histories and politics of the great 'thumb lines' from certain eras and places – US 'Route 66', the 'Hippie Trail', 'Cairo to the Cape' – we would find a rich overlapping narrative. We would discern a tapestry trail of liberation and persecution, defined by the songs, photographs and poetry of those who hitched the route, perhaps offering views and documenting events which might run counter to or be absent from what appears in guidebooks or standard history texts.

An excellent companion piece to *Ben Nevis hitch-hike*, therefore, which develops the idea of a 'thumb line' in a more sociological manner, is the substantial and evocative poem 'Night Highway 99', written in 1956 by Gary

Snyder, about the memory of journeys between Seattle and San Francisco.[4] A friend of 'Beat' writer Jack Kerouac, whose novel *On the road* was published the following year, Snyder brought a wide range of influences to his own writing: his experience of forestry work, union activism, mountaineering, anthropology and Buddhism. He wrote many short personal poems about hitchhiking throughout his career;[5] 'Night Highway 99' is a social commentary on the political history of the landscapes through which the road passed. It begins with a typical Beat theme of young people wanting to get out there and keep moving: 'We're on our way / man / out of town / go hitching down / that Highway 99'. As the journey unrolls like a scroll north to south, we are presented with little staccato snatches of conversation between driver and hitcher: 'Eugene / Ex-logger selling skidder cable / wants to get to San Francisco / fed and drunk / Sutherlin / Guy just back from Alaska – don't like / the States now – too much law'.

Snyder hitched this route many times and fills the poem with personal memories and references to wider social struggles: there's a mention of the 1916 massacre of Industrial Workers of the World activists ('Wobblies') at Everett, Washington ('The Sheriff's posse stood in double rows') and an acknowledgement of the socially invisible migrant workers and marginalised indigenous peoples ('Mount Vernon / Fifty weary Indians / Sleep in the bus station / Strawberry pickers speaking Kwakiutl') but also of the ordinary lives he shares time with: 'Fat man in a Chevrolet / wants to go back to L.A. / "too damned poor now"'.

Gradually the youthful impatience and apparent urgent need of the narrator to get to his destination is questioned. Arriving in San Francisco – 'City / gleaming far away' – there is a realisation that 'NO / body / gives a shit / man / who you are / or what's your car / there / IS no – 99'. Here there is a palpable sense of loss: the experience of the road, which has transformed him, providing a sense of something much more transcendent, has suddenly been ripped away. For Snyder, this journey is a starting point for learning about life differently, to be less goal oriented and materialistic, to slow down, savour simpler pleasures and extend compassion to others.

If there is a lesson here, it is that 'hitching time' allows us to see the politics of the space travelled over, bear witness to struggles past and present within a wider ecological framework. Yet Long and Snyder are both articulate contributors to the social history of the kerbside: what of those whose thumb lines are less visible, who do not shout out in verse so confidently about their connection to the land; those who are less free than others on the road, but still may contribute to its culture, perhaps through the useful application of a marker pen to a light pole or guard railing? What do they think?

Roadside inscriptions

We all used to see hitchhiking graffiti and it could be a welcome distraction from staring at oncoming traffic. Usually scrawled on the back of road furniture or a destination sign, these lively, irreverent and cathartic hieroglyphics had a tendency to comment on the psychological effects of the hours passed standing without being able to partake in 'sex, drugs or beer', with a qualification that the consequences of this were most likely to be hypothermia or death. To emphasise the point, declarations such as 'beware: hitchhiker's graveyard' were prominently displayed, annotated with a mocking skull and crossbones.

These were the 'funnies', next to which there might be more revealing information about persons unknown, those who had taken the trouble to ink some private detail or observation for posterity. Today we'd probably call this process 'tagging', and if it were in the middle of a city it might be a likely source of inspiration for undergraduate student projects on urban culture. Yet for Mark E. Silverstein, of Las Vegas, Nevada, this raw roadside data was more akin to a message in a bottle rather than part of any cultural scene. Since 1992 he has made it his business to collect them and create a digital archive. Often this has been revisiting his own hitchhiking haunts in the American south-west, such as Highway 40 (the old 'Route 66'). He's fascinated by the variety of hastily scrawled biographies, practical 'road' advice, open declarations of love, esoteric literary quotations or demands for political change: why, he asks, of one discovery, would someone take the trouble to lovingly reproduce a poem from the year 1450 called 'Robin Hood and the monk' onto a light pole?[6] Is this a rare visible instance of hitchhiker vulnerability, of wanting to confess and share with others a verse which had moved them in a dark moment perhaps? I like the empathy at the heart of Silverstein's project, to reclaim the marginalia of the motor age, before it is washed from the world (pencil can last fifty years, permanent marker a lot less, judging from his research). If I were to retrace my aforementioned Highland 'thumb line' today, I imagine that most of its equivalent annotations would have long gone, but I would still be wondering about that enigmatic resident of my own home town, Hull: 'The Eyes'.

For a while it seemed that he or she had been everywhere, as each service station or major junction in the north of England bore the trademark graphic of a pair of wide staring eyes in the manner of the Egyptian god Ra. Beneath each ocular depiction would be a clear, organised description of the journey currently in progress ('The Eyes' heads south). Whether they were bound for a music festival such as Glastonbury, visiting friends, or going for a job interview (yes, really, I do recall this), there was a surety about the annotations which suggested a commitment to regular hitchhiking and a connection with others who might be reading them. So, if we are trying to apply a little vagabond sociology, I would surmise that 'The Eyes' was probably in their twenties, male and Caucasian, 'culturally rich, economically poor' in the parlance of today, and, at a time of relatively high unemployment in the UK, had opted for casual work, which suited the itinerant lifestyle which they clearly enjoyed. They would be very much part of the 'gift economy', although it would be some years before the term accrued popular use. Hitchhiking during the late 1980s and early 1990s was still seen as part of a legitimate (albeit declining) youthful activity – supported by just enough cultural memory (or 'capacity') from earlier decades not to be completely written off as a deviant activity.

'The Eyes' was a documenter of these times: a would-be Mark Silverstein, who, for all of their individualistic communiqués on the hitchhiking 'wire', was smart enough to recognise that they were contributing to a broader narrative of travel as social storytelling.

Putting ourselves in the picture

Why take photographs of hitchhikers or collect images of roadside graffiti? Jacob Holdt's *American pictures* contains surprisingly few photographs of being on the road, yet listening to him talk about how he chose to photograph the African American underclasses of the Deep South is a reminder that an ill-chosen shot can reinforce stereotypes and fail to allow the subject a sense of agency. For those of us concerned with documenting the life and times of the groups of people who have travelled the kerbsides, this is highly pertinent to how we remember the past to help inform projects and experiences in the future. In the early decades of the twentieth century there were few official photographs of hitchhikers, and the travellers themselves were rarely wealthy enough to own a camera, so the whole debate about control of images and the politics of representation was largely irrelevant. This changed during the Great Depression in the United States, when photographers from the US government's Farm Security Administration (FSA) such as Walker Evans, Arthur Rothstein, Dorothea Lange and Rondal Partridge were tasked with documenting the migrant workers and homeless itinerants on the roads of America. The purpose was to help communicate the reality of their circumstances to newspaper readers who had not been touched by the after-effects of the Wall Street Crash of 1929. All took pictures of hitchhikers at some point, but it is Dorothea Lange's that linger most in the memory. Many of us know

Figure 2.2 *Young family, penniless, hitchhiking on U.S. Highway 99, California.* Dorothea Lange's haunting 1936 photo, part of the US government's documentation of the Great Depression.

her for the 'face of the Depression' photograph *Migrant mother* (of Flora Owens Thompson and her children under a makeshift awning by the roadside), but the hitchhiking ones are equally stark, particularly: *Young family, penniless, hitchhiking on U.S. Highway 99, California* (November 1936), a rare instance of a photograph of an entire family seeking a lift (Figure 2.2).

It's a low-angled shot, with the father staring off past us, into the dry distance, holding a steady pose, and the mother sitting impassively on one of two small suitcases beside him, cradling a young child. While we may have become desensitised to images of mass migrations, Lange's picture nevertheless evokes the sentiments it was intended to do: the unsettling image of a family cut adrift in a massive space of sky and road, marooned by modernity. The remaining text of Lange's for the picture reads: 'The father, twenty-four, and the mother, seventeen, came from Winston-Salem, North Carolina, early in 1935. Their baby was born in the Imperial Valley, California, where they were working as field laborers.'

We do not hear the voices of these hitchhikers, who remain anonymous (FSA policy), nor glean anything about this particular journey, or the arrangement struck between the respective parties. Even with good intentions, the relationship feels unequal, the subjects passive and the photographic gaze aggressive. In *On photography* Susan Sontag argues that the work of the FSA was to portray a dignity, but in the end it results in a kind of heroic poverty, giving the viewer an imaginary relationship where they can 'take possession of space in which they are insecure'.[7]

When cameras became more available to the general public in the 1950s and 1960s, we begin to see more do-it-yourself roadside anthropology put together by budding photojournalists-cum-hitchers. These were contemporaries of the hitchhiking guidebook writers, emboldened by the belief that the sharing of vehicles was a harbinger of a more empathetic, fairer and less consumer-driven society to come. We see this outlook in Phil Wernig's idiosyncratic and heartfelt early 1970s 'photo-documentary' *The hitchhikers*, unique for its detailed in-action and person-centred hitchhiking shots, juxtaposed with descriptions of the hitchhikers' lives and attitudes, many of whom articulate concerns about how materialism begets more violence and the importance of conversation as an antidote. Leafing through these sepia prints – most of which are from the west coast of the USA – it is hard not to feel as though you've interrupted a series of spontaneous conversations that have occurred by the roadside. From a historical perspective, the variety of hitchhikers is surprising: parents with very young children, solo female hitchers (some with dogs), people thumbing in the middle of cities, heading to the beach with surf boards, or standing in freezing conditions trying out various signs and postures.

If you do an internet search for photographs of hitchhikers there is a uniformity of perspective, even when you get beyond the stock images. There is a tendency to frame the traveller in the close middle distance, which can be helpful for capturing diversity of mood and thumb technique, but less so for culture or context. We don't get much of a sense of what it actually feels like to stand in those spaces, to own them as if in the worn footsteps of a Richard Long, so it was refreshing to stumble across the work of Chris Coekin, who, like myself, was concerned about documenting a declining but important form of transport.

Initially he'd visualised the photography for his 2007 book *The hitcher* as an anthropological artwork featuring a cross-section of contemporary hitchhikers, only to realise that numbers had declined a lot faster than he had anticipated since he'd done the bulk of his own thumbing. Instead, he chose to photograph himself en route to many of the places he'd previously thumbed to, trying to evoke the experience of being by those kerbsides.

Using clever camerawork, he acts out different hitchhiking 'roles' and emotions, depending on weather, time of day, state of the traffic and so forth. If you know the work of Cindy Sherman – adorning herself in the dress and attitudes of different idealised notions of women in history – it's that kind of photography: reflexive and reclaiming of identities and categories. So, we find him, Coekin, looking purposeful, hopeful, pensive, vulnerable, bemused or bored, hot and thirsty (in clothing to suit). Sometimes he is 'caught' by a camera that is 'hidden' in the kerbside grass or on street furniture, which adds to his presence as a legitimate part of the landscape. The diversity of position and mood in Coekin's photographs resists the single objectifying interpretation of what a hitchhiker might stand for.

What we learn from this is how complex and varied the physicality of trying to hitchhike actually is; how strange and vibrant the environment of these apparently banal 'non-places' can be if we stand long enough in them to care. [8] As with Richard Long's *Ben Nevis hitch-hike* we glean the sensations of the moment: beneath Coekin's feet, the splashing puddles, uneven gravel, the soggy cardboard signs and fading marker pens, we feel the turbulence of the passing vehicles, those moments of hope, and of despair, when it isn't going so well. Looking down through his lens, there is abundant evidence of our disconnection with the land that we pass through: the disposable culture of the motor age tossed from car windows, scorched rubber patterns and fragments of glass on the highway, flattened rabbits, the blackened grass.

Equally unusual is the accompanying social archive, of those who stopped their journeys in these landscapes to give him a lift. Each is captured by their vehicle and filmed with eye-catching polarised colours, almost as if Coekin feels the need to 'ink in' their part a bit more solidly, to give them a greater sense of permanence in what is a fleeting arrangement and an eminently forgotten part of history. You feel that moment of social connection with strangers and their apparent reasons for picking him up (which he includes next to the photographs).

Numerous photography-related projects of this nature exist, usually the work of obsessive hobbyists and philanthropists who have been photographing hitchhikers for decades: Doug Biggert's collection of 1970s colour Polaroids in California; Jim Sanderson, the 'Angel' of North Island, New Zealand, who kept log books and albums in his car to show to those he picked up; Tasmanian photo-journalist Giuilo Saggin's book *And so I did*, which captures in stark black and white the lives and thoughts of those who gave him lifts on Australian highways. Technically minded artists have sent mannequins or robots out into the world, expanding the notion of a 'thumb line' in the process: Detroit-based Jim Pallas, testing and mapping out the boundaries of art, commerce and life with his 'Hitchhiker Project' since 1981; the 2014 HitchBOT initiative of David Harris Smith and Frauke Zeller, which was designed to see if humans would harm a cute welly-wearing robot as it hitched across the Trans-Canada Highway, posting pictures of its whereabouts and becoming a global media sensation in the process. Someone watching all of these hitchhiking-related cultural developments has been long-time kerbside advocate and archivist extraordinaire Bernd Wechner

(Figure 2.3), who'd not only done years on the road but had crafted one of the first online memoirs, *Anywhere but here*.

Wechner was an information technology specialist working in Germany during the late 1990s, just as independent travellers were starting to get online. He set up a hitchhiking page at Suite101.com and began building up an impressive collection of short essays on all aspects of the theory, practice and culture of hitchhiking, the first of its kind in English and something of an electronic base camp for what was to come in the next decade. He read and reviewed everything, knew all about Holdt's *American pictures*, and he'd even gained permission from Mario Rinvolucri, who had done his own vagabond sociological interviewing in England during the late 1960s, to digitise his pioneering work *Hitchhiking* (to which we will return in later chapters). He was the closest thing the hitchhiking world had to an official archivist, and he'd thumb to any hitchhiking gathering that he got wind of, even if it meant hours in freezing conditions.

Wechner's enthusiastic web presence and his ability to see the historicity of what he was observing from the roadside caught the attention of his American counterpart Morgan 'Sal'man Strub, a hitchhiker with his own substantial database of road culture. So, by the time Wechner flew into Seattle in November 2002, to attend the First North American Hitchhiker Gathering, the time seemed right to pool resources and present a more unified digital face to the outside world.

Figure 2.3 Legendary archivist Bernd Wechner en route to Vilnius in 1999 for an international hitchhiker gathering. A voracious researcher in the 1990s, his IT abilities gave hitchhiking a significant cross-cultural digital presence.

Hatching a plan in Seattle: the birth of Digihitch.com

To the solitary journalist from the *Seattle Times* and the casual observer, the Hitchhiker Gathering didn't look very impressive – just ten people sitting outside a caravan in Seward Park in the autumnal air, with a couple of identifying signs, swapping stories.[9] Yet in the history of hitchhiking, this 2002 meeting was one of its most important moments: a cross-continental association of key figures, who had put the hours into archiving road culture and were keen to encourage and share more research.

When I began to research hitchhiking in the early years of this century I quickly discovered what Wechner had concluded a couple of years before: that there was a real dearth of meaningful research on the history of hitchhiking. What existed tended to be linked to short-term state interests of a legal or traffic-flow mindset and none of it very recent. However, in 2001 there had been a key attempt at an intervention in the sustainable transport field, with Graeme Chesters and David Smith suggesting in a sociological research paper 'The neglected art of hitchhiking' that, with sufficient research and policy weight, some kind of managed hitching system was possible and practical for many parts of the West. Pondering whether to pursue this further they were told by senior social scientists in the field that nobody wanted to devote funds to hitchhiking and they should pursue something more appropriate to the transport needs of the twenty-first century. They grimly concluded that future work may have to be done by keen researchers on the fringes of the intellectual world.[10]

For all of their mutual enthusiasm, Wechner and Strub had arrived at the same conclusion about researching hitchhiking, but via very different biographical routes. Wechner's hitching career followed a pattern similar to my own: mostly done whilst a student and in more casual employment, tapering off when more permanent work and family responsibilities began to take over free time. Strub (Figure 2.4), by contrast, had a difficult family background, had experienced mental health issues and had not done well at school. Hitchhiking did not just provide an escape from this, but was a personal revelation; he had a real love for those he met on the road, despite an unpleasant debut at sixteen when he was propositioned by a driver. The account of this makes for uncomfortable reading yet remarkably had the reverse effect on him in the longer term. Strub claimed to have always sensed the pain in others and the event eventually emboldened him to follow Jacob Holdt's advice on dealing with difficult situations through empathy: 'love, honesty and acceptance toward others can sometimes keep one safe'.[11]

Amongst those joining Morgan and Bernd at the Hitchhiker Gathering was Irv Thomas, the author of *Derelict days* and the discoverer of our first

Figure 2.4 Morgan 'Sal'man Strub, founder of www.digihitch.com, whose death at the age of thirty-seven robbed hitchhiking of its most proactive American organiser. Here on favourite territory near Fredericksburg, California, heading into Arizona in 1999.

'intentional' hitchhiker, Charles Brown Jr. It was a moot point as to whether he had hitched in more decades than anyone else (six), but he was probably the only seventy-five-year-old still hitchhiking who had an active website telling people about it! From a publicity point of view, Irv Thomas's attendance at this and subsequent events such as the Media Exhibition of Hitchhiking in Portland the following June gave those events a novelty value and a gravitas.[12] Hitchhiking in North America at this point was commonly believed to be non-existent, as a result of all kinds of perceived shifts in public attitude towards risk and media scaremongering (see Chapter 8); a pensioner thumbing to an organised hitchhiking event was unusual and unexpected.

Strub's plan was for his basic site www.digihitch.com to grow into an 'interactive portal' for hitchers and writers everywhere, 'to bring together the stories and resources of the road, to create a community'. He'd already been excited by the energetic travel blogs of Polish hitcher Kinga 'Freespirit' Choszcz and the small international readership following her hitchhike around the world (Chapter 7), so the Seattle meeting with Wechner, Thomas and others gave his own project an injection of enthusiasm.[13]

Even in its early days, the website had a professionalism which took its responsibilities as the most likely first port of call for hitchers very seriously. Mindful of controversy, Strub posted a 'disclaimer' that hitchhiking was not recommended for minors, and all travellers should be aware of the potential dangers (and preferably the legal situation) before setting out. Accordingly, a state-by-state guide to the various interpretations and likely applications of the (often vague) legislation was provided, as were details on the viability of thumbing in a number of countries around the world. Strub then got on with the business of recruiting a series of regular correspondents to add opinions and updates, many of whom began to add to the new sections of 'advice and tips', 'campfire tales' and an expanding database of hitchhikers from previous eras, films, songs, plays and writings about life on the road.

This was significant, as it meant future researchers wouldn't be repeating work already done in film archives or at the Library of Congress. There were plenty of others ready to lend a hand or advocate for the site, including music journalist and troubadour Elijah Wald (author of *Riding with strangers*) and the legendary Russian hitchhiker Alexej Vorov, who entrusted Strub with the responsibility of organising the American leg of the Transglobe Autostop Competition in 2005 (see Chapter 10). As the website took on a more inter-national feel, with regular reporting of races and gatherings in Europe, so the virtual traffic soared, with over 30,000 visits per month at one point in 2006. The forum discussion threads multiplied and it became hard to keep up with all of the postings. By the time that the site was adding its voice to the fiftieth anniversary celebrations for Kerouac's *On the road* in 2007, there was regular sponsorship by online retailers linked with the site's extensive coverage of iconic road music, film and literature. All that seemed to be missing from its thriving pages was an academic archive which wasn't trapped behind a pay-wall (as most academic research tends to be).

Then Morgan developed cancer and died in 2010, aged thirty-seven, leaving a huge hole in many lives and a massive legacy. A bitter battle to save his creation ensued; a tug of war between hitchhiking friends and members of Strub's family who were less interested in or even disapproving of what he had achieved. The dedication of a few saw the site briefly revamped in 2012, but it vanished again under another cloud of accusations. There was a small consolation in that some of the work was preserved via Wechner's website, even though he had moved on to develop his professional work in IT and start a family, after driving the hitchhiking agenda for so many years.

A couple of US travel sites tried to take up the challenge, but there was an absence of anything comparable for years, until the Vilnius-based Hitchwiki. org site began to get into its stride. Today, it fulfils most of the same functions that digihitch.com did, with the additional benefits of being in the midst of the hitchhiking club culture of former Eastern Bloc countries and the Russian Federation. In the years since the demise of digihitch.com, the academic interest in hitchhiking has undergone something of a roadside renaissance: not only does Hitchwiki.org report the latest books and articles in its regular news pages, but it now sports as extensive a bibliography of hitching articles and papers as has ever existed. Occasionally, some of the authors make an appearance on the fringes of major conferences in sociology, leisure studies or transport policy.

If we are to pursue further vagabond sociology, to see the world through the eyes of the hitchhiker, then we need a research institute! Fortunately, we already have the makings of one, in the heart of Slovenia, where one remarkable person has upped the research ante a little with the creation of the world's first hitchhiking museum.

The museum, the mayor, his hat and our future

Miran Ipavec looks interesting. Slovenia doesn't have a massive hitchhiking culture, but it is starting to generate Europe-wide attention on account of the antics of this fifty-something-year-old man in a distinctive white-brimmed hat who insists on thumbing everywhere – even to business meetings. He was a late starter, at twenty-five, but he's made up for it, visiting thirty-eight countries, in 6,000 lifts, covering some 200,000 kilometres and learning seven different languages in the process. Lifestyle-wise, these statistics – which he's still adding to – put him in the bracket of the 'extreme hitchers club' we'll be joining in Chapter 6, but his primary importance in the history of hitch-hiking is his method of documenting some of it: he opened a museum of hitchhiking in 2014 in Kanal ob Soci, a small town in the Soca valley where he had once been the mayor (Figure 2.5). To date, there have been a small number of hitchhiker exhibitions of paintings, films and art installations in several countries, and hitchhiker gatherings on at least four continents, as well as hitchhiking expeditions and lecture tours (mainly conducted by the Academy of Free Travel) and hitchhiking club libraries, yet until this museum opened there had never been anywhere permanent to visit which displays the paraphernalia of the road in such an interactive and evolving way.

Over the years, Miran Ipavec has gathered a tremendous potpourri of hitchhiking paraphernalia from each country he has visited: *liftplaats* signs, flags and scarves, road maps and guidebooks. All these are displayed in cases, along with his sleeping bag and a collection of the white hats which have protected him over the miles. After three decades of roadside solicitations, he's got through a number of log books detailing each journey – the best of which are recounted in his 2014 publication *Hitchhiking tales*. Should you visit the museum and can't afford his book you can always cheer him up by playing one of his hitchhiker road games (such as guessing the flag for every country that he has visited). Television interviews and regular mentions on Hitchwiki.org or at the European Hitchhiker Gatherings (see Chapter 10) have raised awareness of the museum, which Miran went on to relocate to more populous centres – first Ljubljana and now Koper – and there's always talk of promoting hitchhiking through 'pop up' museums in other countries.

Figure 2.5 Miran Ipavec. Prolific hitcher, author and curator of the world's first hitchhiking museum, which opened in 2014 in Kanal, Slovenia, a town where he was once the mayor.

I love the ambition and sense of democracy here, but I also wonder whether in any of these buildings there has been enough space to incorporate a selection of the artefacts and projects which we've name-checked in this chapter, plus some of the archives that others have also assembled. It seems such a fantastic opportunity: to have a small research institute, or a hitch-hiker reading room, full of guidebooks, memoirs, academic papers, binders of photos and maybe a copy of Jacob Holdt's slide show running, just to put things into perspective.

If there's any money floating around, I am going to make a special plea for the loan of a couple of the paintings of Polish artist Edward Dwurnik, to create an appropriate ambience for lateral thinking amongst the next wave of student thesis writers and visiting researchers. Many artists of Dwurnik's 1960s generation hitched, but not many turned their experiences into critiques of Soviet art and the Polish military state! His series of colourful higgledy-piggledy representations of cities (the 'Hitchhiking trips' series) began as roadside sketches – drafted in cafés or on street corners as he 'drifted' through a town – designed to present a more grassroots and 'participatory' view of history and our relationships with one another.[14] These are his 'thumb lines', evoking landscapes full of lived vibrant activities of communities, in close proximity, talking to one another, as contrasted with the orderly State-centred arrangement of an urban grid design, empty of people save the military. They are as much of a reflection on power and exclusion as the photographs of Jacob Holdt which inspired this backpack of hitchhiking culture that we've been filling en route to Slovenia.

So, however we have managed to get to Miran's museum, which ever 'thumb line' taken, thoughts processed about the politics and people we've encountered on the roadside, photographs taken, marker pens wielded: in all that 'hitching time', we've probably forgotten that, at some point, we've been humming a few tunes as well. It is a reminder that one item which is missing from this new vagabond archive is a compendium of hitchhiking songs. In the next chapter we will look at how some of the politics of the road are expressed through the medium of the hitchhiking song as it has played out over the decades – through the eyes of an assortment of troubadours and vagabond creatives. But let's leave Miran and any other curators to decide the best choice of ambient sounds for the museum. I hope it won't be so disruptive as to disturb the work of any recent visitors to the museum – a latter-day Bernd Wechner or a Morgan Strub perhaps – trying to find ways to motivate us all to think like hitchhikers a bit more regularly.

Chapter 3

In search of Woody Guthrie: singing the politics of hitchhiking

Please give me a lift, man

The opening words of the song 'Barstow' are a little unusual: 'It's January 26. I'm freezing. Ed Fitzgerald: Age nineteen, five feet ten inches, black hair, brown eyes. Going home to Boston, Massachusetts: it's four, and I'm hungry and broke.' As hitchhiking songs go, it isn't one which you will be humming the next day should it pop up on your travel playlist. There are no feel-good sunshine moments of roadside liberation, as in The Eagles' 'Take it easy', no optimism of love and a fresh start in the Old Crow Medicine Show's enchanting 'Wagon wheel', or reflections on changing perspectives as with Sheryl Crow's 'Everyday is a winding road'. This eight-minute surreal and edgy blend of folk song and manic orchestration packs plenty of social commentary in its primal evocations.

Written in 1941 by American composer Harry Partch and subtitled 'Eight hitchhiker inscriptions from a highway railing at Barstow, California', the piece was designed to capture the inner world of someone hitchhiking on a winter day during the Great Depression of the 1930s. He'd done enough of it himself to know that Barstow has a bit of reputation for marooning hitchhikers, and situated on the edge of the Mojave Desert it is always prone to wildly varying temperatures. Partch wanted to evoke that rawness in the music he created, to do more than just offer a naturalist orchestral representation of the travelling experience. Listening to it, you'd been forgiven if you thought it sounds 'wrong': Partch believed that to get to the emotional centre of being by the roadside he had to devise an entirely new tonal system, as well as a range of new instruments.[1]

The delivery of the inscription lines by actors is similarly otherworldly, the words rasped out of the temporal distance, almost as a reminder to us that it was possible to starve or freeze by the roadside. Conscious of this, the anonymous second hitchhiker points out to new arrivals that it is possible to get an 'easy handout' (in Monrovia, California). Next up is Marie Blackwell, aged nineteen, of Los Angeles, who, perhaps to distract herself from a rumbling stomach, makes a lively announcement about her destination: 'my object is matrimony'. The fourth hitcher replies 'a very good idea you have. I too am on the look-out for a mate', but gets a ride before being able to leave their own attributes and intentions. Barstow blues hits the next contributor, who waits for five unsuccessful days of counting cars before announcing grimly 'to hell with it, I am going to walk'. Our sixth traveller seems more optimistic, writing: 'Jesus was god in the flesh'! More lonely hearts follow, with 'good-looking' George, the seventh hitcher, 'looking for a millionaire wife'. No doubt Johnny Reinhart, the final inscriber, had a few amorous thoughts on his 'twenty-seven hundred mile' trip from 'Chi, Illinois', but he settles for recounting his two days without food, the rain, the nights in open boxcars and sleeping by the highway, before cheerfully wishing 'all who read this, if they can, get a lift and best of luck to you too'.

According to the Harry Partch Estate, there is good anecdotal evidence that these were genuine inscriptions (the composer regularly carried a notebook for ideas whilst on the road), which adds an extra poignancy to the challenge of trying to convey the experience and politics of the highway as we wait for a lift.[2] Every sub-genre of travelling songs mirrors a movement in the world: sea shanties accompany hard labour with oars and sails, the swirling accordions mimicking the roll of the waves; the rattle of the rails echo the percussive click of the 'train song', the growling rock-and-roll guitar riff urges the motorbike out of the suburbs to beneath the big desert sky.

What does a hitchhiking song tell us? Is it more insightful about our fascination with being nomadic *because* we are not travelling by any of other mode of transport? Does a song sung standing in the shoes of someone by the roadside tell us different things than a song about getting to the beach in a sports car, or is it just a starker way of looking at the same issues about how power can shape our identities?

Documenting all hitchhiking songs is not my intention here. The key criterion is whether we learn anything about hitching in the song, or the social circumstances which produced it, and whether it encourages us to think laterally about who we are and the societies we live in. Many songs of the highway are driven by common themes of liberty and self-reliance – the self-styled 'king of the road' – whilst always being prone to the demands of authority to – in the words of Ewan MacColl – 'go, move, shift'. Issues of migration, land ownership, hardship and persecution are never far from the kerbside and it is through the eyes of Woody Guthrie, who witnessed plenty of these things, that we begin our putative genealogy of hitchhiking songs.

Bound for glory

Born in 1912, in Okemah, Oklahoma, Guthrie's family circumstances were sufficiently complex to propel him onto the road whilst in his early teens. His mother, Nora, suffered from the degenerative and hereditary neurological disorder Huntington's disease and she struggled to run the family home and bring up her children, whilst his father, Charley, traded real estate and was active in local politics. The home pressures and a number of unsuccessful land deals propelled his father to move to Pampa in the Texas panhandle. Woody (Figure 3.1) would hitchhike or freight-hop there during the school summer holidays. He was effectively self-reliant from fourteen years old, odd-jobbing, hanging out with musicians in Pampa, developing his musical skills and beginning to write songs of his own.

A series of family tragedies that occurred whilst Guthrie was relatively young, including his sister Clara dying in a fire aged seven, have led some to suggest that the repeated wanderings of his adult life were somehow connected to a deep-rooted fear of holding on to people and places lest they be ripped from him. Nevertheless, the itinerant lifestyle that he pursued gave him a unique rail-and-road's-eye perspective on the world, evoked in his first book, *Bound for glory* (1943), in letters written to the folk archivist Alan Lomax and in the thousand-odd songs composed before he himself began to be affected by Huntington's disease, in his forties. Some of these he composed whilst waiting for lifts, some he sang to people who let him ride

Figure 3.1 Woody Guthrie, the definitive road bard, whose songs of justice shaped the work of Bob Dylan, Bruce Springsteen and many others. Credit: Al Aumuller/New York World-Telegram and the *Sun* (1943).

with them, others entertained the denizens of innumerable freights or graced the campfires of hobo 'jungles'.

Guthrie's short life (he died in 1967, aged fifty-five) has been heavily mythologised, but the concerns of his art are harder to distort, even if some of the political verses from his most famous song, 'This land is your land', do disappear from songbooks and other people's recordings. What is now, in effect, an alternative American national anthem begins uncontroversially enough: 'As I was walking that ribbon of highway / I saw above me that endless skyway / I saw below me that golden valley / This land was made for you and me'. But we are quickly moved into a different terrain:

> As I went walking I saw a sign there
> And on the sign it said 'No trespassing.'
> But on the other side it didn't say nothing
> That side was made for you and me.
>
> In the shadow of the steeple I saw my people
> By the relief office I seen my people
> As they stood there hungry, I stood there asking
> Is this land made for you and me?[3]

Although there is no actual mention of hitchhiking in the song, the words were penned after a transcontinental hitch west to east in early 1940, and motivated by the extreme poverty that he witnessed en route. According to friend and fellow folk legend Pete Seeger, the moment of epiphany was whilst Guthrie was taking refuge in a Pennsylvania diner one freezing February day and he heard the recently released Irving Berlin song 'God bless America' sung by Kate Smith on the radio. Its cheery words of unity seemed false and he'd set writing about a riposte.

By this time, Guthrie was performing songs that would form his stark and unrelenting collection *Dust bowl ballads*, based on the terrible impact of the clouds of loose topsoil that had corkscrewed their way across Oklahoma on Sunday 14 April 1935. The ruined livelihoods and subsequent evictions and exodus of 'the Okies', to California, has been documented on numerous occasions. Perhaps the most enduring and eloquent account of those events was by Guthrie's own hitchhiking contemporary John Steinbeck, in his book *The grapes of wrath* (published in 1939), which follows the struggles of the extended Joad family as they travel the now much fabled 'Route 66', to discover that they had been lied to about the so-called 'land of opportunity'. The book begins with descriptions of thickening clouds of dust, anxious farmers sitting in doorways peering at the transformed fields and a hitch-hiker, Tom Joad, staring at a truck emblazoned with a 'No riders' sticker. At the time, *The grapes of wrath* was judged as shocking: more because the book had ended with a young mother wet-nursing a sick man after her own child had died than because of the wider indecencies that the author had been trying to portray.

The character of Tom Joad has become an enduring symbol of political fortitude in impoverished times. Woody Guthrie was influenced by Steinbeck's book and included a two-part song entitled 'Tom Joad' on *Dust bowl ballads*, with others in the collection seemingly drawing on the same material: 'Do re mi' recounts the policing of migrants to California, corruption and duplicity; 'Pretty boy Floyd' humanises the wanderer who steals to feed the poor. Guthrie's later song 'Deportee: plane wreck at Los Gatos' identifies with the plight of the thirty-two fruit pickers who perished and were buried without identification in a mass grave (now corrected thanks to Tim Hernandez's research and a new monument).

Guthrie's views from the roadside register on many levels and influenced the politics of Bob Dylan and later Bruce Springsteen, both of whom have periodically stuck out a thumb in their work understanding that it has been a place of both liberation and desperation. In 1995, Springsteen used the memory of the 1930s to raise questions about late twentieth-century poverty and exclusion in the poignant 'The ghost of Tom Joad'. Then, in the wake of the financial meltdowns and economic hardships of 2008, his playing of the title song and renditions of 'This land is your land' took on a much broader racial dimension in the context of election rallies for the President-to-be, Barack Obama.

It was an apt reminder that too often songs of the road which speak of poverty and social exclusion reflect only the experience of the white artists who pen them. This was not the case with one of the first and certainly the most famous blues songs about hitchhiking.

'Nothing in rambling': racism on the road

Legend has it that the lyrics refer to a bargain for musical fame struck with the devil, but there are many interpretations of Robert Johnson's 1936 song 'Cross road blues'. We do know that the location was a typical hitchhiking point on Highway 61 at Clarksdale, Mississippi, where it meets Highway 49 and that he was trying to get a ride. Highway 61 was a common route for black musicians to hitch north on to get work in more cosmopolitan cities beyond the Mason–Dixon line. Just being out alone was a vulnerable business, but the real problem was making sure that the journey was undertaken in daylight. It's not long into his vigil before he's thinking ahead: 'the sun goin' down now boy, / dark gon' catch me here'. This was a potentially

Figure 3.2 Memphis Minnie, in whose songs like 'Nothing in rambling' hitching a ride was tough if you were black and female.

life-threatening situation: he is a black man in a segregated state at a time of curfews for 'coloureds'.

The Great Depression exacerbated prejudice. Mobility was already controlled by the so-called 'Black codes' (which used vagrancy laws to limit the movement of waged and indentured black employees) and the 'Jim Crow laws' (which formalised segregation in public places and on transport). There's a telling Arthur Rothstein photograph from 1937 which depicts six bean-pickers trying to hitch a ride together in Florida, indicative perhaps of the balance of safety versus long waits for a truck.

'Cross road blues' has been covered by many artists and, as with 'This land is your land', often loses its more political nuances in the arrangement. Yet it is still a male perspective of the road. By comparison, the lesser-known oeuvre of Memphis Minnie (Figure 3.2), who was more forthcoming than Guthrie about the experience of racism on the roads, deserves to be heard outside of the orbit of blues connoisseurs and scholars of black feminist history.

Born Elizabeth Douglas in Algiers, Louisiana, in 1897, one of thirteen children, she began playing banjo and guitar early and spent her teenage years busking on the streets of Memphis and touring with circuses before being hired by a record company in 1929. Her blues songs, of which there were several hundred, reflect challenging personal circumstances: being caught up in the worst race riot in twentieth-century America on 28 May 1917 in East St Louis (scores of dead, perhaps hundreds), she lived amongst extreme poverty in southern Chicago (climbing on soap boxes with a guitar to campaign against slum clearances) and had to supplement her own musical income with prostitution. Economic vulnerability was underpinned with the difficulties of travelling as a black woman, segregated on passenger trains until the early 1930s, and in rural areas prone to sexual violence if walking or hitch-hiking. Many black women disguised themselves as men to hitchhike if they had the means. What they thought about it has largely eluded documentation, although since the emergence of feminist and black scholarship, a closer examination of the culture of the time – diaries, poetry and song – has assisted our understanding of the political realities behind individual situations.

The poet and historian Lorna Dee Cervantes tries to unpick the ambiguity in the lyrics of Memphis Minnie songs, pointing out how the reality experienced by black women on the road (including herself) was often only subtly acknowledged:

> rapes were occurring at a phenomenal rate. A young girl, eleven, thirteen, seventeen, travelling, hitchhiking. This was why she dressed herself up as a man. That's what [it] was about. 'Nineteen and seventeen'. 'Twenty-one was tough'. They'd grab you by the hair. Pull you in. These truckers.

And inevitably there would be consequences, so 'In my girlish days' (1941) we follow a teenager hitchhiking away from her family, perhaps heading for an abortion clinic. It is a situation which Cervantes feels adds a heavy interpretation to even catchy famous numbers such as 'Going to Frisco town' (1929), a likely destination for unwanted babies and probable sterilisation of the unfortunate bearer. This was a time when American politics debated and often practised eugenics by stealth, as a way of reducing the numbers of potentially mixed-race children.[4]

It is unsurprising, then, that the oft-covered 'Nothing in rambling' (1941) seems to be giving the clear message that there was no escape from the realities of being poor, black and a woman – the road and where it leads amount to more of the same inequalities and injustices. It is for this reason, some suggest, that there are no road numbers or eulogies for particular highways in the songs of Memphis Minnie.[5] Imagined relationships with freedom down the road are not the same for those who have to live on them.

Three decades later, the growth of the civil rights movement intensified the mood on the roads of the Deep South, as songs of the open road suddenly became part of a national conversation about the principles upon which America had been founded.

Letting freedom ring

In his book *Travels with Charley*, John Steinbeck recounts driving in Louisiana in 1960 and finding himself picking up black hitchhikers who are cautious about him lest he is trying to entrap them. As with Robert Johnson at the crossroads, this was a dangerous moment: progressive ideals about equality had unleashed murderous reactionary counter forces amongst those with interests to defend. The bus boycotts against segregation – which became synonymous with Rosa Parks – had begun in 1955 and boycotts spread into education and other divided areas of public life such as restaurants. The politics of the road were key, since bus routes crossed state lines and segregation on public transport had been declared unconstitutional by the US Supreme Court, something which the southern states openly flouted.

So when northern progressives poured into the South in 1961 to support those campaigning against segregation, the response of conservative white communities to these 'Freedom riders' was ferocious. Roads in and out of southern states became battlegrounds, and buses were attacked and burned out by white mobs, some with full police and even FBI complicity; beatings and mass arrests of protestors were normal.

The scenes were repeated during the 'Freedom summer' of 1964, when campaigners changed their focus to try to encourage voter registration of disenfranchised black communities (which led to the Voting Rights Act the following year). A strong contributing factor to rising public horror was the organised killing by the Ku Klux Klan and local police of three civil rights activists on 21 June 1964, James Chaney, Andrew Goodman and Michael Schwerner. Lynchings and disappearances often went uninvestigated, but this drew national attention, perhaps because two of the men were white northerners. The previous month, two nineteen-year-old black hitchhikers, Henry Dee and Charles Moore, had disappeared without trace in Meadville, Mississippi, picked up by a KKK sympathiser who believed them to be agitators. Their families had been too fearful to report them missing, and the bodies were found only because of the search for Chaney, Goodman and Schwerner.[6]

To the outsider with a social conscience, the road politics of the Deep South in the mid-twentieth century was reminiscent of the fight over abolition the previous century. If one's face didn't fit or one was the wrong colour, any form of transport could be problematic: bus, car, train or thumb. Music was a key marker of the shifts, and whilst black jazz and blues singers such as

Billie Holliday and Nina Simone chilled audiences with their own statements on racism – 'Strange fruit' and 'Mississippi goddam' – the participation of white political songwriters in the civil rights struggles took the issues to an international television audience, and in doing so helped make the New Left more cosmopolitan. Some of the prime contributors to this impetus were Phil Ochs ('Freedom riders'), Tom Paxton ('Goodman, Schwerner, and Chaney'), Bob Dylan ('The lonesome death of Hattie Carroll'), Paul Simon ('He's my brother', a song about Andrew Goodman, whom he had been at school with) and later Neil Young with the searing 'Southern man'.

These were more emotional than physical travelling songs, expressions of outrage (and empathy) that something so inhuman could be occurring on the roads of their own country. If the Beat poets had turned the road into a form of self-expression, now the conversation was more polyphonic, and 'just going', as Dean Moriarty might have put it in *On the road* was no longer good enough. It is unsurprising, then, that Paul Simon started to ask questions as he stuck out a thumb to 'look for America' or that when Janis Joplin sang 'freedom's just another word for nothing left to lose' in Kris Kristofferson's 'Me and Bobby McGee' (1971), it didn't just seem to be about a couple on the road serenading a trucker with their songs and harmonica. Joan Baez captured that wider restlessness and melancholy in 'The hitchhiker's song' (1971) – a 'thousand silhouettes who hold out their thumbs … orphans in an age of no tomorrows', but felt powerless or unwilling to provide a script for those who might want to hoe their own furrows.

The narratives of uncertainty didn't always dominate, but the right to be on the road thumbing a lift as part of the wider cultural imagination was not going back in the bottle. There were metaphor songs – drugs, loneliness, sickness, religion – which the grunge-era bands Pearl Jam and Green Day contributed very effectively to; there were songs with nods to social history which evoked the Guthrie years (Steve Earle had a few of those in the tank); love songs on the road with Dylan as he got 'Tangled up in blue' and Neil Young finding a female hitcher with a dog and a new way of looking at the world in 'Bound for glory' (1986). There were songs which gave agency to older travellers, such as John Denver's under-rated and poignant 'Hitchhiker' (1976), who had been 'a thumbing' for thirty years. There were timeless songs with Christ metaphors, such as Nat King Cole's 'Nature boy', written by eden ahbez, and then there were songs of pure joy, like the much-covered 'Wagon wheel' (2003).

Started by Dylan decades before, the verses found themselves in the guitar cases of the Old Crow Medicine Show, who threw together a backpack full of appealing images on a long day's hitch down the east coast of the USA.

The protagonist is leaving an old life of gambling debts and cold winters in the north, banjo in hand, searching for a lover, for whom he picks some roadside flowers before sharing 'a nice long toke' with a truck driver. We roll along with him, heading for an uncertain future in Raleigh, North Carolina, where (in true Romantic fashion), if things didn't work out, he could still at least 'die free'.

What was less forthcoming in this plethora of paeans to the road was a space for a woman's point of view, someone who would take on the social analysis of a latter-day Memphis Minnie.

Old country roads and patriarchal spaces

There were a few candidates of course, but it was always hard to be heard on the crowded slip roads. All of those men singing about their liberties, the leaving of towns and relationships in search of somewhere more attractive to lean their guitars and hopefully get lucky on the way. Writing about road narratives in the *American Reader* magazine in 2012, Vanessa Veselka notes the disparities in our cultural assumptions: 'A man on the road is caught in the act of a becoming. A woman on the road has something seriously wrong with her.'[7] Indeed, it seems to be wrong for a woman even in the realm of fantasy, judging from the reactions in Republican America to the 1992 Heart song 'All I want to do is make love to you', criticised for irresponsibly celebrating the female gaze and allegedly encouraging women to pick up hitchhikers (or even to try it themselves) and risk getting pregnant! It is telling perhaps that three of the biggest-selling hitchhiking songs – The Eagles' 'Take it easy' (1972), 'Sweet hitchhiker' by Creedence Clearwater Revival (1972) and Sammy Johns' 'Chevy van' (1973) – were simple feel-good endorsements of an easy lay waiting by the roadside.

These were the type of men Joni Mitchell was writing about in the barbed poetry of 'Coyote' (1976), in which she gives the hitchhiker some agency amidst her observations about how love and social differences make us all 'prisoners of the white lines on the freeway'. Mitchell was always an independent-minded traveller, even just watching people's contradictions in the cafés of a new city – the kind of free solo spirit we see in Sheryl Crow's later 'Everyday is a winding road' (1996), where she tries to look through a child's eyes at the world in conversation with the philosophical 'vending machine repair man' driver who gives her a lift. It's a metaphor song with a difference, but one where Crow takes the idea of the freedom of the road to be as much an internal journey as an external one, investing the mundane with the possibility of transcendence.

If there is an heir to Memphis Minnie it may be Ani DiFranco, whose song 'Every state line' (1992) feels like a reminder of the themes of 'Nothing in rambling'. Here the narrator finds herself hassled as a lone woman, first by police at a border crossing in case she's hiding illegal immigrants, later when her car breaks down at night and she's having to brush off wandering hands as a hitchhiker. It is a song that bristles with outrage at efforts to control where women go and how they choose to look – 'fuck you very much' she says, slamming the car door. Forthright, controversial and brilliant, DiFranco is a significant figure in alternative folk music, whose repertoire continues and extends themes from the work of Woody Guthrie, Pete Seeger and other troubadour figures such as Utah Phillips, more so because her language is about sexual identity, women's rights and claiming back public spaces.

Perhaps English singer songwriter Jenna Witts is of similar mind, portraying herself with a guitar at the side of a Devon moorland road on the cover of her album *Hitchhiker* (2013), the title track of which takes the position of a woman driver picking up a genuine female troubadour who 'sings for her supper' and reminds her of her younger self. Their sharing of life and love's travails, is a variation of a nostalgic male hitchhiking 'standard', indicative perhaps that – in the terms of Ani DiFranco – 'every state line' is being challenged, as a right even if it is not every woman's reality yet.

Happily there are also men adding their voices to the challenge to patriarchal narratives that on the road men can act with impunity. The institutional indifference to racist killings and disappearances of indigenous women on Canada's 'Highway of Tears' (see Chapter 9) has generated at least four songs by male artists, and sexism in rape trials involving hitchhikers has been angrily challenged in Attila the Stockbroker's 'Contributory negligence' (1982), underlining the point that hitchhiking should be seen as a legally protected mode of transport where there are no other options to get home. Empathising with why women choose to be thumbing a lift in the first place requires a subtler approach and one fine contribution to this is by the British folk-punk artist and veteran hitchhiker James Bar Bowen, whose 2007 song 'She is' humanises the point of view of a sex worker.

Whilst on tour in New Zealand in 2005 Bowen and his partner picked up a hitchhiker outside Auckland one evening. We experience their conversation in the song as though it is happening in real time, juxtaposing the observations of the driver/narrator with a first-person life story. We learn that she is 'hitching on the Titarangi road', slight of frame, a bit drunk, carrying a suitcase which she'd packed in a hurry – 'running from a nightmare back at home'. The conversation unfolds down the 'Northwestern motorway' that she's a single parent, who works in the sex industry as a dominatrix, and has had enough of an unreliable partner who steals her money and beds other women. But she's philosophical about her situation: 'you're as happy as you decide to be / I'm just a working girl, independent nearly free'. The narrator uses the chorus to underscore their common humanity: 'She is a loving mother / like yours and mine, like no other'. Just as we learn that this could be a familiar abuse story of never quite leaving, the hitcher reveals that she's on her way to see her daughter, for whom she's made some clothes, and this time she has got some savings to help plan a proper escape. The song ends on an upbeat note.

Few contributions to the song book give a marginal figure – an actual male fantasy no less! – quite so much agency – another indication perhaps that our road bards and vagabond sociologists are sometimes in the vanguard of the values of the society through which they travel. Yet how the roads are policed by law or ideology is a fickle business. In the Depression era, a woman travelling across US borders for 'immoral purposes' could be prosecuted under the Mann Act, just one of the catch-all pieces of legislation which governments have introduced over the decades that impact upon hitchhiking or those who choose to live differently.

It's something I had a brief glimpse of on my own roadside travels.

Lochailort, Tennessee

On the cover of the Scottish band Runrig's breakthrough album *The cutter and the clan*, a tiny figure stands by the side of the road, pack set down beside him as he contemplates the vast peaty and rocky wilderness and the possibility of a lift. It is an unglamorous image which suggests itinerant work and uncertainty – rather apposite to a hitchhiking experience of my own, in similar landscapes, during 1986, when I received an impromptu lesson in the persecution of contemporary travellers. It would require a combination of one surplus-to-requirements Royal Navy bus, three student hitchhikers (two of whom were ornithologists called Roger), one tinker encampment and a couple of battle-hardened nomads to enlighten me.

It had all begun on the shores of that most iconic of Scottish waters, Loch Lomond. A small string of English hitchhikers were trying to make the most of the limited standing space where the A82 heads north out of Tarbert, with its picturesque cluster of grand stone buildings, clipped lawns and moored yachts. Already mid-afternoon, with considerable distance still to travel, everyone was mightily relieved at the sudden appearance of a vehicle able to accommodate us all. As we rattled along through Argyll's magnificent mountain ranges, our hosts, Annie and Clive, took every opportunity to pick up other wayside walkers and hitchers. Only when the three of us who'd started out together agreed to share 'crash accommodation' with them at their 'site' at Lochailort, near Mallaig, and we were pitching around the narrow darkened roads of Moidart, did the pair start letting us into their lives a little. I'd already been a little curious about their circuitous route that had avoided the main regional town, Fort William, and the reasons for this were partly vehicle disrepair (a broken headlight), but mostly the resulting harassment regarding their place of residence from the police, if the bus was stopped, which we were assured was likely because they were travellers.

Annie and Clive were in their late twenties, intelligent, articulate, resilient people, committed to their way of life: Clive, wiry, practical and considered; Annie, fiery, beautiful and terrifying, like a character from *Xena: warrior princess*, carrying a knife in her size-nine boots from years of hitchhiking around continental Europe on her own. The previous year, they had been caught up in what has become known as the 'battle of the beanfield', near Stoney Cross in Wiltshire on 1 June, an event which epitomised the polarised and ugly politics of Thatcherism.

By the mid-1980s, the Conservative administration which had won power in 1979 and 1983 had gained the confidence to begin taking on those political forces which were the biggest threats to its neo-liberal economic agenda and its brand of moral authoritarianism. The principal sources of opposition were perceived to be the trade union movement (particularly the National Union of Mineworkers), socially progressive local governments and those alternative communities which tried to live differently or outside the law, such as squatters, travellers and peace protestors. They also began to target what was left of the tradition of free music festivals from the 1970s and the associated New Age pilgrimages to ancient Celtic monuments such as Stonehenge and Glastonbury. These experiments had long been a bane in the eyes of the authorities, but the arrival of a new influx of urban nomads (colloquially referred to as New Age travellers), who were not going to vanish back into the cities after an event, upped the political stakes. Here was another potential 'enemy within', the mobile poor, who were claimed to be trying to bleed the welfare system in the same way that hobos and tramps had supposedly preyed on respectable society in the past. The mainstream media simplified the issues and demonised those involved, spurred on by unhelpful soundbites about 'medieval brigands' from the then Home Secretary, Douglas Hurd – creating the mood for physical confrontation.

So, in May 1985 an assortment of caravans and old buses dubbed 'the Peace Convoy' were heading for Stonehenge with the aim of staying for the solstice (Figure 3.3). The official owners of the archaeological site, English

Figure 3.3 Stonehenge festival. The cultural clashes around mobility and land access during the Thatcher years were aired in The Levellers' searing song 'Battle of the beanfield'.

Heritage, applied for a High Court injunction to place restrictions on access to the vicinity. A significant police presence was mobilised, roads were blocked with gravel and the travellers' vehicles were ushered into a field. Despite some desperate negotiating, what followed was a brutal mass arrest; homes were deliberately smashed, pregnant women and young children injured and some of the journalists present later testified that the police behaved as if somehow the presence of the media legitimated their actions. The English folk rock group The Levellers, themselves part of the travelling communities and advocates for a number of civil liberties campaigns, depicted the events in their song 'Battle of the beanfield' (1991) through the eyes of a hitchhiker travelling to Stonehenge to discover the wider issues at stake: 'Down the 303 at the end of the road / flashing lights – exclusion zones / And it made me think it's not just the stones they're guarding'.

For the likes of Clive and Annie, the most pressing concern in the aftermath of the 'beanfield' were the practicalities of where one could stop a vehicle overnight. County councils began to block off lay-byes, enact by-laws about lighting roadside fires; motorway service stations turned away anyone who looked like a traveller, and any vehicles which appeared to be reconditioned for living in were easy targets for being found 'road unworthy'.

The remnants of the Peace Convoy scattered: some chose to 'winter' in the quieter corners of Scotland and plan for the following summer's festival circuit; others fled to France and Spain to start afresh, away from the clutches of social security officers trying to take their children into care. The legal fallout and compensation cases took many years. The 'battle of the beanfield' soon had an accompanying piece of legislation, the 1986 Public Order Act, which gave the police, the courts and landowners new powers to act against trespassers, limit spontaneous public assembly and impound vehicles. Eight years later, this would be intensified in the Criminal Justice and Public Order Act, which removed the obligation of local authorities to provide accommodation space for Romany cultures (whom they assumed were no longer mobile) or any so-called New Age travellers (whom the documentation disdainfully implied didn't deserve it anyway). This left people on the road vulnerable to trespass laws, which were also strengthened, to prevent any sort of illegal occupation of private land.

Our hosts in Lochailort had been relatively lucky, but as we listened in their cramped caravan by candlelight, sharing food prepared by their quiet companion Rachel, it was hard not to appreciate how frustrated they were with the constant surveillance and uncertainty which Annie assured us was typical even on this remote Atlantic seaboard. It shed a different light on our own relatively benign experiences of 'the road' (which in my case had involved only two incidents of questioning by the police), next to which one night's sleep on the floor of the bus we'd travelled in seemed a humbling reminder of our differences.

Blinking in the Hebridean brightness of a new day, we took in the assortment of caravans, second-hand buses and 'benders' (makeshift tents with tiny chimneys poking through the material). The last belonged to a small 'tinker' community – tinker being of Irish derivation, an elision of 'tin workers' – whom we were told kept their distance from the newer breed of traveller, and talked in their own dialect. Rousing our hosts, we agreed to a quick brew before testing our luck on the quiet highway. A little sleepily, Annie leaned over her ancient caravan stove, stirring the coffee into life, unselfconsciously singing folk songs that could have been written in Mallaig or Memphis. We looked out of the caravan window to the mountainous Isles of Skye, Rum and Eigg, sitting dark against a bright pale sky. It was an idyllic spot, far from any habitation, bar what passed on the road, yet one perhaps shared by hundreds over the centuries. The Scottish travelling communities go back to the early sixteenth century. When people began to arrive they were called 'Egyptians', even though their Romany origins were probably Indian. Whether you were a pearl fisher or a tin smith, just being a foreigner was liable to incur the displeasure of the primitive legal system, with death a real possibility, either sanctioned or through vigilantes.

My first lift out of Lochailort, was of firm political views. To keep foreigners at bay, he said, we needed a strong defence policy, otherwise 'they' would overrun 'our country'.

Whither Woody Guthrie?

One of my favourite contributions to the (as yet unwritten) compendium of songs from the kerbside is 'Hitch-hikers' hero', by the Atlanta Rhythm Section. It is a mid-1970s piece of optimism around the travels of a self-styled community storyteller, who hitchhikes out into the world, then returns to liven up the days of the local children with tales of exotic peoples and creatures. He's the kind of wandering minstrel figure who has an important place in many cultures, but who may need to revise his job specs in the age of YouTube. So, if we set him to work conducting an online trawl of today's hitchhiking songs (maybe using Miran Ipavec's hitchhiking museum in Slovenia as a base) he'd quickly surmise that there seem to be as many being written in bedrooms around the world as when thumbing a lift was a mass movement activity in the early 1970s.

How is this possible? Put simply, there are more potential Woody Guthries and Memphis Minnie's out there recording kerbside tales despite an apparent dip in road bard output during the 1980s and 1990s, when it seemed that the unsympathetic political climate had driven the hitchhiking writer's muse off the road. Nevertheless, there was enough cultural capacity in the idea of the hitchhiker as a character in a song for it to find a new home in genres other than folk, blues and rock; now there are punk, rap and dance music artists also telling their tales, many of them female. What has also facilitated the proliferation of hitchhiking songs this century has been a better-connected primary hitchhiking age group, whose experience of globalisation in travel, work and social media has opened them up to a wider set of musical inspirations and personal transformations than their forebears. As awareness of the consequences of the ecological crisis tightens on each generation, so do travelling songs become linked into more than just the politics of the road, but of society in general. The hitchhiker becomes the lens to look at our own destructiveness: Jamie M. Cooper hitching on down to 'Bundanoon town' (2014) in Australia, where he learns about how it became the first town to ban bottled water and how to think more critically about waste; Eddie Vedder's big-hearted songs from the film *Into the wild*, about the life of Chris McCandless, offer hitcher-friendly insight into the madness of endless accumulation and not treasuring the wonders of nature and one another rather than material objects. It was a tale which, according to the now defunct website digihitch.com, propelled thousands of young people onto hitchhiking pilgrimages across North America.

There is a strange symmetry here in this span of hitchhiking songs across the last century, as we have moved from those which record the experience of the hardship of the road, where often those on it would rather not be, and those whose protagonists choose to get onto it and enjoy movement, conversation and the natural world at a more manageable pace and for its own sake. And yet if one is hitchhiking, these are differences which should be eroded by the camaraderie of the road – travel as community. In her uplifting 'Hitchhiking song' (2014) Australian humanist activist Shelley Segal appears to be channelling Joan Baez as she tries to encourage people to reach across imaginary lines on maps and see beyond ideology, cultural or generational differences. Noting how many strangers have fed and let her sleep on their floors, she challenges artifice and dogma: 'Why can't we live in a world where I can hold out my hand / And you can take me for a ride / And I could do the same for you / And we'd both know we're on the same side.'

The obviousness of cooperation with others just a few miles across some arbitrary line is a common sentiment expressed by hitchhikers in song and in diaries; this is a reminder that, on an anthropological time scale, our world of nations and fixed locations for life and work is impossibly recent – the organisational and psychological consequences of which we are currently struggling with.

In the following chapter, on human nature, we'll explore that slippery slope from being told to 'go move shift' to having to stand firm and cry 'no pasaran' to fascism. Such applicability may explain why Guthrie's star in particular has not waned or been overpackaged, and admirers continue to pay homage in folk clubs and to record his materials. Many of the songs of the Depression era of 'hard travelling' – where jobs were scarce, racial prejudice rife and there was a need to keep moving, to survive – seem only too relevant today with so many millions of refugees on the move across the globe. No doubt that there will be a motorway railing somewhere in Greece or Italy adorned with 'Barstow'-type graffiti, although maybe not in English, just as there will be weary people gathered around campfires listening to a guitarist pluck out some songs about the road back to the homes they have fled in Syria or Sudan. Sadly, Woody Guthrie's 'Deportee' has been all too apposite as national popularism and xenophobia have swept many a country in the West, scapegoating the migrant workers who keep their economies going.

Despite knowing that there may be no glamour on the road, that it can be hard work travelling for many groups of itinerants, our fascination with the mobile lifestyle runs culturally deep. For those of us who have hitchhiked, hearing others document those experiences in song puts us (back) in touch with those larger existential matters: who we are in the world and how we might make a difference through the act of travelling. For everyone else, until we reorganise our transport to share the road more, then it will have to be an imaginative opportunity: to visualise ourselves and those who came before us standing at a dusty crossroads somewhere under a big sky, hoping for good things down the road and maybe humming a Woody Guthrie number to keep up the spirits.

Chapter 4

'Maybe we will meet a nice person': hitchhiking, conflict, human nature

A necessary journey

In early 1940, Woody Guthrie, in his song 'This land is your land', envisaged a 'freedom highway'. Such an idea would become particularly pertinent for some of the Jewish residents of Belgium not many months after he had penned the song, but in rather more extreme circumstances. The military forces of the Third Reich, having already annexed Austria, Poland, Czechoslovakia, Denmark and Norway, were making extensive pushes into France and the Benelux countries, with horrific consequences. As the Luftwaffe strafed the retreating British Expeditionary Force to Dunkirk, and refugees from all urban centres unfortunate enough to be in the path of the German onslaught filled any available trains or staggered hopefully along unblocked roads, those with any kind of Jewish ancestry began to ponder their best course of action: whether to hide, flee or hope that the bureaucratic finger of history would not seek them out for persecution and worse.

Rumours of 'internment camps' in Germany and Poland, the expression of anti-Semitic sentiments through officially sanctioned outbursts like Kristallnacht (night of the broken glass) in November 1938 and in many regions the public humiliation of a yellow star affixed to one's clothing were already part of the collective consciousness. It was not just Jewish people who wanted respite from the brutality and paper fascism which accompanied each occupation – there were many other cultural scapegoats in the ideology of Aryan white race purity: itinerant cultures such as the Roma, homosexuals, the disabled and communists. At any border crossing or port city in Europe, besieged by refugees of all colours, creeds and denominations, those assigned the task of trying to stem the would-be exodus placed labyrinthine paper trails in front of those seeking passage literally anywhere.

On 5 August 1940, on a road heading south out of Antwerp, twenty-year-old newly weds Ida and Maurice Piller, both Jewish Belgians, decided

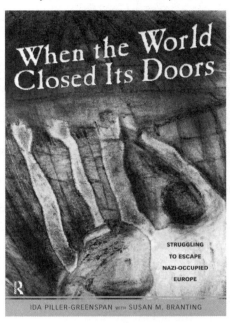

Figure 4.1 The story of Ida and Maurice Piller, just married, hitching for their lives in 1940. The parallels with the plight of displaced people today are chilling but give hope.

to chance their luck. Their story is recounted by Ida Piller-Greenspan in her 2006 memoir *When the world closed its doors* (Figure 4.1). She describes how their extended families had already tried to flee once to the coast, only to get caught up in the chaos of Dunkirk and La Panne, before returning home, by any transport possible, sometimes under fire from German bombers. Ida and Maurice decided to head south instead, hoping to meet up with some of them again in Paris. Carrying one small bag rather than suitcases, to appear less suspicious, they were faced with the reality of hitchhiking on a road with German army vehicles passing them by.

> The truck's brakes squealed as it stopped beside us. The driver, a cigarette pinched between the fingers of one hand, leaned out of the window. Sweat dripped down his nose.
> – Morgen! Ist heiss, nicht? Wo wollt Ihr hin? …
> Maurice and I dared not look at each other. We had to think independently and fast. The smiling German waited.
> Maurice sputtered an answer in awkward German, mispronouncing the words and mangling the grammar, though we both spoke the language fluently.
> – Just fifty kilometres. We're looking for my wife's parents. They're trying to get back to Antwerp, and we're going to help them.
> The German spoke to the thin, young soldier beside him.

– Shall we take them?

– Sure, why not?

The driver turned back to us, where we stood riveted to the road, and spoke loudly and slowly, as if we were children.

– We are going fifty kilometres. We will help you. Get in the back of the truck.

He broadly gestured his cigarette-clutching hand toward the rear of the vehicle.

– Come, come! It's a free ride. Climb into the back.

Maurice, who seemed to have vast resources of optimism, tugged my hand.

So with some misgivings, we walked to the back of the truck where we found, to our dismay, a half dozen soldiers leaning on their rifles and sitting on long benches that ran the length of both sides of the truck bed.[1]

After some awkward exchanges, they opt for silence and the journey passes uneventfully. Renewed in confidence, they flag down another lift, which promptly diverts into a German army camp to deliver some goods. Aghast, they watch soldiers streaming around them, none giving them a second glance. It is only at a checkpoint outside Paris that Ida and Maurice first have to explain themselves, asking for directions to the Red Cross offices, where they find out that their family have already returned to Belgium. The couple do not dally too long in Paris, although they do take in the tourist sites for a while as compensation for the honeymoon that they never had, before heading south-west towards Bordeaux. Hundreds of other Jewish refugees have the same idea.

It takes Maurice and Ida several days to travel the 600 kilometres, during which they have to observe the evening curfews (no one on the streets, let alone hitchhiking), keep their heads down in farm outhouses overnight and avoid army patrols. From Bordeaux they take buses to the foot of the Pyrenees and attempt to cross, only to be turned back, after twenty hours of battling unforgiving terrain, by Spanish border guards (who feed them, but threaten to shoot them if they return). Eventually, after days of waiting in Marseille, they secure short-term transit visas, guaranteed to get them to Portugal for a passage to China – anywhere being regarded as initially preferable – and attempt to cross the Spanish border again, this time on a bus. Time after time, fellow refugees, exhausted and despondent, try to dissuade them, saying that the bureaucratic barriers are made of steel and that it was better to return to Belgium since no one could afford the exorbitant prices charged by the people smugglers. Instead, Maurice turns to Ida in the midst of a despairing moment and says: 'We'll go to the border anyway. Maybe we will meet a nice person.'[2]

Getting off their bus, at Perpignan, whilst a French official is preoccupied with other passengers, they take refuge in a shop, where the owner welcomes them with the news that 'Spain' is across the street and they are able to walk directly to the Spanish checkpoint rather than negotiate with the frowning pistol-holding French officials first. Minutes later they spot their original bus, now in Spain, and they safely re-board it. This takes them to Madrid and then Lisbon in Portugal, where Ida and Maurice endure weeks of visits to the American consulate, motivated by the heart-breaking sight of 500 refugees being sent back to Berlin in a sealed train. Even in the last few days, when their visas have arrived and they are awaiting a ship, they receive an enigmatic summons back to the consulate, which they are too scared to acknowledge. Back home in Antwerp the Gestapo have forced all of their families to wear yellow stars to identify them as Jews. Ida and Maurice board the SS *Nyassa* bound for New York, not knowing whether all of the waiting will be in vain if they are refused entry or the entire ship is directed back to Europe on arrival. Hands shaking, they pass through an immigration barrier that so many of their kinsfolk will never even see.

Theorising the unimaginable

How is it possible to make sense of such events? The German Marxist theorist Theodore Adorno, who himself had fled Europe as the Nazis advanced, famously said that 'after Auschwitz it would be barbaric to write poetry'.[3] Others, such as the Austrian therapist Viktor Frankl, who survived the death camps, used the harrowing experience to develop his branch of psychiatry called 'logotherapy', which emphasised the importance of establishing 'meaning' and purpose for mental well-being, however trying the circumstances of one's life. Although it is difficult to add anything meaningful to so humbling a perspective, I do believe that we can use a journey of survival such as Ida and Maurice's to make some observations about human nature and its relationship to the societies we wish to create.

Human nature dominates discussions of hitchhiking with an intensity not given to any other forms of mobility. This is largely because it appears to be more vulnerable to 'danger' than being on a train or plane, a bike or your own automobile. Accordingly, the possibilities for roadside cooperation are easily displaced into a sinister imaginative realm, reminiscent of when people believed mountain passes were haunted by more than just brigands and outlaws. Such 'liminal spaces' or borderlands have always fascinated us, yet because they frequently lie outside the influence of State and capital, these forces have done their best to populate them with foreboding and dread. This allows us an insight into how 'they' think about human nature, as well as their lasting debt to the philosophical influence of Thomas Hobbes.

Writing at the time of the English Civil Wars and Oliver Cromwell's Protectorate, Hobbes's premise in *Leviathan* was that the historical emergence of the Sovereign State served to keep order and protect its citizens from each other's worst intentions. In return, they had to expect to relinquish some of their freedoms. Hobbes was distressed by the amount of division in the country, much of it along religious lines and, as a secularist, he sought to rationalise a model for how people might live together. He knew full well that he was in the business of myth-making and freely admitted that his tale of the emergence of civilisation from a 'state of nature', where life was 'brutish and short', was allegorical.[4]

Hobbes's assumptions underpinned the emergence of liberal democratic thought during the nineteenth century and the idea of the 'political contract'. They didn't extend as far as addressing the possibility that the actions of the State may themselves be a greater source of harm than any deranged individuals lurking on the fringes of society, or that a rational secular administration itself could be malevolent. We can forgive Hobbes, but today this is a serious sociological matter: some States 'fail' under the weight of complex internal or external forces, or never get the chance to form properly. So how does one judge them in terms of theories of human nature: whether they facilitate our better selves or encourage our worst? Why, when we trace a journey such as that of Ida and Maurice, do we wonder afresh about what might be needed to ensure a balanced, humane society?

Put simply, it is a tale that does not offer simple explanations of human behaviour. It is also hard to locate within the frameworks of myth-making during wartime, which depends on these things. Myth-making requires simplicity. In the following pages we'll see indications that below the flag-waving surface of assumed notions of national unity, or the demonisation of those one is at war with, lie counter-narratives and more complex questions about what binds society together. To meaningfully engage with these matters, we need to depart from the top-down frameworks of those adhering to a Hobbesian view and approach the problem from the roadside and the testimony of those there. This lateral view allows us to see a different reality – what anarchist thinker Colin Ward called 'the theory of spontaneous order' – where communities or individuals organise themselves through mutual aid, springing into life as 'seeds below the snow'.[5] People might be from different cultures, classes, ethnicities (and may even be enemies), but something other than 'orders' (or prejudice) kicks in. They respond to older, more empathic instincts, of being fellow travellers through this world, united by their humanity.

If we accept that this reality is ever present, then how do we translate those latent feelings of mutual aid into building a more just and ecological world today, one where we embrace those fleeing from war, persecution or climate breakdown? How do we stop 'bad States' emerging? Have we made any ethical progress since 1945? If we have, can we truly say that it is enough to reintegrate the possibility of poetry – which Adorno felt was lost to the world – back into it?

Are we the 'nice person' whom Ida and Maurice hoped to meet?

The problem with modernity

It is an uncomfortable truth that the slide into the abyss is frighteningly mundane. Recent estimates of how many German institutions were involved in the supply chains for the Final Solution run at over 40,000.[6] As we read *When the world closed its doors* and live through Ida and Maurice's extraordinary tale of determination, courage and initiative, we begin to see only too clearly how the Holocaust took place away from the death camps: in the railway stations and embassies, carried out by clerks and ticket collectors, in very recognisable 'civilised' contexts. It is this very ordinariness – often mirroring the processes of peacetime – which points to the structures themselves as being capable of 'manufacturing evil'. If it is true that the Holocaust was no one-off event and there is something more fundamental at fault, how are we to act in the world, knowing that such events may keep happening? What exactly is to blame?

Hannah Arendt, the Jewish American philosopher covering the trial of Adolf Eichmann in Jerusalem in 1961, opened the philosophical floodgates with her assertion that the 'evil' in his (and other Nazi administrators') actions was through the 'banality' of the bureaucratic process, in the dispassionate categorising and processing of people, rather than as monstrous individuals as such. The idea was hugely controversial at the time and personally hard for Arendt, because of her background, but it was an analysis of power which has been debated throughout modernity, principally in the nineteenth-century anarchist writings of Pierre-Joseph Proudhon, Mikhail Bakunin, Peter Kropotkin and many others. Theirs was the view that authoritarian social structures themselves would inevitably turn processes of science, administration and governance into forms of tyranny, surveillance and control. Mainstream sociologists such as Max Weber argued something similar: that the 'iron cage' of bureaucracy and 'instrumental rationality' – prioritising the ends over the means – led societies away from their more 'substantive' (i.e. ethical) values. He called this the 'disenchantment of the world'.[7]

It is still perplexing to many that the ideals of Enlightenment thought and all of its benefits to politics, science, technology and medicine can produce something as insidious as genocide in a Western democracy. Not for

Zygmunt Bauman, who, in his brilliant *Modernity and the Holocaust*, argued that the genocide was not an exception, more that it was able to happen because of those elements of progress which allowed people to become detached from the consequences of their actions. Just as societies have evolved greater amounts of differentiation, fragmentation and contingency, so have the uncertainties of living subject to new forms of administration created a sense of *ambivalence* in people towards others. Bauman suggests that this is a coping strategy which sees individuals more likely to bond with the social groups most like them and exclude those with whom they have little contact or for whom they have little empathy. Scapegoating becomes a method of resolving contradictions and perceived injustices within society, made easier by media technologies over which one has little control.

Once the targeting of the Jews became part of a bureaucratic process, huge swathes of the German society were faced with decisions about their involvement in it. How one behaved in the street or at work, whether one laughed at a joke or not: all of these tiny events became really important. Fear for one's own life and livelihood was a powerful motivator, and the cognitive dissonance was made easier by the steady dehumanising of the Jews until they became an official 'non-category'. Bauman argues that the process of *ambivalence* also worked to the favour of the Nazis, who wanted to gain the support of the Jewish ghetto leaders, once the Final Solution was under way and people were being shipped to the concentration camps. Having them believe that most would be saved if a quota were sacrificed would force them to accept the ideology of the more and the less deserving: of dividing the persecuted from one another.[8]

The easy cultivation of *ambivalence* towards others in modernity potentially alters our way of thinking about violence. It may not obviously turn good people into bad ones (although there are famous examples of simulated environments which examine this premise) but it implicates them much more in processes which might cause harm.[9] However, by the same token, no administration can behave with relentless brutality the entire time. Cracks appear in all edifices: people bend rules, wilfully withhold information, arrange ease of passage for the persecuted and so forth. Observing these inconsistencies or small acts of resistance allows us to build hope out of the horrors of organised mass murder.

One of the things we learn through *When the world closed its doors* is that such humanitarian acts occurred on all levels of society. In addition to the official resistance to the Nazi occupations and their networks of safe houses, there were refugee support centres in France, Spain and Portugal. Out on the road, help comes to Ida and Maurice in all kind of ways, including, amusingly, a hotelier who generously provides them with a luxurious room of a rather mirrored décor (they are too tired to notice that it is a brothel). We are reminded, as they are, that most people would rather be kind, are prepared to take risks for others and do not swallow xenophobic propaganda – and such people are to be found anywhere. If I were to give *When the world closed its doors* to a contemporary Syrian refugee (one of an estimated 20 million displaced people) or someone like my friend Claude who fled from the Democratic Republic of Congo in early 2012 and is still arguing about his legitimacy as a sanctuary seeker, they would find some of the language and attitudes remarkably familiar. Claude managed to get to the UK only because of a string of acts of kindness; he couldn't even speak the language of most of the countries he passed through, or pay for transport. Somehow, by the grace of humanity, he found his way to a refugee centre in London.

So, how we think about and respond to such crises and the forces which create them reflects hugely on how we see ourselves in relation to our social evolution; how our natures reflect or resist the political structures and choices we make. At the very least it is perhaps worth repeating Dwight MacDonald's observation that, in a mass media age, where it is possible to whip up hysteria and hatred extremely quickly, societies should fear those who obey its rules more than those who disobey them.[10]

Creating 'banal acts of heroism'

Let's think how we might apply such a perspective to the humble motor car: how we get to work, do the shopping, go on holiday, even have a little fun from time to time. Do those mundane actions resonate with the same ethical concerns about complicity in injustice? Is it reasonable to apply concepts of human nature to driving our kids to school? Are we all guilty in ecocide?

The age of the automobile has been a creeping behemoth, the infrastructure in place for decades, ironically enhanced and perfected as part of the economic growth of societies in the aftermath of the Second World War. Being born into a car-dependent society and being critical of it is one thing, being willing accomplices in its iniquities is quite another. Here the structural *ambivalence* is astonishing: as Winfried Wolf, author of the searing *Car mania* emphasises, no other national transport infrastructure would accept as part of 'business as usual' a total number of fatalities equivalent to dozens of jumbo jets falling out of the sky each year.[11] Few industries before or since have had the power and resources to knowingly damage the lives of millions around the world, be able to fund climate change denial groups and falsify their air pollution and carbon emission results when under pressure to be more responsible. It is no surprise that the rights of indigenous peoples and their environments are frequently bulldozed into the ground in the process.

Shouldn't our response to ecocide be exactly the same as our response to genocide or the persecution of minority groups? At our best we seek to avoid succumbing to the easier choices that modernity allows us to make: to deny ambivalence. In his book *The Lucifer effect: understanding how good people turn evil*, Philip Zimbardo offers a list of benchmarks of behaviour that can ameliorate this: constant personal vigilance, owning up to our mistakes, not putting our security before our freedom, challenging those procedures which make people more anonymous, rebelling against unjust authority, being mindful of future consequences of present actions and not letting desire for group acceptance prevent immoral actions. It is an ambitious list, and well suited though this might be to humanising institutions, Zimbardo suggests that we don't just focus on preventing the slide towards the 'banality of evil'. Instead, we should look outwards, into the world, to consider the far more enduring historical trend which is the 'banality of heroism', the kind of altruistic or helping behaviour which goes unnoticed and yet changes thousands of lives every day. He uses an example of an ex-convict commandeering a bus during the aftermath of Hurricane Katrina in Louisiana during 2005 and taking dozens of people to safety, long before the emergency services arrived.[12]

The hitchhiker may be peculiarly poised in this equation: partially complicit in sharing the petrochemical ride whilst facilitating some of its solutions at a social level. Here the 'vagabond sociologist' comes into their own, as a participant 'bearing witness' to how societies work at their best. Dip into the writings of world hitchhikers of the ilk of André Brugiroux, Kinga 'Freespirit' Choszcz or Juan Villarino and we see 'the banality of heroism' acted out every day through the serendipity of the road, as a more universal form of social currency takes over – the gift economy (Chapter 7). When we embrace those moments, it is far easier, they would claim, to see humanity as a huge family: all of us in adjacent rooms rather than divided by arbitrary administrative lines on the map.

For our wartime refugees, this might appear to be pure philosophical indulgence; yet it is in moments of humanitarian crisis or periods of conflict that mutual aid is strongest – when the *ambivalence* breaks down. This might not even be an act of banal heroism, just a question of not obeying orders because the context is more relaxed and the effort required unjustified. Socially healthier communities are better at welcoming strangers and people revert to their humanity, which was precisely the desperate logic behind 'maybe we will meet a nice person'.

Survival situations are often defined by random and chance elements, as well as the ability to break down a journey or a task into achievable goals. In this story of escaping occupied France, there was so much that Ida and Maurice had little control over, that their positive attitude, in addition to their language skills, had to have been significant. People who are 'lucky' are frequently talked about as risk-taking or outgoing types of people, which is inappropriate perhaps in this context, except that Ida and Maurice placing their trust in ordinary human interaction and a degree of goodness may have made the difference. The couple's faith in their own story of searching for relatives, of soldiers too bored to do anything other than get on with the job of driving and offering lifts, of shops glad of the custom and happy to offer advice, of guards in the Pyrenees who may have been more interested in company and providing a meal for cold travellers in the night than shooting or holding them: all made the probability of success that bit greater. In such situations, one's life may be determined by a mundane stroke of fortune.

During their first attempt to cross the Pyrenees, Ida and Maurice find themselves on a bus heading to the Spanish border town of Pau in the Vichy 'Free Zone'. They knew their documents were not sufficient if a full inspection took place, but the guards at the checkpoint out of German-controlled France poked their heads into the vehicle and asked a perfunctory 'you've all got passes, yes?' question. Everybody nodded.

When we ask questions of our nature on a larger historical scale, such little chinks of light count for something; that sometimes the cognitive dissonance, the *ambivalence* and the willingness to obey orders do not dominate. Given the capabilities of some societies to normalise 'the banality of evil' very quickly and others to institutionalise it slowly, having a theory of social organisation that can avoid 'slippage' is crucial, which means that it is worth addressing some of the usual questions about the pliability or inflexibility of human nature.

How we live with ourselves

The good news about human nature is that the only aspect of it to have changed over the course of the motor age is our perception of it. We've often liked the cultural shorthand of Rousseau's cooperative 'noble savage' pitted against the selfish Darwinian so beloved of free marketers, but the 'hard wired' truth is that both are part of our mix (which makes for harder storytelling). The age of genetics, with the sequencing of the genome, has blurred the conceptual waters even further, as it has identified an intertwining of our aggressive tendencies with the evolutionary need to cooperate to survive, bond and reproduce. According to ethical philosopher Peter Singer, a social trait such as altruism has a genetic base in the bond between kin,[13] and others who have conducted computer modelling of early human group behaviour suggest that the competitive instinct 'follows' more cooperative strategies, to maximise the advantage gained by group cohesion.

The implications of this argument – that cooperative genes which serve collective needs can drive out competitive ones – pose difficulties for Hobbesians, who may want to characterise the last 100,000 years as being dominated by tooth and claw.[14] Instead, the archaeological and anthropo-logical record suggests a more measured pattern of behaviour, indeed, one of relative stability, where small-scale hunter gatherer societies were actually relatively egalitarian in terms of tribal structure. Disruptive individuals could be 'selected out' of the tribal gene pool through expulsion, or by 'levelling mechanisms' by which the power of a leader could be curtailed through group non-cooperation, ridicule or even assassination.[15]

In his books *Hierarchy in the forest* and *Moral origins*, the anthropologist Christopher Boehm describes this as the 'reverse dominance' hypothesis, which he argues helped to maintain the cohesion of groups long enough to lay the foundations for the emergence of empathy and ethics in early humans.[16] However, in hierarchical societies, our bonds of association have become more differentiated, Boehm suggests, thereby reducing the power of our 'levelling mechanisms', yet there is still plenty of malleability within our hard-wired selves to alter the structures within which we live. This is crucial for thinking about how we prevent the 'slippage' into 'the banality of evil' and how we try to create those 'banal acts of heroism'.

What does any of this heavy theory have to do with hitchhiking during the Second World War? Plenty, as it all comes down to the processes of myth-making about what people are capable of achieving. Looking from the roadside rather than from the offices of news companies, politicians and their corporate backers gives us a more nuanced story: one that is validated by the anthropological research of Boehm, Singer, Gintis and others working on the relationship between genetics, cooperation and social structure. So, as we go back to Europe in 1940 to examine other hitchhiking stories, it is worth recalling George Orwell's observation that those who control the past shape the future. Just as some of the acts of complicity in the Holocaust have been covered up, so have some of the daily acts of cooperation and association been ignored, with a number of implications for how we think about and challenge dominant narratives.

Let's start with my own family.

A nation of hitchhikers?

I read Ida and Maurice's tale when I was sorting out old letters and documents from my late mother's side of the family. In a short article for a local
history publication about wartime memories, there was a surprising story
about hitchhiking in Britain. Amidst all of the other tales of rations, the sound
of bombs falling on the nearby Hull docks and seeing Italian prisoners of war
passing by on the backs of lorries was a short account of an event which probably caused a minor scandal on my mother's street. It was the time when the
grandfather whom I never met, Frederick Thompson, went 'absent without
leave'.

Stationed 300 miles away from Hull in Somerset, he'd got wind of the
news that his son was about to be posted overseas and that there was limited
time left to see him. Obviously it had preyed on his mind, so he'd snuck out
of his base somehow and began thumbing, arriving 'in the early hours of the
morning, weary and hugely blistered after having hitchhiked from Weston-
Super-Mare'. In due course, the authorities came knocking, but it provided
my grandfather with a 'few hours to spend with his son, who he might never
see again' and my mother with a 'determined cussedness … [to] place human
relationships and love before the authority or law of any country'.[17]

Trying to make sense of people's decision-making during such situations
is of course difficult, as is discerning an accurate picture of attitudes towards
'the war effort'. A lot of resources, then and now, have gone into providing
a patriotic mythic gloss. Chancing on my mother's account, I was suddenly
taken with the image of maybe countless other soldiers having done similar
things, but it being hushed up or stifled because of family embarrassment.
Being brought up in a Quaker household, I'd heard my fair share of stories
of conscientious objectors in both World Wars, so why should this be any
different?

As with so many others, I'd become used to the standard school-assembly
fare of national unity: the 'flotilla of small ships' sailing out to rescue soldiers
in the retreat from Dunkirk; the 'Blitz spirit' that endured the extensive
bombing of London, exemplified by singing songs with strangers in the
Underground; the heroism of 'the Few' keeping the Luftwaffe at bay over the
skies of England. More progressive reminiscences cited the '(Women's) Land
Army' and 'digging for victory' to encourage more self-sufficiency in food as
part of this. Not only were there no stories of 'the time we all hitchhiked for
Britain', but the largest public participation in lift-sharing in the twentieth
century was in danger of vanishing into oblivion (along with a number of
other more challenging facts about wartime 'solidarity'). Why?

Let's set the picture. On transport issues the British government acted impressively fast following the 3 September 1939 declaration of war on Germany. The cities were full of young children and pregnant women, vulnerable to enemy bombing. Within ten days, over a million of the next generation found themselves 'billeted' in unknown rural villages with total strangers, an event which repeated itself throughout the coming months. The petrol rationing which ensued allowed for a few exceptions – police, ambulances, fire and Air Raid Precautions vehicles – but the rest of the population had to use their swiftly issued petrol coupons wisely. Perhaps anticipating the likely anxiety, newspapers began including photographs of ordinary people hitchhiking, and by November 1939 the Pathé News was showing short newsreels in cinemas that advertised the fact that lift-seeking to and from work was an everyday occurrence. Queues for this alternative to taking the bus became the norm, with regular spots for cars to pull over on the outskirts of towns and cities.

Persuasion of the public was essential. According to historian Martin Pugh, the levels of obedience to the government's preparations for war were far from universal. The hectoring tone of the poster propaganda campaigns was quite unpopular and some print runs had to be withdrawn because of the hostility. Churchill's rallying speeches were less well received than hoped, according to interviews conducted by the Mass Observation researchers at the time, and politicians who had previously been appeasers to Hitler's rise and invasion of Czechoslovakia were now seen as 'guilty men'.[18]

The politics of the previous decade had not helped: unprecedented levels of unemployment and widening polarisation in living standards, health and income between the north and south of England, all sitting on the memory of the previous generation, who had been lured to war in 1914 and been decimated, traumatised and then ignored for their troubles. As fascism grew in appeal, and attracted the interest of sections of the British aristocracy and ruling classes, it was challenged by ordinary people, most famously at the 'Battle of Cable Street' on 4 October 1936, when 100,000 gathered to stop Oswald Mosley and the British Union of Fascists marching through this predominantly Jewish district of London. The heroic duty of 'signing up' for service in the Second World War was never going to be a simple process: there were conscientious objectors, many who found ways to fail medical examinations, and some of those who were drafted found cause, like my grandfather, to abscond when personal circumstances intervened.

The mythology of cross-class unity has been perhaps the most enduring of all the narratives of the period. The politics of transport were hardly straightforward, however: sections of the wealthier classes resented being suddenly told to start sharing their vehicles. Mindful of the unrest of the 1930s, the press tried to be more sardonic in approach. On 23 February 1940, the *Times* leader-writer penned an extensive editorial endorsing the newly formed American RCT (Registered Collegiate Thumber), as an indication that even the most potent symbol of freedom could now be organised into a collective.[19]

No British union of hitchhikers ever got off the ground and the paper had changed its tune three months later, noting on 15 April that the new labels 'Lifts for Service men' which were appearing on some car windshields would do much to 'restore the credit to this ancient form of doing a good turn'. Not that the paper had said much about hitchhiking to date – either in the First World War (when Britain was blockaded by German submarines) or during the ten-day General Strike of May 1926 (when, due to the lack of trains and trams, huge improvisation was required).

Yet the effect of the retreat from Dunkirk was to foster a sense of pragmatism if not necessarily warm unity about transport. Appealing to the middle class's best intentions to share their vehicles actually required the temptation of an extra petrol ration for those who gave lifts within a twenty-mile radius of London. This was called the 'Help your neighbour' scheme, which ran between October 1940 and March 1941, with participants displaying stickers on their vehicle windshields. Anyone entering the Greater London boundary without any passengers was liable to a fine, but (unlike the present-day London Congestion Charge) these were largely exercises in theory. In fact, there were no stipulations that hitchhikers had to be picked up as such; many people prearranged lifts, and according to Mario Rinvolucri's research for his book *Hitchhiking* (1974), the whole initiative came under considerable pressure from the Establishment newspapers, which argued that money was better spent on bus provision than on a handful of lift-givers. (Contrast this with the Geranium Club, which operated in Birmingham beginning in the winter of 1940–1, where enterprising folks made lapel badges and windscreen stickers indicating their membership and just got on with it.)[20]

For those charged with official logistics, it could be a fine balance: the Ministry of Transport kept placing advertisements encouraging people to avoid clogging up the roads, and in fact issued statements as 'late' as November 1944 about the importance of picking up people. Yet as the dark days of 1940–1 began to recede and the war seemed increasingly less 'on the doorstep', so the tone of the debate shifted. Motoring magazines such as *Autocar* and *Motor* moaned that a wave of socialism was sweeping the nation during 1942, with people assuming that they were entitled to lifts regardless, a view which consolidated into wider press reports of people hitchhiking whilst stockpiling their own reserves.[21] The now much-used phrase 'something for nothing' starts to make an appearance at this point, and by the time that the war had ended it was possible to believe that hitchhiking had somehow exacerbated wartime austerity.

Whose collective memory?

That was one way of looking at hitchhiking. Away from the newspapers and official publications, the tone of personal accounts and memoirs was somewhat different. Of course, there was plenty about the practicalities of civic duty and 'making do', as though it was just another thing to be endured along with rationing or the regular 'blackouts' during German bombing raids in the early part of the war. But there was another aspect, especially for women stationed at the forces' bases, and this was hitchhiking being associated with new social opportunities and broadening horizons brought on by the massive practical changes to everybody's lives.

The job of documenting everyday life during the Second World War for the purposes of posterity fell to the oral history researchers at the Mass Observation project, who had been engaged in pioneering recording of daily activities and attitudes since 1937. For all of their valuable gathering of wartime attitudes to rationing, propaganda and work, the material on transport was mostly on rail and bus, with coverage of hitchhiking seemingly elusive. More useful for our purposes are the eyewitness testimonies submitted to the 2004 BBC project *People's War*, some contemporaneous and passed on by relatives, others written decades afterwards, which provide insights into changing attitudes towards gender roles and sexuality. Their power lies in the challenge to the accepted wisdom of a society's view of itself and its past deeds and their ability to reach beyond the statistics and official publications and provide access to the raw experience – in the words of oral historian Alan Dein, 'the remembered event [without] end' – which signifies the bigger changes. In the following examples from the *People's War* archive, we see people becoming conscious of themselves in new ways – geographically freed from the communities which they might have otherwise spent much of their lives in and culturally freed from those communities' social expectations.[22]

Three young women's accounts typify these changes: Heather Simpson, Dorothy Barnes and Betty Bowen. Simpson was a bank manager's daughter from London, nineteen at the outbreak of war and with limited travel experience, who was posted hundreds of miles away in the south-west of England. Working initially as a billeting officer for evacuees in Plymouth, she then moved to the Women's Auxiliary Air Force (WAAF) at Royal Air Force (RAF) base Innsworth, near Cheltenham in Gloucestershire, later transferring to RAF Sidmouth in Devon (where she met her husband-to-be Derrick). During 1942, the dullness of some of the work led her to explore the surrounding countryside on her days off. She dubbed her adventures a 'Grand Tour', but rather than the architectural sights of Europe that her more fortunate ancestors might have experienced, it was the rural romance of the Cotswolds, in a manner not so very different from our proto-hitchhiker the Reverend Tickner Edwardes, back in 1909 (see Chapter 1).

> We went somewhere different each day and we saw these centuries old little towns and villages at their deserted and silent best. We hitch hiked everywhere, mostly in old lorries with red-hot thumping engines. We sat, two or three of us cramped in the driver's cab, looking down on the hedgerows full of delicate dog roses and honeysuckle and out over England's verdant land, made all the more poignantly beautiful by the dangers that threatened it. How very fortunate we were never to see enemy tanks advancing over our green fields or to hear the sound of an invading army marching down our village streets.[23]

Tradition intervened, however, when she was promoted and began to mix with male officers whose status required more formal methods of locomotion, and a dinner table at the 'right' hotels rather than country pubs. Not so with seventeen-year-old Chelsea girl Dorothy Barnes, who also achieved officer status, but who did not have any qualms about hitching once she was a sergeant. Barnes was thrilled by the potential adventures to be had outside London, and when hearing that she would have to wait six months for entry into the Land Girls, when she would then be old enough to join, she cycled across London to register with the WAAF instead.

As with Simpson, Barnes had not previously been too far from home, merely a few dozen miles to Ascot to see her grandparents, yet suddenly found herself on wireless training courses 400 miles away in Edinburgh, then in Cheadle in Staffordshire, before being posted in Lincolnshire, 100 miles to the east. On each occasion she took full advantage of the situation, hitching from Edinburgh to Glasgow one winter afternoon with a friend and arriving so stiff from riding on the back of a truck they had to be helped to alight by the driver. As with Heather Simpson, Dorothy Barnes was not perturbed by thumbing rides on solo hitchhiking ventures, even at night. All of her accounts of hitchhiking resonate with the sense of pressure-free adventure and spontaneity, heading off from Cheadle with her friend Eileen Earls after a long night shift, to go dancing at Blackpool's Winter Gardens, then thumbing south to the holiday resort of Rhyl in North Wales on a long weekend off.

> It took us all day to get there … [and] it was quite dark when we got to Rhyl and we did not know where to look for accommodation so we visited the local police station for advice. There did not seem to be a YWCA in Rhyl, so the police took

us to an Asylum for girls. They took us in – I suppose they had to, as the police had taken us there. We were shown beds in a large dormitory with many females in coarse, white, linen nightgowns. The inmates could not take their eyes off us as we undressed in our WAAF attire.… We did not really have a good night's sleep. We were given a cup of tea and we left – with all haste I may add. After a worrying night we had a lovely day in Rhyl, the weather was glorious.[24]

The constant need for adaptability and understanding in the strange situation which was war preparation was noticed by many of those hitchhiking to and from the bases. Chance events, unusual personal circumstances, all had to be balanced against the traditional need for discipline and punctuality, and yet this was sometimes impossible to achieve, even with public transport. Betty Bowen from Newport, South Wales, experienced this when stationed at RAF Newton Stratton (100 miles away) and tried to make journeys by train and bus to see her parents, but was always cutting it fine on a Sunday afternoon coming back. Once, arriving back very late indeed, she was severely reprimanded but let off the punishments known as 'jankers' (extra cleaning duties), as the commanding officer came from rural Wales and understood some of the logistics involved. The event motivated Bowen to start hitchhiking across country instead and she quickly secured a reputation as 'the hitchhiking Queen of Bicester'.[25]

The whole issue of punishment seemed bewildering, with Simpson noting how detention huts were full of 'girls [who] had done nothing more wicked than overstay their leave because they wanted more time with their husbands or boyfriends'. She found being a young officer a little tricky in these respects and was glad of the support of her senior colleagues, 'who were very motherly towards me, obviously seeing at once that I had no aptitude for the life of a jailer. They were always warning me about possible break-outs, for there were some hard cases amongst them, and devising elaborate schemes for me to foil any escape attempts.'[26]

These may have been the kind of events which promoted the myth of cross-class unity, but for the historians who emerged in the decades after the Second World War and became part of organisations such as the Workers' Educational Association these were times of social revolution. Not only were these events occurring at a time in people's lives when they personally change most anyway, but the speed of ideas matched the reality of the material changes. The sheer number of women working and socialising so freely clearly had an emboldening effect. Nearly half a million women joined the three forces between 1939 and 1945, creating a real sense of disorientation in men at the sudden appearance of 'young, independent women, with money in their pockets, in public houses and other public spaces'.[27] Then there were the issues around sexuality, which proved a headache for the authorities.

It wasn't just because of the arrival of the Americans in 1941, who are disproportionately remembered for creating sexual tension on the home front; there were plenty of other nations – Canadians, French, Poles – adding to the novelty of new people and places. Hysteria amongst the upper echelons of the forces about declining moral standards led to widespread issuing of condoms to servicemen (although not to women) to prevent venereal disease. Even in the relatively chaste accounts of Dorothy Barnes and Heather Simpson, there is a strong sense of the emotional juxtaposition between humdrum life on base and the relative whirlwind of socialising with visiting pilots or officers. With so many prospective husbands liable to disappear, be reposted to other bases, or simply vanish presumed killed in action, seizing one's opportunities just made sense.

More than a few memoirs from the *People's War* archive talk of having 'a good war': brief moments of independence and excitement, which remained an important memory through the years when women were expected to become dutiful housewives in the post-war economic boom. From a hitchhiking point of view, Simpson, Barnes and Bowen were the ones who passed on the baton to those who set out in the post-war years. What we gain from their accounts and those of their contemporaries is a sense of the variety of the roadside journeys of countless thousands, even millions – on the way to work, the allotment, the base, to escape the nightly bombing, or to see relatives and sweethearts. Most importantly, this is a moment when we see a crucial change in the social image of hitchhiking brought about by the war, going from that of a 'lone working man down on his luck thumbing in the open countryside' to 'the normal habit of the suburbanite'.[28]

What happened during the 1940s indicated something else: that it was possible to 'socially engineer' acts of mass cooperation very quickly by tapping into something which was already there.

Nurturing the seeds of empathy

Survival is a strong motivator, but institutionally driven hitchhiking at times of crisis tells us something else: that there may be more trust in 'the people' than is sometimes acknowledged.

When you nudge a culture in one direction, other things occur – the law of unintended consequences – and there is no better example of the benefits of wartime cooperation on a massive scale and its subsequent nurturing of our better selves than the impact of evacuation. In his book *Empathy: a handbook for revolution*, Roman Krznaric argues how moments of identification with the plight of others can be vital for the social evolution of societies.

Imagine, for a minute, the scene in hundreds of village halls up and down Britain in the autumn of 1939, as the rural middle classes were suddenly presented with lines of new arrivals of children from the cities. Many of the children standing there, name tags and all, were poor and undernourished; their new guardians had to quickly bond with these youngsters, take them home and support them for many months, through the emotional traumas caused by relocation. Such scenes did not take too long to percolate into the consciousness of politicians; indeed, long before the famous 1942 Beveridge report (seen as the start of the Welfare State in Britain), there were new initiatives to improve school meals, provide cheap milk for children and expectant mothers, and include vitamins in household rations. Yet as Krznaric notes, there was little evidence that those who had 'instigated evacuation had any intention of sparking a change in child welfare policy'.[29]

The accumulation of these individual actions created a momentum which led to the formation of the National Health Service and a commitment to using tax payers' money to benefit education and transport structures. It was a model driven by a more compassionate public-welfare-minded form of economics – Keynesianism – and one that translated into the policy of other north European democracies for at least the next three decades.

Cooperation for the general domestic good is often a fragile truce between vested interests and those most likely to be the ones who experience its reality. In the aftermath of the Second World War, the semiotics of hitchhiking became even more complicated – with news desks and opinion formers caught between emphasising the new narrative of post-austerity whilst being aware of the cultural memory of lift-giving when it came to picking up those completing their National Service. All kind of cultural anxieties would emerge – especially around young travellers in continental Europe in the 1950s – but the 'something for nothing' rhetoric in the UK was not really backed up by anything legal, unlike in the USA, where there were established vagrancy laws which could be employed if needed.

Meanwhile, in the background, the practice of hitchhiking continued – in smaller numbers, but still embracing a cross-section of the population, including school children in rural areas. As the generation who had hitched in the war as young service personnel gradually became car owners, so they became the new lift-givers, nurturing the memory of their own highs and lows by the roadside, thereby ensuring that for the next thirty years there would be a steady supply of drivers to support a hitchhiking culture.

In political theory, this process is called 'capacity building': the production and continuity of ideas through families, regions, workplaces and social environments. It is why I intuitively knew that it was possible to hitchhike in the early 1980s (and how to do it). For those a little older than me, that knowledge had been more tangible: retired Bristol teacher Harriet Wordsworth had an early memory of being in the back of a stranger's car, hitchhiking as a child in the 1950s with her mother, and hearing her cheerfully announce that 'we all used to do this in the war'. That recollection was a key ingredient in her subsequent twenty-year hitchhiking curriculum vitae: from chancing her arm as a student around continental Europe, then in western African countries as a trainee teacher, later with her young son in rural parts of south-west England close to her home, before switching to car-share schemes when she was in her late forties. Few of Harriet's generation lasted so long by the roadside, but the fact that she believed hitchhiking was a legitimate way to travel for over two decades says something significant about mid- to late twentieth-century values (as well as her own).[30]

Empathetic environments need to be nurtured. Most of the structures which drive the contemporary world hold the potential to go awry, which means that without 'banal acts of heroism' or an understanding of how to create moments of 'reverse dominance', there is always the risk of a slide towards the 'banality of evil'. The digital age has underscored this, and any would-be Zygmunt Bauman updating *Modernity and the Holocaust* will not be short of material to work with.

When the world closed its doors (again)

After their abortive efforts to escape Belgium, Ida and Maurice Piller's families believed that it was better to stay put in Antwerp and wait out the Nazi occupation than to flee. Unfortunately, they were wrong. So, whilst we rejoice in the liberty of Ida and Maurice, there is a grim epilogue to *When the world closed its doors* which details how most of their extended families, including Ida's father, mother and sister, were deported to Auschwitz and killed there.[31]

It took Ida forty years to tell her story in full, so deep was the trauma of what had happened to her family, and she did so initially through the medium of art, in which she had become a lecturer and exhibitor. When she learned she was about to become a grandmother, Ida decided to create a pictorial diary using stark impressionistic charcoal drawings of incidents from the journey. These eventually formed an exhibition, which prompted a series of interviews about her experiences, one with Susan M. Branting, who wrote the book around Ida's pictures and memories. Ida also contributed in 1997 to Steven Spielberg's Visual History Foundation archive 'Survivors of the Shoah', which gathered hundreds of recollections, as part of the process of trying to understand how genocides happen and what they do to people.

Reflecting upon the courage of her parents, Ida and Maurice's daughter Rosie Piller noted how they had set 'their grief and anger aside' and as she had learned about the Holocaust at an early age, 'the focus was not on hatred but on the lessons to be learned regarding resistance to oppression and compassion for the oppressed'.[32]

As the number of those still living who survived the Holocaust becomes ever smaller, the political lessons which we may not have learned from it are amplified by work in the field of epigenetics that notes how the trauma of the concentration camps has been passed down and can be detected in subsequent generations.[33] What then of the potential long-term damage which the wars of the Middle East and sub-Saharan Africa may have on the millions of people displaced, often corralled together in camps and on boats in desperate survival situations, or walking for weeks to get anywhere? How are we going to offer healing and empathy when some of the State responses to the so-called 'migrant crisis' have been horrifyingly familiar?

In 1990 I watched a BBC human rights drama called *The march*, which envisaged a massive migration of displaced or poor people across North Africa to the Straits of Gibraltar and Europe. They were depicted marching under the slogan 'We are poor because you are rich', a message with significant implications, coming only six years after the Ethiopian famine, which had exposed the hypocrisy of the politics of development, with food flowing out of some parts of the country or being withheld from the starving in other regions. In the drama, the marchers are tired of being victims of war, exploitation and economic mismanagement, so they choose to come and claim some of what has been taken from them. As the boats start to land on the Spanish coast and events get out of control, *The march* ends with a fudged message about empathy. The protagonist journalist, reporting to the world in breathless, earnest tones, grasps the reality that the Western game is up, but 'we're just not ready for them yet'.

I've thought about that film repeatedly, as images of overladen leaky boats or columns of exhausted footsore families winding their way through fields or along motorway verges in central Europe have filled our screens since 2014. How ready are we for this? Judging by some of the responses from governments, there is a different kind of preparedness, with Hungary leading the xenophobic charge, building walls, changing laws, erecting razor wire, unleashing paramilitary policing and giving carte blanche to vigilante groups to patrol remoter potential border crossings to 'deter' more refugees.[34]

Whether the migrants are actually seeking political asylum or they are 'just' fleeing for their lives, the political language about them uses terms like insects and vermin or terrorists. There is a long history of this in Western media and it is exactly how the Nazis treated the Jews, as Bauman outlines in *Modernity and the Holocaust*. More subtle have been the machinations of the political bargaining process, of 'packages' and 'deals' between nations, trading people's futures and lives, eerily similar to the 'ambivalence' that allowed those providing the infrastructure for the Holocaust, indirectly, at a distance, to live with themselves.[35] Children have been pawns in all of this too. For example, the British government patted itself on the back for allowing a few hundred Syrian children into the country, making comparisons with the *Kindertransport* in 1938 – which was actually an exception to a hostile immigration policy at the time.[36] Reports of families crammed in trains on the Hungarian border with limited sanitation or food or water made me recall one of Ida's paintings, *The Sealed Train*, depicting children's faces pushed against windows as they were sent back from Portugal to Berlin, and probable death.

The grassroots refugee support groups have understood the parallels, mobilising very publicly in cities across Europe. Nowhere was this more poignant than in Germany, when crowds gathered at railway stations to greet the first influx of Syrian refugees, with 'welcome' banners, singing, applause and food in February 2015. Six months later there were street rallies and marches across Europe.[37] The same mindfulness of history has also been utilised (albeit very differently) by 'No Borders' networks and 'safe passage' groups who, in actively assisting refugees to get over borders and providing safe houses, have likened themselves to those helping US slaves escape through the so-called 'underground railway' in the nineteenth century.[38]

Hitchhiking has become a curiously potent and multifaceted symbol in all of this. The same kerbsides may contain migrants thumbing out of necessity, plus 'ordinary' European hitchers, as well as those participating in autostop club races. In such an environment, extending the hand of friendship becomes vital and something which Hitchwiki.org now advises upon to avoid potential flashpoints or legal conundrums. To date, many European hitchhikers have relied on the Schengen agreement, a piece of legislation which has assisted hitchhiking across international borders, yet the solidity of this arrangement has become increasingly undermined or challenged to gain political leverage in the management of refugee destinations. Some countries are 'criminalising decency' in the words of children's author Lisabeth Zornig, who was arrested and fined for picking up hitchhiking Syrian refugees in Denmark, a country considered progressive in so many social justice and environmental areas but one which native Jacob Holdt (see Chapter 2) now regards as more outspokenly racist than white supremacist enclaves in the US southern states. In this way, accidental and ordinary acts of compassion, such as giving a lift and buying the passenger a meal, become regarded as 'people trafficking'.[39]

Bleak though this slide into more 'ambivalent' ways of thinking is, there *are* more inclusive visions out there on the highways, representative of our better natures, where we think and feel as though we already live in a border-less world.

An extra pair of boots in your rucksack

Most hitchhikers carry what they need for the journey in question, although some travel empty-handed because they are too poor or they have left their homes in an appalling hurry, driven by warfare or domestic violence; others, just occasionally, pack more than they need. When I look for signs of hope beyond the current cacophony of nationalistic populisms, I think about a number of young people converging upon a European capital in October 2015, having hitched there with a pair of walking boots in each of their rucksacks.

They were part of the European Alternatives network, an alliance of groups, projects and events committed to free movement, the promotion of participatory democracy, sustainable economies and respect for all mi-norities and cultural identities (including, notably, the Roma). Appropriately, they held their yearly Trans-European Festival in Belgrade, a pinch-point for refugees arriving from Turkey and Greece, because of the aforemen-tioned problems in Hungary. The organisers called the event 'Beyond the fragments', hoping that it could be a symbol of hope and unity. Knowing that many festival participants were hitchhiking there, often across several national borders, conference activists consulted with local refugee support groups as to the best way the attendees could assist those stuck in bureau-cratic limbo. As so many refugees had tough days of walking ahead, the word went out to those coming to Belgrade to make space in their rucksacks for an extra pair of boots. It would be a highly meaningful symbolic gesture and an important addition to the clothing collection points and accommodation spaces which were already in place in the city. In addition, hitchhikers were asked to document meetings they had with refugees en route and to ask their drivers about how they made decisions about lift-giving.[40]

It wasn't an isolated event. Belgrade has many initiatives working for peace and justice, generated in the aftermath of the Balkan wars of the 1990s. One of these is the Serbian Travel Club, formed in 2005 by a handful of hitchhikers and 'free travellers', who were motivated to use the difficulties of post-conflict mobility – because of poverty and prohibitive visa arrangements with surrounding countries – as a means of connecting people. Modelling themselves on the Russian Academy of Free Travel, the Serbian activists regard hitchhiking journeys as social adventures which promote cultural understanding. Their philosophy – that direct and unmediated contact with others is the best means to 'fight against prejudice, stupidity and hatred, against borders around us and within us' – has had an influence in the country. The Travel Club now works with the Serbian Ministry of Sport and Youth as well as schools and community groups to promote some of these values. They also do 'outreach work' from a 'pop up' social centre or 'Travel House' in another European city once a year, to which many hitch from elsewhere on the continent.[41] Such projects might be thought of as the building up of empathic 'capacity' amongst a generation of travellers, to prevent 'slippage' in the values of our societies: to insure ourselves against future conflict.

Peter Kropotkin was fond of saying that the best example of mutual aid in human societies was the lifeboat, staffed by volunteers who were prepared to risk their lives to save others. It is an image that may seem too close to the bone, as humanitarian activists have flocked to help on the shores of Greece and Italy in recent years, to assist struggling migrant vessels or those too weak to pull themselves out of the shallows after harrowing days at sea in crowded leaking vessels. But the point is that they did; despite all of the media filters and the actual geographical distances between themselves and the refugees, something moved and motivated them, if not to get in a lifeboat, then to coordinate food and clothing collections and then travel hundreds, even thousands of miles to refugee camps, because they felt a sense of solidarity with their fellow human beings in their hour of need.

When people look back at this time in decades and centuries to come, I hope that there are stories which reflect this surge of outrage and compassion. The heroism of the Berlin airlift in 1948–9 was celebrated for decades because it fitted a Cold War narrative of the humanitarian West. Similarly, the spirit of Dunkirk fitted with the idea of being an embattled island nation. Yet, as I watched footage of the Calais refugee encampment, 'the Jungle', being dismantled in October 2016, I tried to imagine a 'flotilla of small boats' heading out from the English coastline to show a solidarity and compassion that had seemed absent in the appalling blame game between governments as to who was responsible. Maybe if we followed Roman Krznaric's suggestion that each of us be encouraged to accept a refugee into our homes, in a re-run of the wartime evacuation, it would help us all reconnect with our commonality as citizens of the world.

There's a story too about 'the time we all hitched with a pair of boots in our rucksacks'. It might not have happened quite like this, but I like to imagine pairs of boots exchanging hands in a public square or park in Belgrade, between men or women, of similar ages who have all travelled huge distances, perhaps even more in their minds than in reality. And maybe there is a young couple, perhaps only just married, who've had to leave everything in a hurry, their families scattered, fate unknown, for whom this encounter allows them to think positively about humanity and gives them strength in the days ahead.

Chapter 5

The great European adventure trail: hitchhiking as a measure of freedom

The lightness of liberty

It was one of the most profound thoughts of Alison Prince's long, eventful and creative life, one which startled because of its sudden strangeness, at the end of a day's hitchhiking. Thumbing a lift had nothing to do with it – that had just been the mode of travel – and she did it a lot in the 1950s. This was different, a sense of freedom inextricably linked to a situation of apparent vulnerability. 'Lying under a hedge one night somewhere in France,' she said, 'and realising that not a soul in the world knew where I was gave me a curious sense of security that has never quite gone away'.[1] Words written with such confidence over fifty years after the event tell us something deeply philosophical about ourselves: that we easily confuse our liberty with our security, as surely as Jacob Holdt realised that being without money is not a barrier to travel. To be so at ease with the world, whilst travelling alone, is to see the forces which shape and often overwhelm us for what they are: as much the product of the mind as the harshness of material circumstances.

For many, the end of the Second World War had meant something far less weighty, just a breathing space to feel fortunate in and to hope to find a less painful future. Alison had good cause to think about freedom in those days, even before she would take that independence of mind into publishers, television studios, schools and readers' hearts as a writer of children's fiction (television as well as books). Moved by an advertisement in the *New Statesman* in the summer of 1953, posted by 'Jutta, a German Jewish girl, whose parents had fled to Australia before the war', she had been struck by the desire to help and challenge herself at the same time. Jutta 'was on a pilgrimage to find out what members of her family were left (very few, it turned out)'. Their hitchhike into Germany felt as though they were crossing into a quarantine zone:

> We had some strange experiences in the war-battered cities and countryside before reconstruction got going. Youth hostels were rough, often with no facilities

at all, and sometimes we slept in the fields, but we never felt that we were in any danger.... Truck drivers were incredibly helpful, often buying us a meal in a transport café or sharing sandwiches in the cab. We never had any trouble with car drivers apart from the odd unrepentant Nazi – and then only on political grounds that were desperately upsetting for Jutta.[2]

Hitchhiking is arguably the most personally liberating form of transport, but there are inevitably places and times when one person's freedom becomes another's licence to enact horror, which is why the discussion on human nature in Chapter 4 underpins any debate about the 'right' to go where we please in the manner of our choosing. So, how we think about liberty matters for the kind of communities, nations or ecological futures we choose to build, and in the following pages we will follow Alison Prince's generation heading out across Europe, to test our notions of liberty, to feel the lightness of spirit and insight which sometimes comes from experiencing other cultures in an unmediated, even innocent, manner. Many of these mid-twentieth-century journeys were too early to be tainted by the templates of mass tourism but were, rather, genuine meetings of strangers of the kind that have always existed – and in those spaces we can see the opportunities to think more expansively about our mutual paths. The imaginative energy of the voices we'll be hearing is undeniable, but these hitchhiking decades are so mythologised, so subsumed into somebody's *idea of a time* that they also garner lazy thinking. Yet it is by listening to the voices of those who completed their latter-day Grand Tours or who ventured on to the fabled Hippie Trail – whether naively or confidently – that we can glean insight about the full extent of the liberties we live by or aspire to.

A new sense of the world

'Suddenly you could go anywhere.' So begins Ian Rodger's post-Second World War recollections *A hitch in time*, a book that captures perfectly the rising expectations of a generation with greater access to education and disposable income, who wanted to stretch out their thumbs to see for themselves the places that seemed the 'products of propaganda and received nostalgia'.[3] Hitchhiking was second nature to this generation, and it wasn't something that those controlling the narrative of post-war recovery in the UK could do much about, except occasionally to use it in the press as an example of the evergreen political theme of 'the decline of national standards'. If you lived in a rural location with poor bus provision, then it was the only option, so seeing school children hitchhiking was perfectly ordinary. Boarding school students incorporated hitchhiking into their lives, using the now long defunct tradition of 'free days', when pupils would 'sign out' and head off for a spot of local sightseeing or stick out their thumbs and see how far they could get in the allotted time.[4]

Ian Rodger typified that way of thinking. He'd been an evacuee from London and was in Worcester during the war. He was hitchhiking at fifteen, and was still hitchhiking as an RAF recruit in 1945 and later as a student at Durham University, racing his college peers back to London at the end of term. The relative liberty of the post-war era also brought a greater social diversity of people accessing the 'great outdoors', with hitchhiking as integral to the walking and climbing scenes as membership of the Youth Hostel Association.

Although there was a strong novelty pull of continental Europe, many were happy even without crossing the English Channel; young men and women tapped into the new cultural activities that were now possible closer to home. Retired college lecturer Barbara Noble of Minehead was one of them. Recalling her debut journey in 1949, she said: 'a party from our Church Youth Club decided to visit Devon and Cornwall. We hitched in pairs of one male to one female … [and] most days we managed to get to the relevant youth hostel.'[5] It was not unusual to see members of the Scouting Association on the road then either, with young leaders such as Donald Cole from Leeds thinking nothing of hitting the road with a couple of his teenage charges to get to their summer camps. Once, remarkably, and just for the hell of it, he dragged some along to have a go at the John o' Groats to Land's End hitchhiking challenge. The crofters they stayed with at the time couldn't believe it either.

Others chose different springboards. For those who were in the armed forces, or in the newly established programme of National Service, this was simply the way one travelled. Welsh engineer Martin Evans described the strange social physics that took place around hitchhiking: 'Somehow, many hundred airmen got collected and delivered all over the country on a Friday evening (from Yatesbury) and amazingly all of them duly delivered back on the Sunday evening'.[6] The confidence which being in uniform provided led many to follow their peers out into the world once their period of service had ended.

One of these was Derek Foxman, a maths teacher from London who left school at eighteen in 1947 and thumbed for a couple of years whilst in the RAF, before undertaking a series of summer-based hitching adventures as far as Turkey and Israel (where he taught for a while) in the late 1950s. The daily diary which he kept for six weeks in August and September of 1957 – in flowing fountain-pen script – seems to epitomise this era of spontaneous 'eyes wide open' vagabonding, where one headed off, armed only with a couple of road maps, a sketchy knowledge of likely accommodation and the eye of an anthropologist. Here he is, a few years and miles already under his belt, observing his fellow travellers as he sets off again towards Dover aiming for Greece.

> Wednesday 21 August 1957: (third lift) Fiftyish woman, cultured. Talk mainly on international politics. Has lived in Africa. I liked the way she did not merely say 'yes' to a theory or comment. [On the] boat – met what later proved to be an Oxford History Undergraduate. Easily spotted (beard, glasses, cultured voice)…. Leftish leaning. Yugoslavia seemed to be his model country. His political theory had a basis in utilitarianism: his version – 'greatest opportunity for freedom for greatest number'. I showed him that the freedom which one was allowed to have came from above.[7]

Two days into his journey, thumbing along the Loire valley, he meets 'Professor Lucas', a 'middle aged French teacher in an old car … loaded to the eyebrows', who ropes his rucksack to the roof and with whom he exchanges 'information about our respective educational systems'. Foxman, a teacher himself, is appalled to hear about contrasting values in France, where access to teaching is 'very compliqué and mostly a matter of politics not policy. The communists are in control of many schools and in order to get an appointment one must apply to one's union. Heads have no say at all.'

To us, these might seem curious outbursts: but the context is everything. Travelling anywhere within post-war Europe was to find oneself shaped by the politics of the Cold War (1956 had just seen the Soviet invasion of Hungary) and it became a lens through which many situations were defined by the three main travellers we'll be journeying with here – Foxman, Rodger and Sharon Stine. We see a very obvious reaction against the idea of absolutism, which Rodger, writing with hindsight in *A hitch in time*, sees as indicative of the legacy of the 1930s: 'The folly of the faiths had been exposed and it was therefore no accident that we preferred the uncertainty of hitchhiking which never guarantees arrival.'[8] There's clearly more to it than this rhetorical point: in those early post-war years, these travellers had very little idea of what they would find on the road, or of the likely reaction of those they encountered, let alone what to think about it.

Rodger's initial experience of France had not been without difficulties, and he even wondered whether 'they would understand hitch-hiking on the Continent'. He wandered into his first French town proper, Rouen, in 1951, his head dancing with visions of café society, and conversations about Proust or Proudhon, only to splutter on the sharp wine and then get into a mix-up about ordering milk (a drink rationed to children at the time) in a shop because he had been told that French water is hazardous. Next day, his introduction to the romantic myth of 'gai Paris' was rather too literal and it took him a whole evening of drinking in cosmopolitan clubs with three American dentists to realise that he was being picked up. A little out of his depth, he fled to the edge of the city and sought overnight refuge on a building site wrapped in a tarpaulin.[9]

Fortunately, his cultural negotiations were more successful out on the kerbside in the coming days.

The international school of roadside diplomacy

Today there would be a 'light bulb' joke about it, such is the improbability of hitchhikers being able to agree on anything. Hitchhiking may appear to be an entirely individualistic mode of transport but, over the decades, it has also been defined by codes of conduct and assumed etiquette. After his nocturnal adventures in Paris, we find Ian Rodger, a little tired and thirsty perhaps, at the famous Fontainebleau Obelisk, the prized junction on the south side of the city and a notorious hitchhiking bottleneck (Figure 5.1). As he quickly discovers, the constant flow of international travellers through this point, heading on the N6 (now A6) for Lyon, the Rhône valley and the Côte d'Azur required a degree of hastily arranged diplomacy. The fast straight road beyond the junction militated against simply 'walking on' and hoping

Figure 5.1 'Suddenly you could go anywhere'. In the 1950s the Fontainebleau Obelisk became a meeting place for many international hitchhiking 'delegates', heading south from Paris to the Mediterranean.

for a lift a kilometre down the road. It's something which those who have hitched in the era of motorway slip roads in the UK, with all of its legality issues as to where one can stand, may recognise.

What usually transpired was a bizarre enactment of 'game theory', where each individual or couple acceded to whatever tactic worked for the general good. In those days before motorway service stations, where it was not so easy to wander off for a coffee and hope your 'competition' had secured a lift on your return, hitching bottlenecks were important meeting points, with valuable advice to be gained about tactics, accommodation and each other's circumstances. Diplomacy was an asset, as it was highly probable that one would meet the same people further into your trip, something which was facilitated by the greater visibility of 'foreigners'. As Rodger notes, one could presume it would be possible to meet up in Nice, say, even if one had no 'idea how big places like Nice were ... [as] you could go into a café and ask them whether they had seen an Englishman recently. They could usually tell you.' Accordingly, he quickly became sensitive to the necessary negotiations, sometimes based on swift cultural assessments:

> The common condition also brought out interesting national differences. The easiest to persuade towards a plan were the Danes, the Swedes and the Dutch. The Belgians would get bored and go to sleep. The New Zealanders would try to organise a camp-fire or a sing-song and the French, conscious of being the hosts, would fetch out their small knives and share out their bread.[10]

These temporary alliances were often points of 'first contact' and inevitably cultural stereotypes were applied, confirmed or found wanting, as each hitcher regarded the other 'in the manner of explorers. As we talked we would note how we dressed, how our boots were sewn differently, how we rolled our cigarettes.' Much to his bemusement, as an Englishman, Rodger is assumed to know what he is doing by many of his international fellow hitchers: 'had not the English won the war? Were not the English going to tell Europe what to do about the peace?'[11]

Not all of the new alliances and meetings felt liberating, with some travellers still burdened by the prejudices of the past. Many a youth hostel conversation touched on the tactical benefits or risks of backpacks bearing one's national emblem. Not everyone was quite so accommodating of the English either: one hitchhiker who wrote to me, David Watts, recalled how in the summer of 1959 he was chased and berated by a pitchfork-wielding French farmer who despised the English for their abandonment of his nation at Dunkirk! Perhaps the signs that Derek Foxman noticed in many hotels and bars, 'English spoken here', were striking a conciliatory tone but, as he drolly observed: 'We could find no one who did!'

Encountering German hitchhikers on the road sometimes amplified the sense of cultural unease for British and American hitchers, as Rodger notes the lukewarm reception given to strident and boisterous young Germans with whom he and his associates shared youth hostel accommodation in Italy. The prejudices set up by the war could lead to aggressive police searches at borders, yet yield many moments of shared humanity: peasant farmers would come up to Rodger and say 'English good' and marvel at his passport. Once a bus full of orphans each demanded to shake his hand as they passed a cemetery full of Allied dead, leaving him tearfully humbled: 'the electric shock of war was being earthed. I was taking it away.'[12]

Six years later, attitudes seemed to have moved on, with Derek Foxman noting how, amidst the Kiwis and Australians at the Ravenna hostel in Italy, 'there was a curious group consisting of twenty Germans, seventeen Danes, and one Norwegian. I think they had met in Germany the previous year and decided to go on holiday together.' Today, after decades of 'gap year' travelling and the open borders of the European Union, it is easy to overlook the raw immediacy of these meetings, done without a script as to how to conduct oneself to whom and why. It was at places such as the Obelisk, or in the cab of a truck or in communities visited en route, that all of the homilies about travel as educational could be subject to some unsettling tests of one's character.

The politics of gender was a case in point. Heading to the Mediterranean, alongside a group of Belgians, Rodger realises that he is not in agreement with those male hitchhikers who view their female counterparts as a useful possession to secure lifts, like 'a brand of stove'. Talk about using women 'as a decoy for lecherous drivers' makes him feel that there is something 'a little dishonourable' going on, a view that haunts him on his return journey, as he is complicit in encouraging a woman with whom he and several others are hitching (as part of a race between Amsterdam and Paris) to earn some money working in an 'exotic' bar for a night. (She is physically unharmed, but it is a strange and sordid business that all parties regret later.)[13]

Foxman for his part is similarly surprised by the sexism he encounters, although less complicit in events. Ten days after leaving Paris, he has breezed over the Alps, through Lombardy to Venice and is heading south through Tuscany. There he teams up with an all-female Australian and Canadian duo and they help each other acquire lifts: 'the magic word "amico" worked again', he observes. As dusk falls on a hilly road south of Siena they accept a lift from a truck, and whilst Foxman enjoys the cooling breeze under a starry sky from the back of the vehicle, things are going less well inside. At a rest stop they tell him that things are 'getting "very hot" in the cab' with the two

Italian drivers (which has simply not occurred to him as a possibility), so he says something to the drivers and a few minutes later they are all dumped by the wayside. Still well short of Viterbo, some locals witnessed their plight, 'plied us with excellent wine and refused payment', and pointed them in the right direction for cheap accommodation some kilometres distant: 'We set off for the pensione, the girls singing their favourite songs which seemed to be out of light operettas.' They refused lifts that would have meant splitting up, 'as gracefully as possible', before being stopped by a car coming in the opposite direction: 'the driver was from the pensione and had been sent out by our friends!'[14]

If the roadsides were a raw mobile laboratory for how to negotiate with fellow travellers and those who offered lifts, they were also a sharp reminder of the relative liberties which all those involved shared, or had yet to enjoy. So, whether it is the male assumptions about the sexual availability of female travellers or Westerners' apprehensions of communist countries and their representatives, it is worth having a closer look at how we think about liberty.

Freedom is a state of mind

Everyone likes the idea of freedom. It is, as philosopher Isaiah Berlin remarked in his classic 1958 essay 'Two concepts of liberty', 'so porous that there is little interpretation that it seems able to resist'.[15] For Berlin, writing in the Western liberal tradition of the 'political contract' between the State and individuals, freedom was an expression of personal ideals and possible actions as set and mediated by the laws of the land. The State protects citizens from each other's worst behaviour, by ascribing limits to what they can do ('freedom from') whilst providing spaces in which individual independence can flourish (the 'freedom to'). Foxman may not have ever read Berlin, but he is channelling those philosophical distinctions in his debate with the 'Oxford man'. It is a beguiling argument: that the democratic freedoms enshrined in law and accountable to an electorate are the perfect model of liberty. However, there is a big 'if' underpinning this assumption!

What we have learned in the previous chapters is that Berlin's duality is stretched considerably by the actions of the State itself. Our journeys on the roads of the Deep South of the USA with Memphis Minnie and then through some of Europe's occupied territories under Nazi administration with Ida and Maurice Piller show perfectly well how the freedoms guaranteed by the 'political contract' can be susceptible to systematic indifference and active denial, based on poisonous ideology. As we saw in the work of Zygmunt Bauman, particularly *Modernity and the Holocaust*, it is very easy within a bureaucratic and 'ambivalent' society to manufacture 'otherness' for political purposes, leading in the worst extremes to ethnic cleansing and genocide. Freedom becomes an illusion maintained by might. So, if these things can happen in a representative democracy – with people voting for them, as they did in 1930s Germany – surely we need to ask some fundamental questions about what principles of liberty we are basing our societies upon.

This is the contradiction at the heart of Western democracies' view of themselves: that freedom is a set of conditions or values, to be arbitrated by judges, politicians and (increasingly) by corporations, and handed out to their citizens, almost as a reward for good behaviour after a bit of gentle discussion. The main issue with this is not the alleged innocence of power but the assumption of stasis – denying the reality of the struggle *for liberty*, which can take decades or centuries of great suffering before 'rights' or 'justice' are eventually yielded by the powerful.

So, a more useful approach is to see freedoms as part of the lived relationships between people in a society, indicative of the strengths and weaknesses of the bonds of communities and networks which connect us. How we speak of, organise and fight against forms of injustice and prejudice says much about the power of ideology to shape us. The figure of the hitchhiker, as an embodiment of the disparities within a society, can therefore offer insight into how new narratives of freedom emerge and nudge societies in a hopefully more progressive direction.

It is clear from the memoirs of those hitchhiking and youth hostelling in the 1950s that they could see some of the changes occurring and that they – like every other generation of young travellers – wanted to test out their ideas with strangers at the end of a long day. This was particularly true for female travellers, epitomising many of the post-war benefits of a growing economy, an expansion of higher education and having career aspirations as a possibility rather than as wishful thinking. This was also a cohort of social adventurers, with their outlooks broadened by consumer identities, the world of rock 'n' roll, television and a widening political awareness of foreign affairs. Some social theorists of the time, such as Abraham Maslow, began to talk about the emergence of a new kind of confident individual, indicative of a more affluent society, who was freer to engage in the process of 'self-actualisation', if their more basic needs for sustenance, shelter and company were met.[16]

Sharon Stine from California embodied this new sense of independent possibilities, and her memoir *Gypsy boots* is one of the most eloquent accounts of what the world looked like from the roadside in the 1950s. Going to Europe by herself was daring enough in the eyes of family and peers, and learning to hitchhike was definitely not on the list of approved travel options for middle-class women in 1958, when she began her journey, aged twenty-three.

Hardly off the transatlantic liner, she is persuaded of the viability of hitchhiking by fellow hostellers, advised about use of destination signs and national emblems, and sets out from Den Haag with a woman she has met at sea. Determined not to resort to 'Claudette Colbert' tactics of rolling up skirts (see Chapter 1), they manage a quick getaway on the road to Amsterdam, with Stine on the verge of the epiphany ('I'm hooked') as their first driver buys them a coffee and makes them feel welcome. Over the next eighteen months she hitchhikes 25,000 miles, through seventeen countries, much of it with Ruth, a German woman she meets early in her trip, all of which is a massive undertaking for someone whose post-college horizons were dominated by family expectations about marriage and raising children. Dispensing with her heavy suitcase, Sharon quickly realises that 'with only the possessions in my rucksack, I am no longer burdened by the ways I thought young American women should travel in Europe.... In my wildest imagination, I never thought that I'd do this.'[17]

This personal sense of liberation from the very real social and psychological expectations of their time was apparent in many women's accounts; they discovered in continental Europe what their wartime counterparts had found when posted to military bases in England and Scotland. Describing herself as a self-confessed 'hitchhiking addict', young history teacher Antonia Lister-Kaye, from England, 'loved this economical and interesting form of transport in the early to mid fifties … and all those people met with, from Calais to Naples via Basel, and several times round Germany … the nights spent in barns, convents and even a brothel! … I have travelled a lot since those heady days but it has never been such fun and never have I had such a sense of adventure.' Both Stine and Lister-Kaye describe the subterfuge necessary to hide the fact that they were hitchhiking, the latter noting that her father 'hated the whole idea of me hitching. Deception was difficult as he knew I had virtually no money but he would get postcards from Paris, Geneva, and Florence in less than a week.'[18]

Stine refuses to be deterred by the fears of family and becomes irritated with fellow travellers' assumptions that certain places are unreachable by thumb, such as Lapland, in northern Finland. Remote roads, rough accommodation and adjusting their bodies to the length of an Arctic day becomes its own adventure ('I wouldn't be anywhere else in the world'). Pushing on into Norway, the quiet roads end at the small natural harbour of Hammerfest, where Ruth and Sharon make a decision that would have horrified their selves of twelve months before: hitchhiking on fishing boats down the coast to Trondheim, with all-male crews, Spartan conditions and little real idea of how long the journey will take. It is the supreme test of trust, but by then they have developed a knack of spotting danger and on ship they are treated 'as if we were crystal glasses that might crack'. Rolling a cigarette for a driver as they leave the North Sea coasts behind, Stine reflects on her adaptability: 'Now it seems normal. He is offering his friendship. I realise that I've moved some place else, more spacious, less judgemental.' She hopes that returning to suburban America will not mean a loss of perspective, or of 'the need to understand'.[19]

Gypsy boots gives us a woman's view of freedom, representative of those who were spirited and able enough to take the opportunities presented to them. In so doing, those women who embarked on such adventures not only became more open minded and compassionate people because they were able to glimpse how other societies conducted themselves, but arguably became more political as a result. Other representations of hitchhiking at the time communicated a less progressive but possibly more appealing set of messages.

Over to you, Jack.

On the road politics

The late 1950s is of course associated with one monster best-seller book purported to be a bible of hitchhiking, to which we must pay homage for precisely this misapprehension. Why *On the road* by Jack Kerouac has accrued the mythic status that it has is because it expresses an idea of a time, rather than it being a representation of what hitchhiking was actually like for those doing it. Subsequently, it has become a form of cultural shorthand which keeps perpetuating itself, name-checked by everyone.

No one disputes the book as a literary achievement: the conveying of a certain kind of restless post-war youth culture identity, hedonistic and individualistic. The form is as wild as the content, mirroring a break from their parent's generation, in the same manner as the film *Rebel without a cause*. It's just 'a startlingly bad blueprint for travel', observes the American travel writer Rolf Potts in his essay 'We don't (really) know Jack'. There is actually very little hitchhiking in *On the road*, and even less actually said about it; for all the energy that Dean Moriarty and Sal Paradise devote to 'just going', the 'somewhere' that they want to get to and the cultures and landscape travelled through seem largely ignored. Most travel classics, as Potts notes, encourage people to 'slow down, to linger, to listen' and contain an element of roadside anthropology about them, however small.[20] Fellow Beat writer Gary Snyder packs far more hitchhiking content into his poem 'Night Highway 99' than Kerouac does in the whole of *On the road*.

However, for all of these misgivings, and the pretty appalling attitudes towards women in the book, we should express some gratitude for the fact that Morgan 'Sal'man Strub, the founder of Digihitch.com, was personally inspired by reading *On the road*, even altering his name to acknowledge the influence. More broadly perhaps, Kerouac's name has a prominence among the 'baby boom' generation, fulfilling a nostalgic role in constructing an allegedly 'benign' period of hitchhiking, predating the supposed slide into 'darker times' (see Chapter 8). For cultural analysts such as Jeremy Packer, *On the road* offers 'a bridge' from the immediate post-war generation to the more politicised values of the 'counter-culture', where mobility can't be seen just in terms of individual rights.[21]

The travel memoirs of Rodger and Stine give that generational 'bridge' some substance in terms of a transformation of values: an emerging awareness of inequality through the 'shock' of encountering other cultures without the kind of preparation that many later travellers would have available to them through guidebooks. Neither of their books are activist rallying cries as such, more a documentation of personal social and political awakening. For Stine, the contrasting fortunes between herself and those she meets are most starkly exposed when she reaches pre-Wall Berlin, where the lack of basic amenities is still apparent years after the war. In a café, she and Ruth encounter a group of East German teenagers and Sharon notes: 'nothing in my past could prepare me for the trapped helplessness and the ominous political future people in the room describe. I live such a privileged life.'[22]

More social divisions await them in the comparatively benign houses of Zurich, where they become aware of the role of unofficial foreign workers, as they while-away the winter accepting arduous work as maids for the Swiss upper classes. Back on the road, the class contrasts within Spanish society are less hidden and more pronounced. A remarkable example of generosity from an affluent Franco-supporting Spanish family, who provide a long lift, accommodation and a horseback tour of their estate, leaves Sharon uncomfortable as to what she witnesses in the space of a couple of days:

> I can't get rid of the image of threadbare people kneeling in the street while a priest drives off in a shiny Buick.... I feel out of balance as I search the ragged edges of this journey, trying to understand what matters. It's not as simple as cathedrals or Goya's paintings. This journey isn't destinations and historic sites, but unplanned encounters with people and places that have the power to tangle my thoughts.[23]

Spain was also notable in the accounts for its conservative attitudes towards women, after a patchy flowering of gender awareness in some Republican areas during the Civil War and Revolution of 1936–9. As independent-minded cosmopolitan people, Sharon and Ruth are very visible, especially when they make a decision not to travel 'tourist class' on trains or ships. Ian Rodger travels solely by thumb, but he is also uncomfortable with what he sees and how places are portrayed by travel writers to potential visitors, hiding the realities by writing 'about the landscape and its people from the vantages of hotels and villas' and allocating 'aspects of mystery and exoticism' to the peasants and fishermen and waiters.[24]

These new political discoveries reveal something else: a questioning of the values that they have brought with them and their own understanding of 'freedom'. Exposed to other nationalities on the road and in the hostels, the Western assumptions of Cold War foreign policy are suddenly put under scrutiny, with Stine noting how the brutal French occupation of Algeria crops up when conversation turns to the threats posed by the Soviet Union. So, as her thumb turns towards Greece through Yugoslavia, the thriftiness and generosity of the locals make her think more universally of what unites rather than divides people, and she reflects that she has 'been programmed to think a certain way, a patriotic American way. Now I am uncertain about many things … the word communist doesn't carry the same threat anymore.'[25]

Exposure to ordinary acts of kindness and compassion whilst travelling not only makes a mockery of the political assumptions that her generation has become accustomed to, but their journeys become barometers of an emerging internationalism and globalisation long before these were everyday concepts. As an American, Sharon is assumed to hold particular opinions about race: arriving in England in 1958, she reels at the prejudice amongst hoteliers who believe their 'no blacks' policy will impress her and, by contrast, in educated French company she is horrified that people somehow assume her attitudes will be those of the school segregationists whom civil rights campaigners were challenging in Little Rock, Arkansas.

What these journeys show us is a view of history as process, of freedom as something that is *fought for* – with travellers as diplomats and ambassadors, not just of where they come from but as an embodiment of ideals that are not yet fully realised. The end of *A hitch in time* leaves one with a strong affirmation of this, as Rodger lists a series of international events which he had sensed as inevitable just from listening to others on the roadside and in the cabs and coffee houses. Accordingly, he invites the politicians of the future to adopt the perspective of a hitchhiker, and take a turn negotiating with each other at the Fontainebleau Obelisk, as though the immediacy of those interactions and what we learn on the road from the 'real people' we meet is instructive of how we should conduct our politics.

As for his own peers, many who had set out defined by the absolutist political philosophies of their parents returned with a greater sensitivity to other ideas, changed by the inequities and complexities of what they had seen: 'Some caught the vision of a new kind of internationalism at the roadside, ended up in the service of UNESCO and the UN and have never mentally returned to their homes.'[26] We'll pick up some of these wider notions of liberty shortly, but for now let's allow ourselves a bit of a theoretical rest and take a romantic detour to consider some of the more sensuous aspects of the 'freedom' of travel, which is also part of the story of hitchhiking, as with every other form of mobility!

Why don't we do it in the road?

For such a practical aspect of life, transport can pack quite an erotic punch. It's always been there of course, rooted in our origins as migratory beings, the body brushed by the rhythms of the world; survival and reproductive instincts colliding in the urge to move. Modernity has paid its imaginative dues with its literary erotic tropes: the Victorian railway carriage, the Regency stagecoach, even the elevator – anywhere the anonymity of place meets the temporary freedoms of association. The motor age has extended this with the perfect synthesis of personal space and limitless mobility, accruing as many cultural anxieties as it has new sexual opportunities, plus an inexhaustible supply of imaginative fictions. Into this social space comes the perfect fantasy figure to liven up the banality of the drive: the hitchhiker.

There are plenty of on-the-road liaisons in the hitchhiking literary canon from before the Second World War, even if the motor vehicle was not quite so culturally and erotically charged as it has subsequently become. Well worth the effort (for many reasons!) are the wondrous colonial-era travelogue exoticism of Frederic Prokosch's *The Asiatics*,[27] Russ Hofvendahl's vivid and quite explicit Depression memoir *A land so fair and bright* and, most eloquently, Laurie Lee's retrospective account of pre-revolutionary Spain in *As I walked out one midsummer morning*. These memoirs and travelogues quite beautifully evoke the enduring romantic appeal of the itinerant entertainer or worker who passes through a community and alters lives, regardless of what mode of transport brought them there.

The affordability of the automobile in the burgeoning economic boom of the 1950s and 1960s changed the whole tradition of courtship and codes of conduct: it was perfectly possible to meet a future partner or conduct a temporary fling in the random roadside universe, especially when it became the *modus operandi* to attend music festivals. Such was the intersection between hitchhiking and lifestyle in the 1960s that (male) guidebook writers such as Ed Buryn devoted sections of their books to 'sex and love', offering health advice and advice on cross-cultural attitudes towards sexuality.

For our 1950s European adventurers, being away from families and in more cosmopolitan surroundings nurtured social confidence. In *Gypsy boots*, Sharon Stine tells of her daring purchase of copies of Henry Miller erotica banned in the USA but available in Denmark. She relishes being able to hitch spontaneously with a young man whom she meets at the youth hostel, enjoys café society with strangers and only fleetingly wonders about whether she might be seen as 'fast'. It's a refreshing perspective on the 'road as educator', with classic Romantic views of identity in the process of transformation. Understandably, writers (or maybe their editors) of this era vary in how forthcoming they are about casual sex or romantic dalliances: Rodger's *A hitch in time*, for instance, gently hints at on-the-road affairs throughout, before eventually revealing the full extent of the promiscuity within his group of temporary road mates, and suddenly the 'swinging sixties' are happening a decade too soon and the possibilities of what one can do on the back of a moving flat-bed truck acquire new significance.

The male travel writer delivering his tale with a sexual swagger and a few self-admonishing literary quips is something of a cliché, and there are plenty of hitchhikers who have done the same.[28] Perhaps this is at least part of the explanation for the success of Tom Robbins's 1976 novel *Even cowgirls get the blues*, a hitchhiking tale of female agency and sexual expression. This tale of Sissy Hankshaw, the supreme hitchhiker with a big heart and oversized thumbs to match, portrays a woman open to experience and sure enough of herself to glide to and fro over the North American continent for the hell of it. Written as philosophical comedy, the antics of Sissy Hankshaw have had a significant cultural impact, inspiring artistic projects, extensive commentary and a lot of independent women.[29] Less known, however, is the darker beauty of Iva Pekárková's 1992 novel *Truck stop rainbows*, which puts her hitchhiking heroine, Fialka Jourová, in some remarkable dilemmas about sex on the road in the former Czechoslovakia. She is a free-spirited student and environmental photographer, who likes hitchhiking and having sex with truck drivers, but her best friend's diagnosis of multiple sclerosis motivates her to try to earn the money for his wheelchair in this way, leading to considerable soul searching (and some far from glamorous encounters).

Outside the realms of fantasy erotica or pornography, it is unusual to encounter female authors writing about the experience of sex whilst hitchhiking, especially as a form of personal liberation against social conformity and political oppression. Yet Pekárková does more than just this; the 'rainbows' that her heroine is seeking are moments of serendipity: spontaneous, colourful, enriching and liberated. Whether it is having sex, or a philosophical discussion, or wandering in unspoilt natural surroundings, Fialka tries to find the aesthetic and emotional security of the temporary as a bulwark against the ongoing psychological and ecological totalitarianism and conformity which surround her. The rainbows are a symbol of the permanence of a moment of social value, however fleeting their actual incarnation.

Truck stop rainbows is perhaps the most conceptually innovative fictional representation of hitchhiking, as well as a worthy documentation of the more amorous aspects of 'the road as teacher'. It also leaves us with a sense of transcendence and possibility, where individual liberation as glimpsed from the roadsides can lead to more collective changes. This reworking of Romanticism became synonymous with the generation of independent travellers who ventured eastwards from Europe in the 1960s and 1970s onto the imagined landscapes of central Asia, where they were forced to test many of their ideals about liberty.

The politics of the 'Hippie Trail'

It was a substantial undertaking, however one traversed the route. Many began thumbing from as far away as Western Europe, or took one of the low-budget transports that linked 'hip' European destinations such as Amsterdam, Athens and Copenhagen with Istanbul. Others packed themselves into the now legendary split-screen VW camper vans and did it this way too, with all of the logistical problems of keeping a vehicle in roadworthy condition. Hitching the entire 'Trail' was unusual, as sections of the route through Turkey and Iran into Afghanistan could be traversed using incredibly cheap local buses, and in other areas a local lack of familiarity with the practice guaranteed slow progress.

Separating myth from reality is important. From the mid-1960s, when doing 'the Trail' was starting to become popular, it began to accrue its fair share of negative publicity, usually around drugs and clashes of culture. Thousands could be on the route at any one time, and there was plenty which could go wrong just in terms of dealing with the practicalities of massively contrasting temperatures, hydration, diet and illness. The travellers' grapevine and an emerging 'Trail' industry covered some of the information gaps, but the psychological demands were considerable.

Why people were drawn to such undertakings was complicated. The overland route to India had until the late 1950s been something only a wealthy adventurer or a mountaineering expedition would undertake for fun, but as mass tourism began to take hold of the Mediterranean coastlines, it seemed to push a network of bohemians and 'backpacker-drifters' (as sociologist Erik Cohen called them) eastwards.[30] These were the now fabled 'baby boomer' generation, some of whom began to reject the aspirations of the stable consumer society of the 1950s which they had grown up in.

In his book *The making of a counter culture*, historian and cultural theorist Theodore Roszak tried to understand the psyche of those who chose to embark on 'the Trail' as a statement or a form of pilgrimage. He argues that it was one cultural expression of the search for 'non-material' needs, this being an era when many basic requirements linked to scarcity had been met, leaving energy for personal development and exploration of new desires. The huge social transformations brought on by rock music and youth culture, more liberal attitudes to sex and politics, and the role of television in reporting it around the world created a rising climate of possibility for much deeper shifts. The Vietnam War, the civil rights struggle, the Prague Spring and the General Strike in France in May 1968 became international touchstones for the wider analysis of what 'life in the West' was predicated upon (and what the alternatives might look like). For many, Roszak argues, the liberties available through consumerism seemed hollow – receptacles for the 'surplus repressions' created by civilisation to control people. By way of response, the so-called 'hippie counter-culture' offered new forms of community and lifestyle – communes, free music festivals, alternative media and art spaces – in which ideas could be shared, conventions challenged and re-evaluated.

In this climate, hitchhiking took on an almost allegorical status – a way of responding to the violence of 'the system' through human contact, reducing impact on the environment, carrying each other along. John Francis ('the Planetwalker') even renounced hitchhiking and took to walking everywhere after witnessing the impact of an oil spill off the coast of California (he also took a vow of silence). Yet, despite an emotional engagement with the world worthy of the Romantics, the alternative lifestyles did not always translate into much-needed shifts within the economic and political realm, nor magically resolve the multiplicity of demands for greater freedom within wider society. For some on the roadsides of Afghanistan heading for Kathmandu or the beaches of Goa, the answers to the lack of liberty in the world were not to be found on the boulevards of Paris. As Theodore Roszak despairingly observed, for all of the iconoclasm of the era, the experiments and expanding political consciousness, there was a strange intellectual turn amongst progressives towards mysticism.[31]

It had happened before: revolutionary moments slipping away, with some of their principal players opting for something less tactically complex. When the French Revolution began to go awry and the Jacobins lost their allure, some of the Romantic poets turned to nature for inspiration, shying away from the human foibles exposed by the heat of the moment. At the end of the 1960s, however, the defection from rationalism was much more complete than two centuries before, with countless thousands veering into millenarian traditions, cults and repressive communities.[32] For others it was just great business: the Beatles' dalliance with the transcendental meditation guru Maharishi Mahesh Yogi in 1967 the perfect simulacrum of rebellion. But then again, some of the Beats hadn't really helped: Jack Kerouac and Allen Ginsberg dabbling with Hinduism and Zen, imbuing Mexico and North Africa and 'simpler' indigenous cultures with a degree of mysticism and idealisation.

It is unsurprising then that tucked into rucksacks on the 'Hippie Trail' and at music festivals the world over were copies of *The Tibetan book of the dead*, the *I Ching* or one of the mystical philosophical quest novels by Hermann Hesse (*Siddartha*, *Journey to the east*) which enjoyed a new popularity amongst these audiences. If hitchhiking through countries with massive levels of inequality was odd enough, to choose to soak up theologies vastly different to one's own, some of which enforced caste systems or the inferior position of women, was maybe indicative of how lost (or uncritical) some people felt.

One might regard some of the conversions and experimentations on the Trail as a theological version of the Stockholm syndrome. Cultural guilt aside, there wasn't much spiritual karma for would-be acolytes clogging up embassies on the Trail itself, or incurring the ire of locals on the Indian coasts. There were clashes of culture (especially around nudity and drugs) but some of the strongest reporting of so-called 'hippie invasions' occurred in places that were aspiring to be more tourist orientated. Also well documented were tales of imprisonment on the Trail, the forced shearing of locks at border crossings and infamous warnings, such as a legendary sign at the Afghan embassy in Tehran which encouraged people not to try to secure relevant paperwork 'with hair like that of beetle'.[33]

'Not till we all are is anyone free'[34]

This was not everyone's experience of course, and amongst those who didn't make the press for the wrong reasons were Michael and Sheila Hall from Northern Ireland, relative latecomers to the Trail in 1976, but representatives perhaps of the kind of ethical or environmentally conscious traveller of the future. They were politically minded people, had been in Paris during the student protests of 1968, and were happy to take a break from the religious prejudices they'd encountered as a result of their relationship (she was Catholic, he Protestant). Already seasoned hitchhikers, with college degrees behind them, getting out and seeing a bit of the world was more important than planning a career or a mortgage.

Being on the Trail was something they'd heard lots of scary tales about, but they were mainly concerned with the practicalities of what to take and whether they had raised enough money working in the Netherlands beforehand. As for their 'hippie credentials', the Halls approached the idea of travelling through Asia to India and beyond with the 'mood of self-sufficiency ... [and] confidence in one's own ability to adapt and survive' that was typical of the time. Perhaps inevitably, they had 'delved into Zen, meditation, yoga, and most potent of all, experimentation with the mind-expanding drug LSD' but found the hippie scene 'shallow and little different from other fads'.[35]

Michael Hall's memoir *Remembering the Hippie Trail* is typical of many an adventure written up years later from copious diaries, photographs and travel paraphernalia, framing events with hindsight and reflecting upon how much life on the road had changed the author. Hall's, Stine's and Rodger's books are observations by intelligent, articulate and literate people, who probably represent some of the most open minded of their generation. However, what is striking about the Hall's account of the couple's eventual nineteen-month journey is how their assumptions about travel altered when they moved beyond Europe.

> From the minute we stepped ashore in Asia we had experienced few esoteric musings and no preoccupation with developing inner awareness. We had simply taken each day as it came, soaking up every new experience to the full, and when thoughts intruded they were more often worldly, more likely to be concerned with how the ordinary people we travelled among managed to cope with the numerous trials and tribulations which so constantly beset them.[36]

As with our 1950s hitchhikers, their book is full of the usual stories of impromptu kindnesses by poor families, but we also see bewildering encounters of a more complex nature, such as one in eastern Turkey, where they were detained by army officers near a military base and accused of spying for Greece. (This is a common traveller's tale.) It was very unsettling and at one point Sheila, outraged at the preposterousness of the charge, shouted at an army officer in the street. The gathered crowd, mostly Kurdish, with little love for the Turkish military, looked on approvingly, but it was a situation which could have easily got out of control.

In Turkey, gender politics were never far away, and if a confident woman could confound in some situations, this was offset by the perennial expectation that 'the sexually liberated image attached to Western women meant that anyone was free to touch them up'. Amazing to the Halls was the response to a rebuke, which was along the lines of a game: a case of 'Oh well, I tried and failed; now I can just be friendly again'.[37]

Some travellers more than others are at the sharp end of the disparities between their 'freedom to go' and how it might be shaped by forces beyond their control. Patriarchy defines so many presuppositions, as does financial inequality, and the flows of people on the Trail – estimated to be 10,000 at any one time at its high point[38] – brought with them another manifestation of global culture apart from preconceived ideas about women: the image of a traveller with endless amounts of disposable income. By the time that Michael and Sheila Hall arrived on the Trail, it had become such an industry that the possibility for 'genuine contact' and suffusion in the gift economy had been eroded by the apparent uniformity of any overseas visitor, traveller, tourist or hitcher: relatively speaking, they were all business opportunities for the fraudster, the fake-gemstone seller, the over-friendly money exchanger, the guru in the Emperor's new clothes.

To the hitchhiker wanting to by-pass the formal economy and engage in something more meaningful, this seemed a disappointment. Yet is this so bad? Ian Rodger's response to dealing with the changes that more travellers and tourists made to an area was to head away from it, to find somewhere more authentic, but perhaps by staying one learns how to instigate change. Let's not forget that many countries encouraging tourism and the companies who are providing them with it do not always have issues of equality in mind: trying to understand, emphasise and connect with others as directly as possible should surely be the goal, as an alternative to the systematic injustices perpetuated by the status quo.

So where does this leave our models of freedom? In grossly unequal societies, even the illusion of state-brokered rights (i.e. freedom *to* and freedom *from*) is a luxury, so how one embraces the *freedom for* liberties of self-determination is particularly tricky. What right, the Halls ask at the end of the book, do we have to brush off street traders like insects or fail to ask permission to take photographs in potentially sensitive situations (on the back of a truck in the company of conservatively dressed Afghan women for instance)? Addressing their children's generation, they suggest a philosophy of travel that observes the maxims 'Take nothing but photographs and leave nothing but footprints' and 'Take with you an open mind and leave behind you a sense of international friendship'.[39]

It became tricky to do these things on the Hippie Trail for a couple of decades, as 1979 saw both the Iranian Revolution and the Soviet invasion of Afghanistan effectively close off the region to Western adventurers. Cheaper aviation routes altered the travel culture in the intervening years, by which time there had been all manner of memoirs, films and journalistic nostalgia pieces, either focusing on the drug-taking and guru-searching or lapsing into the easy copy of 'we were young and naïve and now we have grown up' variety.[40] As with Kerouac symbolising a rebellious sensibility, so the Hippie Trail became the embodiment of an 'idea of a time', a passing phase of social experimentation, eccentric travel and colourful if misguided behaviour.

An alternative, more constructive view of such times, however, sees their bursts of creative energies as part of an evolving societal transformation: an 'ecology of freedom' which ebbs and flows, with its failures and successes, but always towards a more empowered and egalitarian future.

Flowers in the asphalt of history

Thinking about freedom is hard work. Yet so much of our time is taken up by clinging on to freedoms which have already been fought for – the right to vote, speak out, have free health care and education – or trying to manage the overwhelming 'tyranny' of too much consumer choice that there is precious little energy for anything more. The idealism of 'not till we all are is anyone free' creates a problem for how we begin to model what we have seen and construct a workable sense of the *freedom for* now that we have seen the insubstantial nature of the *to/from* view from the centre of politics.

Hitchhikers are of course no freer than anyone else, but there is nothing essentially 'freedom-poor' about being by the roadside; it is, rather, that being on the margins facilitates ways of connecting and identifying with others who have shared the same spaces over time. For writers such as the anarchist thinker Murray Bookchin (*The ecology of freedom*) and cultural critic Greil Marcus (*Lipstick traces: a secret history of the twentieth century*) there is a whole millennium or more of groups flowering in the historical margins, defining new notions of liberty through forms of political, religious, cultural and sexual practices which rub up against the mainstreams of the time. We could substitute 'hitchhiking hippies', for argument's sake, with any number of medieval or Reformation-era heretic communities, including the Diggers or Ranters, or, later, some pirate communities, the utopian communes of the industrial era, collectives during the Spanish Civil War, squatting movements, peace camps, and the Occupy and Climate Justice movements of the last decade or two.[41]

The evolution of our notions of freedom begins in movements such as these, on the margins, in a dynamic and dialectical relationship with the mainstream. From there, the vagabond sociologist sees history in those terms, witnessing the ebb and flow of groups and individuals advocating the *freedom for* new ideals weaving through the centuries, sometimes coalescing into major historical moments, at other times influencing quiet corners of the world to be more autonomous and self-organising. It is an uneven process, subject to the contingency of history: every era has its successes and failures, dead ends, failed experiments; for every Tom Paine and Mary Wollstonecraft, a Robespierre or Napoleon; for every thriving self-managed community, a squandered opportunity or fraudulent guru. The difference between these positions can sometimes come down to our starting premises and how accountable we are to each other in our aspirations for liberty. And, it seems, how we link this to nature.

In recent decades, our understanding of the struggle for freedom has become increasingly associated with philosophies such as 'social ecology' and 'deep ecology', fostering debates about how human societies sit within (or in opposition to) the self-organising and mutualistic 'laws' of nature. For me, the writings of Murray Bookchin are key here: premised on the idea that social and ecological aspects of liberty are interconnected, with much of the damage a result of human societies 'choosing' to evolve their own forms of social hierarchy over the last ten millennia.[42] As with the arguments of the anthropologist Christopher Boehm – whose 'reverse dominance' theory we met in Chapter 4 – Bookchin looks to the endurance and stability of small-group societies where empathy and forms of egalitarianism were able to thrive through mutual interest. There is, he believes, an inherent drive within all life to flourish and 'actualise its own potential', including the ability to correct any imbalances which work to its own detriment (in this case, the dysfunctions created by hierarchy). For human societies to fully realise their own potential, there needs to be a rebalancing of structures towards more participatory and democratic ideals and in their relationships with nature. Truly free individuals are possible, he argues, only if they embody that balance. Today, many social ecology ideas now reside in green parties around the world, anarchist and cooperative movements, and even in 'free' parts of Kurdistan, not so far from the old 'Hippie Trail'.[43]

How we organise our transport should be no different, so if we bring this back to hitchhikers, then they are in a prime theoretical position to see the relative mutualistic 'health' of the social ecosystems through which they are passing. Obviously, hitchhikers themselves are part of that system – something the generation of the counter-culture was trying to 'actualise' – with people such as Jacob Holdt and his utter faith in the mutability of the universe being the embodiment of the empathic cooperative ideal of a Bookchin or a Boehm: a microcosm of the world as it should be.

These are difficult and contentious concepts and not all of the hitchhikers in this chapter would see it quite this way, but I have a hunch that most of them would endorse the general sentiment.

Like a Belisha beacon lighting up an entire lifetime

In June 2009, a letter in the *Guardian* newspaper motivated an eighty-three-year-old man to sift through a lifetime of papers and memorabilia, walk down to his local London library to photocopy a sheaf of inky pages and post them to a complete stranger. For a moment, as he was feeding the pages through the machine, he pictured himself back on the roadsides of Greece and Italy many decades before and marvelled at how he'd managed to travel so far, so easily and for so many years.

Four hundred miles away, on the Isle of Arran, a writer paused in her plans for the day, scanned the same newspaper, which had landed on her doormat, and found herself typing something entirely different from what she had intended; she wrote instead of an intuition about the world that she had found in the place where she had least expected it, sleeping under a hedge by the roadside on her own many decades before. She thought about how that feeling still informed her days, what she wrote about in her 'Greening Arran' column for the local newspaper, how people thumbed around her island and shared cars because there was little public transport, especially in winter.

Both of them found it hard to focus on anything else for quite a while.

The response to my request for accounts of hitchhiking during the mid-twentieth century was quite overwhelming and those of Derek Foxman and Alison Prince were just two of the stories which impacted on me. I'd asked for memories, diaries, articles written, and these came so thick and fast that I spent a month dealing with the correspondence alone. It was quite an emotional process, filtering all of those experiences which at some level the writers were still trying to make sense of, not because those were their 'salad days' or 'happy times', but because their experience still felt socially meaningful in the wider scheme of things.

Existentialist philosophers argue that we interpret our past through the lens of the ideas gained over the intervening years. One after another, my respondents reiterated a narrative which compared the more managed travel experiences of their children with the raw exhilaration of their own, each of them believing that the new infrastructure of tourism and leisure emerging since they had withdrawn their thumbs from the road had diminished that sense of freedom. This was most telling in terms of certainty and pre-planning. Antonia Lister-Kaye reflected on how her own children 'preferred the relative certainties of Trail Finders and local buses' but she felt that 'they lost out in many ways, not just money, but that element of surprise encounters and not quite knowing where you were going to pitch up'.[44] Lesley Morrison, who hitched across Canada in the late 1960s, considered her feelings about what she learned on the road and the different expectations and interactions four decades later:

> People are potential friends until proved otherwise, and cars (as you say) are a luxury to be shared. We've encouraged our kids to believe that. When my nineteen-year-old daughter currently travelling in the south of Spain, mentioned that she'd been hitchhiking, did I feel an initial tremor of concern? Yes. Was it soon replaced by a feeling of (a) pride and (b) envy? Yes.[45]

Sociologists have suggested that the generation of the 1960s was involved in an 'expressive revolution', and, regardless of their political successes and failures, had embraced more emotionally driven ways of thinking and talking about being active in the world. It may be entirely coincidental that the boom in those areas of public sector employment which require the most communication and empathy, the emergence of people-centred approaches to learning and the application of mediation and counselling to structural as well as individual problems all occur at the same time as this wave of hitch-hiking. There seems something homologous about it all: they are part of the same evolution of human ideals, a blossoming just as with the moments of Romanticism during the Enlightenment. Those more comprehensive ways of thinking about liberty, of the politics of hitchhiking, of our relationship with the environment and each other, in a newly global world, are vagabond viewpoints more generally.

It is not a coincidence that some of our hitchers went on to do the things that they did. Michael Hall became a writer and political activist, penning substantial publications on the importance of mediation and building community resilience in conflict situations, at the time when Northern Ireland finally began to change for the better. Sharon Stine's book ends in a moving epilogue about the impact of her long adventure on her life, the importance that she had attached to landscape as an artist, academic and traveller, how she still felt that those roadside experiences with her friend Ruth (whom she stayed in touch with) lived inside her. Such emotional investments in those moments of freedom translated into oft-repaid debts to my own generation, without whom the road would have felt a much more daunting place.

Many of the people in this chapter hitched into their late twenties or early thirties, and looking through their eyes and hearing their thoughts help us appreciate the kind of worlds which are imagined if not always pursued. The baby boomer generation and their most immediate inheritors were arguably amongst the 'freest' people of the last century – whose ideas of liberty have percolated deep into our culture. For others, a few years on the road becomes more than just a way of informing life off it, but the springboard for a different way of living altogether. In the following chapter, we will be meeting some of these people – who share a common denominator in having braved the cold winds and difficult psychological truths on the Alaska Highway. Amongst their number are some of the most legendary long-distance travellers on the planet, whose lifestyles have to be regarded as a little unconventional – even crazy – but whose vision of social justice, ecological balance and how we live as though the future matters may turn out to be the truest of all the hitch-hikers in this book.

But first, let us cheer ourselves up, with one more warm-hearted European anecdote – a sliver of optimism and possibility for those who have tasted that remarkable feeling of freedom that one can get only from hitchhiking. Here is writer and journalist Ian Martin reflecting on one of his life lessons on turning sixty years old: a 'rainbow' of freedom to inspire our collective roadsides.

> It was 1968. Early summer evening. A Saturday. My mate and I were hitching home in the Essex countryside. We got a lift from a happy couple in a boaty car that smelled of leather and engine oil. We were fifteen, they were proper old, twenty-ish. Relaxed and so very much in love. They treated us as equals, laughed at our jokes, we smoked their cigarettes. 'Walk away Renee' by the Four Tops came on the radio. We sang along to the chorus. I felt a blissful certainty that life as an adult might genuinely be a laugh. The entire encounter lasted no more than ten minutes. I have thought about that couple every day since. Every day for forty-five years. Imagine that. A Belisha beacon of kindness pulsing through the murk of a whole life.[46]

Chapter 6

The Alaska Highway hitchhiker visitors' book: the personality of the 'extreme hitchhiker'

Hearing the call of the wild

It takes a special person and a good reason to stand at 'Mile 0', Dawson Creek, British Columbia, Canada, thumb outstretched beneath a destination sign reading 'Fairbanks 1523 miles'. The Alaska–Canada Highway, or 'Alcan' as it is fondly known, may not have an official appreciation society like the legendary Lincoln Highway, but it has had many more books devoted to its place in road history. It taps into all of the myths of the American north that have been constructed by white explorers, settlers and fortune hunters over the centuries. Much of the route tilts east–west but the iconography and language of the road are firmly etched out as north and south, anchoring the meaning of fabled locations of various gold rushes ('the Klondike' in Canada's Yukon Territory), oil towns and trading posts of the trapping industry. It is easy to understate the extreme isolation, weather and terrain that define such places: winter comes early to most of the route, and ice may still etch the surface of lakes above latitude 60° in May. Frost damage and flooding mean that the summer months are ones where road repairs are constantly required to keep nature from reclaiming sections of it in the winter. The difficult stretches may have been straightened out and the modern traveller no longer has to deal with quite the same quantities of slippery gravel that defined some sections until full paving in 1992, but it is still a psychologically demanding drive, and for cyclists and motorbikes a major undertaking. One can often be fifty miles from the nearest roadhouse or fuel pump, and summoning aid is made difficult by vast cell-phone 'dead zones'. Electronic reconnaissance courtesy of Google Earth merely reinforces this, with large sections of the road resplendent in benign summer colours, with not even a hint of harsh winter hazards. Look at a few minutes of videos from holiday road trips posted online and you realise not only how narrow the highway can be but how few vehicles seem to be coming the other way.

The remoteness is of course part of the appeal – vast mountain ranges which anywhere else would each have a national park status assigned to them, pristine glacier-fed lakes, abundant wildlife visible from the roadside, including bears, moose, coyotes and even wolves. It is of course a landscape popularised by Jack London novels – *The call of the wild* and *White fang* – which are often mis-associated with the narrative of American progress and Frederick Jackson Turner's 'Frontier' thesis, celebrating the power of the all-conquering individual over savage landscapes.

The experienced hitchhiker can expect to spend three to four days travelling one end to the other, with the likelihood of long waits in the upper Yukon beyond Kluane Lake through to Tok Junction in Alaska (including the uncertainties of the international Canada–USA border crossing, where one must prove one's financial as well as bureaucratic worth). Despite the staggering beauty to be enjoyed from being stationary in such places, the time waiting can be defined by two notorious factors: the cold and the maddening presence of hungry insects (the 'no-see-ums' in local parlance).

People who hitch the Alaska Highway are part of an elite bunch of travellers, free spirits, often perpetual adventurers for whom many of the normal rules for choosing to strike out for somewhere do not apply. They also usually journey alone. When they open an atlas, they are looking at the same topography as you and I, but devising road trips of a different order of magnitude. Instead of a few hundred kilometres, they are sizing up the crossing or circumnavigating of a continent. For such people, 'doing' the Alaska Highway is not an isolated event, more a single part of a series of bigger journeys, perhaps heading across the Trans-Canada highway to Nova Scotia, south through the Americas or catching a plane from Alaska to Russia to begin other challenges in Asia. Some of them may even be part of a hitch-hiking competition, of the sort organised by European clubs (see Chapter 10), but it is a journey that none of them forget, and many are entranced by it enough to repeat it.

For the purposes of differentiating them from those equally elusive beasts 'the ordinary hitchhikers', let us enrol them into a hypothetical 'extreme hitchhikers' club', whose members' determination and ambitions are worthy of extra psychological enquiry, in the same way that we might speculate about the motives and drive of adventurers and explorers of the climbing Everest or crossing Antarctica variety. The practical environment of Highway 97 does require a certain ambitious psychology to make it through to the official end at Delta Junction, just short of Fairbanks, and reading some of the accounts of the journeys it's hard not to feel a pang of amazement and admiration, perhaps tempered with concern for their sanity. Winter aside, it may not be as daunting as it once was, although a disagreement with a driver could leave one in unforgiving terrain. Also, the bear attacks on campers and walkers are highly exaggerated!

In this chapter I will explore two aspects of the personality of the 'extreme hitchhiker': their psychological 'makeup' as adventurers and arguably social pioneers of one sort, and, relatedly, what the journeys of these individuals say about the societies from which they have been motivated to leave, albeit temporarily. So, in the first instance, if we use the Myers–Briggs personality type indicators as a rough guide, it might be true to say, as Stephen Franzoi did in his comprehensive study of over 100 'cross-country hitchhikers' in the summer of 1973, that they are mainly 'impulsive and autonomous, having a high degree of tolerance for complexity and change, with strong interest in interpersonal relations'.[1] His findings were that, in the main, people undertaking long journeys shared a similar profile to those who train to become counsellors. They demonstrated a strong interest in those who picked them up, often equal or greater than their feelings towards the landscapes through which they were travelling. These conclusions provide a fascinating starting point to consider the relationships between individual motivation, societal structures and the health of our world, with the Alaska Highway serving as allegory.

So, as we relive some of the hitchhiking history of this legendary road, we will find these issues increasingly intertwined. As with our 'Hippie Trail' hitchhikers in the previous chapter, these travellers must have a basic level of adaptability to the physical rigours of the journey and plenty of mental resilience, regardless of the reasons for why they are standing at Dawson Creek heading north.

But before we meet our club members and hear their individual motivations, let's just remind ourselves how psychologists have portrayed hitchhikers in the past.

The rites and wrongs of passage

The odds have always been slightly stacked against us, from the initial attempts to understand the mind of the hitchhiker in late 1920s America. According to the historian John Schlebecker, the first frame of reference was 'quirky but harmless adventurers', but once we get into the Depression era and transport companies start to lose money, the focus begins to be on the danger to the public presented by criminal elements in society. This shift facilitates a raft of anti-hitchhiking legislation, backed up by a lot of editorial commentary but little actual clinical evidence. It was enough, Schlebecker argues, to create doubt in the minds of some of the motorists, even if the numbers of hitchhikers on the road made the proposition that they were all criminals absurd.[2]

The starting premise for any serious studies of the minds of hitchhikers has been that any problem may lie with the individuals concerned rather than the society through which they may be travelling. This is reinforced by a common belief in the West that hitchhiking is not actually a *form of transport*. Predictably perhaps, when social scientists began studying youth subcultures and new forms of deviance in the 1950s and 1960s, hitchhiking could sometimes be found alongside other forms of 'resistance' to forms of authority. This was particularly true of studies of young offenders institutions, church or special education schools, many of whose own histories are now blighted with abuse scandals (raising questions as to why so many young women tried to abscond).[3] One clinical psychology report from 1978 noted that female hitchhikers were more likely to be unconventional and non-conformist than non-hitchhiking women, which raises questions about how public space can be so easily gendered (a point we will revisit in Chapter 9).[4]

The predominant assumption behind most post-war studies of hitchhiking psychology is that it is part of a life cycle moment – a rite of passage. Mario Rinvolucri's UK-based research on hitchhiking over several weekends in 1968 was not just driven by some of these assumptions, but it affected his whole methodology, choosing not to interview anyone over thirty years old. A keen hitchhiker himself, who had first done it as a form of rebellion, he conducted some remarkable road-based research interviews, kitting out a van with table and chair for interviewees whom he and a friend went in search of on the (as then) new motorway network. The urge to hitchhike, he deduced, was largely based upon 'stretching, if not slicing, the umbilical cord' and that the practical arrival of children and the 'necessary' car diminished the desire to express one's freedom through that mode of transport.[5] Rinvolucri's interviews are engaging but we don't learn much about how these journeys might have transformed those undertaking them as people, or added to their social or political outlook.

By comparison, deciding to ask hitchhikers about how they acquire information, make decisions and relate to others in the world is a more useful approach to understanding motivation and belief. This was the thinking behind Stephen Franzoi's decision to use the Myers–Briggs Type Indicator (MBTI) when he set out in his van to find hitchhikers who stated that they intended to be on the road for at least a week. Based on Carl Jung's work on 'archetypes', the MBTI is now largely used to assess potential candidates in employment situations. The test evaluates responses based on a combination of four polarised scales or dimensions: introvert/extrovert; sensation/intuition; thinking/feeling; perception/judgement. Using this process, one can arrive at sixteen possible personality 'types', popularised through easily identified societal roles: entertainer, logician, advocate, commander, adventurer and so forth.

Over half of Franzoi's sample fell into the two categories which *most* emphasised intuition and feeling (which was higher than similar studies of college students and the general population), the archetype of these interviewees most closely matching 'mediator' and 'campaigner' roles within society.[6]

I'm not surprised by this, given the parameters of the study. Clearly, no accurate 'psychological profiling' could capture the entire history of hitchhiking in terms of personality, due to the complexity of reasons for being on the road over the decades. However, Franzoi's findings seem a useful touchstone to explore the more empathetic qualities of a select group of Alaska Highway hitchers, whose outlook and ambition appear to have implications for how we might relate to each other as people more generally.

But let's stop hitchhiking these conceptual terrains for a bit and get out onto the Highway itself.

Welcome to the club - look who's here!

After the extensive forested flood plains of the River Liard leading to Watson Lake at Mile 632, we get a remarkable sight of human connectivity: a dense 'sign forest' comprising tens of thousands of metal place names attached to wooden poles representing all of the different nationalities of travellers who have passed through this self-styled 'Gateway to the Yukon'. Now complete with a visitor centre, the practice has become so enshrined in the legend of the road (started in 1942 by a homesick soldier Carl T. Lindley) that many add their own plate as part of the ritual of 'doing the Alcan'. I like to imagine that, hidden amongst this strange microcosm of humanity, is a small pine shelter containing a few wooden chairs, a small library of travellers' tales and a prominently displayed thick paper tome with the words 'Alaska Highway hitchhiker visitors' book' scribed in large friendly letters. It will be much thumbed, a little worn and yellowed, and an unknown custodian will have divided the sheets up into columns in which to note 'name', 'words to describe yourself' and 'messages for other hitchhikers'. It has quite a membership list too, this extreme hitchers' club, full of record breakers and pioneers, eccentrics and visionaries.

Some of the names are already familiar to us and others will become so: Alexej Vorov (1992), Kinga 'Freespirit' Choszcz and Radosław 'Chopin'

Figure 6.1 André Brugiroux, believer in a world without borders and top of many 'greatest traveller ever' lists.

Siuda (1998), 'Alexander Supertramp' (1992), Benoît Grieu (1995), Matthew Jackson (1997), Alyssa Hoseman (2010), DeVon 'Rocketman' Smith (1957), Kenn Kaufman (1972 and 1973), Macdonald Stainsby (2003 and 2009). We'll catch up with some of these folks in due course, but one name immediately leaps out. On one unspecified day during November 1967 there will be a note in the visitors' book that André Brugiroux ('world traveller' – Figure 6.1) from Brunoy, near Paris, passed through, wishing everyone 'good fortune'. This, for historians of hitchhiking, would be akin to a young musician finding Elvis Presley's autograph on a guitar in a junkshop. Brugiroux is a legend amongst hitchhikers and long-distance travellers – often regarded as a

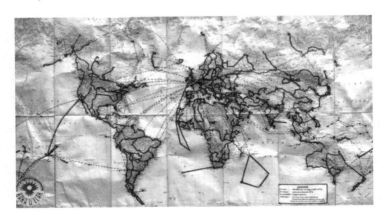

Figure 6.2 A map of a human heart. Between 1955 and 1973, André Brugiroux hitched over 250,000 miles and has now visited every country on Earth.

twentieth-century Marco Polo – and the fact that he passed through Watson Lake in winter conditions merely confirms his reputation.

Leaving home at seventeen in 1955 with the ambition to visit every country on Earth, Brugiroux amassed over 250,000 miles in 135 countries over eighteen years, with nearly 2,000 individual lifts on land, sea and air (Figure 6.2). The book of these adventures, *One people, one planet*, is a powerful evocation of the humility generated by contact with other, poorer societies and the welcome that most give, as well as something of a template for how many later accounts by world travellers pan out. Brugiroux flinches at the squalor of lives in the shantytowns of Panama, insidious anti-communist paranoia throughout the Americas and the senseless violence that he sees in Southeast Asia in countries affected by the Vietnam War. Despite suffering significant weight loss, repeated arrests, imprisonments and deportations, as well as being mistaken for Che Guevara, Brugiroux did not return home and lock the door behind him; rather, he has continued to journey and has now visited all 239 countries and territories in the world. The time away merely consolidated a view of seeing the world as home and its many peoples as fellow citizens rather than potential enemies. Accordingly, and as with many other world travellers, Brugiroux became determined to contribute to those societies less fortunate than the one that he set out from and has subsequently engaged in extensive charity work.

The temperatures on the Alaska Highway during November 1967 dropped as low as −49° Fahrenheit (−45°C). Only a handful of hitchers have voluntarily endured such temperatures and many of them more recently, in the era of Thermafleece and breathable fabrics. Clad in a modest anorak, Brugiroux proceeds up the Alcan, leapfrogging from garage to diner and staying off the open road, where the cold sears the lungs and the touch of a car door would leave layers of skin on the metal surfaces. He is reminded that a human hand was 'found' the previous year, all that was left of a fellow Frenchman who attempted the same journey, and why, so the story goes, residents of remote settlements do not lock their doors at night – for fear of being welcomed by a corpse on their porch the next day. Accordingly, Brugiroux crouches in doorways nursing cups of coffee, waiting for the three or four vehicles that pass each day. By the time he arrives in Fairbanks, one of his rides has broken down and he is feeling incredibly lucky to have arrived in one piece, but it doesn't deter him from hanging around airports trying to thumb a plane to the Arctic Circle and see the sun set in early afternoon over the Beaufort Sea and the remote Brooks Range mountains.

André's long journey prompted me to wonder whether these sensibilities signified something deeper, on an evolutionary level? Could his drive and desire for connection be a unique development of our older migratory ancestry perhaps, where we are propelled to connect with others, not to trade or conquer or spectate upon, but to exchange understanding and heal division at some more fundamental level? Rather than thinking about this in terms of individual rites of passage, maybe it is worth seeing these characteristics of our extreme hitchhikers as facilitators of a *societal rite of passage* to greater tolerance and empathy, a kind of empathic outrider of a future social evolution. We're familiar with the arguments that there are certain gifted scientific personality types whose unique knowledge, focus and abilities are one of the driving forces of civilisation (the Alan Turings of the world); what then of the huge upsurge of interest in empathy in recent decades and how this might link to our desire to travel?

Globalisation has certainly amplified our capacity to stand in another's shoes, as so many pioneering social reformers have done over the last couple of centuries. Our impact as a species on the planet and each other – through tourism and consumerism as well as war and resource exploitation – has become an inescapable challenge to us as adaptable creatures. The lens for this has been the work of primatologists and conservationists – the likes of Jane Goodall and Frans de Waal – but empathy has been at the heart of understanding our own differences, such as the leaps forward in understanding people on the autistic spectrum. Those who study social movements would point to the proliferation of principles of non-violence derived from Mahatma Gandhi and Martin Luther King, which utilise a range of different skills in problem-solving through listening, consensus and by example. Some protest events now have 'empathy tents' as spaces for personal reflection on the effects of campaigning on difficult issues.[7]

Reading Brugiroux's memoir, it is hard not to empathise with his very high ideals about the obviousness of caring for each other regardless of our superficial cultural differences; indeed, some sections of the book are a humanitarian's roll call of places with entrenched conflicts (e.g. Israel–Palestine) or bewildering instances of patriarchal brutality (female genital mutilation in Somalia). Whether these sensitivities derive from the influence of his inspirational outward-looking mother, whose early death affects him deeply, seems possible, as do his feelings of being shunned by his traditionalist father (who couldn't cope with André's extensive reading). Brugiroux wouldn't be the first wounded or emotionally troubled traveller to head out into the world wanting to promote more social understanding, but maybe it is more useful to think less about what he is running away from, and more about what he or any of our hitchhikers here are using the Alcan to head *towards*. Looking at the websites of long-distance hitchhikers, the inspirational quotes which are often used are those derived from Buddhism, the Quakers, or in André's case the Bahá'i faith, all of which emphasise human compassion, tolerance, connection and humility.

But before we explore these characteristics in others from the 'club', let's back up a little now, and think about the road itself, as a product of its time, what it symbolised and how the very first hitchhike on Highway 97 took place.

'Here be female hitchhikers': Gertrude Baskine and Lorna Whishaw

The origins of the Alaska Highway are of course as shadowed in mythology as are the various gold rushes and land grabs that were visited on the frozen parts of Canada and the USA the previous century. One name that comes to the fore is that of engineer Donald MacDonald, who in the 1920s dreamed of a hypothetical (Pan-American) link between South America and Russia, via the USA and Canada, and set out to plot a potential path through the Rocky Mountains. Imaginative and practically possible, it was financially a non-starter for the politicians, despite MacDonald enlisting the support of visionary entrepreneur Slim Williams, who used dog sleds to ride a route that maximised the use of the Rocky Mountain Trench. The plans ground to a halt.

In December 1941, the indifference shown by governments to the scheme was swept away after the Japanese bombing of the American base at Pearl Harbor, Hawaii. Suddenly, the vulnerability of the Pacific seaboard became apparent, with the double insult of an attack on the Aleutian Islands in June 1942. The 'Highway' paperwork sped through, focusing the minds of the American and Canadian governments as to the logistics of mapping and supplying a route that twisted through dense forests, vast swamps and massive mountain ranges.

Using Williams's and MacDonald's ideas as blueprints, aerial reconnaissance attempted to guide the many ground survey teams who had trekked for months through the dreaded muskeg tussocks, subsisting on parachuted-in supplies. Meanwhile, thousands of troops and temporary labourers were posted to four distinct points along the route to begin work simultaneously, with a preposterous timescale of twelve months set. Driven by patriotism and the individual rivalry of contract teams, the actual 'join up' was accomplished four months early (at Soldier's Summit north of Kluane Lake in the Yukon). It was not without its costs: there was a constant battle with the spring thaws washing temporary bridges away and, as with earlier engineering achievements such as the rail passes through the Rockies, many men died in its construction. The extensive winding character of some stretches of the road have been mythologised as a heroic attempt to deter potential Japanese bombing runs but were probably more likely the result of poor surveying.

At Dawson Creek, there is a symbolic archway, a commemorative plaque in honour of those who built (and died on) the road, and a number of flags fluttering to note the start of the route. For those tourists 'doing the Alcan', this is the first and most famous photo opportunity. There is no reference anywhere to Gertrude Baskine, its very first documented hitchhiker, whose book *Hitch-hiking the Alaska Highway*, published in 1944, both reinforced some of the mythologies about its heroic construction during wartime and also blazed a trail for independent female travellers in quite socially unforgiving circumstances.

Already a seasoned international traveller, Baskine, a Canadian journalist, musician and poet, was on a lecture tour of the prairie provinces when she boldly announced her intentions to expectant audiences that she would 'hitchhike the Alaska Highway'. Drawn by both the appeal of northern wilderness and 'the human element to be found in … pioneering circumstances', she appeared to be unconcerned that travelling the length of the route was 'impossible', as she was subsequently told at every turn.[8] Undeterred, confident and opinionated, she secured a permit into what was effectively a military zone even though she had no actual role in the construction of the road or its administration. This turned her 'hitchhiking' into a series of innovative side steps through regulations and protocol, seeking out lifts at each camp on the road, constantly expecting to be arrested or packed off back to civilisation. Baskine travelled in military supply convoys, log-carrying 'semis', jeeps and even by horse over ground in the White River area where the Highway had yet to be constructed. She's not actually thumbing as such, and somehow the book's cover montage of her standing roadside with a large army kit bag doesn't really do justice to the complexities of what she goes through in terms of the negotiations of asking for transport at each stage of the journey.

Gertrude Baskine is quite a force. Right from the opening pages she is challenging male assumptions about what women can do and she is a firm believer that if women were making big political decisions there would be no wars in the first place. As a piece of social observation and storytelling about the logistics of the operation and how some of the remarkable engineering was achieved along different sections of the route, it is a vivid and effective account, not least in discussing the sexual division of labour in the camps. However, it was rightly criticised as wartime propaganda, and certainly there is little mention of social inequality or the deaths of workers, and comments on First Nation individuals or tribes often resort to stereotype. Nevertheless, as an insight into women in a man's world, *Hitch-hiking the Alaska Highway* is where the account is strongest, not least some of her reflections on spending two storm-blasted days marooned on an island in Kluane Lake with three weathermen, whom she spontaneously decided to accompany, and their reactions to her. As the wind blows and rain lashes down and they huddle around the spluttering fire, she's thinking how 'respected and safe' she is that none of them would break convention (they're all married) and put their arm around her, until one eventually yields and she is able to make a grateful and wry observation that it was the 'least romantic of the three' who was the most daring![9]

Seemingly cut from the same cloth, and encountering similar levels of incredulity, prejudice and chivalry was writer and linguist Lorna Whishaw in the summer of 1955. Restless at the travels of her geologist husband, she packed her own rucksack, left her ten- and twelve-year-old children with the housekeeper in Kootenay (British Columbia) and repeated the route (going beyond Anchorage, to Seward). In actual hitchhiking terms, hers is the more impressive journey, and unlike Baskine, for whom the various officials along the route seemed to arrange accommodation, she has to develop a different type of road sense (when to pack in the hitching and get a room for the night; when to bed down under the stars; when to keep walking, etc). *As far as you'll take me* (Figure 6.3) is a faster-paced book, conveying the excitement of each new conversation, right from stepping out of her front door and listening to

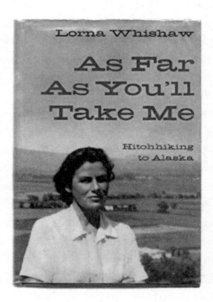

Figure 6.3 'A little insane, by the standards of my fellow housewives and friends.' Lorna Whishaw's lively account of her 1955 hitchhiking expedition is still read and reviewed today.

the first driver lecture her about what had happened to a woman whom a friend of a friend of his knew! Although there is less social observation than in Baskine, simply because Whishaw deals with fewer people, the insights into the haulage industry at the time, the long days and dangerous road conditions are brought alive by the friendships that she strikes up with two or three drivers along the route (who manage to 'rescue' her rucksack when she becomes separated from it for three days and 600 miles at one point due to a misunderstanding).

In total, she is away for three months, covers 2,670 miles by hitchhiking and a considerable number on foot, when she takes time out from her main journey to spend time in the Kluane mountain ranges with a couple of game wardens, whom she stumbles across by the roadside. As with Baskine on her island, Whishaw's account of her camping trip into the bush with two strangers is the kind of passage which would see many a present-day reader arching their eyebrows at in amazement, as incredibly trusting and 'risky' behaviour. It turns into a mutual learning session about their respective lives and observations, some of which is also brought on by moments of hardship whilst in the 'wild'. Whereas Baskine made jokes about her 'wolves with no fangs', Whishaw reserves her anxieties not for the camping trip or even heading out to climb a peak on her own, but a walk in the dark to a hot spring with one of her already familiar lorry drivers, close to the end of the journey.

At this point in road history, it was not unusual for women to hitchhike long distances, but these particular journeys are worth seeing in terms of the already existing tradition of female exploration, and the challenging of social as well as geographical boundaries. Yes, it is true that, as with our Edwardian gentlemen in Chapter 1, Baskine and Whishaw were adventurers within a particular educated class, well connected, adaptable and resourceful. Their psychological motivation to explore the natural beauty of the Arctic seems linked to their desires to stretch conventionality, with the challenging natural and social environments seemingly interlinked. It is difficult not to read both books as feminist texts, so frequently are Baskine and Whishaw judged in terms of their perceived female temperaments, family responsibilities and (in)abilities to adapt to situations largely defined by men. Outside of their comfort zones, Baskine and Whishaw's reflections upon their more difficult moments serve as fine sociological testimonies to the relative progress of feminist ideals, and also of their psychological adaptability.

One passage of *As far as you'll take me* finds Whishaw tramping a remote stretch of road heading for Fairbanks, oblivious to how long she has been out, as night and a new snowfall catch her in a moment of self-doubt, and she wonders whether she was paying a 'high price' for her curiosity; whether she 'was a little insane, by the standards of my fellow housewives and friends to have left my home and my children'. In the same breath, seemingly, she is humbled and inspired by the power of the situation:

> Although this turbulent night robbed me, briefly, of the symbols whereby I identified myself, it also improved, for all time, I hope, my perspective. I don't think I shall ever forget how slight these symbols are, how mighty is solitude, how welcome its embrace.[10]

Few accounts of an extreme hitchhiking situation are quite so eloquent, and it is clear from both books that Lorna and Gertrude are very much within the profile identified earlier in the chapter: autonomous, adaptable, tolerant, empathetic and imaginative. Nor are these lengthy ventures either rites of passage or permanent attempts to flee from society: these are the type of journeys or goals which pioneering and unconventional women might undertake as part of how they operate more generally in the world. Whishaw is in her late thirties at this point, feeling claustrophobic and unfulfilled, wanting to push herself; Baskine already has several impressive adventures to her name (including Cadiz to Constantinople by car in 1928 with a female companion). Both women are acutely aware of being caught between convention and their own progressive ideals; both include tributes to their husbands, with the subtext that 'this will make our relationship better', and Whishaw dedicates her book to her housekeeper, for looking after the children.

In her writings on female hitchhikers in 1970s Canada, feminist historian Linda Mahood refers to psychometric tests which suggested that many women who thumbed lifts during those years were confident, optimistic and defiant people, who were claiming the road for themselves, even if it was not necessarily for very long.[11] Today there are hundreds of such solo travellers, like Baskine or Whishaw, hitching and roughing it around the world at any one time, made easier by shifts in attitude and work patterns of the sort that their forebears did not always have the luxury of. One of these, fellow Canadian Alyssa Hoseman, whom we'll meet in Chapter 7, used the Alaska Highway as a 'test run' in 2010 for her solo hitch down the west coast of Africa. Even now, regardless of how we may utilise personality types to classify long-distance hitchhikers, the politics of our societies are such that many 'ordinary' travellers and members of the public would raise questions about the sanity of such people.

Dromomaniacs anonymous

How long should one hitchhike and vagabond for? What seems reasonable in this or any day and age? Do those who keep going across continents, racking up tens of thousands of kilometres every year, deserve our admiration or our pity? In an era of mass migrations and globalised employment, characterised by uncertainty and flux, can one still talk about the kind of life-cycle stages of the mid-twentieth century, where one 'settled down' in one place to pursue a career for life? People undertake travel at different times in their lives now, and middle-aged 'gap years' are as common as the 'rites of passage' journeys of earlier decades. Those bitten by the travel bug today who possess transferable trades may ply them for a few months before moving on to another country or continent. Others just travel and hope to find work on arrival, in common with innumerable migrant workers the world over.

This matters, as there has always been a temptation to pathologise adventurers, mystics and idealists – those who have pushed things too far in terms of obsessions, sometimes risking their own or others' lives in the process. As Sara Maitland argues in *A book of silence*, the list of those seeking forms of enlightenment through solo yachting or wilderness pilgrimages and then coming unstuck is extensive, just as it is becoming clear with hindsight that many great explorers and leaders were defined by psychological ailments, such as bipolar disorder. In an age where travel is ubiquitous, the things which we might be 'escaping' from or looking to re-energise ourselves in elsewhere are as diverse as those setting out. The spaces on the map may now be largely 'known', and we fill them instead with our own personal challenges, but the questions still remain as to how these journeys align with our evolutionary inheritance, and whether they are pioneering on an empathic level as well as a practical one.

There is a clinical term for those apparently addicted to the desire to keep moving: 'dromomania'. The condition was identified in the nineteenth century, when it was linked to sleepwalking and inherent restlessness (sometime with memory loss), but the term has since been applied to a variety of behaviours, including wanderlust. Sometimes unkindly referred to as 'mad traveller's disease', there is an implicit assumption that the desire for movement is somehow an unnatural state of affairs, rather than perhaps an extension of a natural process, hardwired into us. A number of travel writers have wrestled with this conundrum, notably Bruce Chatwin in *The songlines* and, more recently, Richard Grant in *Ghost riders: travels with American nomads* – a vivid survey of perpetual movers over the centuries from 'mountain men' to recreational vehicle (RV) owners, tramps, hippies and hitchhikers. A key question persists as to the relationship between our distant ancestry as nomadic hunter gatherers and the extent to which the agricultural revolution, the emergence of city states and forms of social hierarchy quelled those tendencies entirely. Clearly, something has persisted in the desire of people to become scouts, trackers, drovers, merchants, explorers, religious missionaries or even to live unchanged in a nomadic ethnic group such as the Roma community. What then of the roadside traveller, keen to meet others, to share experience and advocate wider human connectivity irrespective of cultural differences, age or gender, whose views on national boundaries and political divisions may run counter to those in the countries which they pass through?

The thousand-star hotel

Few of us – hitchhikers or not – think about ourselves in terms of global citizenship. Somehow it is too much of a conceptual stretch, even if the heart is willing to extend our empathy to others for limited periods of time. We're still living within the frameworks of modernity which were about social and economic differentiation, and narratives of national superiority – quite a burden to shake off suddenly. Universalistic embracing of peoples everywhere implies a different type of global governance and, as we saw in Chapter 4, it is so easy to engineer the opposite: to structure *ambivalence* to the other; to create less deserving categories of humanity with the tools of bureaucracy; to imply a natural separation of peoples, however absurd it seems on an evolutionary timescale.

One of the ways in which some hitchhikers counter these artificial boundaries is to rethink their ideas of what 'home' means. It is something which the photojournalist Matthew Jackson had cause to reflect upon when spending four years hitchhiking around his home country in the late 1990s. In *The Canada chronicles* he talks about the 'serendipitous, almost karmic goodwill' that he constantly benefited from in every corner of his country. Whether he is ruminating on the contradictions of the Inuit world 70° north, meeting a fishing blockade in New Brunswick or enjoying a touching romance on the prairies of Saskatchewan, Jackson describes his time on the road as shifting his view of himself as a person of the world rather than of Canada particularly. Suddenly 'home wasn't any single place anyway, but rather a state of mind, a feeling of belongingness that I could experience anywhere if I let myself appreciate the similarities I shared with others'.[12]

We see these ideals of global connectedness expressed through some of the hospitality communities such as the Quaker-affiliated Servas network, or travelling festivals like the Rainbow Gatherings, which some hitchhikers may dip in and out of, particularly in North America. Yet being on the road for more than a few months means striking a balance between embracing the revelation of one's more migratory ancestry, with some of its consequences, in a society not usually set up for perpetual wanderers. One hears of casualties of the sort represented in Agnes Vardes's gruelling 1985 film treatise on nomadism *Vagabond*, which is perhaps why others 'structure' their journeys over the course of the seasons, taking a little time to recharge.

Enter Benoît Grieu, a self-declared modern-day gypsy, one of the most prolific hitchhikers of all, who amassed over 1,500,000 kilometres through 170 countries between 1979 and 2011. A perpetual traveller who funded his ventures by medical experiments and selling his blood, he was that rare Westerner, one comfortable heading into the most inaccessible places with cultures least similar to his own. In the summer of 2009, for instance, he racked up 13,500 kilometres between Paris and Beijing, winding his way through Iran, south-east Russia, China and the Hindu Kush region of Pakistan. Unsurprisingly, there are plenty of references to him in the Vilnius Hitchhiking Club's record books, one of which is to his fleeting experience of the Alaska Highway, traversing the entire route in one lift, having being picked up in Anchorage and taken to San Diego, a distance of 6,000 kilometres, one of the three longest lifts ever.

Grieu's love of travel and other cultures meant he was described by some as akin to a chameleon, able to speak five languages fluently and with a working knowledge of several more. Happy to eschew accommodation if none materialised at the end of the day, he'd often prefer to stay in a 'thousand-star' hotel, where he could see the night sky. Shrugging off the notion that his constant travelling is a 'hitchhiking addiction' he claimed: 'I like better to live my dreams instead of dreaming my life. That's why I can't fall asleep for long hours because I know that my reality is finally better than in my dreams.'[13]

Few people can have ever been so at ease with themselves to frame their own life in quite this way – to feel free from the obligations of a fixed base, a career or attaining a certain level of consumer status. Grieu's attitude and itineraries seem consistent with both the history and philosophy of 'voluntary simplicity' and low-impact living, as well those longer migratory traditions explored by Bruce Chatwin and Richard Grant. Perhaps it was the Buddhist in him, but Benoît's attitude to possessions was uncommonly functional, giving items away as quickly as he acquired them from the roadside, in skips or charity shops, a traveller confident enough to lose himself in other cultures all year around and not be bothered that sometimes this meant carrying his road gear in a large hessian sack. The rest of us may look askance, but we are also easily entranced by those who embark on unusual challenges on the fringes of society, our imaginations (and subconscious) stirred because they present us with fundamental questions about the value and meaning of our own lives, questions which we sometimes do not want to address.

Benoît remains a massive inspiration for his achievements and his approach to living exactly as he wanted, sometimes prioritising travelling rather than writing about it. This is our loss, as sadly, in August 2011 he disappeared in the Indian town of Hapur (near New Delhi, in Uttar Pradesh), and his family and friends posted 'Missing' statements on a number of news platforms. To date, no information regarding his death has been forthcoming. It was horribly ironic, as only days before he had issued a rare caution to fellow Westerner travellers about entering Pakistan's North-West Frontier Province (in the wake of the death of Osama Bin Laden), where he had experienced active hostility from both bureaucrats and residents. That someone so adept with people should be so concerned for others in the light of this seemed not only typical of the empathy of the man himself, but perhaps as good a marker of the relative dangers of travel at certain times and places as any other source.[14]

Most people have not heard of Benoît Grieu, or any of the other 'extreme hitchhikers' in this chapter, and sometimes the first one learns about their lives is when the news media focus on the occasional disappearance. Of all of the misfortunes to befall hitchhikers, few have captured the international imagination in quite the way that Chris McCandless did. Many of the themes of this chapter, from the psychological drives which send people out on the road to the challenging critiques of society which some take with them or develop on the way, can be read through the interpretation of his life and death.

The relentless pursuit of authenticity

In April 1992 a well educated twenty-four-year-old man hitched from South Dakota to Alaska, gathered a few supplies in Fairbanks, including a low-calibre rifle, bought a book about the local flora and fauna and headed excitedly away from civilisation. In the previous two years, he had led an itinerant existence of casual work and soup kitchens in the south-west of the USA, living in alternative communities such as 'Slab City' (Niland) in California, exploring and walking in the wilderness, travelling by thumb, freight train and canoe under the assumed name of Alexander Supertramp. Many of those he'd met along the way knew more about his plans to go to Alaska and live wild than his own family, with whom he'd had almost no contact and who'd been mystified as to why he'd donated his substantial trust fund to charity.

Unlike other adventurers from our visitors' book, Alexander Supertramp (real name Chris McCandless) did not return to society some months later with a head full of inspiring tales. Instead, he starved to death in the Alaskan wilderness, provoking an acerbic debate between local backwoodsmen, newspaper editors, mountaineers and eventually Hollywood directors as to the relative foolhardiness of trying to live off the land, whether he had just been unlucky or had been doomed because of ill preparation and naivety. His story has been told many times, brilliantly by Jon Krakauer in *Into the wild* (1996), with an intelligent film written and directed by Sean Penn of the same name further cementing opinion some years later.

Media debates about McCandless's death and responses to the book and film tell us more about the society producing them than about what is believed to have happened to him.[15] People who reject the American dream are often regarded with suspicion, and any liberal urbanite encroaching on the 'place myth' of the macho Alaskan frontier as zone of economic opportunity, where 'we do things differently', even more so. Yet the internet has merely enhanced interest in Chris McCandless, and every year people are drawn to seek out the abandoned bus on the 'Stampede Trail' where he had lived, leading to accusations of 'cultish' behaviour around his death.[16]

Many interpretations of the case are possible, but all seem to be linked by narratives of violence of one form or another. The most revealing account is by his sister Carine McCandless, whose book *The wild truth* reveals the extensive background of domestic abuse and deceit that Chris and she grew up in, a factor in his eventual opting for a very different kind of existence. Her account adds the psychological dimension to Krakauer's politicised claim that McCandless was 'relentlessly pursuing a form of authenticity', in seeking genuine relationships free from the societal expectations of career aspirations and respectable consumer lifestyle. It is telling, too, that McCandless's attitude to belongings was not unlike Grieu's: highly utilitarian and critical of the way we chain ourselves to places and things (new cars seemed absurd, an offer of a plane ticket to Alaska 'cheating'). It does take a certain mentality to view consumer society as a form of psychological violence, but we forget just how relatively recent the mass marketing of desire and choice is, how subtle our slavery to peer expectations and digital forms of branding. By contrast, the 'authenticity' that Krakauer refers to are the honest face-to-face relationships which Bauman argued became squeezed out by the ambivalence of modernity (see Chapter 4).

Chris McCandless was hardly the first to seek out the wild in this way (comparisons are often made with Everett Ruess, another well educated hitchhiker and thinker, who disappeared in the Utah desert in 1934), but it is easy to forget that the most nature-centred Romantic is fundamentally a social being, propelled to seek out the unpopulated reaches of the world for a while, perhaps for aesthetic reasons, maybe as a result of an injustice or an inability to cope with some aspect of industrialised society. We shouldn't forget that the radical ecological tradition in American politics, from Henry Thoreau to Murray Bookchin, is full of these dialogues about how to achieve a just balance between the social and natural worlds. Sometimes in the pursuit of that cause, activists have become eccentric or a little unhinged – John Muir famously survived many escapades in the wildernesses – but rarely do they become hermits or wanderers for long. As Krakauer noted, McCandless referred to the 'joy of new encounters [and] an endlessly changing horizon' as his road philosophy, and reflected, as he made his attempt to return from the wild, that 'happiness is only real when shared'.[17]

Had he lived, it is very possible that Chris McCandless would have eventually penned a book of reflections on his nomadic lifestyle and maybe received plaudits about 'showing another side to America and the way we live'. What we glean from the snippets of writing which have survived is both a perennial exasperation with the psychological limits of materialism and a horror at the sense of entitlement which business and governments demonstrate in their use of the natural world. For all of the accusations of Romanticism thrown at McCandless, his sense of injustice in the world overlaps with the views of his own hero, Jack London, whose socialist ideals are also downplayed and depoliticised in the clamour to fit him into a (more heroic) 'frontier' view of the Yukon and Alaska.

Behind the endorsement of the wilderness in his fiction, London wrote books about the class struggle against fascism and capitalism (*The iron heel*, 1908) and about trying to live in balance with nature in new forms of community (*The valley of the moon*, 1913). Certainly, he, like McCandless, would have had a lot to say about one particular industrial development, which both reproduces all of the social problems of earlier eras and contributes to a much more extensive set of ecological ones in the future.

But there are other hitchhikers and Romantics who take up this particular baton.

The view from the Tar Sands

At the end of *Hitch-hiking the Alaska Highway*, Gertrude Baskine offers us visions of global highways that connect people in new ways, but with the corollary that this requires us to have a global thinking to go with it. Inspired by what she had seen on the Highway, and as the Second World War began to turn towards Allied victory, she sensed 'the possibility of a world community … to develop tolerance, understanding, and finally, sympathy', suggesting that the highways of the future must bring not only trade and communication but 'expression of thought, of culture, of reciprocal sentiment and good will'. No longer will we be able to ignore others' plight: 'the eyes of the starving will be too close to us', she says.[18]

Baskine's optimism as to what the human spirit can potentially turn its collective attention to is stirring in any era. For all of the hope and empathy she expresses, it is an example of what we now call 'technological determinism': where material advances and 'progress' are assumed in and of themselves to automatically alter our consciousness about particular social matters. Often the mantra of its wealthiest promoters, it is invariably a view of technology as liberator – more roads lead to greater freedom, more internet access generates better communication – with any (known or assumed) negative consequences glossed over or left back at the office.

In the seventy years since the Alaska Highway was built, attitudes towards cutting huge swathes of highway through wilderness areas have altered significantly. Environmental concerns and indigenous people's rights now ensure that no project in Canada receives an automatic go-ahead, except, it seems, where oil is concerned. The discovery of bitumen under the boreal forests of the Peace River basin in northern Alberta in the early years of this century has turned a Florida-sized portion of the Canadian wilderness into a toxic lifeless desert with global consequences. The so-called Tar Sands development, centred on the new boom town of Fort McMurray, involves the extraction, refinement and piping of enough oil to satisfy a lot of North America's perceived future fuel needs and energy independence. It has not been the first controversial development in the region – the oil terminal at Prudhoe Bay on the Arctic coastline drew plenty of criticism in the late 1970s – but the timing of Tar Sands epitomises competing visions of humanity's future itself. Since the site underwent a major expansion in 2008, its global stock has multiplied, as has the belief that further fossil-fuel projects in the Arctic are possible, something regarded by most environmentalists as ecocide.

One person in the latter camp is the self-declared 'writer, hitchhiker and revolutionary', Canadian campaigner Macdonald Stainsby, who, since his teens, has seen the importance of linking how we get around with the way we treat the ecosystem. It'd be fair to say that his politics lean towards the anarchist and social ecological end of the spectrum and hitchhiking is, for him, an important ingredient in the vision of a more cooperative, egalitarian and non-violent society. He has an intense look about him, a 1,000-yard political stare, but there are a couple of YouTube clips which deconstruct all of this – demonstrating a comical 'hitching technique' which (when desperate) involves a curious hopping backward and bowing movement to present a sense of humility.

Figure 6.4 Connecting the issues with empathy: hitchhiker, writer and campaigner against the Tar Sands, Macdonald Stainsby on the Alaska Highway near the Liard River in 2009.

In the early years of the century, Macdonald was a prolific and enthusiastic contributor to the newly established Digihitch.com website, filing detailed reports on the quality of the hitchhiking on many of the roads of British Columbia, Alberta and the Yukon Territory. He's done the Alaska Highway several times (Figure 6.4) and is a huge fan of the wild places through which its 'spur', the Dempster Highway, passes through en route to Inuvik and the Arctic coastline.

The first time he saw Tar Sands, it chilled him to the core – that people could do so much damage to the landscape. He'd seen plenty of ugly 'clear cutting' of forests in the past, but this was on a different scale – tens of metres deep as far as the eye could see:

> This was feeling the stench of death reach into every pore of the visible world, completely taking over the air, the water, everything. The first true moonscape views, right near the Syncrude refinery itself, were absolutely jaw-dropping. The whole thing feels utterly military. Everywhere we went, it was clear you could feel the triumph of nothing where somewhere there had been something before.[19]

But this wasn't 'just' an ecological disaster. It was a social one too. Anyone who spends road time in British Columbia and Alberta quickly becomes aware of the difficult political relationship that indigenous First Nation cultures have with the wider governmental forces in terms of their economic and social well-being. This enrages Macdonald Stainsby, who, since starting campaigning on the issue in 2008, has made it his business to document each injustice as it emerges, whether it is doctors mysteriously being fired for speaking out about the disproportionate clusters of unusual illnesses, or those objectors imprisoned for putting their bodies in the way of the machinery, or attacked by 'disaffected' sections of the contracted white workers on the projects. He's also mapped out the 'money trail' – along with an indigenous activist, Dru Oja Jay – which links the oil industries with charitable trusts which buy off more moderate environmental opposition or cleverly 'front' top-down public relations exercises to advocate more 'managed' approaches of 'saving' some land without challenging the basic premises of oil extraction.[20]

Macdonald Stainsby's concerns chime with the wider sense of empathy expressed by activists involved in climate-change politics. Historically, many indigenous communities around the world were politically isolated, bought off or brutalised out of view when a mining, logging or dam-building project was being proposed. Today their plight is seen as symbolic of a wider civilisational malaise, with the Tar Sands extraction having united ecological protestors, Black Lives Matter activists, financial divestment campaigns, Hollywood celebrities and ex-army 'protectors' at Standing Rock in North Dakota where the pipelines from Alberta are to cross Lakota tribal lands.[21] Never has the Hopi concept of *koyaanisqatsi* ('life out of balance') felt more palpable.

Another way of putting this would be to reprise our discussion of freedom from the previous chapter in the light of Tar Sands. So, if we think about the democratic ideal of the 'freedom to' enjoy particular rights or liberties and remain 'free from' harm, it is immediately evident that individual States frequently fail to protect their citizens from the short- and long-term consequences of many industrial developments. This is the contradiction at the heart of attempts to 'green' the capitalist system – the incommensurability of ideas of social justice and ecological responsibility as realised through the liberal theory of rights within Western democracies. If we recall the model of social ecology advanced by Murray Bookchin, from our 'Hippie Trail' discussion, this is the suggestion that notions of 'freedom' need to be *for* a set of values that reflect the experience of those most directly connected to the perceived problem (i.e. not interpreted for them by politicians or corporate interests). For Bookchin, the domination of nature is rooted in and inextricable from the domination of humans by other humans; any environmentally sustainable society is necessarily an equal one, without the hierarchies that perpetuate the problem.

Macdonald Stainsby and those campaigning against Tar Sands know this. I've no idea whether he or any of his hitchhiking associates are typical 'mediator' or 'campaigner' 'personality types' (according to Franzoi's research) but their willingness to act in ways which are beyond what is socially comfortable for most of us – perhaps the best criterion for judging the personality of our extreme hitchhikers – is a worthy source of speculation and hope for the future. It is comforting to know that sometimes this can emerge from the most unlikely of circumstances.

In recovery from Western civilisation

There is a beautiful moment in Kenn Kaufman's cult ornithology book *Kingbird highway* where the now internationally respected author, then aged only nineteen, completely flummoxes the outlook of a young woman who gives him a lift. It is 1973 and Kaufman is chasing around the North American continent on what birdwatchers call a 'Big Year', where one aims to see as many species as possible during the course of the four seasons. Unlike some of his record-pursuing peers who use cars, or even hop onto a plane at the merest rumour of a sighting, Kaufman is hitchhiking, which by his own admission he is neither very technically assertive about nor socially comfortable with. Of all the people we've met on Highway 97, on one level he seems the least inspirational: he is flat broke, with long lank hair that often bears the signs of the dust or leaves which have provided the previous night's accommodation. He is also embarrassed to declare that he is a birdwatcher, which must have taken quite a toll given the number of conversations he has on any given road day.[22]

Doing a 'Big Year' involves considerable planning and resources. The process is very tactical, depending on all kinds of local knowledge and anticipation of bird migrations throughout the continent. Getting to Alaska's rich avian crossroads, for instance, is key to having a chance at the world record, but hitchhiking the 'thousand miles of gravel', as Kaufman calls it, has to be done at a time when enough species will be there to greet you, and the weather is bearable enough to spend long periods out in the open. In March 1973 he's biding his time ticking off easier targets, whilst waiting to head north on the Alcan. Then he hears rumours of a rare flock of Mexican crows that have snuck over the border into Texas, so he hitches southwards towards the border town of Brownsville where the birds may have been sighted. Still some miles short of his destination, a woman in a yellow Mustang screeches across three lanes of traffic to give him a lift.

Diana is in her twenties, heading into town to pick up a friend and go shopping for quality fabrics and clothes patterns. She quickly finds Kaufman's vague answers to her polite questions somewhat irritating.

'Look, if you don't want to tell me why you're going [to Brownsville] you don't have to.'

'Actually I am going to the city dump at Brownsville to look at some crows.'

Her expression right then was priceless: 'Wow, far out … but look, you didn't hitchhike all the way from Arizona to look at these crows did you?'

'Not exactly, I left Arizona in the middle of January, and I went over to Florida and up to Maine, and back down to North Carolina, and then over to Kansas, and I've been down here in Texas for about a week now.'

'I'm almost scared to ask,' she said, 'but did you do all that hitching around just so you could look at birds?'

'What other reason is there to travel?'

'Wow. You're out of you're mind.' The way she said it, it didn't sound like an insult. 'But that it is weird enough to be cool. I mean it is really different. None of my friends are interested in anything.... I've got to find out if you're kidding or I'll always wonder.'[23]

An hour later they are standing amidst mountains of garbage, with innumerable birds of all shapes and sizes (and some rats) hopping around. They share binoculars to try to differentiate the sound and markings of the Mexican crow from the Chihuahuan ravens, which they eventually do by the formers' smaller body and 'macho' croak, as Diana puts it. Then they notice that several of the workers have downed tools and are watching their antics, so Diana grabs his hand and they lark around enjoying the moment, playing to their audience's impression of being there on a date!

Hitchhiking literature is full of these spontaneous moments of wild imagination. We may never know whether or not Diana became a great recycler, or did amazingly innovative things with cloth or simply started looking at nature in a new way, but the fact that someone as unprepossessing as Kaufman could pique her interest is heartening. Reading this passage now, five decades later, there is something rather allegorical about looking for hope amidst the ruins of our own environment – so many bird species declining, or in danger of extinction, often in spite of the work done by bird-watching conservationists such as Kaufman.

Kingbird highway is not just the story of a Big Year: it is a documentation of a young man in the middle of a rising ecological consciousness in North America who maintained that he learned to be a better birdwatcher because he had chosen the kerbside as his mode of transport. At the end of the book, we find Kaufman watching a surprisingly depleted flock of migrating myrtle warblers that have been caught up and decimated by an unexpected snow storm. He notes how inured we are from the shock of the real world, living 'enclosed in artificial structures with controlled climates, synthetic food, and purified water'.[24]

For some of our Alaskan Highway hitchers this is the Faustian bargain of the kerbside: the more one travels and is uplifted by it, so there will be the distressing moments when human societies seem to be bereft of compassion for the lands they exist within. In the years since Kaufman did his four transitions of the Alcan, ecologists, feminists and poets have begun to frame this disconnection in terms of grief and social paralysis. Macdonald Stainsby's reaction to Tar Sands, for instance, is in keeping with the eco-psychological writings of people such as Lewis Mumford, Theodore Roszak and Chellis

Glendinning, who talk about how technology and instrumental attitudes towards nature mediate our perception of the likely consequences of our actions.

The *koyaanisqatsi* factor need not be a Tar Sands project: it can be as everyday as travelling up Highway 97 in one of many hundreds of RVs that make the same journey which our hitchhikers have done on an annual basis. Of course, it's a road trip to die for: an almost empty thoroughfare, with the occasional pit stop for petrol or a bite to eat, music and microwaves and DVS players on board; everyone is pursuing their own dream of being free in the 'wilderness', the myth of which is reinforced at every diner and gas station. Such journeys play to an individualist consumer mindset, where one can experience nature without engaging properly with it or the social history of those who live there. For writers like Glendinning, this is where the technology is in control, so if one were to break down in a blizzard in the Yukon, the uncomfortable reality may be that all of the gadgets in the world will not help if one is dependent on Google rather than the ability to light a fire or know what to do to preserve body heat out of doors.

The Alaska Highway was built in a crisis and designed to bring people together for a common purpose (to prevent a military attack). Today one can travel it and see evidence of some of the ravages which the motor age has bestowed on the region through global heating – more forest fires, swollen rivers endangering bridges – and we can only hope that the global mindset which Gertrude Baskine envisaged can be adopted now, on the brink of the point of no return. Healing ourselves and the planet from destructive technological systems needs the kind of inspiring voices we've been listening to en route, those able to get out with their thumbs and who are willing to share ideas and thoughts, the ones who know how to bed down by the roadside and who think of 'home' more as a state of mind than as a fixed destination.

Back in the apocryphal small pine shelter at Watson Lake, amidst the sign forest, someone's been busy with the visitors' book. They've added another section, for 'friends' and 'supporters' of Alaska Highway hitchhikers. Perhaps it's Macdonald Stainsby just popping by and feeling more optimistic about our ecological future; maybe it is a Kenn-Kaufman-inspired new breed of ornithologist, more interested in observing bird habitats at a slower pace for the collective good rather than individual name-ticking glory; it's more likely, though, that it's a would-be vagabond who's looking for a bit more adventure than they are getting from their current road trip and they've just chanced on the shelter and let their imagination run a little.

We can't all travel for years at a time like André did, nor do we have the nerve of Gertrude or Lorna; nor do we feel able to challenge so many aspects of Western civilisation or social conformity in the way that Chris or Benoît did. Each of them offers a little bit of the hope we need to empower ourselves to make our societies more sustainable and compassionate: to be as brave as they were at reaching out and listening to others with whom they shared the road; to stretch themselves to think not of profits and possessions but of the adventure of being alive in the wild with a viable common future. This is why I like to think of the extreme hitchhikers' club as 'empathic outriders' of a society yet to be fully realised, but existing here and there, motivating us out of our complacency, detoxifying the stale ambivalences of the world, and re-enchanting our relationships with nature and one another, whichever imagined landscape it is taking place on.

There are plenty of pages left in the visitors' book, but maybe your name is already there.

Chapter 7

The power of the gift without return: hitchhiking as economic allegory

The Zambian minister for hitchhiking

Long-distance lorry drivers heading through the town of Luanshya in northern Zambia en route to Congo during 1999 could be forgiven for thinking that the brightly coloured hitchhiker was just another prostitute touting for trade, as this was a common sight in that part of Zambia. Anywhere close to national borders brought out its fair share of poor young women, making the most of the considerable waiting times for drivers whilst their paperwork was sorted.

This hitchhiker was different. Like many in rural sub-Saharan Africa, she'd asked for lifts before, simply because the lack of access to transport and the price of taxi or bus fares meant that sometimes it had to be done, and fending off sexual propositions was part of the job. But on this occasion she'd dressed as though she was expecting clients, storing her normal teacher's clothes in a large bag that also contained packets of condoms and a copy of her HIV test results. She opened the cab door of the first of many large rigs with a confident nervous energy.

Born in 1977 into a relatively affluent Zambian family, Princess Kasune (Figure 7.1) grew up in a community which was beginning to lose people to a then unnamed illness that claimed her baby sister and both of her parents whilst she was still at school (then later her brother). It fell upon Princess and her extended family to try to support the remaining brothers and sisters, but the limited property rights that women had in Zambia meant that, for her, marriage became a matter of priority. Following what she called the 'sugar daddy' tradition of young women marrying much older men, she found herself pregnant at eighteen, to a controlling man who had had four wives previously. Whilst working at Luanshya Hospital with the dying, she became appalled by the silence and stigma that attached itself to HIV and began to read about it, concerned for her two children's future well-being. Arranging

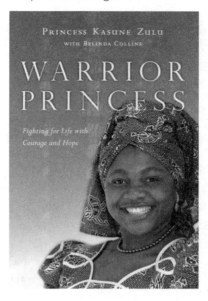

Figure 7.1 Community health from the kerbside. Princess Kasune's hitchhiking with her HIV test results and a bag of condoms in 1999 altered Zambian society and made global headlines.

to have an HIV test in Zambia required the consent of one's husband, however, and it took months of persuasion before Princess managed to secure a joint appointment at a clinic.

The first person Princess told about her HIV-positive status was the driver who picked her up hitchhiking back home from the clinic and who propositioned her anyway, whilst her husband walked to work in the other direction. The experience provided her with a motivating image 'of Africa as a woman, with cars and trucks spreading the cells of the virus through her body … and I knew this had to be part of the solution'.[1]

Zambian society had barriers enough of its own, in its post-colonial struggle for social and economic well-being. Once a global leader in the copper trade, but paralysed by the independence war in adjacent Zimbabwe, its own self-determination had been marred by the typical 'development debt spiral' of new governments borrowing from Western banks, leading to corruption, debt and subsequent public service cuts brought on by the International Monetary Fund's 'conditional' support. In a country with deeply conservative attitudes towards women, sex workers and health education, the financing of any schemes for altering the behaviour of a large itinerant male workforce was going to be particularly difficult.

'Sir, I have to tell you, I am on a mission. I have got into your truck to tell you about a disease called Aids!' Once drivers had recovered from the shock that they had picked up an HIV-positive political activist rather than a prostitute, the conversation followed a pattern: the driver exclaiming that she didn't look ill; Princess presenting her test results and explaining that it was not the virus that killed you; then a discussion about the respective needs of the lonely driver and the young women who needed protecting through the use of condoms. Attitudes varied, but for her, even if one or two drivers changed their behaviour and a handful of lives were spared, then that was worth the social discomfort that she felt juggling her roles in the community. If fortune favoured her, Princess Kasune Zulu fitted in three hitchhiking trips a day. She also began to target large companies, sometimes turning up unannounced to distribute information about HIV, then thumbing home before her husband, who knew nothing of her campaigning, returned. One afternoon, behind time and desperate that her alternative existence was about to be discovered, her panicky technique attracted the attention of a prestigious-looking car, the driver of which was a national presenter of television and radio programmes on health issues.

Intrigued by her tales of being a 'freelance Aids activist', he asked her to come on to his radio show and openly declare her HIV status. The impact of this appearance (and later that of her husband) generated a huge amount of attention, leading to her own radio programme, *Positive living*. The story of her hitchhiking became the hook which drew the international media and – as with fellow hitchhiker-activist Jacob Holdt, campaigning on poverty and racism in the USA – Princess found that she gained notoriety and influence within a very short time. Stirring liberal sensibilities in Washington, DC, and Chicago helped to secure direct funding for many more HIV treatment centres in Zambia and beyond. Like Holdt, she was a little sceptical of the political machinations, appalled that her own politicians had been at those tables before and not done more for her people, and later disappointed that the Bush administration had insisted the funded projects preach abstinence rather than providing sexual health information for all, or support for the sex workers themselves.

Princess's story, on the surface, appears to have little to do with economics, but this is a conceptual difficulty. In all of our obsessions with the arbitrary assignment of value to an object, based upon bundles of coloured pieces of paper or numerals on a computer screen, we forget that at the root of all trading is something more fundamental to human history: communication. Our current way of organising the financial world is less than 300 years old, and for all of its material successes, to some it has been one of humanity's weakest inventions, formalising our worst instincts, denying or underdeveloping our better cooperative natures and in the last forty years wantonly disregarding knowledge about the threat it poses to the planetary system which sustains us. If we are to give ourselves a chance of rethinking the global economic system in order to alleviate runaway climate breakdown, then hearing stories which shift our consciousness away from growth economics will be critical; we need to think less of the things we own or carry with us and more about the connection we have with others.

In the coming pages we'll be bottling some of our Alaska Highway empathy to look for inspiring people and human-scale initiatives which can return hope to economics, to think about longer-term human advancement, less from the algorithmic perspective of Wall Street and more from the perspective of those who might be standing waiting to gift the future with more tangible social contributions on the dustier roads of the world.

The secret history of trading

In his influential critique of the failure of centralised planning *Seeing like a state*, the anthropologist James C. Scott talks about the pivotal role which 'practical knowledge' of local geographical and cultural circumstances can play in the long-term social health of a place. He contrasts the benefits of hands-on management of agriculture and transport by those it affects most with that imposed from thousands of miles away. Reading Princess Kasune Zulu's autobiography, *Warrior princess*, one is struck by how communities can suddenly be galvanised into acting and thinking differently if an issue is communicated in a way that makes sense to those whom it affects most. Her tale of local agitation against silence and structural injustice is a powerful message of how we might transform our own communities, a narrative foil to the storytelling behind the modernist visions that Scott describes and the latest 'scramble for Africa' going on in the boardrooms of international trade and development agencies.

There is something deeply allegorical about going back to the continent on which *Homo sapiens* as a species is believed to have evolved its sense of empathy, to look afresh at how we trade with one another and why. Travelling informally through the kind of places that many have an opinion about but not necessarily an understanding of can help us by-pass conventional ways of thinking about the value of goods and see cooperation differently, especially if we have to negotiate the mode of transport ourselves. Often when we travel, somebody else does this, because at every stage a price has been arranged and there is an infrastructure around the act of travelling – ticket checks, administrators, call centres, places to stay at the end of the journey. If we are hitchhiking then another dimension to economics opens up – the 'experiential value' – where it becomes hard to explain the conversations and negotiations in terms of 'use value' or 'exchange value' (i.e. the practicality of an object and its worth on the market). Once we take on the idea that a conversation has an intrinsic value, albeit different, then questions about its worth to a society multiply rapidly. How might we 'do business' differently if we started paying attention to its potential benefits in shaping how we and our goods and services get around?

Anthropology is a useful ally here, providing us with a long lens to consider other trading systems, such as those which have employed the economics of the 'gift', where the exchanging of goods is inextricably bound up with a myriad of social obligations to culture, kinship and locality. Most of human history has involved small-scale economics carried out face to face within a relatively limited geographical area. Mass production, distribution and global consumption have altered our relationships with objects, one another and (most obviously) the ecosystem. The shattering damage caused by only a few decades of models of trading based on disposable goods and short-term profits now warrants proportionate questioning of its underlying assumptions. What, we have to ask, is economics *for*? What is it supposed to *do*?

Much of what we are taught about how economic systems help to lift people out of poverty rests on the assumption that this requires globe-spanning digital infrastructures and complex mathematical modelling: trade as advanced technological system as opposed to being rooted in the social fabric of society. It is a conceit reminiscent of the days of the 'civilising projects' of late nineteenth-century colonialism, when Western anthropologists visiting indigenous cultures in Africa, South America and Polynesia saw themselves as part of a more advanced intellectual system because it was based on science and rational notions such as that of the market, as opposed to the 'primitive' trading networks apparently founded on time-consuming rituals of exchange and superstition.

Departing from this view was French socialist Marcel Mauss, who suggested in his book *The gift: forms and functions of exchange in archaic societies* that economics is always based on complex symbolic meanings within a society, which could sometimes be unfathomable to the outsider. He noted how the Māori place a spiritual value or *hau* on artefacts which alters their meaning, so that even after goods have been handed over, the *hau* continues, leaving the recipient with a sense of responsibility and form of debt to the giver. A few years ago, a friend 'gave' me one of his guitars, believing that it would improve my song-writing. Although he was unlikely to ask for it back, my respect for the 'loan' was such that I try to maintain it to the best of my ability, keep him up to date with my progress and sing better songs at our 'open mic' nights! Such emotional investment is not that unusual: think about the huge significance which we attach to objects with deep family connections. What is missing perhaps, in the world of mass-produced capitalist goods, is a social connection with (or obligation to) those who make, market and then sell us the objects in our lives.

For anthropologist David Graeber, what Mauss's work on the gift economy offers us is a chance to rethink our economies as a 'total social phenomenon', where we make less distinction between 'interest and altruism, person and property, freedom and obligations'.[2] Another way of putting this is that everybody in a community takes responsibility for everyone else, a principle which has underpinned the *Dama* trading system of Mali, which is thousands of years old. Here, the entire population of a village donates their time to cook, clean, look after children, support visitors or mend houses as they see fit; when extra effort is needed, it is provided by volunteers, and no one goes hungry or lacks a roof over their heads.[3] The endurance of the *Dama* is proof of what is possible if the desire to ascribe special status to material acquisition for its own sake does not dominate, or if communities are so sizable that it is hard to coordinate action.

Today, the priorities of the 'experience value' of all life on Earth requires us to rethink archaic frameworks such as gross domestic product (GDP), which assumes infinite planetary resources and that one can judge the health of a society based on how much it sells to others. The relevance of the long tradition of 'voluntary simplicity movements', 'intentional communities' and visionary thinkers such as the economist E. F. Schumacher – all emphasising the beauty of small communities and low-impact lifestyles – is now apparent. 'Happiness' is, though, now part of the language of economists, a trend begun in the 1970s by Buddhist thinkers who had witnessed the appalling effects of globalisation on sustainable societies such as Bhutan and Ladakh. They proposed a new measure, the Gross National Happiness Index (which has been written into the constitution of Bhutan). This links mental health, freedom of expression and association, the rights of women and minorities and access to nature to basics such as whether one has enough to eat or a place to live.[4]

Most of us understand that consumerism for its own sake is a chimera. It's one of the reasons why we do charity work and volunteer and why we help our neighbours. It is why films such as *Amélie* and *Pay it forward* are so popular: they remind us how easy it could be to revitalise our societies and economics with a different vision. According to the French philosopher Jean Baudrillard, the 'power of the gift without return' is a revolutionary act because it changes the nature of desire, it inverts the symbolic order of ownership.[5] If so, then we have to learn (or perhaps remember) different narratives: when we join the Freecycle movement, take part in a 'Give It Away' or a 'Random Acts of Kindness' day, we are following in the old tradition of 'potlatch' – a Kwakiutl practice of gaining respect and status by redistributing things rather than accumulating them.

When hitchhiking, conversation becomes the 'gift without return', contributing to a much broader sense of 'economy' – Graeber's 'total social phenomenon' – where the *hau* of an encounter may even influence a lifetime. This is much more in keeping with the thinking of feminist interpretations of Mauss, such as that of Genevieve Vaughan in her edited collection *Women and the gift economy: a radically different worldview is possible*, who suggests that reciprocity for its own sake may not be enough; instead, we should think of our relationship with nature and those in the world we treat as other. So, to bring this back to Princess Kasune Zulu (tackling patriarchy on a number of fronts): the diffusion of her conversational gifts to individuals may be hard to calculate, but the informal manner of their delivery and effects on the fabric of Zambian society might be regarded as allegorical for how we could think about 'development' and political economy from a kerbside perspective.

A cooperative gift map of Africa

There is a long history of Western map-makers distorting the real size of Africa. It took a lot of trendy posters produced by the *New Internationalist* magazine in the 1980s for my generation to realise that the squashed continent in the centre of most of the maps we'd grown up looking at was not the same size as Europe, but actually larger than North America. Somehow, this alternative cartography – the 'Peters projection' – which attempted to rectify the balance only seemed to accentuate the fact that fifty-four countries and all of their diversities across 12 million square miles had been marginalised in the world system. Representations matter. In his classic analysis of literature and colonialism *Culture and imperialism*, Edward Said argued that the absence of any kind of voice of 'native self-determination' in the portrayal of another culture has huge consequences. Fortunately, the post-colonial era has generated its own response to these imbalances, with Africa-centred literature and film reaching wider audiences and thriving, even as news features about Africa have been disempowering, focusing on negative topics: famine, unfathomable ethnic conflict, corrupt officialdom and, more recently, Islamic terrorist enclaves and people-trafficking.[6] Coverage of these topics invariably fails to point out the long hand of colonial power and financial interests implicated in bloody resource wars over oil, diamonds or coltan, and the indifference to slave labour behind an innocent bar of chocolate.[7] Equally, poverty is never linked to the effects of cuts in public services because of pressure from the International Monetary Fund, or migration to a climate breakdown that most of its population are not responsible for. Above all, we hear almost nothing about what people might be doing for themselves, to alleviate any of these problems through their own collective action.

One starting point from our perspective is to think about Princess's image of Africa as a woman's body. Instead of seeing it criss-crossed by HIV-carrying transportation capillaries, let us try and re-visualise it in terms of a network of cooperative antibodies, electrolytes and social nutrients, which draw upon pre-existing knowledge and help to revitalise the continent's ailing systems. The inspirational *Dama* gift economy is an example of grassroots people-centred forms of trading, but in recent decades there has been a flourishing of the cooperative sector across much of the continent, often linked to the International Labour Organization (ILO), as well as pioneering initiatives such as the Green Belt Movement – where women in particular have tried to take control of their communities. These offer a different perspective on the 'problems of Africa': a more positive 'economic body image'.

The Green Belt Movement, started in Kenya in 1977 by Professor Wangari Maathai, began with the premise that communities needed to address the increasingly severe consequences of deforestation for the ecosystem and that those who worked most closely with the land, mostly women, had the know-how to prevent the water courses drying up. By preserving streams (and therefore vegetation), women had to travel less far for firewood, the ground became more fertile for crops and there was greater social and ecological stability. These early initiatives spread to other countries, working successfully at a local level, in a way that the modernisation of agriculture and village design imposed by Julius Nyerere's Tanzanian government of the 1970s has been seen to fail at, because of its 'one size fits all' model (drawn out of the Soviet ideological play book).[8] It is something only too apparent in Zambia in recent years as the government signed up for extensive Chinese-funded and distantly administered agricultural and mining schemes about which grave concerns continue to be aired.[9]

Initiatives of the type promoted by the Green Belt Movement have been internationally praised for being able to help preserve the carbon stocks locked into the continental biomass and helping to meet climate change goals – unlike indiscriminate logging and monocultural cash-crop production.[10] Studies also show that the model of producer-owned cooperatives, which have risen alongside the Green Belt Movement, yield similar results in terms of food security, by keeping money (and some of the produce) within a locality, as well as supporting democratic initiatives and (although not always) the rights of women and children. Cooperatives have had a long history on the continent and, according to an assessment of eleven countries by the ILO, employ around 7 per cent of the working population. The ILO report, *Co-operating out of poverty*,[11] also shows how micro-financing has increased social cohesion in rural parts of Rwanda through the network of People's Banks that aim to reduce tension in the wake of the 1994 genocide. The authors also note how the transport union Assetamorwa (the Association de l'Espérance des Taxi Motos au Rwanda) managed to bring motorbike hire or ride services together in helping to distribute HIV information to passengers and their communities, creating a better working culture and helping to avoid price wars and resentments about monopolies.

South Africa has seen plenty of these flashpoints, which became quite serious in 2009 in Port Elizabeth, with a row erupting between overcharging taxi firms and hitchhikers. Those normally commuting to work by taxi voted with their thumbs instead, which led to road blocks, violence and the provincial government stepping in. Given the long history of transport-related strikes connected to poverty or apartheid, including bus boycotts,[12] it was unsurprising that policy-makers in the Eastern Cape took an inclusive approach, commissioning research and demanding business plans from the taxi firms, but remaining largely supportive of the right to hitchhike in designated places.[13]

As an indicator of the necessary levels of daily cooperation on transport issues, the government report was stark: for example, 80 per cent of households in the Eastern Cape had a minimum fifteen-minute walk to a taxi rank in 2014 – which meant that there were some large niches to fill, given the lack of investment. The reality of cooperative transport in many African countries is often an innovative combination of official taxis and rickshaw motorbikes and the informal and negotiated. Semi-regulation seems more of a default position. Take the Matutu taxi system in Kenya, which provides thousands of daily commuter journeys into and out of cities such as Nairobi, and is perceived as dysfunctional and unregulated: in fact, the Matutu Vehicle Owners' Association manages to negotiate between local government, the drivers and the public when controversies around fares, competition and congestion arise. It's an ad hoc association, not exactly a union and a long way from a cooperative, but it is not untypical: something similar operates in Nigeria, where those who drive the *fula fulas* (pickup trucks and reconditioned buses) are informally regulated by the National Union of Road Transport Workers.

Such arrangements have often evolved to suit particular local needs and conditions, and are usually an expression of more general political and economic turbulence and uncertainty, onto which international organisations such as the World Bank too often try to impose 'one size fits all' transport schemes. Looking at its policy documents from 2008 to the present, it is clear that the narrative of what (in the Bank's words) 'African cities need' is a uniform model of mass-transit systems, designed to improve the economic viability of crowded but 'unproductive' cities, in turn lifting the GDP of the countries in question, and 'opening doors to the world'.[14] These schemes, usually partnerships with the African Union, European Union and the UK Department for International Development, have good intentions but leave one wondering whether they are just another corporate investment opportunity, the benefits of which will be minimal to those most affected. What always seems absent in the rush for straighter lines and faster movement is the human cost: the removal of all of those inconvenient obstacles blocking the roads, such as pedestrians, livestock or market trading, that are part of the life of a community (however cumbersome to the outside eye). This is the *modus operandi* of those who see transport solely in terms of use and exchange value, who regard 'slow' bus services that wait until they are full before departing as inefficient, who never consider vehicle-sharing in any form and who ignore the reality of thousands of ordinary people hitchhiking every day in any one country. The same World Bank also calculates deaths lost to air pollution in its annual statistics on mortality whilst apparently encouraging more car use!

Any planner or transport policy-maker worth their salt knows about the impact of Jane Jacobs's seminal critique in the early 1960s of modernist design, *The death and life of great American cities* – a book that chimes with ecological ideals about the need for urban regeneration to prioritise the social well-being of those already there. Her argument was that approaches which favour the private car and regimented street patterns strangle the life out of cultures that have evolved over time. This seems to be part of the message of a telling piece of interactive art outside Durban in South Africa (one of the cities earmarked for the World Bank template) called *Rush hour: acknowledging everyday practices*, by local architect Doung Jahangeer (Figure 7.2).

It's a hitchhiking shelter – and a large one at that! Positioned close to where many locals thumb onto the busy N3 motorway from the poor (and polluted) suburb of Cato Manor, the (permanent) installation is made out of the bodies of cars culled from Durban scrapyards. For Jahangeer, architecture should aspire to be 'without walls', so if car culture creates divisions between communities, then having a shelter for travellers outside a suburb with a brutal history during the colonial era and under apartheid is highly

Figure 7.2 Doung Jahangeer's hitchhiker shelter/art installation *Rush hour: acknowledging everyday practices*, at Cato Manor, Durban.

symbolic.[15] *Rush hour* is also a reminder of the intersection between how to think about economics and our role as travellers and the extent to which we have meaningful (i.e. 'gift economy worthy') interactions with others and the landscapes which we pass through.

Jahangeer intended *Rush hour* to be a meeting place as well as a commentary on the limitations of our car culture, so let's expand on that to think of it as fulfilling the kind of function that the Fontainbleau Obelisk (Chapter 5) did, with its revolving door of different cultural representatives, each able to contribute something to the cosmopolitanism of sharing the road. Durban already has plenty of hitchhiking spots dealing with daily commuters, but maybe this work can and does serve a slightly different purpose, apart from a shelter from the rain. Perhaps it creates a space where independent travellers can intersect with local communities, forging bonds which are outside the remit of the mainstream tourist industry. There is room enough for the odd market stall and the scrap-metal supports are ideal for posting fliers!

Any opportunity to access the gift economy of another country is even more rewarding than discovering it in one's own, as it confirms something any regular hitchhiker knows to be true: that the only currency which matters in the world is human decency. It is a lesson which hitchhikers visiting the African continent have been attentive to for over half a century, so it is worthwhile backtracking to look at some of those early 'thumb lines'. In the remainder of the chapter, we'll be shadowing a number of hitchhiking ambassadors, whose philosophy of travel has been to savour the 'experiential' value of their interactions with others, whose motivation is to connect, empathise, learn and 'pay forward' their discoveries to those who might benefit most from them. We'll begin in London in the autumn of 1949, with three adventurous young women about to embark on a 10,000-mile hitchhike from London to Nairobi, Kenya, at a time of stirring independence movements in the colonies of the imperial powers.

Respectful lines of exchange

The account of that journey, *Trio's trek*, starts, incredibly perhaps, with an advertisement in the *Times*. The adventure-minded Nancy Blessley requested 'two female companions for a bus-cum-hitchhike via France, Spain, the North African coast, Egypt, the Sudan, Uganda and the Belgian Congo to Kenya. Low costs.'[16] Joy Daneman and Mary Jaques-Aldridge (the author of the book) join her, the latter being informed by telegram, winning the last place ahead of thirty others interviewed!

They were typical of the post-war generation, for whom the possibilities of travel had expanded, although few of our great European adventurers in Chapter 5 ventured quite so far afield. It would be fair to say that the trio were, as with our Alaskan Highway duo Gertrude Baskine and Lorna Whishaw, resourceful, independent-minded women, whose hitchhiking and willingness to board 'native' transport constantly turn heads. Sometimes the uneasiness of others empowers them, and there's a sliver of excitement as Mary notes how 'as we waited about for lifts at various roadsides … the fresh wind of freedom blew exhilaratingly and I felt that the wide world lay before me … new countries, new people, new experiences. I felt that no one could have a more stimulating future to look forward to than I.'[17]

If we see past the sensationalist chapter titles (e.g. 'Don't get your throats cut'), the real drama is in their social adventurousness: the book reflects a genuine inquisitiveness about Islamic culture and the rich histories of the North African coastline, including the independence of the Berber cultures. This is all gleaned from those they meet on the road, especially during the three days they spend with Abdul and Ali, two independence activists out for a drive near Bône (now Annaba) in northern Algeria. The pair stop for the trio and express concern that they have no planned accommodation. So they all put up at the next hotel and a mini road trip ensues, crossing into Tunisia, strolling through the Arab quarters of several towns, visiting cinemas and mosques, attending a Muslim wedding, partaking of various intoxicants in cafés, all the time conversing in broken French and English. It is incredibly innocent and dignified, yet punctuated with serious debates about the role of women in their respective cultures, which on occasion segue into the need to gently rebuke romantic proposals and establish a 'pact' of *abstention totale* where matters of *l'amour* are concerned! There are mutual attractions that remain unresolved, and a growing awareness that this is an unusually intense moment in their lives, far outside of contemporary cultural expectations, and maybe what they are likely to encounter in the future. Ali and Abdul, like many other of the trio's lift-givers, request postcards to confirm their journey's eventual success (perhaps a testimony to the depth of 'value' of the exchange). A final roadside picnic takes place on the coast road between Tunis and Sfax; tears are shed and Ali sings a farewell song of his own composition, aimed mainly at Mary. All three women don rucksacks and 'set off down the road … immersed in our secret thoughts'. The tune lingers in Mary's head for days.[18]

Some reviews of *Trio's trek* by late twentieth-century hitchhikers have overemphasised aspects of its antiquated language, but, on balance, the actions of Mary, Joy and Nancy were very respectful of cultural difference and they regarded any form of apartheid with revulsion. That they chose to finish their journey with a lecture at the United Kenya Club in Nairobi – 'the only place in Kenya, with its strong racial prejudice, where Africans, Asians, and Europeans may meet on equal terms'[19] – sums up the progressive nature of their incredibly brave undertaking. Given the appalling brutality of British rule in Kenya, it is a hard tale to forget and a heartening riposte to the attitudes of the time.

If there's a common thread with Wendy Myers' *Seven league boots*, it's a preference for avoiding ex-pat communities and imperial apologists; the author opted to rough it even more than the 'Aldridge girls' did, to see what the road brings. Her 'thumb line' through Africa is just one of many on a seven-year journey across 100 countries, a feat that at the time rivalled that of fellow globe trotter André Brugiroux; her map of the world was also inscribed with a maze of meandering lines.

It is a vivid and modest account, from the moment she sets out from England in 1960 aged eighteen with parental blessings and money saved from the bank job she has just given up, to her reflections on return that the globe is her home as much as any country. This worldliness is marked out as much by her observations on the demise of the colonial era and how this affected travellers as much as it shows how one can adapt to and respect most things which another culture might present one with.

As the independent-minded white traveller moving between different social classes and ethnicities, she is constantly asked about her perspective on wider colonial transformations, which she finds exasperating and bewildering, being unused to so much hatred. The racism of apartheid Rhodesia (now Zimbabwe) and South Africa utterly flabbergasts her, as do the segregation in the USA, religious missionary attitudes to indigenous cultures in South America, and abandoned babies and infanticide in Iraq.

Arriving in Zambia, after months of hitching through half a dozen southern African countries, white colonials tell her bluntly that any overland trip across (the then) Republic of Congo would be suicide, because they have heard news of instability and rioting in some cities. Wendy takes it in her stride – as she's been party to many conversations about independence movements and anti-apartheid activism already, aired by those who have projected their own anxieties onto her. Her 1,000 miles on train, boat and by thumb pass uneventfully. For all the good hospitality, the racial politics are always there, with some of her Congolese hosts trying to gain her approval with diatribes against the local Pygmy tribes for not wanting to 'progress' like them. Arriving at the border finally, she has a more uplifting encounter:

> the immigration officer in Libenge … expressed great interest in my travels, and presented me with a letter which asked all police, soldiers and frontier guards 'in all the countries west' to do whatever they could to help me on my way. Some months later I wrote to this man, thanking him for his kindness, and was touched by his prompt reply. 'You are the first white person of intellect who has ever treated me in such a way'.[20]

Time and again, in hitchhiking autobiographies such as Wendy's there are accounts of this nature, where a quiet confidence, respect for one's environment and a peaceful demeanour appear to work social wonders.

It's tempting of course to write these mid-twentieth-century journeys off as innocent and unconnected with the practical realities today, but this would be to misunderstand the geography and politics. For all of the talk of mass-transit systems and modernisation at the level of policy-makers, the sheer size of many of these countries is such that random and beautiful encounters on dusty roadsides are not only entirely possible, but far more frequent than one might envisage. Sometimes this may be helped by the *modus operandi* of the independent traveller just confounding people – as though the bizarreness of someone emerging out of the jungle with just a backpack resets any likely suspicions to a default position of mutual aid.

These minor 'gift economy' moments count, too, in terms of the transferable value of 'experience' as an economic measure – they seep into the wider cultural hinterlands both of where they take place and of the people involved. We don't know how those moderately successful travel books impacted on the public, or how the authors' journeys affected those they met, but it is something which, in the digital age, becomes more immediately obvious. Tracing out the 'thumb lines' of responsible travellers onto a cooperative gift map of any continent provides a way into thinking about the importance of 'experience value' as a small counterblast to dominant economic narratives that can pay forward to give hope to others in the future.

Following in Kinga's footsteps

In the summer of 2009, during a lunch break while on a hospital vacation job, Alyssa Hoseman, a young Canadian student, had a small epiphany. With one year of college left, she was thinking ahead – looking for travel inspiration online. What she found was an article recounting the hitchhiking life of Kinga 'Freespirit' Choszcz, a motivational figure to those who'd followed her five-year vagabonding journey around the world (between 1999 and 2003) or who had read *Led by destiny*, the book of those travels with her partner, Radosław 'Chopin' Siuda. What piqued Alyssa's interest was the thought that 'I didn't even know that hitchhiking was a viable means of transportation in the 21st century, let alone hitchhiking the world'. There was also the small matter of Kinga's 'My Africa' blog, which detailed her (mostly) solo adventures from Morocco to Ghana in 2006, through Mauritania, Mali, Burkina Faso, Niger, Gambia, Guinea, Sierra Leone, Liberia and Ivory Coast. Transfixed by this, Alyssa began devising 'a new plan for my life' and figured that before her final exams she ought to do a 'test run' for any future travels.[21]

We met a lot of amazing people in the previous chapter, but none of them thumbed the Alaska Highway as part of their very first hitching journey. Alyssa decided to head out of Toronto and get to Dawson Creek via much of the Trans-Canada Highway first. Some adventure-orientated hitchhikers would regard *either* of these roads as lifetime ambitions – Alyssa did both on her first trip, noting by the time that she arrived at Whitehorse in the Yukon that it was 44° Fahrenheit below zero! Once the Bachelor of Science certificate has been secured, she set out for Africa in early 2010, aged twenty-two, with no return tickets or timescales, taking in half a dozen European countries en route.

Three and a half years before, any hitchhiker who used the independent travel websites would have heard the news that Kinga 'Freespirit' Choszcz, aged thirty-three, from Gdansk, Poland, had died after contracting cerebral malaria in Accra, Ghana, on 9 June 2006. Judging from the hundreds of tributes which had poured into the Digihitch.com and Virtualtourist websites, it would have been clear to Alyssa that here was a person who exuded such remarkable joy of life, self-belief and vision that it was hard not to be carried along with the idea that any problem which the road presented could be solved.[22] Photographs of Kinga communicate this assurance – standing on roads the world over, always in orange and red clothing, her calm demeanour belying the speed with which she's taking in situations with her sharp brown eyes. As a teenager she'd solo hitched, inheriting the legacy of post-war Polish travel culture from her mother, who'd done the same.

Whether one is reading *Led by destiny* or the 'My Africa' blog, Kinga's rich anecdotes of the random beauty of the road in the quieter parts of the continent shine out. Here she is, away from the relative certainties of accommodation through the likes of Couchsurfers or the Hospitality Clubs, slipping into the more random state of mind where the road 'decides'.

> I get off the truck in the middle of some dusty Gambian town. A guy grabs my backpack.
> 'Hey, where are you going with my backpack?'
> 'I'll help you carry it to the bush taxi station.'
> 'I'm not going to the station. I'll spend the night here.'
> 'You have a place to stay?'
> 'Not yet.'
> 'Come to my house.'
> He doesn't want any money. He's not hitting on me, either. He's a twenty-three-year-old road construction worker who works twelve-hour day shifts for the equivalent of one Euro a day. He doesn't understand when I ask him why he invited me. Isn't it self explanatory – I'm a stranger in his town, I have no place to stay. Isn't it the most obvious and natural thing that he should invite me?[23]

One needn't go to West Africa to experience the simplicity of offering assistance or spontaneously putting up a stranger, but it's something of a stark reminder how alienated people in richer parts of the world can be from this kind of generosity. Cross-cultural studies of the willingness to help strangers tend towards places where the pace of life is somewhat slower, economic productivity is not so high, population density is lower and where social obligations are placed above personal aspirations.[24] This is where the power of 'the gift without return' comes into its own, where we access that inner 'Amélie' in others and find mutual aid networks which are often lost to us in the bustle of a big city.

Knowing how to find these things as a traveller, when so much is set up for the mass tourist experience, can be as much of a skill as the generosity of others is a surprise to one who is not used to it. The popular American writer and broadcaster Rick Steves has tried to bridge some of these distances in his book *Travel as a political act*, in which he advocates using local, small-scale operators and networks, which benefit people directly, and not some distant McTourist corporation. Responsible tourism keeps money and decision-making within the region, and allows local people to devise their own scripts when guiding visitors around their neighbourhoods. He argues that touring officially approved sites of interest rarely benefits one's understanding of a place and is unlikely to alter popular prejudices.

The spaces which States make

Back with Alyssa Hoseman in 2010 (Figure 7.3): hers is a similar desert route to Kinga's four years before, heading south from Morocco into the less 'touristy' areas of West Africa, where lifts and accommodation seem to generate their own cooperative momentum. Impressed by the Mauritanian tradition of opening one's door upon waking, to welcome in the world (*teraanga*), she finds that such generosity to strangers extends down the road, almost as if those who help her see it as part of their responsibilities to ensure safe passage, and setting up contacts for her is part of some unwritten rule of their 'exchange'. Over the border in Senegal, a couch-surfing contact from the previous week comes good – the daughter of the great uncle of a friend of her associate (!) and she is welcomed into Rosso, whereupon she spends 'six days with Mama Falla and her family … walking in the nearby villages, learning to cook ceep-o-jenn (rice and fish), getting in a little Senegalese Bré (wrestling), and even a few afternoons of high school English and French classes'.[25] It's indicative of the ebb and flow of her fifteen-month journey, becoming part of a community for a few days or weeks, being guided by those whom she is staying with, then moving on to see what the road brings next. If there's no

Figure 7.3 'A new plan for my life'. Canadian Alyssa Hoseman in 2010, solo hitchhiking the gift economies of West Africa. The experience motivated her work supporting victims of conflict in Afghanistan.

prior contact and no driver offers accommodation, she gets out at the next obvious village, asks the tribal chief for permission to stay (which always works), or on other occasions just beds down in the bush, off the road.

Spending time in 'ordinary' homes may sound an underwhelming tourist experience, until one does it, but immersing oneself in all aspects of the family life and traditions of a very different culture is arguably more educational (and character-building) than touring the usual famous cultural sites and landmarks of the powerful on a well trodden 'Grand Tour'. Not only is this experience of 'opening a country' (as Anton Krotov calls it) incredibly enriching on an interpersonal level, but there's a growing awareness of also being party to traditions, trading networks and social structures which do not necessarily conform to official 'State spaces' as recognised in the corridors of power far away. Sometimes one just wanders over the border, unchallenged, for a social event, as Alyssa does for a couple of days from Rossa, attending a music festival in a remote village back across the river in Mauritania; other times, all roads and tracks are policed and full, up-to-date paperwork is required. Predicting one's reception can be especially tricky.

When the European powers drew their lines on the map at the Conference of Berlin in 1885, they were not factoring in the nomadic peoples found across Africa, who have been for centuries trading, driving livestock or migrating with the seasons outside the borders of recognised States. Nor were they contemplating the lie of the land or how they might manage it from distant capital cities. Human societies, as with much of the natural world, do not align themselves with straight lines; many of the boundaries inked on maps cut across ethnic as well as obvious geographical features, storing up trouble for the future.

Here the work of anthropologist James C. Scott can help us again. In *The art of not being governed*, he examines the other side of what the 'State sees', namely the 'self-defining' histories of those ethnic groups and communities who always exist on the margins of the nation State in upland parts of Southeast Asia (his main case study) but also in the case of the Berber cultures of the Maghreb in Morocco. Scott's thesis is that these long-lasting traditions have resisted the 'internal colonialism' of State governance and taxation from far away lowland capital cities, because they have successfully learned how to manage their resources, climate and local alliances to their own convenience. These small sustainable societies trade with others across the uplands, some of which may include the nomadic herding communities and traditions (such as Tuareg and Maasai). Upland societies may also not operate at the same speed as their counterparts nearer the coast, something that is not lost on those hitchhikers with experience of how 'time' can reflect political economy.

The time thieves' reprieve

The cross-African visa system is notorious and idiosyncratic – some visas one can gather ahead of a trip, but others one has to apply for when one arrives at a border. Many last a standard ninety days upon issue rather than from the date one enters the country, yet there is so little unanimity about provision that almost every independent traveller encounters a problem at some point. It's an issue which the business networks are currently taking very seriously, impacting as it does on trade and the flow of potential migrant labour. The rhetoric of there being 'one Africa' – similarly to the Schengen agreement within Europe – is subscribed to by no less an organisation than the African Development Bank, which believes that, in the long term, minimal borders will discourage migration from the poor to the rich countries, enhance equity amongst their populations and reduce conflict (which could be business-driven wishful thinking of course).[26]

We know that time can be 'slow' on parts of the African continent, in terms of pace of life, but time is also prone to specific 'controls', dependent on national policies, economic disparities, the legacy of war and so forth. For our hitchhikers arriving at a border, perhaps oblivious to some of these issues, two possible forms of 'time' seem to shape their experiences. One is what social scientists refer to as 'clock time' (see Chapter 2), historically specific to modernity and aligning itself with mainstream economics, politics and the bureaucratic mentality. This shapes, or perhaps imposes itself on, the organised travel experience, often inhibiting the adventurous, spontaneous and personally negotiated encounter. Alternatively, what I call 'hitching time' is not defined by money and control, but is more organic, negotiated, non-linear, mutualistic and empathetic; here, the needs of the moment can produce long-lasting 'gifts' of time.

Are 'hitching time' and 'clock time' irreconcilable? No. I would suggest that the view from the kerbside seems to suggest that 'clock time' can be stretched or moulded by the raw immediacy of an encounter between two strangers. Here's Alyssa again, in one of those classic visa 'chancing it' moments, having walked for miles to get to the border of Senegal and Guinea:

> I had no idea what kind of reception I would receive considering not only (thanks to the upcoming elections) that Guinea is currently rated by the government of Canada to be as dangerous as Somalia, but also because I was attempting to enter without any of the required documentation. I walked into the town, told the gendarmerie about my trip, and they'd soon stamped my passport, brought juice, fresh bread and mangos, let me have a refreshing shower and given me a personal hut for the night; they even changed my CFAs into Guinean francs at a better-than-normal exchange rate.[27]

Some weeks later, at a quiet checkpoint on the Cameroon and Gabon border, both visas having expired, the direct approach doesn't work. She loses her ride and for an hour 'the chief soldier' tells her that she will be arrested, taken back to the capital and repatriated to Canada. After listening respectfully, Alyssa provides some 'vivid descriptions of the "severe malaria" I'd had, along with a clear indication that I wouldn't be handing over any bribes [upon which] they fed me bread and candies and helped me hitch a ride onwards'.[28]

Even without knowing the politics of visas or migration in the respective countries, perhaps the simplest explanation for this is the desire to avoid paperwork and conflict, when a spot of humility and respect will suffice, no egos are bruised or national reputations tarnished. Maybe the willingness to help was born out of boredom or even war fatigue, given how much conflict has blighted many of the countries our hitchhikers here travel through; perhaps there was time just on that day to 'negotiate' the most obvious 'human' outcome. Either way, it allows us an insight into some of the rhythms of 'hitching time'.

Alyssa calls them the 'meant to be' factors: events which unfold after a glitch in the journey, or when unnecessary, frustrating waiting has ensued, such as the above border encounter:

> Passing through a town, my ride decided to stop to buy drinks at a bakery where, as if perfectly planned, the mayor of the town also stopped by. We were intro- duced by my driver, and after explaining a little of my plan to head southbound through the bush, he gave me contacts in villages all along the way, including a bar where drinks were on his tab, a village halfway where I could spend a night, and the contact of the mayor of Oveng, the last small town on the map before the border.... Upon arrival I was warmly welcomed by the entire family – it's days like that when a cold bucket-bath and a hot meal go the furthest. To top it all off, surprised that I was on foot and impressed by the fifty km [I'd walked] ... the mayor offered one final token of the greatness of Cameroon – a motorcycle and his nephew to take me the sixty or so kms along the tiny, winding, jungle-dirt track leading to the frontier. And of course, being the guest of the mayor meant no more questions about my expired passport. Just to think, none of that would have happened without that briefly annoying stopover with the military, combined with the perfect timing of the mayor's need for a croissant.[29]

Hitchhikers the world over will recognise that peculiar ebb and flow feeling of time working in different ways, of there being a balance to how events unfold, of the incredible generosity of people blotting out the memory of a long hot dusty road or a cloud of hungry insects. The generation of the 1960s and 1970s may have called it 'karma', but really it is more of a 'reward' for being respectful of others and choosing one's lifts and locations of travel shrewdly. Some of hitchhiking's positive qualities, its laws even, are more visible in the remoter corners of the world, where 'clock time' impinges less on the huge distances, and the generosity of the road more easily aligns with the idea of a 'gift economy'.

Nevertheless, there's something highly allegorical here: an all-of-life-in-a-sliver-of-time moment; for all of these random acts of kindness and examples from anthropology, we still struggle to visualise time as an empowering social resource, because so much of it which we live is owned, shaped and sold back to us by others. It is reminiscent of Michael Ende's cautionary tale *Momo*, where a sustainable Mediterranean society is seduced by the arrival of the bureaucratic 'Time Thieves', who promise its population more time saved in the 'Time Bank' if they work harder, travel faster, demand more 'things' and rely less on each other and more on outside experts.

Any sustainable egalitarian future requires us to stop 'stealing' it from our children's generation, regardless of their location. Weaning ourselves off the damaging aspects of 'clock time' in our economic practices requires more imaginative utilisation of 'the gift' – to visualise our actions as part of a 'total social phenomenon', in keeping with the theories of Marcel Mauss, David Graeber and others.

Je suis Africa

Changing the story is going to be tricky, because there is a new one already being spun by the international financiers and petrochemical industry executives. Capitalism is riding to the rescue of the collapsing ecological system, promising a more responsible approach to business as usual. All that is needed is a bit of new investment, a shifting of market priorities and there will be more jobs, growth and freedom. We the public need not worry too much, as long as we keep on buying.

Next to the rhetoric of development projects sponsored by the World Bank and designed to make cities more 'open to the world', or distant investment in large-scale agricultural projects which benefit those holding the patents rather than the spades, the economy of the gift looks impossibly insignificant. Yet it is far stronger and a lot less financially fickle because it is usually rooted in the complex social fabrics of a community, which allows it to evolve more organically, thereby encouraging accountability and participation. We just need to see such ventures as far more universal than may be occasionally presented, through mainstream broadcasting, as a cute story. All of those narratives of hope we started this discussion with – Princess Kasune Zulu hitchhiking with her HIV results and a bag of condoms, the many self-organised transport cooperatives, or those women from the Green Belt

Movement who sought to sustain their lands and livelihoods: they are just the first few pinpricks on our new cooperative map. This will trace alternative landmarks and social topographies, identify where gift economics are present or mark the societies which aspire to calculate 'quality of life' according to non-GDP criteria. Maybe it will soon look similar to the incredible thermal map of hitchhiker-friendly parts of Europe devised by Hungerian hitchhiker Ábel Sulyok which I came across recently.[30] We might also scribe onto the palimpsest a spidery web of transport arrangements – not unlike the annotated routes from the old hitchhiking guidebooks – where it is possible to see the most viable options for shared transport. Perhaps there is an Android app which does this kind of thing already.

Responsible economics and sustainable travel are mutually supporting and if sufficiently small in scale facilitate greater cultural exchange and understanding. During her journey, Alyssa encountered at least 100 locally managed educational and community health projects and initiatives with international environmental and justice goals. It is easy to be critical of charitable projects if there is any element of external financial dependency, but a more pronounced problem is doing away with destructive economic policies which are less transparent and possess no philanthropic sensibili-ties at all. This is where our vagabond sociologist on the look-out for gift economies needs to bear witness to what the corporate world and complicit governments try to hide from the general public.

An individual on the kerbsides is rarely able to do more than bear witness, as we have seen throughout the previous chapters – from Jacob Holdt's encountering indentured labour in the USA to Macdonald Stainsby on the Tar Sands industrial atrocity in Alberta – and in many African countries the chances of coming across an example of Western corporate mismanagement is always a possibility, given the respective legacies of new and old forms of colonialism. Its ugly face has been recently revealed in the instance of child slave labour in the cocoa trade, where, unbeknown to many chocolate lovers in Europe and America, the contracting out of work drops to new lows. Coming across economic inequalities like this on the road would test anyone, the idea of challenging it as a solo female traveller highly inadvisable, but not, it seems, for Kinga Freespirit.

Hitching through Ivory Coast in May 2006, she suddenly becomes aware of the unpleasant hold that this market has on the life of poor families, whose children can get press-ganged or bribed or bought from parents who may have few economic alternatives. Many come from other adjacent countries, smuggled over borders. The conditions and treatment received from the plantation owners are appalling. Horrified, Kinga tries to make enquiries to charity workers and the authorities, with little success, and whilst she is waiting in Abidjan she witnesses another layer of 'slavery', with children in domestic service in the wealthier parts of the city. Determinedly she 'buys back' a servant child, Akua (for $150), whom she has befriended, and they hitchhike across the border into Ghana, with Kinga planning to get Akua back into school.

At this point, Kinga falls ill, and it is her partner, Chopin, who delivers Akua safely back to her parents, whilst conducting his vigil at Kinga's bedside. Later, her family and friends set up the Freespirit Foundation, designed to help the education of children from poor families in Ghana, through literacy and the promotion of Ghanaian culture. Now, a decade later, there are strong cultural links and exchange programmes with art and dance centres in Gdansk, and involvement in campaigns for the rights of children. The Foundation has a centre in Mooden, the village of the family of Akua. In that time, the Fair Trade movement has made some impact on the structural issues of child labour.[31]

For 500 years, people in the northern hemisphere have benefited handsomely from food and resources extracted from the African continent, often without any contact or knowledge as to what goes on 'there'. The transparency possible in the age of globalisation allows us to stand in others' shoes, to visualise the 'labour behind the labour' as one organisation puts it, engage with the issues and seek alternatives to it. Re-imagining this process as a 'total social phenomenon' often involves tales of individual bravery and initiative, whether it is women taking control of their community's needs or an outsider shaking up the status quo. What unites these things is the sense of empathy with others – linking those 'come to my house' moments with the desire to 'open a country' to cooperation not short-term investments – to find out what we've always known, but not always felt: that there is a common humanity that can be accessed beneath whatever divisions have been imposed upon us.

After fifteen months of hitchhiking, Alyssa comes to the end of her journey and, standing on the shores of the Indian Ocean in South Africa, gives a sigh of relief:

> which wasn't so much for myself, because I still don't credit myself for making it this far; it was for Africa. For all the preconceived notions that fought to keep me from travelling here, hopefully a single woman hitchhiking across the entire continent, never staying in hotels or sticking to 'safe' places, and arriving safely, in perfect health, and without any excitingly dangerous stories to tell, will open at least a few people's eyes.[32]

Regardless of which continent one is travelling on or trading with, we need a global sense of *Dama* to underpin what we pay forward to future generations, whilst we look after the current ones. For Alyssa, and many other hitch-hikers who become involved in so-called 'development issues', this becomes something of a life calling: two years later, she leaves Canada again, lands in Europe and hitchhikes east, again on her own, to Afghanistan via Turkey and Iran. The new plan for her life now includes working for a development charity looking after orphans of war in Kabul.

If you have dealt with the realities of conflict and poverty, you are open hearted enough to know that the world is driven by goodness and possibility; that trust in one another is ever present and binding in all kinds of incredible circumstances. So it may come as a surprise to know that there is a narrative, pivotal to debates about hitchhiking, which suggests that there has been a decline in trust in the world and that we live in much more uncertain and risky societies than ever before.

Chapter 8

The myth of the great decline: hitchhiking and the *increasing* levels of trust in the world

Save our hitchhiking post!

Salt Spring Island is the largest in the Gulf Islands archipelago between Vancouver Island and the Canadian mainland and is pretty proud of its independent spirit and sense of community, to the extent that the residents were applying to the provincial government for municipality status when the 'hitchhiking post' story broke in June 2017. Almost certainly this was coincidence, but the strange preoccupation of regional transport officials with installing a few metres of metal barrier outside Embe Bakery in the small town of Ganges did not go down well with those who had been used to standing there thumbing lifts at 'Salt Spring's bus stop' for as long as anyone could remember.[1]

Hitchhiking on any of the Gulf Islands is a way of life. Pender has official 'car stop' signs. Bowen Island offers a 'casual carpooling' system based on colour-coded 'lanyards' which correspond to a specific area of the island, so that any foot passengers coming off the Vancouver ferry can wait for someone heading in the right direction.[2] There is a presumption on Galiano Island that anyone walking on the road may require a lift and with plenty of hikers visiting from the mainland, stopping and asking is just part of one's daily driving experience. The demographics on all the islands, but particularly Salt Spring, may have shifted from the hippie enclaves of artists and philanthropists who moved there in the 1970s to a more upmarket retirement profile, but there has been enough 'cultural capacity' – all of the everyday activities and beliefs that are needed to keep anything in life going – to ensure that thumbing a ride is still regarded as a legitimate form of transport.

There were over 100 protestors assembled outside Embe Bakery on 6 June to defend their long-standing 'hitchhiking point',[3] with teenagers addressing the media as well as single mums, pensioners and plenty of middle-aged artisans in bright tie-dyed and hemp clothing. Anyone who had not signed the 1,000-strong online petition to be delivered to their member of parliament were encouraged to do so. Scepticism over the official Department of Transport media line that barriers would make it a safer stopping point was rife; for most, the whole exercise was unnecessary, disproportionate and more to do with police crackdown on hitchhiking. The provincial law says you can't signal for a lift in the road, so at the hitching point everyone stands on the dusty side of it; a barrier would prevent stopping and force the hitcher to act illegally. At the rally there was talk of people being ticketed more often in the Islands and across British Columbia.

One word seemed curiously absent from all of the media conversation: trust. Usually, hitchhiking news stories can't resist speculating about why they believe that this ever-present yet elusive binding force within society has suddenly vanished. So, by implication then, trust must be doing something right on the island, along with the 'cultural capacity' which keeps hitchhiking viable! But what do we mean by 'trust'? How is it that we are so keen to declare when it is absent without always thinking about how it might be present or just differently manifested? Why might I feel more comfortable hitchhiking on Salt Spring, or one of the Hebridean islands in Scotland where I have received many a lift, but feel nervous doing it in more urban areas? How can I feel happy logging onto a couch-surfing website and then camping out in a stranger's living room a few hours later, but react with suspicion if someone knocks on my door with products or ideas to peddle?

Trust tropes

The primatologist Frans de Waal has suggested that it is the global dimension of contemporary life which poses the biggest challenge for us as a highly tribal species.[4] Ever since there have been large settlements and impersonal systems of administration, we have had to find ways of dealing with strangers in our lives and placing them in our imagination. The emergence of distinct urban ways of living in the industrial era prompted many artists and intellectuals to speculate on whether or not it may affect our compassion for one another, a sensibility now intensified by the narratives of globalisation.

So, as 'what killed hitchhiking?' began to be a popular topic for the newspaper supplements in the 1990s, often with quotations from those who had thumbed the kerbsides of the 1960s, trust and globalisation were key players in the mystery. In all of these accounts, the roadside rot seemed to have set in just *after* the hitchhikers had hung up their cardboard signs, with the reasons cited for the decline impressionistic, driven by speculations about the role of the media and a perception that the world was suddenly more violent and divided. It was a catchy tune and many institutions, including the hitchhiker's former friend the publisher Lonely Planet, hummed along to it (as we will see).

I am going to call this nostalgic and melancholic narrative 'the Fall'. It might be said to loosely correspond with the end of the OPEC crisis of 1973, when we began to see the emergence and reshaping of the world by neo-liberal economics, and the favouring of individualistic and consumer-driven attitudes towards social problems. There are other changes going on, such as the 'disembedding' of people from long-standing geographical and class-based communities in the West, which saw shifts in the labour markets to include more women and migrant workers. These patterns parallel the economic eclipsing of the West, the ongoing psychological consequences of loss of empire by European nations, and an apparent unravelling of some of the moral and social bonds which hold societies together. Headline-grabbing books which try to make sense of these shifts are Robert Putnam's *Bowling alone: the collapse and revival of American community* and Anthony Seldon's *Trust: why we lost it and how to get it back again*. Both speak of the impact which some of the new forces of consumerism, suburbanisation and media technologies have had during this period on political participation and our sense of community.

These have become familiar and fatalistic tropes in trust commentaries, sometimes linked to the belief that these structural transformations have also produced a substantial and damaging decline in 'deference to authority'. There is a tendency to focus upon the perceived negative consequences of challenges to an institution such as the Church (i.e. a decline of religious teaching) rather than its benefits (more open attitudes to marriage and sexuality); there are deterministic readings of new cultural activities (the atomising effects of television) and an under-acknowledgement of the movements which may be emerging with a progressive agenda and different ideas about trust. Decline theorists have a tendency to look into the past, with trust seen as an educational and cultural superglue that can be readily applied to any perceived societal dysfunction through a bit of 'sweetness and light', as Matthew Arnold put it long ago in *Culture and anarchy*.[5]

Trust and social cohesion are not this simple, argues sociologist Karen S. Cook in *Cooperation without trust?*, noting that moral accounts underestimate the effects of social structures and tend to fall back on assumed facts about human nature, or rely on opinion polls which are framed towards more emotive subjects.[6] Social cohesion, she argues, is more subtle in its composition, so rather than seeing a healthy society as defined by good manners, respect for authority and traditions, it is more useful to think about whether it is held together for the common good: with effective public services, accountable politicians and regulators, and a responsible business culture.[7] That trust issues invariably are ones of social justice and empowered populations is also central to the logic behind Richard Wilkinson and Kate Pickett's argument in *The spirit level* that more equal societies almost always do better.

Our hitchhiking campaigners on the Gulf Islands seem in a strong position here: able to mobilise resources on the basis of having solid associations defined by geography, community participation, good quality of life and crime rates so low that a misplaced bike may make the evening edition of the local paper, the *Driftwood News*. Yet it would be so easy to see this story of community transport as a relic from a sadly disappearing age of cultural innocence, rather than a sign of hope for what can be achieved with the right political will, if we 'upscale' from examples like this. So, before we work through some of the reasons for hitchhiking's decline in many parts of the world, it is worth considering how such an 'upscaling' has been recently achieved and why this might alter how we think about trust in the future.

Learning from Cuba

It is one of the best kept hitchhiking secrets. Only Poland has had anything like the same success at mobilising people by the roadside, for so long. Yet until the Obama administration took a more relaxed and conciliatory approach towards the island, most of the mainstream news about Cuba was in terms of political repression, poverty, propaganda and homophobia. In varying degrees this had been the case since the overthrow of the American-backed Batista regime in 1959 by revolutionary forces led by Fidel Castro and Ernesto 'Ché' Guevara. Cuba is the classic example of a Latin American country which experimented with a form of socialism whilst effectively under siege, but we hear less often about its generally positive record on education, health and literacy rates or the remarkable transformation of the country's transport and agricultural systems since 1990, when the Soviet Union oil imports dried up.

The logistics were akin to those in Britain in 1939 after the declaration of war on Germany, when speedy solutions were required to the problems of moving people and food around whilst expending the least possible amount of fuel. Urban areas of Cuba were served by innovations such as the 'camel' bus, essentially a tractor pulling passenger trailers, alongside an organised hitchhiking scheme monitored by government employees, the *amarillos*, which still operates throughout the island. Dressed in bright-yellow jackets and trousers and patrolling most major road junctions on the outskirts of towns and cities, the *amarillos* flag down vehicles and arrange lifts for those 'hitchers' who converge there (and who pay them a small fee). The low

Figure 8.1 Urban hitchhiking and carpooling points became essential to the Cuban economy after the collapse of the Soviet Union in 1990 and the drying up of its oil supplies.

percentage of private cars practically guarantees that many lifts will be on the back of trucks, along with other passengers heading in the same direction. Unlike hitchhiking anywhere else, the probability of failure is remote, and with relative high levels of respect for women in Cuban society, this form of hitchhiking is regarded as a safe option for them.[8]

So ubiquitous is the system that it also functions *within* towns and cities, with *amarillo* waiting areas, supported by local food and water traders, functioning as an alternative bus station (Figures 8.1 and 8.2). There are no forms to fill in and no insurance companies to be seen. Outside of office hours, when the *amarillos* have gone home, more usual hitchhiking takes place and

Figure 8.2 Hitchhiking without an app or ride-share board in sight: Cuban *amarillos* (to the rear) organise a queue of young passengers (foreground).

it becomes beneficial for drivers to voluntarily give lifts as they can pocket the small fees that hitchhikers would expect to give to the *amarillos* during daytime. Whether or not the government vehicles which are exempt during the day for business reasons cash in a little is not known!

Ironically, in the USA during the 1973 OPEC crisis a similar behavioural change in the public was required, albeit for only a short period. As the petrol flows slowed, prices rose and amidst television footage of huge queues at gas stations and reports of pistol-wielding motorists, 'carpooling' became the norm, as did a lot of respectable-looking folks hitching to work! One of these was Californian Richard Vane, who used the moment to lobby Congress for the establishment of a formal (Polish-style) register of hitch-hikers and 'hitch-pickers', who would benefit for each mile they assisted a traveller (through vouchers which could be cashed in). Perhaps due to the FBI anti-hitchhiking propaganda of the time, the proposal never made it through the Congressional Assembly Transport Committee,[9] and it wouldn't be the last time that a proposal to adopt an organised hitchhiking scheme would fall at the first hurdle. Yet out of that crisis moment, researchers at the University of Denver obtained some National Science Foundation funding and began interviewing participants in the highly successful Fort Collins carpool, which had 2,600 members, to test the feasibility of something which looked suspiciously like the organised hitchhiking which was now officially called 'casual carpooling'![10]

Any discussion of the manifestation of trust within societies requires us to see it as an organic process, that is defined by and responds to local sets of circumstances, as much as it might to policy decisions. Sometimes there may be 'trust centres' which run counter to the general trends of a country, perhaps due to a surge of energy and creativity from a section of a population. The Cuba example is a reminder also that the discussion about the decline in trust is a conversation within some parts of the rich world as it responds to its own transformations. It is largely irrelevant if one is a hitchhiker in transport-poor Zambia or the Eastern Cape, or in a war zone such as Palestine and Israel, where 'tremping' continues to be practised irrespective of age, background and social status because it is seen as a key part of maintaining normality. With all forms of transport vulnerable to attack, providing good deeds (*mitzvah*) which express *chessed* (loving kindness) towards fellow citizens is a vote for a more hopeful future.[11]

So, instead of seeing trust as dissipating from the world, I like to think of it in terms of displacement, as though one had pushed down on the side of a balloon and sent the cooperative air off somewhere else (which we'll go in search of later).

The empty slip roads

The evidence was irrefutable, yet impossible to put an exact date on or to name a likely location. By the time I began hitchhiking in Britain, in 1982, the decline was underway, although the picture is distorted somewhat by the still busy slip roads and kerbsides out of London, Bristol, Leeds and Glasgow, and the summer music festivals spilling many weekend hitchers on to the M5. One noticed it first at motorway service stations: there were fewer rucksacks propped against barrier railings and fewer cardboard destination signs left for the next traveller; the cheery marker-pen messages on the back of exit-ramp road signs were a little less fresh perhaps.

Student culture, so long a backbone of the hitching scene, had changed too, with fewer chancing their arms over longer distances, unless it was for an annual charity event. The University of Lancaster, where I studied in the mid-1980s, had its very own thriving local hitchhiking system between the campus and the town, three miles away. It was easy, obvious car-sharing, mostly involving fellow students picking one another up, but was often socially awkward, with little time to get conversation going. Yet even then I began to feel like a lone evangelical when I headed off down the motorways on Friday afternoons for a 'proper' journey.

How, within a single generation, such a long-lived practice could have vanished so rapidly remains a sadly under-explored topic of discussion. One sympathetic analysis by sociologists David Smith and Graeme Chesters tries to think from the point of view of a student family member, whose response to a suggestion that hitchhiking might be an option to get home from college in 2001 was: 'Dad, it doesn't work like that'.[12] For them, the 'it' here is that question of 'capacity' I referred to earlier: which factors work in tandem to whittle away the public perception that hitchhiking is a viable activity.

'Capacity' is perpetuated by many things: the values and beliefs of family and friendship networks, passed over the generations, perhaps reinforced by locality, tradition and geography (as in the Gulf Islands and Cuba). The more fragmented some of these relationships become, the less likely the idea or practice will be to continue. So, in the early decades of the motor age, everyone hitchhiked – young, old, men, women, rich and poor – and this was sustained by the necessities of economic recession, the rise of youth movements (including the Wandervögel and the Scouts), 'hobo' newspapers, songs of the road, college culture and even mainstream films such as *It happened one night* (discussed in Chapter 1). In the years after the Second World War, the memory of that obligation established a momentum, helped by the liberal and communitarian attitudes of the 1960s, all of which allowed the number of hitchhikers to rise.

A high proportion of my lifts followed this tradition or were provided by professional drivers who had experience of thumbing with their trade plates or 'tacographs'.[13] Those joining me on the slip roads may have seemed pretty diverse then, but in reality there were fewer thirty-somethings than in previous decades, rarely anyone in Her Majesty's services, no families, fewer single women and almost no one who was black or from an ethnic minority. Hitchhiking had become the practice of niche groups: political campaigners such as peace activists, the punk and squatting scenes, climbers, participants in music festival cultures (legal and illegal), other nationalities on holiday and the unemployed. The general trend was towards car ownership, and this is a very persuasive explanation for hitchhiking's numerical slide. The proportion of the UK population who had access to a vehicle leapt from 137 per 1,000 in 1960 to 515 per 1,000 in 2002.[14] Another way of putting this is the key shift between 1971 and 1981 which saw the number of households with a car leap from 50 to 60 per cent, according to census data.[15] It was a story repeated in other European countries, Australia and especially in the public-transport-unfriendly USA, where the proportion of the population with access to a vehicle had risen to 80 per cent by 2002![16]

Key factors here were the lobbying power of the automobile and oil industries on governments in favour of private transport, the mass production of smaller vehicles such as the Ford Fiesta (in the USA), the Mini and Citroen 2 CV (in Europe), but most of all the normalisation of vehicle ownership as a marker of one's place in society. By the 1980s, learning to drive and aspiring to own a car were becoming increasingly common amongst students, and those who could not team up with their peers opted for the expanding network of intercity private coach carriers such as National Express (even as publicly funded rural services declined alarmingly). There was nothing new about coach travel in the UK, however, as it had a huge boom in the 1960s, when plenty of folks were hitchhiking, and there were no mass defections then.

Rail travel has focused the attention more, in particular the introduction of the European 'Interrail' ticket system in 1972. This has sometimes been linked to the decline of hitchhiking, as it allowed young people the opportunity to travel relatively cheaply around the continent for a month, without roughing it as our post-war hostellers in Chapter 5 did. Given the lack of investment in the railways in the UK since the 1960s (and its notoriously high fares) it is not really an argument that holds much credibility, and for Simon Calder, the legendary hitchhiker and travel journalist, it can probably be better explained as a marketing opportunity than as a political conspiracy.[17]

During the twenty-first century, the key dynamic between the normalisation of car ownership and the perception that those who hitchhike are outside of acceptable society appears to be consolidating. Polls suggest that drivers are reacting to *something*, as the willingness to pick people up appears to be losing momentum, according to regular surveys by the UK Automobile Association (AA) in association with National Liftshare Day. The annual questionnaire is distributed to 15,000 recipients, and poses several scenarios about lift-giving. The results revealed how the number of those prepared to offer lifts to a hitchhiker dropped from 25 per cent to 9 per cent between 2009 and 2011.[18] The really telling statistic here concerns the eighteen to twenty-four age group, who were least likely to pick up and almost none of whom had actually hitchhiked themselves (93 per cent); meanwhile, 88 per cent of the twenty-five- to thirty-four-year-olds had never hitchhiked, whereas 48 per cent of fifty-five to sixty-four-year-olds and 52 per cent of those over sixty-five indicated that they had tried hitching at some point in their lives.

If the study confirms the 'capacity' argument, it also shows that willing-ness to pick up was strongest in the remoter parts of Scotland, Wales and Cornwall and Devon, these being the kind of landscapes which draw inter-national visitors, have scant public transport and where hitchhiking usually works. Affluent rural areas and poorer urban conurbations were the least supportive of picking up strangers.

I rarely noticed much change throughout the 1980s and the above 9 per cent estimate as late as 2011 was actually better than my own numerical rule of thumb: that one in every twenty cars might be prepared to stop! If there was a reduced philanthropy on the roads, it didn't tally with my own statistics, which remained consistent right into the late 1990s, when I stopped regularly thumbing, but perhaps it looked different to those who were starting out. Anyone picking up a *Rough guide* at the time would have noticed that, compared with other European nations, Britain was seen as a divided and 'autocratic' society, not somewhere which was enhancing the potential of 'capacity' for empathy with strangers. This, if anything, was the so-called 'Thatcher factor': a shift away from collective compassion towards individualism and consumer sovereignty.

The cultural historian Joe Moran adds an intriguing technological argument to the oft-reported claim that somehow the British prime minister had killed off hitchhiking as well as the notion of society. He proposes that the design of cars in the 1980s provided a technological cocoon which effectively endorsed the individualistic mantra of 'I'm alright Jack'. By comparison, drivers in the 1970s 'would probably have welcomed the company of hitchers to distract them from the boredom and discomfort of their dodgy suspen-sion and badly equipped cabins. Now cars have ergonomic driving seats, remote-controlled iPods and automatic temperature controls. Why would we invite a sweaty stranger into this snug haven?'[19]

It's a good argument, although prophecies of the death of interaction and community have accompanied many technological changes (the aforementioned Putnam and many others on television for instance). Clearly, many do identify more with the freedoms their vehicle gives them (women and the differently abled in particular) but most people's relationship with their cars is purely functional. It could be me, but I suspect that only a handful of gadget-happy drivers may have been lost in the technical upgrades that Moran describes. A more useful technological angle may be the growth of online ride-share schemes, which AA chairman Edmund King, an ex-hitcher himself, noted were important for those who were not confident enough to thumb a lift in the traditional manner, owing to the safety fears which have been 'drummed into us'.[20] It is strange, then, that the same survey which he was commenting upon revealed 61 per cent of motorists were willing to stop to assist someone who had broken down by the side of the road.

So, if mutual aid still appears to be at a high level and it may be possible to engineer moments of mass cooperation, then why is there what Jeremy Packer, a scholar of communication, calls a 'popular truth' that everyone knows why nobody hitches anymore?[21] Media negativity may be everyone's favourite explanation for its numerical decline, but many amongst the hitch-hiking communities and commentators themselves suggest that there are other reasons to consider, such as the role of the law and the shackles of litigation culture. So let's be more conspiratorial-minded and look at some of the occasions when people really have had it in for hitchhikers.

Just because you're paranoid....

In the aftermath of the Second World War, there were a few attempts to get hitchhikers off the road, mainly because in those countries where hitchhiking had been part of the 'war effort', to do so would send the wrong signals during a time of economic recovery and rising expectations. Opposition was quite gentle in Britain – a case of 'don't you chaps know the war is over' cartoons in national newspapers – and it was too late: the habit was already ingrained in the collective psyche and the generation with whom we travelled in Chapter 5 were already taking advantage of the new freedoms of the road and countryside.

None of this stopped Mr E. St John Catchpool, head of the England and Wales Youth Hostelling Association, from addressing an international conference in 1950 and warning how hitchhiking could lead to moral problems, lack of respect in young people and a tendency to discredit the hostelling movement.[22] The image of Britain abroad mattered, as it sought to maintain its economic and cultural power at a time of declining empire, a predicament curiously played out in the letters page of the *Times* during the summer of 1955. The context was a renewed interest in hitchhiking sparked by a month-long rail strike.[23] Throughout August and early September, twenty (mainly positive) letters reflect a microcosm of post-war anxieties. For some, hitchhikers seemed to represent the antithesis of what was required to rebuild the national psyche. Shouting loudest was R. G. Cooper, of Churt, Surrey, who bemoaned (but could not elucidate upon) 'the change in standards of conduct from those of thirty years ago' and that – 'bumming a lift' should be presented as 'normal, and no shame attached to it … [even] enterprising' (24 August). A. J. Evans, of Billingshurst, Sussex, concurred that this was 'yet one more example of the present tendency to "get something for nothing"' (29 August). Others warned about unwashed campers, pickpockets and those foreigners who besmirched the good name of the Royal Family (Alan M. Allan, London W1, 29 August) or the need 'to refuse lifts to any (unknown) men or youths, especially on lonely stretches of road … in view of the crimes of violence reported almost daily' (F. L. M. Cockerell, Aldermaston, Berkshire, 2 September).

The *Times* editorials were often fairer than the letter-writers, and pointed to the need to repay 'war debts', to assist the economy by providing lifts for migratory workers, but respecting Britain when abroad, not making 'nuisances of themselves by expecting to be transported, housed and fêted, free, gratis and for nothing, from Cairo to the Cape' (3 September). There would be lots of criticism of hitchhikers in the late 1960s in the press, particularly around stop and search under the Dangerous Drugs Act 1967, which the independent academic Mario Rinvolucri argued felt like a law against thumbing, but his own research reveals only one mid-twentieth-century attempt to ban it in Britain. This came from a Staffordshire road safety committee in 1957, which incurred the unexpected wrath of the *Daily Mail* for trying to interfere with the freedom of the individual![24]

France was worried about its tourist beaches and fearful of wild campers and public disorder. Consequently, it began to police those arriving on the Mediterranean coasts from the late 1950s. Concern grew too amongst anti-prostitution campaigners that hitchhiking would become a gateway for the trafficking of any female travellers, particularly teenage runaways. During 1964 and 1965, the multilateral network Action Teams Against the Trade in Women and Children lobbied politicians, transport unions and the media to change the minds of any women thinking of going to France from other parts of Europe for hitchhiking holidays.[25]

None of these developments impacted on the rising hitchhiking numbers. The Dutch, renowned for their famous communal 'white bicycle' initiatives in the 1960s,[26] responded with a policy of accommodation, situating official *liftplaats* around university towns, many of which are still there, even though the government made public transport free for students in 1991. The Germans have also pursued an inclusive agenda, both before and after reunification, with hitchhiking often part of conversations about sustainable travel and a tradition of *Liftershalte* signs, including a 2015 addition in Kiel. The Dutch added one in Oldemarkt the following year.[27]

North Korea is currently the only country with an outright ban on hitchhiking. Most nations which have expressways forbid people flagging down vehicles on the roads themselves, so one is expected to try from 'on-ramps' leading up to the main thoroughfare. The current US laws date back to the anti-vagrancy campaigns of the 1930s, devised to prevent itinerant workers, tramps and hobos 'loitering on sidewalks', lighting fires by the roadside or trying to 'solicit lifts'. However, from the 1950s and 1960s the growth of the Interstates and turnpikes required some clarification as to who or what ought to be allowed onto them: no pedestrians, horses, bikes and so forth. The Uniform Vehicle Codes, which are common to all state highway legislation, mostly include a variation of the phrase 'no person shall stand in the highway for the purpose of soliciting a ride from the operator of any private vehicle'. In reality, this is open to interpretation by individual police officers or prosecutors, which may explain why some states include the sidewalk in their definitions (thus making Nevada, Idaho, Utah and New Jersey the only states to make hitchhiking fully illegal).

The cultural agenda in the USA was pretty tough too. The post-war economic boom was much earlier than in Europe and was built around the car, suburban living and new consumer identities. Although hitchhiking was tolerated and still extensively practised, it gradually became a symbol of austerity and out of sync with the mood of the times. According to Packer, representations of hitchhiking began to switch from a discourse of civic duty to helps others, to it being a dangerous option for the motorist. Publications such as *Reader's Digest* begin featuring stories of hitchhiker murders from 1950,[28] with one involving a 'mysterious' hitcher who assaults newlyweds on their honeymoon and ties them up, before they are rescued by a passing policeman.[29] This 'stranger in the car' urban myth bore some similarity to Ida Lupino's 1953 film *The hitch-hiker*, and there were plenty of other movies of the time reinforcing the idea that the road had become an 'amoral space': *The devil thumbs a ride*, *Detour* and *The postman always rings twice* (where the male protagonist Frank is a vagabond loser). For film noir analyst Mark Osteen, you can see 'the fears of post-War Americans, their terror of invasion and loss of freedom' in these hitchhiker and *femme fatale* narratives.[30]

By the time Hoover made his personal address to the 'American Motorist' on the 1973 'Death in disguise?' poster, there'd been plenty to terrify the respectable family out for a drive. Presented with an innocent looking hitch-hiker, drivers were urged not to 'pick up trouble': 'is he a happy vacationer or an escaping criminal – a pleasant companion or a sex maniac – a friendly traveller or a vicious murderer?'[31] J. Edgar Hoover might have added 'or a communist', as this was one of the anti-hitchhiking tropes which he had used to stir up resentment against civil rights activists travelling to the southern states to encourage black voter registration and oppose segregation on the buses a decade before (see Chapter 3). Packer's assessment of the period suggests that the hassling of hitchhikers has been under-theorised, not least given the serious attempts in 1970 by a number of municipalities to ban all hitchhiking in California. The pretext was the danger to young hitchhikers (often treated as runaways if under sixteen) from drug-pushing drivers. The application of local laws was deemed unconstitutional after campaigns by hitchhikers, but there were still mass arrests on roads such as Telegraph Avenue in San Francisco and raids on houses in political neighbourhoods to intimidate those doing it.[32]

Hoover's relentless work may have created a negative image of hitch-hiking in the USA and maybe stayed in the mind of those enforcing the law over the decades, but there was one good piece of legal news: a reversal of fortunes in Wyoming in 2013. Thanks to Senator Leland Christensen, there has been a relaxing of that state's inflexible interpretations of what constitutes 'soliciting a lift', to allow standing on the sidewalk to signal as a legal option. Such a small gesture may have now elevated a notorious 'bummer' state in 1970s hitchhiking vernacular (usually those in the mid-west) into a more middle-of-the-pack experience.

Don't let a werewolf into your cab

The law may be a little fuzzy in places when it comes to the legality of hitchhiking, but so is the imagination of some of the professional drivers on the road as to why there are fewer people doing it. Try logging onto one of the many truckers' forums and perusing the posts, many of which deal with the changing camaraderie of the road, the politics of shorter contracts but longer working hours, and greater competition from international hauliers. Yet, amongst all of the bawdy bravado and emojis, there is usually a contri-bution about giving lifts that runs along the following lines: 'I used to pick up hitchhikers back in the day. Now it's too risky. I am probably not insured, and anyway, this happened to a friend of a friend of mine...' (cue gruesome story, probably including a reference to *The Texas chainsaw massacre*). Driver insurance and urban myths may be strange bedfellows, but trust me on this one! Here is a story which I heard in three different cabs during 1994. If it had appeared in Jan Harold Brunvand's book of cautionary tales *The vanishing hitchhiker*, it might have been called the 'Female con artist':

> A female hitchhiker gets into a cab with a long-distance lorry driver at a motorway service station. It is daylight, an ordinary weekday. Not far into the journey she asks him for money, and when he refuses threatens to scream rape. Frightened and angry the trucker turns off the motorway, heads straight for the nearest town, pulls up outside the police station and honks his horn until somebody comes out. The woman is charged and it is discovered that her clothing had weak seams and could be dramatically ripped to appear as though she was a victim of assault. She asks for dozens of similar offences to be taken into consideration.

Over the centuries, urban myths or cautionary tales have projected many a social anxiety onto an archetypal 'stranger' figure. The female con artist may not represent a plague-carrier or wild pedlar of ideas, but there will be an older template where another traveller has their assumptions of trust tested on a different mode of transport. Here we see a male space under threat when an act of compassion is turned into a threat. Gone is the female hitchhiker as an object of desire; now we have the assertive manipulative woman able to play a legal system that has become an unwitting instrument of feminism. So, regardless of the unlikelihood of prosecution in this scenario, it becomes a story which can be told to assuage any potential guilt about not picking up a hitchhiker and to further erode the cultural capacity needed to maintain sharing the road with one another.

If these myths of the road are about masculinity in crisis, then hitchhikers have accumulated a few urban myths themselves. Circulating in the 1980s, but almost certainly not originating there, were: the 'penitent thief' who has to be beaten with a cane by the hitcher to compensate for stealing from his boss; the driver with a sock fetish who requests a single item from each hitcher and has a glove compartment in his car full of them; or the male driver who nips home to 'check on something' only to re-emerge in women's clothing in the wink of an eye.

The wider point here is that although the roads of the global era are becoming places of greater social and, by extension, sexual diversity, the specific stories tell us that male work identity has been eroded so much by the deregulatory forces and lack of social solidarity that only a man's sexual confidence and pride are left. These allegories become conversational resources in the strangeness of a hitchhiking encounter, serving to reassure both parties of their normalcy, to forge a trust bond against the 'mad world out there'.

Insurance is just an excuse here. As an explanation for the decline of hitchhiking and trust it doesn't work on its own. People have been using this argument since the Great Depression, when the 'No Riders' stickers that Tom Joad sees on a prospective lift at the beginning of *The grapes of wrath* were very prevalent. For all of the shrugged service station responses of 'Can't carry anyone, mate', drivers always have their own criteria about whom they might pick up if the loneliness or boredom becomes too much, and most companies have to be pragmatic, as insuring only the driver creates problems if there are fellow workers or the driver's family who need picking up.

Litigation culture on the road has not been universally binding and there are as many national variations as there are interpretations of them: Spain for instance decided in 2011 on a blanket ban on lorry drivers picking up hitchhikers; in Germany the insurance is for the vehicle and all its occupants, with the caveat that if the passenger injures someone (opening a door, say) then that is their responsibility.

Even if we rule out insurance as having much of a role in the decline in hitchhiking, it plays a crucial framing role in how we think about travelling, and the extent to which trust relations have come to be connected with form-filling to improve our experience and keep us safer.

Are you insured for nostalgia?

We are all in love with the past: as individuals we reinterpret our own histories to face current uncertainties; as societies we reinforce our own national-ist, ethnic, religious or political identities by selective story-telling and the creation of mythic golden ages. The process is so ubiquitous, such a default reflex, that it appears akin to an evolutionary function, one which unfortu-nately brings with it a distinct lack of critical thinking about the realities of our societies as they change.

In his classic work on nostalgia *Yearning for yesterday*, sociologist Fred Davis suggests that there are three forms of the condition: the most common is 'anecdotal nostalgia', existing through personal emotional reminiscence; the second is a more 'critical' version where one thinks from the point of view of what has been learned; and the third is a more interpretative or psycho-analytic perspective, which tells us what is 'missing' in the present to us as individuals, and by extension society as a whole.

We've already seen from the letters pages of the *Times* that anecdotal nostalgia can be an easy default position for many retired hitchhikers. Those who had the time to write memoirs like Ian Rodger or Sharon Stine (see Chapter 5) were more critical of what they had seen in terms of the politics of race, gender and poverty, even if their generation was a little prone to regarding the time before motorways and mass tourism as the 'golden age' of hitchhiking. This is easy to understand: there were fewer people hitching and sometimes it *was* aesthetically preferable not to scramble for position on motorway slip roads. However, the conundrum posed by the era of the Fall is how to explain why the reduced numbers of hitchhikers on the roads has produced such negative connotations, rather than someone thumbing being seen as a special kind of traveller (like someone on a tricycle). What, if anything, has changed? Here's where the publisher Lonely Planet becomes a key player in the decline thesis, as its story arc encapsulates this second, 'critical' type of nostalgia, but with an unsettling narrative.

Once upon a time there was an adventurous couple of the baby-boom generation called Maureen and Tony Wheeler who travelled across central Asia in a camper van and devised a guidebook to tell everyone how great it was to meet people and do so with very little money. The publication of their first book, *Across Asia on the cheap*, in 1972, tapped into the same currents of authentic adventure-seeking that we met on the 'Hippie Trail'. The aims behind what morphed into the Lonely Planet guides were to encourage responsible travel and to forge meaningful relationships with those whom one encountered. For the emerging demographic of young educated Westerners looking for a few months of independence, the shoestring approach of the guides was ideal. The phenomenal success of the series during the 1980s meant Lonely Planet was able to open up a second front in Africa, but the organisation's credentials were already being tested by accusations that the tourism its readers practised exacerbated ecological problems and reinforced the inequalities between the developed and developing worlds.[33]

At first, hitchhikers had been favoured readers but as the books became more of an international brand, and small businesses from Istanbul to Bali sought to secure the accolade of 'as seen in the Lonely Planet guide', so a more respectable tone was adopted. Litigation culture undoubtedly hastened matters, and soon disclaimers began to appear in the guidebooks along the lines that 'hitchhiking is never entirely safe and we cannot really recommend it' (this even appears in the current guide to Cuba). Unlike a scuba-diving accident, hitchhiking cannot be covered with insurance, so endorsing it as a good way to travel around a particular country opens the organisation up to liability (although no case has ever been filed, to my knowledge).

What galvanised Lonely Planet into its new position was the global media coverage of the 'Australian backpacker murders' in the early 1990s. This concentrated series of attacks – all occurring along the Hume Highway between Sydney and Melbourne during a four-year period – represented a significant blow to a crucial part of the economy. The savage nature of the murders, carried out by Ivan Milat (and a probable but unknown accomplice), and the fact that four of the seven victims had been travelling as pairs – usually regarded as a safe option – had an understandable chilling effect.[34] Widely syndicated press statements from Lonely Planet journalists echoed the UK Foreign Office advice, couched within a new narrative about road history, including the remarkable claim that: 'these are not the Kerouac days of old. The culture of hitchhiking has changed dramatically in the Nineties and we feel it is so dangerous we would rather people didn't take the risk.'[35]

Exactly who or what had facilitated this purported shift and where it occurred were never said. Delivered under pressure (and much repeated), the comments seemed designed to evoke a 'feeling' about the world rather than comment on hitchhiking per se. What on Earth were the 'Kerouac days'? In a sense, it didn't matter: the point was to restate the role and responsibilities of Lonely Planet as mainstream travel operator. In the distancing from its alternative history was the Newspeak of the consumer: services, contracts, liability, reliable operators and safe locations.

With Australia as a popular site for 'gap year' travellers, and somewhere always in the global media, the image of the country seemed to suffer in line with the narrative of the Fall: the arson attack on a backpacker's hostel in Childers, Queensland, in 2000, which killed fifteen young people; the 2001 murder of Britain Peter Falconio and the abduction of his girlfriend Joanne Lees on a remote stretch of the Stuart Highway. None of this was helped by the financial success of the film *Wolf creek* (2005), which posited a brutal rural macho culture behind an easy-going international tourist image.

Each time an attack on a Western traveller was reported, there would be statements from police, community groups, women's organisations and news columnists about travel safety and hitchhiking, wherever it took place. All references to thumbing a lift in the UK were expunged from the 1993 'Highway Code' drivers' manual, and the respected UK women's safety campaign the Suzy Lamplugh Trust trotted out the new mantra of danger: 'What was once a safe and fun way of travelling is now, sadly, a kind of Russian Roulette. There is simply no way of knowing whether you are getting into a car with a friendly local or a psychopath.'[36]

No one had any evidence: it was all anecdote and rhetoric, as though everyone were living in one of the 'hitchhiker from hell' films rather than a relatively safe, rich country. It was precisely the disempowering terrorising by the tabloids which sociologist Frank Furedi has written extensively about in *The culture of fear* (1997) and *Therapy culture* (2003). For him and many others across the political spectrum, the litigation culture, which has paralleled and fed off the decline thesis more generally, has endangered our judgement on all kinds of issues, affecting whether we trust ourselves to experience the world without a signed-in-triplicate paper trail or an electronic comfort blanket. Our lives have become so mediated by others that those speaking on behalf of the global tourist sector or from Foreign Office press offices have to be uniform and clear. The idea of consulting with real hitchhikers to talk about trust and their (possibly differing) views of the relative dangers of the road would not be even on the agenda.

Interviewing one highly educated political hitchhiker, Harriet Wordsworth (from Bristol, England), who'd hitched Europe and West Africa as a young teacher in the late 1960s, it was apparent to me just how seductive the easy answers are. Even after years of solo hitching in the 1970s, including with her kids, she slipped into taking lift-share schemes in the 1980s and now believes that she would hate any of her family to stick their thumbs out (or they for her to try again at the age of sixty-three). Ruefully she admitted the pressures of conformity and the narrative of a more dangerous society, even though she could see no obvious decline in trust: 'I guess I have believed the media'.[37]

Trusting in grassroots energy

The Fall serves a purpose: it creates anxiety, provides marketing opportunities and cleverly obscures a counter-intuitive version of events: that the same period has seen an *increase in trust* rather than the reverse – it just depends where one looks for it! This is how Fred Davis's more psychoanalytic third level of nostalgia (what is missing from us as individuals and our societies) can be used, as an active remembering of our skills and collective potential.

There are two ways of thinking about this. Firstly, let's not dismiss the power of communities where trust ties have been seen to fail and folks are apparently unable to reach out to help their neighbours. Since the 1970s, many countries have seen their trust-building capacities undermined by a concerted series of economic and political interventions which Naomi Klein calls 'the shock doctrine'.[38] The UK under prime minister Margaret Thatcher has been one of the most strident advocates of this, the complex effects of which are easily overlooked by more morality-focused 'loss in trust' theorists, such as Anthony Seldon. So, despite the impact of these policies on the social fabric of life, inspired by the likes of Milton Friedman, some communities in the worst hit areas – such as the pit villages of northern England in the 1984–5 miners' strike – managed to form extensive mutual aid networks, largely driven by the women, to share resources and support other public-sector workers (dockers and print workers) under attack by the same forces.[39]

These years saw plenty of other communities around the world responding positively to sudden economic and social pressures. In Campbell River on Vancouver Island in 1981, a number of residents set up an alternative economy based upon a 'bank' of local skills, in order to allow everyone to keep working in a severe recession and to maintain social ties and stability. This involved an early 'virtual currency' which allowed the value of each task (e.g. fixing a roof) to be determined by the people themselves. The Local Exchange Trading Scheme (LETS) initiative – popularised by environmentalists after the 1992 Earth Summit – fed into what later became the Transition Towns movement (see Chapter 11) to assist communities, to empower themselves in the move away from economies based on fossil fuels (and to cope with austerity after the 2008 international financial crisis).

Such latent trust energy also manifests itself in transport issues in double-quick time. Witness what happened in November 2012 in the wake of Superstorm Sandy, when many East Coast American cities were flooded and their public transit systems taken out of action. To fill the gap, carpooling spontaneously took off, just as it had in 1973 during the OPEC crisis, with the mayor of New York, Mike Bloomberg, creating something of a stir with the suggestion that people should start trusting strangers in order to get to work. Writing about these events in the *New York Times*, cultural theorist Ginger Strand argued that, in the light of this public spiritedness, America needed to revisit its sense of trust and 'relearn' hitchhiking.[40] Maybe the release of the film version of *On the road* helped move the *Zeitgeist* along, because two years later policy-makers in the Kansas town of Lawrence set up a new rolling ride-share scheme CarmaHop. This utilised an app that catered for all kinds of hitched lifts, with participating drivers being issued stickers for their windshields and the hitchhikers a fold-up waterproof sign to identify themselves if they presented themselves on the sidewalks.

These initiatives happen because we have a more informed, networked and critically engaged public. People have always been capable of such community mobilisation, of course, but during the period of the Fall there has been a deepening of trust relations in the world based upon a *second factor*: the decline in 'deference to authority'. The term is often used pejoratively to describe youthful disregard of their parents' generation's laws, but it might be more productively employed to explain the *raison d'être* behind the proliferation of non-governmental organisations in the last fifty years addressing the complex impacts of technology, consumerism, militarism and unfettered corporate power on the planet. For all of their different histories and priorities, the political effect of the rise of ecologism, feminism, anti-militarism, indigenous rights, lesbian and gay liberation and animal liberation has been to challenge the iniquities of the political economy of modernity. At the heart of many of these ongoing challenges to the institutions of modernity – the 'expert systems' that Ulrich Beck described in *Risk society* – is a need for a more accountable, participatory and non-exclusionary set of structures to cope with globally interconnected problems. Climate events such as the aforementioned Superstorm Sandy and Hurricane Katrina reveal the deep justice issues behind how the resources in our societies are organised and why trust issues are so contested.

If we take a long view of this, our adaptation as a tribal species to globalisation has been to evolve trust-based social networks across distance to match the impacts of our technologies and practice of political economy. Fighting for our species' survival against vested interests in growth economics and the fossil-fuel industry has become the ultimate 'levelling mechanism' which Christopher Boehm argued in *Hierarchy in the forest* was so important 100,000 years ago for how groups maintained the stability of their tribes when the well-being of all was threatened.

The small-scale transport initiatives that well up to deal with particular crises within the overall system are an indication, too, that the more a society prioritises bureaucracy and hierarchy, the more wasteful it will be in terms of both human and natural resources.[41] This is at least part of the reason why many of these movements emerging during the period of the Fall have employed more participatory decision-making processes – the politics of consensus goes hand in hand with the politics of trust.

In a sense, there are always 'hitchhiking-type people' and the arguments about trust in an era of globalisation and neo-liberal policies is more indicative of the disappearance of some of the certainties which defined the world of the baby boomers than a shift in the human cooperation. Even if it is not the capacity of hitching per se that is passed down over the years, maybe those mutualistic sensibilities become part of other 'trust centres', such as setting up a local food cooperative, a refugee support network or a carpool club.

For those of us who have largely retired our thumbs from the road, it is always heartening to chance upon those who are just starting out in the sharing economies of the world and are transformed and enchanted by the road, just as I was forty years ago.

Passing the electronic baton

I met student charity hitchhikers Tom and Alex at Dover ferry terminal in March 2013, bleary-eyed after a night in a bus station and trying to assess their chances of negotiating northern France, on what was their debut journey: to Zagreb, Croatia. Twenty years old, articulate, well presented and unerringly optimistic in the full flight of adventure, they had already experienced the hitching 'karma' of a lift from a single woman who had also (to their amazement) made a donation to their charity, Link Community Development.[42] Their unmediated sense of ambition and enthusiasm were a poignant reminder to my middle-aged self, on a more limited 'inter-railing' tour of Europe with my family, of what was still possible.

As the French shore slipped into view, I found myself having a somewhat surreal historical 'moment', thinking about the countless travellers who had been in Tom and Alex's shoes, hanging on the rail and eyeing up the possibilities of lifts that would hopefully take them to distant parts, or at least beyond the concrete façades of Calais. My daydreaming quickly imploded with the brutal reality of how little advice I could give these debutants in terms of the actual road networks that would present themselves. My recent reading of the 1950s memoirs of Ian Rodger and Derek Foxman and dim recollections of what was in the now-much-dated guidebooks of Simon Calder and Ken Welsh were not going to be of much use, I reasoned, so I blabbered out some website names, hoping that these would have it covered. But as we gazed across the grey-and-glass expanse of port buildings and road architecture, Alex grasped the moment perfectly: 'This is our first decision then'.

Everyone's entry into the trust economy is different, and for many the emergence of 'couchsurfing', devised by American Casey Fenton in 2004 as a way to live cheaply on a holiday to Iceland, has been a more likely port of call than hitchhiking. Today, countless thousands of 'couch nights' are logged every year; couchsurfing is a recognised term and the organisation Couchsurfing has around a million members. Predominantly undertaken by so-called generation Y, it has spread across all ages, with a sizeable number of pensioners opting for it as a more interesting (and obviously cheaper) alternative to booking into a supposedly more appropriate and comfortable hospitality option. There are offshoots – Trustroots and BeWelcome – which were troubled by the more commercial feel that Couchsurfing had adopted with registration fees and sponsorship.

For Tom and Alex's generation, the myth of the Fall envisaged by the baby-boomers is nothing more than a faint echo of what their own doubting peers trot out. It is not the final answer to the question of 'what killed hitchhiking? and certainly no explanation for the 'trust issue' either. As children of the age of global connectivity, they are not even asking the same questions – they encounter the world, and more specifically the road, as they find it. In the San Francisco Bay area, thousands of young people of their age use the casual carpooling schemes every year, for whom the official signage and queues of people are enough to reassure them that this version of thumbing a ride is safe and fulfilling. Some of these 'pools' have been going for thirty years.

In 2009, at the same time as the UK Automobile Association had reported that only 9 per cent of drivers would pick up hitchhikers, the media were celebrating the travels of one Water Aid charity campaigner, Paul Smith from Newcastle, dubbed the 'twitchhiker'. He had set himself the challenge to get to Chatham Island off New Zealand with no money, on the basis of what he could organise on Twitter no more than three days ahead of time. Nervous of what the ether would throw up – despite having around 1,000 followers – he eloquently 'blogged' about his trepidation, largely it seems on account of the fact that he had never actually hitchhiked. He makes it of course, securing free flights, hotels, just through asking, and perhaps talking up the charitable work he is involved in.[43]

Reading his story, I wondered whether this is really any different from Simon Calder's suggestion at the beginning of *Britain: a manual for hitchhikers*, written in the mid-1980s, that the best way to restore your faith in human nature is to head out of town and wave your thumb at the passing traffic. The trust economy is always there on the open road, as it is in the ether, between neighbours, campaigning for resources for one's community, identifying with others across the globe with whom you might have common interests or concerns. Globalisation has required us to adjust to thinking about trust differently, rather than it being absent. We are able to be inspired by others by watching online as projects as large as the Cuban *amarillo* system continue to thrive, or the hitchhiking point outside the bakery on Salt Spring Island gets a reprieve, with plans drawn up to install a bus shelter but still allow hitchhiking.

There *is* more trust in the world, I am sure of that, but regardless of the optimism many hitchhikers feel about the strength of connections between people, in order to properly advocate the sharing of the road, we do have to seriously consider the complexities of danger relative to who you are and where you are travelling.

Chapter 9

Climatic dangers: hitchhiking and the relative realities of risk

Hitchhiking for peace

Pippa Bacca set out, with her friend and artistic associate Silvia Moro from Milan, on International Women's Day, 8 March 2008, dressed as 'Brides for Peace'. Their intention was to hitchhike through the Balkans, across Turkey, Syria and Lebanon to Israel and the Palestinian Territories, interviewing and collecting information from people who had lived through war. Giuseppina Pasqualino di Marineo (known as Pippa Bacca) was thirty-three years old and had been hitchhiking since she was a teenager; it was a family tradition and a key part of her identity. An earlier performance art piece, *Beyond*, held in Perugia in 2004, also focused upon a hitchhiking journey and included contributions from people encountered en route. For the 'Brides' tour, the two women designed dresses containing symbols or patterns which represented each of the countries visited. They believed that hitchhiking between those communities – with such an ordinary experience as a metaphor – could build new peace networks across borders.

An interactive part of this performance was for the artists' hosts each night to add something to the dresses or to design the cardboard destination signs for the next leg of the journey – thereby passing their goodwill down the road to the next set of people. There was to be an exhibition later, which compiled all of the interviews and stories from the road, and juxtaposed the wedding dresses, marked by the hard dusty graft of the journey, with unmarked copies back in Italy (perhaps symbolising the pure ideal of unity without effort). The pair stayed together until Istanbul and arranged to meet up later on the route.

Silvia hitchhiked all the way to Tel Aviv, but Pippa was raped and killed by a lorry driver in Gebze some forty miles from Istanbul, three weeks into her performance. It was a news story which drew international attention and outrage from artistic and feminist groups in Turkey, who marched through the streets of Istanbul, and later organised a bilateral conference of artists and an exhibition in Pippa's name. The public outcry was not just to condemn the killer, but because the tragedy exposed the deeply entrenched culture of male violence against women in Turkish society.[1] The response was evidence of a more cosmopolitan and secular generation of activists within Turkish society who were challenging the old patriarchal narratives of public and private spheres.

One of these progressive voices was that of investigative documentary filmmaker Bingöl Elmas. She was also in her early thirties and had been so moved by Pippa's story that she decided to continue the unfinished journey herself and make a film true to the same ideals as the 'Brides for Peace' performance, whilst raising questions about masculinity and power in Turkish society.

Exactly a year on from Pippa's death, on 31 March 2009, Bingöl stood in the village where Pippa's body had been found, dressed in a black wedding gown that had been made by a designer whose own daughter had been murdered. Attached to it were little messages of hope and the names of others who had suffered violence. Bingöl set off hitchhiking, as distinctive a figure on those roads as Pippa had been, also carrying a small camera, on which she recorded conversations about the artist's journey and the reactions to her rape and death. The aim of making a film was to try to understand but also challenge the 'mentality that doesn't seem to want or be able to solve the problem of violence against women'.[2]

Those sentiments quickly become clear to her in the apparent invisibility of women in public life in the communities which she passed through on those 1,000 miles across Turkey. The only women she saw were the sex workers on some of the roads outside of the bigger towns (and with whom she was often confused). As a documentary maker, Bingöl was used to challenging situations, but this was doubly difficult: the hitchhiking alone was impressive, even though she had a GPS device and a support car filming when possible; and not many journalists flag down lifts and then ask difficult questions about gender roles in their society.

The collected interviews and observations were edited into a forty-three-minute documentary, *My Letter to Pippa*, which played at film festivals in Turkey, Italy, France, Romania, the USA and India during 2010. Remarkably, Pippa's own footage had been salvaged and put to good use, in another documentary, made with the help of her family, by Joël Curtz (*The Bride*, 2012), who attempted to give her hitchhiking peace message a new poignancy.

At the time of Pippa's murder, the Turkish president, Abdullah Gül, rang his Italian counterpart, Giorgio Napolitano, to express his sense of shame, a sentiment shared by some newspapers, although others pointed out that had the hitchhiker been Turkish, the blame would have been attributed to her instead of Pippa's attacker. Sadly, this is precisely the kind of disparity which makes any discussion of the relative risks of hitchhiking a highly political and gendered matter.

So far in the book we've seen the importance of having counter-narratives to dominant views of the world – whether in terms of human nature, freedom, trust or economics – and heard inspiring examples to demonstrate what people are capable of achieving if they put their minds to it. Questions of risk are more problematic: it seems hard to tell optimistic tales when the job of documenting the nastier side of road history invariably leaves one with stories, such as Pippa's, which linger, irrespective of the statistical odds against such a tragedy. Nevertheless, it is our responsibility to bear witness, challenge victim-blaming narratives and tell alternative ones which address the structural issues behind attacks on hitchhikers: misogyny, racism, economic inequality and social alienation.

As we'll see later, with the First Nation communities in Canada – who have suffered disproportionately in this respect – some of the collective responses to hitchhiking tragedies have been particularly empowering. Learning from these can be helpful in how we think about tackling the overarching issue on the question of risk and transport – how we respond to the climate crisis in ways which do not reinforce the existing inequalities of the road.

Hitchhiking has a part to play in the solutions, but first let's take a closer look as to what we mean by risk.

Perceptual games

We think we intuitively know what risk is. Most of the time we are dealing with short-term or immediate dangers, but how our body anticipates or responds to a situation is based on adrenaline and primal imagination, rather than reasoned assessments of what might harm us over a longer duration. Complex information-driven societies mediate our anxieties – sometimes to frightening effect in the age of social media – but we have been engaging our rational brains about risk since we learned to store food for the winter or to expel disruptive people from the collective. Avoiding danger can be as much about the political will to plan for the long term as it is to stay safe in the fight-or-flight rush of the moment.

All of us have what the transport geographer John Adams calls a 'risk thermostat', which involves managing our behaviour depending on scientific information from governments, individual experts and the gut feelings and common sense of those around us.[3] We absorb these positions and weigh up a course of action based on the likely rewards of a specific 'risky' activity, judged against what we know of the potential harm that could come to us. The politics of this, of course, is that some groups or individuals may be more likely to be impacted by an issue than others; some 'risks' may not even be defined as such due to the pressures upon governments by corporations not to regulate them – a key strategy which the fossil-fuel industry successfully deployed to delay for decades any action on global heating (and one earlier used by the tobacco industry in relation to smoking).[4]

How do we judge the risks of hitchhiking? In a chapter in his co-edited book *Cities and risk*, Adams devises a typology of transport safety based on the amount of control one has over the mode of mobility. So, a car driver deals with 'applied risks', chiefly other road users, speed limits, street furniture and so forth; a cyclist negotiates a 'diminished' version of the same, but is more exposed to environmental factors and dangerous driving; then there is flying, where one has 'no control'. Finally, Adams offers a more 'low tech', 'voluntary' risk category, which would include walking, where one is exposed to some environmental dangers but is freer to make one's own decisions.[5]

Hitchhiking is a hybrid of these: part of the 'applied' category yet with additional 'voluntary' aspects to this too. Each traveller has to make choices about clothing, time of day to set out, whether to stand by the roadside or walk, which roads to use and if some conversation topics are best left off the agenda: all of which may pose risks in and of themselves. Some female hitch-hikers would argue that these decisions are the same ones that women have to make all of the time in public. So, in a country where lift-giving is normal and women's role in society more equal, then hopefully the relative risk is lower; conversely, a more patriarchal society where women have far less freedom and fewer opportunities could pose dilemmas for visiting hitchhikers.

Many of the people we have been travelling with in this book are loath to avoid a part of the world simply because it might be decreed dangerous or too politically sensitive by Foreign Offices and major news outlets, preferring instead to travel amongst ordinary people and see if the 'universe will take care of you', as Argentinian Juan Villarino is fond of saying. Just occasionally there are interventions, like Benoît Grieu's in 2011 telling people to stay away from parts of Pakistan after the USA's assassination of Osama bin Laden (see Chapter 6).

After over two decades of hitchhiking, Juan Villarino, the founder of the Argentina Autostop Club, is quite a good judge of which places and situations can be difficult, but he also feels that we are looking in the wrong places. Horrified by the impact of the collapse of the Argentine economy in 2000 on his parents' circumstances and well-being, he reflected that 'the 12-hour workday is more dangerous than hitchhiking', which was a major motivator to try to pursue a more compassionate life than chase the acquisitive capitalist dream.[6] Villarino shelved his psychology degree, then began odd-jobbing abroad to fund his new life as a nomad whilst sending money back home.

What sharpened his personal vision was the US invasion of Iraq in 2003, when every news story he heard seemed to be a one-sided Western account of the people there: defined by sectarian religious violence, or corrupt and failing social structures. So Villarino set out in 2005 to prove that the countries dubbed by the Bush administration the 'Axis of Evil' (Iran, Iraq and Afghanistan) would still open their car doors to strangers, share tea by the roadside or put him up for the night, just as he would expect if hitchhiking anywhere else in the world.

This they did, assisted, Juan believed, by his obvious lack of political association and the ambition of his plans. The sheer complexity of Afghanistan's recent history – occupied in turn by the Soviet Union, CIA-backed Taliban insurgents, a US-led alliance after 11 September 2001 and then a wave of United Nations and development NGOs – made him feel a little edgy on occasion and he tried to adopt a strategy of 'look powerless and see what happens'. A lone traveller, not obviously part of these forces nor of any of the different ethnic groups, may invite some suspicion but also generate curiosity and support, he reasoned: 'people get behind you … because they feel that it is necessary that you continue doing what you are doing, precisely because of the quixotic nature of the quest and perhaps sometimes because they feel your dream is also theirs'.[7]

Perhaps Juan conveyed the parallels with the destabilisation of his own country well enough to those he met to help solidify a bond of mutual aid: the common story of people baling one another out in a crisis. His account of his journey, *Hitchhiking in the axis of evil*, sold thousands of copies and turned him into an inspirational cult hero. Not long after its publication in 2011, three men tried to mug him in a Buenos Aires street, but upon recognising him decided to give him money instead and tell him to watch out on his travels as 'hitchhiking is dangerous'!

Problem-based learning

Hitchhiking 'well' does depend on more than the science of reading the road right: there is a level of intuition and grasp of body language involved, backed up by knowledge of the cultural traditions or geography of the place one is travelling through. It was always the intention of the guidebook writers of the

1970s to 'pay it forward' as we'd call it now, passing on gifts of knowledge to increase another's future safety. The digital age has cemented these possibilities, yet too much information may be counterproductive: travel requires an element of curiosity and exploration. Someone on an ordinary package tour may have their holiday so mediated and cocooned by company staff and policies that it reduces their capacity to respond to a crisis. Someone travelling by thumb or couchsurfing may appear to be more vulnerable, but could be thought of as being in a position of strength because it is closer to the heart and culture of a place.

Few hitchhikers believe that the risk increases the more you do it, and those who do would do well to absorb Bernd Wechner's discussion of the 1984 German Federal Bureau research into hitchhiking-related deaths and attacks. Here, the police themselves speculate that the reason why the majority of the casualties appear to be those engaged in short-distance urban hitching after 7 p.m. is that these are infrequent travellers, who are less practised at choosing lifts sensibly or less conversationally skilled at defusing situations (made worse by alcohol, they also suggest).[8]

Risk minimisation when hitchhiking starts with preparation. If it is your first time, you do your homework on road layouts, travelling etiquette, local customs and traditions, dress sense (for men as well as women) and 'thank you' phrases if it is not a language which you normally speak. Following the blog of a seasoned globetrotter has helped many, and there are few with quite the depth of experience as the Croatian hitchhiker Ana Bakran (Figure 9.1), whose book, *What's wrong with you?*, is an empowering travelogue about all the

Figure 9.1 Prepare for everything. Croatian super-hitcher Ana Bakran, here in Iran in 2015, has a list of forty tips for women hitchhikers to feel more confident on the road.

things which might occur if you choose to hitchhike 33,000 miles between Europe and Western Polynesia![9]

Based on these experiences she has compiled an eye-opening list of forty tips, each of which deals with a common question or situation that solo female hitchhikers might encounter en route. Planning is prudent: wear a fake wedding ring with a believable story attached to it; decide on a religion to adopt if asked (which can be sometimes safer than being an atheist); learn to trust your intuition about the many scams travellers encounter; find a diplomatic way of dealing with excessive generosity without offending those who want to fill your backpack to the brim with food and gifts (a 'nice' problem to have perhaps). In Iran and other Islamic countries, the advice is to always cover one's head and have a destination sign in the right language to avoid confusion about what you are doing by the roadside. There is also a stark piece of rape-prevention advice: to always wear sanitary pads if in a country where men will not have intercourse with women if they are menstruating.

Most advice in the hitchhiking literature on managing risk points to good communication strategies and listening skills. Diffusing tension before it arises is seen as key, such as keeping the conversation on the driver's life (however dull) rather than one's own, but if in tense situations to project calmness and use disarming conversational gambits to alter the mood of a sexual predator ('Jesus loves you my friend', or announcing 'my boyfriend's meeting me at the next service station'). Sometimes no matter how many discursive sleights of hand one has acquired, evolutionary instinct may decide the day. In the memoir of Irish poet Rosita Boland, *Sea legs: hitchhiking the coast of Ireland alone*, she tells of the moment she's offered a lift by a driver who claims to have the 'day off' and is 'just driving around'. It produces a 'purely animal instinct of warning … that I could not explain logically' and made her 'absolutely determined not to get into the car'. Boland's senses may well have been correct – the driver sat and watched her until she began noting down his licence plate number.[10]

How one plans for such situations is tricky: should one 'arm up' as a woman, be fast on the draw with a mobile phone, or a knife? Is taking a self-defence class, as many student hitchers on 1970s campuses did, a sensible starting point? Often the preparation for a journey means having strategies in place for potential flashpoints. Some hitchhikers immediately take photos of the vehicle that pulls up. Others, like French solo hitcher Nina Nooit, try to humanise themselves by sharing family photographs as early in a ride as possible, especially if it is the kind of long journey across central and southern Asia in which she seems to specialise.[11] Hitching with a child or a dog has often been regarded as another humanising technique which reduces potential dangers. Ana Bakran wears a visible (rape) whistle around her neck and carries a pepper spray to use if someone won't let her out of the car (which, in a confined space, is a powerful deterrent).[12]

We rarely hear about hitchhiking in such proactive terms and these are vital lessons for planning to share the road more collectively and responsibly in the future, but it is worth a sobering look at some of the relative dangers of the automobile itself – whether in the hands of one problematic driver or a whole society of them.

A short history of death on the road

Sigmund Freud argued that civilisation is necessarily based on denial, a view which he certainly never applied to transport, although subsequent therapists have done so in terms of how we refuse to confront our own impact on the planet. There's something very apposite about the detachment from reality and the behavioural changes which being behind a wheel can bestow on the mind of the driver. The cognitive dissonance involved in all of those obsessions with brand identity, other people's driving skills or the limits to individual liberty posed by speed cameras or high car parking charges is breath-taking: all whilst we continue to participate in the longest, bloodiest undeclared war in history.

It all began with the unfortunate Henry Bliss, run over in New York City on 23 September 1899, whilst helping a fellow passenger descend from the trolley bus they were riding on. He was the first of 57 million to die over the following century, 3 million of whom were Americans, with 30,000 annually adding to that total. The World Health Organization put global annual road deaths (including pedestrians and cyclists) at 1.35 million in 2018, the eighth highest cause of death for all ages.[13]

The Earth presently bears the toxic burden of over a billion cars – that's about one for every seven people, irrespective of age or cultural appropriateness. 'Motor mania' may have peaked in many Western nations, but everywhere else the corporate global propaganda that individual car ownership equates with progress is opening up new fronts, forcing cycling nations such as China, India and Vietnam to adopt the car more. Mega-cities such as Lagos, Jakarta, New Delhi and Mexico City are now almost permanently gridlocked, yet few want to talk about individual carbon footprints and collective responsibility for the 8 million annual global deaths attributed to air pollution caused by the burning of fossil fuels (the UK alone attributes 200,000 deaths per year to air pollution).[14] It is no wonder that several of the major car manufacturers have been caught trying to falsify their vehicles' emissions data.

Such is the lobbying power of these companies that the known ecological and health damage caused by the automobile is rarely presented to the public, nor are counter-narratives that campaign for more awareness about the costs of the freedom to go. Is anyone advocating an ecological awareness component to the driving test, or that police visit schools to talk about auto-addiction, or pressuring the makers of popular television motoring shows to provide a pre-show health warning about the disturbing nature of their subject?

Compare this to the occasions when the relative dangers of hitchhiking are discussed in the media: there's a curious tendency for official organisations to project the impression that they had access to some substantial body of research evidence, compiled by a crack team of international statisticians. The truth is that there isn't one. Even the FBI at the height of Hoover's counter-cultural paranoia rarely utilised statistics, preferring to scare the public with posters and press releases of 'America's Most Wanted'. If the FBI have a hitchhiker body-count database, then it is not telling anyone! Hats off, then, to the Californian Highway Patrol and its now legendary research report *California crimes and accidents associated with hitchhiking*, which has become a bit of a lodestone of statistical reassurance in pro-hitching debates.[15]

Written in the aftermath of the fuel shortages of the 1973 OPEC crisis this was a pragmatic study that looked at the possible (future) dangers to motorists and hitchhikers alike of so many people by the roadsides of California, and it assumed that numbers might be increasing. Assessing all of the road-related offences and accidents, the author deduced that hitchhikers were involved in 0.26 per cent of all road accidents and 0.63 per cent of all road crimes at the time (many of which were simply thumbing in an illegal position). Two hitchhikers are recorded as dying during the six-month study period, out of a total of 5.2 million hitchhiking journeys. By comparison, the total number of automobile and motorcycle fatalities exceeded 2,500. Since the Highway Patrol researchers collected data from each of the local police departments, we can assume that these hitchhikers were the only known fatalities (i.e. one death for 2.6 million journeys). There are many ways of spinning statistics such as these, but a sociological study at the University of Wuppertal from the late 1980s led by Joachim Fielder seemed to indicate a similar negligible risk of hitchhiking. The report, *Anhalterwesen und Anhaltergefahren unter besonderer Berücksichtigung des 'Kurztrampens'* ('Hitchhiking from the specific perspective of "shorter journeys"'), was a sustainability study looking at the part hitchhiking might play in a rural transport economy. Based on extensive questionnaire-based interviews of young people who were currently hitchhiking and groups of older radio listeners who had also hitchhiked, the researchers estimated that the chance of a female solo hitcher being raped was one in 10,000 rides.[16]

Compare that to the early decades of the twentieth century, when a combination of rough roads, unqualified and unregulated drivers and lack of taboos around drink driving probably made hitchhiking a pretty scary business. Or the reality of life on the roads during the Great Depression, which brought many dangers: poverty and illness on the road, violence from railroad 'bulls' and vigilantes, and being the target of vagrancy legislation. In the high plains or mountains at the wrong time of year, being escorted by the police to the city limits could actually be a death sentence.

It is useful to remember this when engaging with those overly preoccupied with the lingering legacy of the serial killer in the (American) imagination, and how it has distorted debates about the relative dangers of hitchhiking.

A world not full of serial killers

Serial killers are not a complete fabrication of the entertainment industry; neither are they evidence of some new nadir of human nature lurking solely in 1970s California. On a criminological level, their emergence as an alarming new phenomenon lay in changes within the FBI, which, under Hoover, had become more professionalised, utilising specialist departments to tackle key aspects of an investigation rather than having a generic team approach. Accordingly, the FBI was catching more people and by involving the media through poster campaigns and television bulletins, the FBI managed to transform crime into a form of entertainment whilst having a hand in shaping public opinion. However, on an ideological level, the publicity around people such as Ted Bundy and the 'Zodiac Killer' (who was never caught) during these years may have unintentionally served to fulfil a much older patriarchal trope – keeping women under control by implying that violence and danger lay only 'out there', in the form of some psychopath on the Interstates.

Serial killings comprise less than 1 per cent of homicides in most countries, and despite the best efforts of popular culture to convey the opposite, they have been falling dramatically in number due to more effective psychological profiling techniques, which have allowed more potential serial murderers to be caught before they can go on to commit further acts.[17] When we look at those killers whose victims included hitchhikers, only one appeared to target them specifically: Edmund Kemper, who abducted four of his six student victims hitching near to or on the Santa Cruz campus. The profiles of William Bonin ('the Freeway Killer') or Henry Lee Lucas (subject of the film *Henry: portrait of a serial killer*) were of opportunists who would kill anyone and who struck in parking lots, broke into houses and murdered their own family members. Yet having one of 'America's Most Wanted' as a murderer of hitchhikers served a number of purposes: it helped to deter more people from trying it – let's not forget that Hoover thought hitchers were communists – but it also helped to foster an apocalyptic amoral landscape in which it was easier to intervene politically.

The road system itself assisted this process. One of the reasons why Ted Bundy evaded capture for years was because he didn't always kill locally, as is often the pattern, but used the new Interstate network, which split investigations and created the impression that his crimes had been done by separate killers in different states. The out-of-town labyrinths of underpasses, storm channels, stanchions and scrublands were also ideal places to dump a body, regardless of where they had been killed. This increased the chance of 'road-based' explanations, so, if hitchhiking was part of the victim's lifestyle, even if they had been abducted elsewhere, it might feature in the media reports. The phrase 'last seen hitchhiking' became part of the grim reporting culture, first used in conjunction with seven unsolved killings on Highway 101 near Santa Rosa between 1971 and 1973.[18]

All of this facilitated a switch in media narratives, according to Jeremy Packer in *Mobility without mayhem*, from the 'homicidal hitcher' to 'asking for it'. Depictions of naïve young women at risk from sexual predators behind the wheel began to appear in publications such as *Newsweek* and *Good Housekeeping*. One film, *Chastity* (1969), cast the pop singer Cher as a troubled runaway heading for disaster with the wrong driver. The imaginative power of a potential 'Charles Manson' lurking around the next corner to keep people off the road may have suited some political agenda, but a more realistic danger of the time may have been drivers 'under the influence', as contemporaneous novels such as Don Mitchell's *Thumb tripping* (1971) vividly depict.

By the time the UK had its own nadir of the reporting of hitchhiking in the mid-1990s, there had been two decades of internationally popular slasher and 'road trip gone wrong' cinema. These films impacted on the public perception of thumbing a lift, not least the image of John Ryder (Rutger Hauer) stalking the kerbsides with a shotgun in *The hitcher* (1986). Crime fiction was on the up, and innovative serial killers were becoming ubiquitous within drama, so any road-related tragedy that hit the newswires was likely to fall into a pre-existing press narrative, which usually revealed the classed, raced and gendered nature of reporting.

In December 1995, a visiting French student, Céline Figard, was found murdered in Worcestershire, England, on the way to a temporary Christmas job. It was the first reported hitchhiking murder in the UK since the unsolved case of Finnish nurse Eila Karjalainen in 1983, but it opened up a national conversation about the wisdom of anyone, especially women, trying to thumb a lift in Britain.[19] Whilst the police sought her murderer, the press began speculating about the existence of a 'Midlands Ripper', making connections to the cases of nineteen women who had gone missing or been found murdered near major roads over the previous five years. Many of the victims were sex workers or vulnerable itinerants, whose disappearances had gone largely unreported. It was a grim time to be reading the news, as, only a few weeks before, the press had been covering the trial of mass murderer Rosemary West, whose husband Fred had picked up and later murdered two hitchers, Therese Siegenthaler and Juanita Mott, in 1974 and 1975, respectively. Like Ted Bundy, the Wests were opportunists who preyed on vulnerable young women across a wide geographical area, at a time when many thousands hitched every week.

The tone of much of the press coverage of the time was to reinforce the 'decline in trust' thesis (or 'the Fall' – see Chapter 8), which tended to emphasise the innocence of the past, when hitchers had taken unnecessary risks, even as some of the same crime reporters were also covering the advances in DNA technologies and forensic psychology which made it *less likely* that any modern-day Bundy or West would be roving the roads for very long. In addition, there was another reason why the roads may have been safer than they had been in the mid-1970s: there was less lead in the air, in buildings and in people's bodies.

It was a controversial thesis at first, because it was medical and simple, rather than a more complex sociological picture of risk factors and socio-economic circumstances. It also undermined vested narratives about the effectiveness of policing, or prison policy or the dangers of certain lifestyle choices (e.g. drug-related gang violence) in explaining crime rates. The 'lead-crime hypothesis' was a combination of two separate pieces of research by Rick Nevin (an economist working in the US housing sector) and Jessica Reyes (an academic studying the effects of chemicals on pregnancy). The years-long research established links between the rise in car ownership in the post-war period and the possible effects of lead (which had been added to petrol to improve engine efficiency) on the population, which twenty years later appeared to show a huge rise in violent crime.[20] These followed a similar pattern in most large US cities and in other Western countries, including the UK and Canada. There are no safe levels of lead in the blood, which affects brain development and cognitive ability and disrupts the normal inhibitors of our natural aggressiveness. The lead levels were highest where urban traffic was densest and the affected groups the most at risk of falling into crime for all of the usual socio-economic reasons (moreover, housing was often contaminated with leaded paint). When lead was taken out of petrol and environmental legislation tightened in the 1990s, the rates of violent crime plummeted across the board.

Aware that this cause–effect explanation would be regarded with scepticism, the authors made sure that they had mapped out against the more sociological reasons for rising crime rates in particular locations – population rates, policing strategies, availability of drugs – but concluded that none of those data sets matched the rise and fall as closely as their own. The work may turn out to be a portent, given what we already know about how industrial pollutants have impacted on human health, and the increasing numbers of studies raising concern about the effects of air pollution on the brains of those living in heavily industrialised and traffic-congested parts of urban areas.[21] At the time of writing, this relationship between urban populations, air quality and proximity to industry and major roads had become part of the conversation during the COVID-19 pandemic – a disease that disproportionately affects black and ethnic minority groups.[22]

Perhaps the love of driving was already poisoned anyway. Transport historian Kurt Moser dates the end of the motoring ideal in the USA to the OPEC crisis, when fuel shortages, carpooling and speed limits stymied the drive of the heroic motoring individual central to the myth-makers.[23] Ginger Strand goes further in her *Killer on the road: violence and the American Interstate*, arguing that the cultural preoccupation with the road as a dangerous place is a manifestation of the demise of the belief that the road and the automobile are able to bring prosperity for all. For her, the soulless structure of the Interstates, both geographically and psychologically disconnected from communities, becomes its own signifier of how we have chosen to imagine the worst in ourselves rather than elevate and build upon existing transport cooperation.[24]

A few days after Figard's death, *Guardian* reporter Maggie O'Kane conducted an impromptu survey of fifty drivers at a motorway service station and could find only one who had ever hitchhiked. On this basis she claimed that Céline's death marked 'the end of the road for hitchhiking'.[25] Apart from being caught up in the gloom of the moment, it was a strange assertion about transport politics of the time, which had taken a turn for the environmental. If anything, hitching was enjoying a tiny spike in popularity, with a wave of environmental direct-action protests against the Conservative government's 'Roads for Prosperity' scheme sweeping Britain. Protest camps were everywhere, to which activists were hitchhiking or using one of the first online car-share schemes, Freewheelers. There was plenty of research which suggested building roads rarely eases congestion in the long term and usually divides communities. The car-orientated government, lobbied hard by industry, kept framing the debate in terms of the rights of the motorist to determine their individual futures and cut travel time, even if it meant bulldozing ancient woodlands, wetlands and Neolithic monuments. No one was suggesting interviewing relatives of the 3,621 people who had died in car crashes that year about the dangers of getting into a vehicle.

Prisoners of the white lines on the freeway?

Neither was anyone using the 'asking for it' argument in the press coverage of Céline's murder, but there were vox pop suggestions in some quarters that anyone thumbing a lift had no respect for their own life. It was reminiscent of a comment a couple of years earlier by the managing director of Electric Pictures, Liz Wrenn, on the importance of their film *Henry: portrait of a serial killer*: that it was 'valuable and justified for a number of reasons. Not least for reminding women how vulnerable they are. Any woman seeing it will never hitchhike again, never open the door to a stranger.'[26]

Cultural policing of women in their public lives can be so ubiquitous as to be invisible. In the UK, the BBC interactive television series *Crimewatch* became notorious in the 1980s and 1990s for its glamorised reconstructions of cases where women had been alone at night engaging in allegedly risky and (by implication) inappropriate behaviour. Just as they had been told they had no place in the factories, in trade unions, political parties or the armed forces, they had no business being out alone. Such individualised and victim-blaming representations had been the motivation behind the 'Reclaim the Night' marches which emerged in the late 1970s across a number of countries, to make a stance on male violence and demand justice for the often hidden victims of it.

For some solo hitchhikers, the right to thumb a lift is part of the same conversation as why women should be free to walk, run, have a solitary drink or just drive without verbal, physical or legislative persecution. In her essay 'Why I continue to hitchhike', the Paris-based travel writer Nina Nooit – who has hitched in sixty different countries – reflects that dwelling on the risks to those on the road is to ignore the normality of forms of sexual violence meted out to less confident women elsewhere.

> During all my hitchhiking time, I was verbally sexually harassed a lot, but I was groped only twice (both times in Iran). And I can say I am by far not as traumatised by what has happened to me when hitchhiking, as I am traumatised by the things that were done to me by men with whom I flirted, went on dates, or even had relationships.[27]

Feeling welcome on the road, then, is a key issue even before one gets into a vehicle. The roadside is a disorientating place at the best of times – many injuries and fatalities have occurred throughout the world to people just standing in the wrong place or hitching in the dark, or walking with their back to the traffic. Ana Bakran urges female hitchhikers to watch for the U-turning car, as it is often a sign that someone doesn't think that you should be there and a dangerous situation could be about to unfold. The same sense of male entitlement crops up when occasionally drivers 'flash themselves' at a female hitchhiker. This is not a new issue but, she speculates, could be connected with the mass availability of online pornography and stereotypes about women hitchhikers, which requires additional preparation:

> the important thing is not to freak out as you might freak them out and then they might do something stupid out of the panic. By the look on their face you'll notice they don't really know what the hell they are doing. It's the look that's saying: I've seen this one on YouPorn and I wonder if it works…. I'll let my penis out for few minutes and see what happens. Tough news amigo, nothing will happen.[28]

I have never tested myself as a hitchhiker in the kind of climes that Ana and Nina have; I lived a charmed kerbside life, free of aggressive incidents, but I knew male hitchhikers who had been propositioned. I find it hard to imagine how I would react to being groped, exposed to another person's sex acts or worse, which is all the more reason to respect the testimony of those female hitchhikers who have been sexually assaulted but continue to keep travelling on their own.

The Dutch academic Barbara Noske, who solo hitched for thirty years before documenting her experiences in *Thumbing it: a hitcher's ride to wisdom*, was so determined to continue her chosen method of transport after a harrowing assault that she managed to find a way of rationalising it in her anthropological work on the physical and emotional boundaries between the animal and human worlds.[29]

Most people's immediate reaction to this would be incredulity: how could anyone even think about doing this? It is easy to lose perspective here, since many of the women in this book are hitchhiking 'activists': confident, resourceful and assertive travellers, perhaps able to use self-defence or coun-selling services. They largely chose to be by the roadside, whereas many others do not have that luxury. In some parts of the world a hitchhiking journey maybe no different from those endured by numerous women on underground metro systems of the West today – where some kind of assault is a real possibility but there are no other transport options available.

Nowhere is this more evident than in the recent history of one of the most beautiful and remote stretches of road on the planet: Highway 16 in

British Columbia, Canada. Nowhere has the treatment of female hitchhikers triggered such a far-ranging debate about the politics of the road, nor galvanised such a fightback against systemic violence.

Reclaiming the 'Highway of Tears'

To the outside observer, it all seems surreal. Canada enjoys a reputation as one of the most welcoming and easy countries in which to hitchhike, with its long history of migrant communities coexisting in a vast landscape and its relatively benign provincial and national governments. Surely it should be a role-model society for ecological living and transport, what with its long liberal agenda, including legalising homosexuality in the 1960s, welcoming Vietnam War draft dodgers from the USA, and the legacy of one Pierre Trudeau, arguably the only Western leader ever to advocate the educational benefits of hitchhiking whilst in office.

All of this is true: there is a rich legacy of hitchhiking culture, including some substantial academic work by Linda Mahood, whose book *Thumbing a ride: hitchhiking, hostels and counterculture in Canada* is a unique depiction of life on the road during the Trudeau era. Yet the people in Mahood's book are of a kind: largely white, Caucasian, resourceful and self-reliant; they see hitching as part of life's great adventure. They didn't have to regularly hitch lonely stretches of highway to school, work, college or medical appointments because there was no public transport and they were too poor to afford a beat-up motorbike or old car to share with their neighbours. They are a stark contrast, then, to the reality of First Nation men and women living on reservations along the 725-kilometre highway between Prince George and Prince Rupert, whose stories of the road have come to international attention only in this century.

First Nation people have been there for 9,000 years, the last few hundred of which have been defined by extermination, disease, exclusion and corralling into reservations by European colonisers. Positive media representations are infrequent and coverage of life on the reservations is limited to individual moments of tragedy or when these communities rise up to challenge potentially damaging developments such as the Coastal GasLink pipeline which runs through Wet'suwet'en territory to the north of Highway 16. There is a long history in Canada of the negative impact of new 'oil rush' towns on indigenous communities, with popular stereotypes of men being workshy, lazy and drunk, and the women being 'easy'.

The trigger for much of the debate within the last two decades has been the extraordinary number of disappearances and killings of young indigenous women on or close to Highway 16 (at least seventeen in all, with some estimating thirty), many of whom were hitchhiking. Yet it took the disappearance of a white woman for the global media to realise that a rather nasty structural problem existed in this corner of an advanced Western nation.

Back in June 2002, the Highway 16 corridor was experiencing an influx of seasonal tree planters, which provided many young people with a little cash-in-hand income, and a sense of adventure far from the cities in which many of them studied. Due to the infrequent Greyhound bus services, hitchhiking to and from the jobs made practical sense if there were not lifts available from fellow workers. One of these young tree planters was twenty-five-year-old Albertan Nicole Hoar, who set out hitchhiking from Prince George, heading west for Smithers, some 300 kilometres away, to visit her sister, but never arrived.

The mystery surrounding her disappearance drew extensive national media attention, whose reports began to include images of five indigenous women (Delphine Nikal, Ramona Wilson, Roxanne Thiara, Alishia Germaine and Lana Derrick), who had died in the early 1990s. Most of the victims were regular hitchhikers, so it was inevitable that there were media speculations about truck drivers and the possibilities of more than one serial killer operating in the province (due to the dates and spacing of the disappearances).

Blaming the victims was harder to do, as the sheer volume of the attacks indicated something much deeper rooted within the society than the Canadian government seemed willing to address. In 2004 Amnesty International issued a report entitled *Stolen sisters*, which claimed that indigenous women between the ages of twenty-four and forty-four were five times more likely to die as a result of violence than other Canadian women of the same age. Four years later, the United Nations warned the government that it needed to review its treatment of indigenous communities,[30] and in 2013 Human Rights Watch took the Royal Canadian Mounted Police (RCMP) specifically to task for its 'aggressive policing, neglect and allegations of sexual abuse' when dealing with the Highway 16 communities.[31] Accusations of institutional indifferences were hardly helped by comments from the then prime minister, Stephen Harper (a 'Big Oil' advocate, incidentally) who infamously said that holding a public inquiry into the murder of 1,186 indigenous women (between 1980 and 2012) was not 'really high on our radar to be honest'.[32]

The Highway communities themselves had begun to mobilise much earlier, motivated by two more deaths: those of twenty-two-year-old Tamara Chipman, who disappeared whilst hitchhiking in September 2005, and fourteen-year-old Aielah Saric-Auger, who was found on the roadside outside

Prince George in February 2006. In April 2006, First Nation activists called for a multi-agency symposium where the politics of the road could be debated more systematically in the public eye. Not only was this a key moment of community empowerment, with their voices and stories at the forefront of publicity, but one which addressed the complexity of the injustices rather than actions of the individual victims. Presentations to the symposium outlined how transport poverty was perpetuated at an intergenerational level, whereby the older generations in these under-resourced communities had little choice but to watch their young people hitchhike to get anywhere.[33]

The symposium concluded that a number of practical interventions were needed: more 'at risk' group information, emergency call boxes along the road in cell phone 'dead zones', safe houses in case hitchers were stuck en route, and, of course, substantially improved public transport. Market forces seemed to have constantly impacted on the latter, with a distinct absence of subsidised local shuttle buses or dial-a-ride options of any longevity, until 2017, when a supplementary service to the intercity Greyhound routes (which pass down the road once or twice a day) was unveiled, using Burns Lake (a mid-point on the road) as a hub. However, only a few months later, the Greyhound services themselves were cut from Highway 16, along with those on other major routes in northern Canada, raising concerns about women's safety and the ability of indigenous communities to access basic medical and educational services. Fortunately, the lack of official resource is not mirrored in community passivity, with many public rallies and 'Reclaim the Highway' walks; indeed, the indigenous youth have literally sung out loudly, encouraging a more positive self-identity through music videos, including telling their side of the 'Highway of Tears' experiences.[34]

For long-time researcher on the subject Professor Jacqueline Holler, status is a key element in trying to understand the problems faced by those in the reservations. She notes that not only do the communities have high rates of domestic violence of their own (often taboo), but indigenous women also receive disproportionate levels of sexual violence at the hands of non-First Nation men. Holler sees the culture of violence as a potential vicious circle, where lack of self-worth and resignation to systemic abuse and indifference mean that incidents are not reported, which in turn may even act as a signal for those wishing to enact violence. How this translates to the road is a complex question, although Holler's research suggests that sexual violence against hitchhikers within British Columbia has been dropping since 2008, perhaps as a result of greater awareness of the 'Highway of Tears' issues.[35]

In addition, perhaps because of the pressure it was under, the Royal Canadian Mounted Police adopted a more pragmatic approach in 2013, issuing advice leaflets as to how to stay safe on the road, rather than commit-ting resources to trying to deter those they perceived as 'at risk'.

Earlier in 2013, a far more idealistic response to solving some of the safety concerns was put before a meeting of Prince Rupert Council, by André Virly, a psychologist and environmental campaigner based in British Columbia, who felt that there was much to gain from implementing a variation of the organised Polish hitchhiking coupon system. His proposed scheme, the North West British Columbia Autostop, would involve registering regular drivers on the Highway and supplying them with logbooks and identification, and to encourage hitchhikers to purchase or be supplied with exchange-able vouchers which they would hand to their drivers. This could occur at recognised places en route and the drivers could cash in their vouchers later, or use them against vehicle maintenance or insurance costs. As an answer to safety concerns and as a means of uniting different parties in a collective problem-solving exercise across the region, the proposal had a lot to offer.[36]

Sadly, after the initial publicity, this disappeared without trace; perhaps there were too many recollections of the early 1970s, when it seemed that Pierre Trudeau had effectively institutionalised hitchhiking. More likely it was just one of many 'Highway of Tears' proposals which got lost in funding battles between federal and provincial governments or political differences about indigenous rights. Indeed, at the time of Virly's intervention, none of the symposium's recommendations had been take up, although the commu-nities themselves were increasingly vocal and mutually supporting of other campaigns around Canada where First Nation women had been killed.[37]

The dangers of hitchhiking are rarely so complex yet stark in nature. Those who continue to hitch on Highway 16 may play a very small and vulnerable role in attempting to reclaim the road – as do those protestors who walk the length of it – but largely these are people at the bottom of the social hierarchy, who have very little influence as individuals. What we need are more voices, including those of men like Virly, not just with practical suggestions but with the courage to call out male violence and some of its root causes to help make the roads more equal.

More men needed for hazardous journeys

Few countries outshine New Zealand when it comes to the viability of hitch-hiking, with governments repeatedly striking a pragmatic balance between being alarmist and blasé about its relative dangers. Even before the country experienced a massive boost in tourism as a result of the *Lord of the Rings* and *Hobbit* film franchises, it was relatively at ease with the idea that backpacking culture often involved people thumbing beside some dusty roadside miles from anywhere. It makes sense, with huge tracts of sparsely populated land on both islands not served by public transport, so over the decades the Tourist Research Council has actually logged anticipated or completed hitchhiker journeys. There's an ongoing interest now, with the challenges posed by climate breakdown, in including hitching as part of a sustainable transport policy, hence the debates about the wisdom of establishing official 'hitching points', such as the one at Hutt outside Wellington.[38] Unsurprisingly, there is press interest if it is the local politicians who are doing the hitchhiking to work, in suit and tie, as councillors Aaron Hawkins in Dunedin and Sheldon Nesdale in Tauranga have made a habit of doing.[39]

A bit more challenging is Project Wildman – initiated by Wellington builder Rob Cope, who in 2013 decided to hitchhike around the country raising awareness of mental health issues in men, with a fridge. In it were copies of his book *Men wanted for hazardous journey*, an honest account of coming to terms with the reasons why his marriage had failed: his inability to talk about why he had felt lost or angry or powerless in his life. We get years of formal education, he reasoned, but nothing on the emotional preparedness of being a parent, a husband or a true friend: men exist behind a mask of machismo that Kiwi society does little to challenge. For Cope, the fact that half the population could not talk about their inner struggles was a public health crisis – all those feelings of depression, loneliness, failure and shame held hostage by a Lone Ranger stereotype who solved problems by action rather than communication. The consequences of these repressed feelings were likely to be forms of domestic or public violence.[40] So, after a few meetings with friends around a campfire talking these issues over, Cope decided to take the book on the road and be amidst the very people who might well be suffering from those conditions: men alone in their vehicles.

Best-selling author Tony Hawks might have popularised the 'fridge' idea as a hitchhiking gimmick, but for Cope it was an icebreaker for some potentially difficult interactions. He doesn't frame it in this way, but there is an overlap with the 'Brides for Peace' performance with which we began the chapter: Cope is enacting a piece of political theatre which challenges the dominant narratives of male power and public space. Some commentators on Pippa and Silvia's performance had made the uncomfortable connection with the history of feminist body art and experimental figures such as Marina Abramović, who sometimes pushed the boundaries and 'tested' the potential brutality of an audience on herself, the performer.[41] Putting one's body on the line as civil disobedience is a challenging thought in this context – there is a long tradition of peace activists and hunger strikers doing this – but prior to the 'Brides for Peace' tragedy no hitchhiker had died for their art as far as I know. Rob Cope reported nothing but good reactions, but a different messenger could have received a beating for being 'unmanly' perhaps.

Just as Bingöl Elmas felt the need to complete Pippa's journey – as a fellow artist trying to offer a more positive vision of human capabilities and to generate further debate – it is clear from the reactions to Cope's fridge tours (two in New Zealand, one in Australia) that he knew he was becoming something of a spokesperson for a much-needed emotionally literate masculinity.[42] Project Wildman became about enabling others to set up groups in which men could discuss their emotional difficulties and by doing so also contribute towards reclaiming the road as a safer place in the long run.

When we talk about hitchhiking and its risks, we are having a conversation about the distribution of power: who controls the narratives of the road, who are the people travelling on it and how important are their lives and stories to society. There may be less lead in the air, and hitchhikers may be more savvy about safety and have more technologies to facilitate this, but ultimately the reason why hitchhikers occasionally do get killed is that men have a problem of perception shaped by the unequal, divided and misogynistic societies into which they have been born and usually not prospered in. Often the victims are those who also suffer from social and economic uncertainties and structural inequalities and whose names do not make the headlines.

Focusing on and debating these points is important, in terms of bearing witness, but it is not hitchhiking itself which should be centre stage. Media attention to relative risk on the road is a massive distraction and hitchhiking provides the lens to help us adjust our vision about what is structurally dangerous and those things which can be managed with knowledge and mutual support. With the climate crisis requiring us to put these issues into practical perspective, we'll touch on some uplifting examples from the transport history of the former communist world in the coming pages, to look forward to a less risky world in the future. It might require you to join a hitchhiking club though.

Chapter 10

Good news from Vilnius: the rich life of hitchhiking in former communist countries

Last amongst equals

Jona's team came towards the end of the pack. The race across Ukraine hadn't been easy. It was a World Championship preliminary round and their German team had been up against the experienced Russians, folks used to airing their thumbs in snowy temperatures likely to worry even an Alaska Highway veteran. The freezing rain that had accompanied them for most of the seven days and relatively sleepless nights in October 2012 had been a little dispiriting at times. Then there had been the small matter of 'the rules', which ran to several pages, detailing race etiquette, kerbside protocol and how to negotiate course checkpoints in the correct manner. The bureaucracy, much greater than in their own National Championships, had been enough to deter some of Jona's compatriots, who found it a culture shock. By contrast, Jona Redslob was a keen enough racer not to be fazed by such matters but nevertheless it was not his day job; as a 'purist hitcher' he hitched everywhere unless it was absolutely necessary to do otherwise. To some, races may still seem a bit of a novelty, but as a growing phenomenon on the hitch-hiking scene, it is something one *has* to have an opinion on.

Jona cuts an impressive figure: blond, gangly, with a big smile, the kind of healthy-looking traveller who always does well with lifts. Jona's hitching started with the proverbial missed bus whilst still at school in his home town of Magdeburg; then, as an exchange student in Latvia, he acquired a taste for the quieter non-autobahn journeys available in the former Soviet Union. Extending his horizons from journeys to visit family and friends within Germany, to Morocco, the UK and Siberia, he then tried his hand at competitions every six months. Soon he was attending and then helping organise the annual summer European Hitchhiker Gathering, and he was actively involved in planning the events in Portugal (2010) and Bulgaria (2011). It has left him pretty adaptable to what the road reveals. Even coming last in competitions may have distinct social advantages, he muses: 'Hitchhiking competitions differ from normal [sport] racing competitions, because in the latter whoever arrives first is applauded the most whereas at the former the later you arrive the more you are applauded simply because the people who arrived before you are there to cheer for you.'[1]

To the outside world, organised competitions must seem curious and paradoxical: hitchhiking suggests individualistic and self-directed activity but which is also completely dependent on cooperation and sharing. One academic writer on 'slow travel' and alternative mobilities, Michael O'Regan, argues that cooperation is so central to hitchhiking that competitive racing may be antithetical to the spirit of what hitching is all about.[2] Some events test this premise more than others: on the one hand, there are German races such as those organised by tramprenn.org, which raise money for humanitarian projects in the developing world; then there is the controversial Belgian and Dutch race Route du Soleil, which enjoys considerable corporate sponsorship and is as much a travelling roadshow which non-hitchers can enjoy as a 1,000-kilometre hitchhike. All participants gravitate eventually to a purpose-built beach village (with shuttle buses on hand to the nearest town) where award ceremonies, corporate giveaways and serious partying take place. It's an approach which was not well received by some in Jona's own hitchhiking circles, for departing from the social and economic values which hitching is seen to embody.

So how did hitchhiking become so interesting and diverse? Is this just digital interconnectedness revealing pre-existing nuances and contradictions? Do hitchhiking cultures automatically align with specific political or economic ones, and if so what can be learned for our future benefit? Is the problem of thinking in opposites such as cooperation and competition more of a hindrance to progressive transport ideals than just accepting that life is more complicated (regardless of our local political culture)?

The illusion of individual brilliance

Hitchhikers have always raced, in one way of another. As far back as the 1920s the *New York Times* was perfectly happy to cover the long-distance competitions organised by the Scout Association of America (see Chapter 1). It adds an extra incentive, drawn from that more competitive part of our genetic makeup, to supplement the camaraderie and social novelties of different people and places. If the weather has taken a turn for the worse, there is nothing as satisfying as arriving ahead of a projected coach or train time, or a hapless fellow hitchhiker! In the days before mobile phones, there was always an extra level of mystery to the whole process, not knowing how one's peers were faring on the road. Today, with relative declines of hitchhiking and lift-sharing culture in many countries, it is possible that for some young people their *only* experience of hitching might be through a charity race event such as the 'Prison Break' (furthest away from one's 'confinement' in twenty-four hours wins).

In the 1980s and 1990s, the annual *Guinness Book of World Records* included hitchhiking in the category of 'human achievements' (though later classified it under 'travel'). Persuaded by the self-promoting Ilmar Island, a resident of Key West in Florida, to recognise his five-day hitchhike to Fairbanks in Alaska (a distance of 5,200 miles) as a 'record', the researchers began logging other committed accumulators of miles and times, eventually awarding an honorary beer mat to Stephan Schlei of Ratingen, Germany, for being the World Champion Hitchhiker. His eventual tally of 1,000,000 kilometres (often following the Liverpool football team) certainly outstripped the achievement of the flamboyant and innovative previous title-holder DeVon 'Rocketman' Smith[3] and puts him maybe third or fourth in the all-time list, behind Benoît Grieu and Alexej Vorov (about whom more below). With the new millennium, Guinness either bought into the 'stranger danger' thesis or decided it needed more space in the book for speed donut eating or pedalo racing, and so deleted the hitchhiking categories. Fortunately, the responsibility for record-keeping and assigning hitchhiker champion status was already in the capable hands of the Vilnius Hitchhiking Club, which has become an epicentre for hitchhiking gatherings and race events such as the annual epic 'Baltics' race (1,000 kilometres), which criss-crosses at least one of the three Baltic nations.

Few hitchhikers wake up with plans to break records, although the way that Guinness logged the statistics – you start counting the 'time' from the first lift – clearly pandered to those desperate enough to afford to wait for the 'right lift'. Some record holders may have even become overly precious about the numbers game. Why else would Peter W. Ford have attempted to do the Land's End to John o' Groats return hitch twice (1974, 1976) if it hadn't been for John Frederick Hornsey knocking an hour off his fifty-seven hours in between! One can also only wonder whether between 1985 and 1995 Bill Heid and Stephan Schlei were keeping tabs on each other as they kept leapfrogging each other's 'world record' tally, but I suspect that they were above such egotism (if they even knew about each other!).

Many individual achievements accrue simply because of the huge amount of time spent on the road. Vorov has had some of the largest annual totals *and* the longest waits. The humour is not lost on the archivists in Vilnius, who encourage hitchers to be 'happy for our colleagues … not to be envious', a sentiment underscored by including records sent in by supporters which no one would ever actually *attempt*, such as the minimum and maximum temperatures experienced by a hitchhiker (–61°C and +55°C). When super-statistician Robert Prins, holder of the twenty-four-hour record announced that, at 11 a.m. on 2 February 2011, his lifetime's worth of hitching amounted to the distance that light travels in a second (299,792.5 kilometres), it was a gentle reminder to think about the bigger picture.

To the average Western hitchhiker, the idea of being in a hitchhiking club is still pretty unusual. It is more likely that, for a group of friends, who share a musical or political taste or affiliations, hitchhiking becomes one part of their 'scene' or collective identity, not its main purpose, and probably not for very long. By contrast, clubs in former communist countries are numerous (Russia has dozens), enjoy considerable longevity and retain their members: the Vilnius Club has its origins in the hitchhiking section of the Vilnius Engineering Construction Institute tourist club, in 1987; the St Petersburg Autostop League dates back to 1978; the Moscow School of Hitchhiking, founded by Valery Shanin and Anton Krotov's Academy of Free Travel (AVP), began in 1995. These clubs have been organising races or expeditions for several decades. Not to be outdone, the Polish (with clubs in Gdansk and Wroclaw, as well as Warsaw) now claim to run the largest international race, with up to 500 participants from seventeen nations at last count. The infrastructure is often pretty impressive too, with those turning up to compete in the 2010 hitch from Sopot to Prague finding an entire public park kitted out for the registration process, complete with food stalls, bands, balloons and even a climbing wall for competitors to warm up on!

Hitchhiking health and safety: sign here please

If hitchhiking clubs seem bizarre, wait for the bureaucracy! If you are enrolling in one of the above events, there's more to it than quickly scribbling the phone contact details for you and your race partner at the start line. You'll be asked to submit evidence from your hitchhiking CV to the race arbitrators as part of the registration process, and there are quite a few stipulations, as this section from a 2007 document posted on the Vilnius Club website indicates:

1.3. PARTICIPANTS

1.3.1. Applications for participation may be submitted by:
– every member of a hitch-hiking club, which has an official number;
– a probationer, who will get a number after the competition.
Any application may be refused up until 12 hours before the start.

The probationer, who aims to get an official number, must have 5000 km of experience for summer competition. Moreover, during the period of probation a probationer must get over 1000 km alone or as the leader in a pair. The route to work or a place of study cannot be considered to be part of that experience.

To compete in winter, a probationer must have 5000 km of winter experience. Every kilometre made in summer counts on 0.5 km in winter, so 5000 km of summer experience equals 2500 km of winter experience. 1000 km made on your own in winter can not be replaced by any summer experience.

1.3.2 The organisation committee has a right to reject a probationer's application for the competition.[4]

If that looks a bit daunting, there's a good reason for it: some of the conditions are akin to winter orienteering, with entrants expected to be versed in first aid and survival training. Many competitions encourage the use of the 'professional hitchhiking suit' designed by Alexej Vorov – a remarkable bright yellow and red invention, made out of recycled parachutes (see Figure 10.1) – which is warm, waterproof and visible in headlights at 250 m. On matters of safety, Alexej Vorov's voice counts for something. When one hears him talking about preserving food in extremely low temperatures or not running after cars for fear of one's breath freezing, then suddenly the

Figure 10.1 Hitchhikers united. Russian and German sports hitchers compare race rules and latest road wear in Berlin in 2017. Left to right: Jona Redslob, Alexej Vorov, Stefan Korn and Elizaveta Tezneva.

idea of having a few competitive rounds – of the sort which Jona Redslob was participating in – before embarking on a year-long race makes sense!

Beyond these safety protocols, many of the competition rules revolve around road etiquette towards other teams and filling in the paperwork. Western hitchhikers will recognise the taboo of arriving at a roadside and standing in front of hitchhikers already there – now imagine this in a race context! However cuddly one feels towards one's fellow travellers, tempers are likely to flare if it is pouring with freezing rain. So, the 'who arrives first gets pole position' rule maybe the most important one of all, assuming that most entrants will not 'cheat' by fixing up lifts with friends or catching a bus through a slow part of town. At the finish line, one's due diligence is hopefully rewarded, providing one has gathered the designated codes from every checkpoint visited and noted down the details of each ride taken, including the make of cars ridden in. After several days in the open air, getting disqualified for not paying attention to the small print may be quite a downer!

But how did hitchhiking culture evolve in such a different way from that treasured by Western popular culture – where an imagined Jack Kerouac figure cuts a solitary, independent presence? Are these contemporary racing teams from former communist countries any less individualistic and competitive than their North American counterparts? Or is it a matter of whether some societies are more absorbing of political difference and able to celebrate diversity a little more openly? To find answers to these questions we need to dip back into some of the post-war histories of Poland and Russia in particular, and how a way of sharing the road and supporting those on it emerged out of austerity and division.

'A river of young people bubbling with joy'

In the aftermath of the Second World War and the realignment of Europe, the governments of those nations which comprised the Eastern Bloc were faced with the problem of how to offer some kind of psychological outlet for the wanderlust of their youth. A policy of 'containment' prevailed, with travel to the West highly restricted, available only to specific Party members or special delegations. Instead, programmes of 'patriotic' tourism began to be cultivated, initiated in Moscow, with travel-writing becoming a new form of propaganda, singing the praises of looking inwards, as the holiday sector adjusted its infrastructures to fit the new mindset.[5] For instance, Polish leaders needed to find a way to energise the younger generation with national pride after the trauma of losing a sixth of its population in the war and over 20 per cent of its land to the newly established Soviet Union.

As an established transport tradition, hitchhiking was ideally positioned to fulfil this, linking a programme of economic recovery with an encouragement for those taking to the road to visit war memorials and concentration camps such as Auschwitz to underscore the sacrifices that had been made for their generation's freedom.[6] Pivotal in delivering hitchhiking as part of a transport policy was the progressive Polish head of state Wladyslaw Gomulka (1956–70), who set up the Social Autostop Committee to administer the voucher (or coupon) system in 1957. Would-be hitchhikers were expected to purchase, in advance, a cheap book of coupons at one of the estimated 260 branches of the PTTK (Central Board of the Polish Country Lovers' Society), at official youth clubs and even at some border checkpoints. Along with the coupons, detailed road maps were sometimes given on which were marked routes of different distances (20 kilometres, 50 kilometres, etc.), totalling 2,000 kilometres. The coupons were handed to the driver, who could then cash them in and be entered into a national lottery draw, which was regarded as an important economic incentive by the authorities.[7] Such a positive synthesis of politics and transport resonated well with international socialist observers in the 1970s who turned the system into a *cause célèbre*, even though within Poland itself the management of the autostop scheme received some resistance from purist hitchhikers.

Being told that it was forbidden to hitch at night, or further than the 2,000-kilometre limit of the tokens, or outside the official hitching season (May to September) seemed antithetical to the liberties of the road. Accordingly, many hitchers ignored the rules or refused to take part, just as some drivers would waive 'payment' so that hitchers could extend the use of their coupons. The age limit created a headache too, as it led to under-sixteens forging certificates that would allow them to benefit from cheap easy travel.

At the outset of the coupon system, the Polish authorities were trying to deal with an emerging youth counter-culture, which mirrored those based around music, fashion, motorbikes and narcotics in the West. The constant overlapping of these interests with hitchhiking meant that the authorities had to walk a fine line around issues of public acceptability. For historian Mark Keck-Szajbel, Poland has to be viewed as a barometer nation in East–West relations. The hitchhiker was posited as a 'chimera' figure: praised for citizenship, damned for 'loose' attitudes to authority or sexuality. It was common for letters from outraged parents to appear in the travel magazine *Dookola swiata* ('Around the world') about the evils of the road. Yet in this flowering of youth identities and liberal political outlooks, there was exactly the same kind of generational optimism and enthusiastic questioning of received wisdom that Westerners such as Ian Rodger, Sharon Stine and Derek Foxman had expressed a few years earlier. Keck-Szajbel saw these new mobile idealists as 'a river of young people bubbling with joy'.[8]

One song captured the *Zeitgeist*, 'Jedziemy Autostopem' ('Let's go hitch-hiking'), by the popular pioneering rock band Czerwono-Czarni (Red and Blacks). The lyrics (in translation) include: 'We go hitchhiking, we're auto-stopem/ This way you can ride bro Europe/ Where the road white thread, go ahead and get out there bro/ And do not worry about what will happen next'. Reflecting upon the impact of the song, which won a national music award, the band's singer, Karin Stanek, noted that one of its first performances, at the 1964 Opole music festival, had been particularly striking, since so many of the audience had arrived there by hitchhiking. Stanek's memoir is one of dozens in the substantial anthology *Rideshare Poland: communism and modernity*, edited by Jakub Czuprynski, which also includes an extensive range of poems, literature, sociology, art and political comment inspired by autostop over the previous four decades (first published in 2005, the book awaits an English translation).

An estimated 35,000 hitchhikers went through the books of the Social Autostop Committee during an average year; many hundreds of these were visitors to the country. The popularity of the scheme survived the period of martial law between 1981 and 1982 although it began to fade when Solidarnošc and Lech Walesa came to power; it eventually folded in 1995. Its enduring relevance to what is possible today is nicely expressed in some lovely propaganda of the time:

> Polish autostop is a purely social organisation. It is self-supported and represents a democratic form of tourism in the widest sense of the meaning.... it develops self-dependence and accustoms young people to hardships and surprises of the journey, develops the ability to cope with various conditions.[9]

Beware of beatniks and bohemians

Not everyone was quite so enthusiastic. As it began to find its feet, the autostop system was being watched by some of Poland's less liberal Eastern European neighbours, who saw it in terms of the emergence of progressive youth movements elsewhere in the communist world. On the Czechoslovakian campuses of 1963, for instance, conflicts erupted between students and Party officials about a range of lifestyle matters, from the influence of Western music and fashion to the reading of the early humanist writings of Marx rather than the correct scientific socialism approved by the Party. Travel became part of this dialogue and one of many mobilising points or cultural shifts which would gradually coalesce to become the Prague Spring of 1968, when the country fought for its independence as its reforming leader Alexander Dubcek battled the hard-liners in Moscow. For the older generation of Czech communists, hitchhiking evoked the negative memory of the inter-war years of beatnik hikers and bohemian clothing (worn by 'soft males'), so they wanted to use the Polish system to control the mobility and ideas of sections of the Party Youth (or Komsomol).

Unlike Poland a decade before, the narrative of the voucher system as a unifier and educator on 1960s Czechoslovakia didn't fit with the rising expectations and cultural expressiveness of the young, so plans for it were quietly shelved. An official explanation finally surfaced claiming that the narrow national roads were unsuitable for the autostop system to function safely, an argument also used by the tough East German government. The students were less volatile there, but hitchhiking was so much a part of the culture that the long-serving post-unification chancellor of Germany Angela Merkel, who grew up in East Germany, remembers being more terrified of staying in a Western hotel for the first time than any of her time on the road in her youth![10]

Tolerance of or support for hitchhiking varied greatly across the whole of Eastern Europe. Poland continued to draw attention for its relaxed summer-season visa arrangements (the Borders of Friendship treaty of 1972), but other countries were less keen on the idea of such hitchhiker-friendly bureaucracy and the prospect of thousands more people on their roadsides. Pragmatics, however, meant that the less-economically developed countries, such as Hungary, Bulgaria, Romania and Yugoslavia, had to balance any anti-hitchhiker sentiment within government against the economic realities of low levels of car ownership and unreliable or limited public transport systems. We have to remember that all of these countries were transitioning from largely rural societies to industrial ones and there were many variations of transport culture, with drivers in some places (e.g. Romania) asking for payment. Serbia today may have a thriving hitchhiking culture, but in the years of the former Yugoslavia it was patchy; outsiders saw Yugoslavia as a friendly and quirky place to hitchhike through, but not in a hurry.

It's to Russia we turn now, as a country with a very long tradition behind its current position as a centre of world hitchhiking. As with Poland, there was a culture of sharing to meet a national need, and this, too, has filtered down into contemporary hitchhiking clubs and their outlook.

Meeting the professionals

There is a popular story which attributes the official recognition of hitchhiking in the Soviet Union to the visit of first secretary Nikita Khrushchev to the

USA in 1959, where he was 'inspired' by hearing about their way of doing it! Here the mind boggles a little: did his limousine break down, or was he given a copy of Kerouac's recently published *On the road* as a diplomatic gift? The truth of the motivation aside, the coupon system (with prize incentives for drivers who had 'collected' the most kilometres) began in St Petersburg (then Leningrad) shortly after and enjoyed popularity in the surrounding Baltic States, with over 90,000 people having signed up by 1965.[11]

It wasn't exactly a conceptual revolution. Hitchhiking was well established due to the realities of geography and transport scarcity, so formalising it along the same lines as its Warsaw associates was a handy means for the Kremlin to appear benign (after the Stalinist era) whilst still exerting some control over youth activities. Given the rising student unrest in Czechoslovakia the thinking is clear, although it didn't appear to pacify the more alternative 'hippie' counter-cultural networks springing up in Estonia, who organised an independent coupon system and integrated it into their do-it-yourself lifestyles and burgeoning music festival culture.[12]

The Russian coupons are long gone, as is its poor reputation as a hitch-hiking destination for international travellers, with pragmatic officials now taking a remarkably relaxed attitude to would-be visitors thinking of extending their palms (rather than thumbs) into the road. Many post-Soviet developments have actually suited hitchhiking: an expanding road network, easier access to land previously closed to the public and greater diversity of media coverage on travel issues. The legacy of the communist era has included something else too: an attitude of adaptability and empathy with others, which helps explain the longevity of the practice decades after the fall of the Berlin Wall. As Alexej Vorov, the president of St Petersburg Autostop League, explains: 'Everyone knew that there was no sense to rely on the State or other service providers. You had to find another way. Moreover, only a few had a car, so hitchhiking was possible and it was a pleasant way of getting to know other people.'[13]

Whether one is listening to Vorov, Anton Krotov (Academy of Free Travel) or Valery Shanin (Moscow School of Hitchhiking), each of the three club figureheads is equally expansive about this relationship between scarcity and cooperation. For Shanin, hitchhiking is enough of a 'way of life' for it to be worthy of discussion in his classes as a psychology lecturer at Moscow University. He's keen to get students thinking laterally about the social and interactive benefits of travelling with very little money – something he has over 900,000 kilometres' experience of – as well as the history and culture of hitchhiking more generally. When he organised the 1995 Russian National Championships, there was a note in the publicity that this event was taking place close to the seventy-second anniversary of the 'start' of hitching (which he attributes to the famous 'Drifter' piece in *The Nation* – see Chapter 1). It was an observation born of the time when new generations of travellers were heading out from former Soviet Union countries and learning about how their activities aligned with the rest of the world.

One senses this in terms of how the Academy of Free Travel (AVP) presents itself. It's founder, Anton Krotov, is probably the most famous Russian hitchhiker, partly on account of his sheer productivity: not only has he provided important advice in *A practical guidebook for free travellers* (which sold 140,000 paperback copies) but he has written at least forty other books based on his expeditions. As we noted earlier, regarding competition rules, the seriousness of the geography and climate underpins much of the talk about hitchhiking in Russia. It is the largest country in the world, covering 17,000,000 square kilometres across nine time zones, with many different ethnicities and cultural traditions between Kamchatka and Vladivostok on the Pacific Rim and the more populated parts beyond the Urals towards Europe. In between, transport routes and options are few, with most of the habitation close to the principal east–west road and rail lines. Vast areas of tundra define the northern latitudes, giving way to forests and mountain ranges in which you could lose several European countries, south of which is an extensive arid belt (which includes actual desert). Listen to anyone who has hitched through the stunning scenery of north-eastern Siberia on the Kolyma Highway and all of those 'obvious' guidebook questions suddenly take a different meaning if three cars a day is normal. Hopefully you won't have to give your last morsels of food to a passing bear to save your skin, as the renowned zoologist Vladimir Dinets did whilst waiting for a lift on this road some years ago!

For the adventurous souls at the AVP, adaptability in these climes is critical and hitchhikers have to become proficient in utilising freight trains, cargo planes, barges and boats, as these might be all that are available to keep moving (and not freezing). For this, a different set of skills is required, which is why the AVP is adamant that 'free travel' is not necessarily about the absence of money (*halyava*) in a transaction (and stowing away is forbidden), but the ability to overcome or negotiate around social and bureaucratic 'restrictions'. Here the AVP aims to educate its club members to take charge of their experience of travel more directly, dispensing with the need for third-party guides, insurance industry operatives, hotel chains and purpose-built tourist enclaves. If one avoids these 'restrictions', by adopting a confident attitude and open mind, the true nature of a place and its people can be revealed. This is how one 'opens a country', accesses its trust economy, a technique which can be assisted by showing one's letter of recommendation from the AVP club president, which explains your willingness to be of service in exchange for a lift.

Western readers might raise an eyebrow at this unusual approach to travel, which is a remnant of the Soviet era and the need to justify one's movements. We have to remember that for many millions of people the idea of venturing beyond their national boundaries, or even going very far within them, was as much of a culture shock as that faced by some of our post-war hitchhikers travelling into North Africa or on the Hippie Trail. When Krotov wrote the first edition of *A practical guidebook for free travellers* it was 1995 and the legacy of travelling with an official chaperone or with a Party-approved script was still part of the cultural memory. In addition, he knew that it was going to be read by teenagers, so he framed some of his FAQ with their parents' anxieties in mind. One sociologist of youth movements, Dennis Zuev, suggests that the new political culture into which the AVP emerged was one of accommodation towards unusual ('drop out') organisations, many of which were given a semi-official status despite holding unorthodox attitudes, just to 'fit' into the new culture.[14]

So, when we read the aims and objectives of the Academy, the terminology feels reminiscent of a scientific research institute from a different era, because it is aiming for a respectability of purpose, yet it is also revealing of how isolated its originators felt as they conceived a plan for how to engage with the land beyond their borders:

> 1. To collect information about the world, its countries and regions and their peculiarities;
> 2. To organise hitchhiking expeditions, rail journeys and treks in various parts of the globe and Russia;
> 3. To educate people on the properties of the surrounding world and the possibilities for independent travel.[15]

If this tradition is a variation on the old adage of the road as an educator, as Zuev proposes – comparing it to the Western obsession with the cultural authentic and unspoilt wildernesses – then it is one that the AVP takes very seriously, demanding that its members provide talks on their return from expeditions. This 'outreach' work is another aspect of Russian free travel which harkens back to traditions from the twentieth century.

Hitchhiking 'outreach work' and its discontents

In the late 1920s, Russian citizens were encouraged to identify with the figure of the 'proletarian tourist', who mixed with real people, learned about politics and became fit through participating on walking tours. The idea flourished under a number of different guises and societies, some of which seemed to double as border patrols on Russia's perimeters.[16] During the inter-war years, more self-organised alternatives were available, such as the practice of 'wild tourism' (*turizm*), which served as a low-budget alternative to Party-run package tours to 'heroic' and educational cultural sites. If the latter were designed to serve up 'rituals of reassurance' to the general public,[17] 'wild tourism' was nothing more elaborate than what we would now call 'backpacking', but it was more liberating in terms of what one learned and where. Hitching and hiking were inextricably linked as families and groups of young adults explored the countryside using a network of hostels and cheap lodgings. Although this practice dipped in popularity during the 1950s, according to historian Anne E. Gorsuch – possibly due to lack of support under Stalin – it was back in time for the emergence of youth cultures and alternative lifestyles during the 1960s, after Khrushchev's conversion to hitch-hiking and the idea of voucher or coupon systems.[18]

Dennis Zuev considers the work of the AVP as being part of that 'wild tourism' tradition, with its many hitchhiking expeditions across Russia to propagate the ideals of free travel and peaceful coexistence, but also through its latest manifestation: the 'Home for All' (HFA) project. This sees the AVP renting a property well away from its Moscow base, which then becomes a springboard to encourage knowledge of 'free travel' in the neighbouring community and to show that people can live communally and manage them-selves outside of the official tourist industries. The HFA project encourages social mixing between visitors and locals, to prove that people are the same; no matter where the outreach work is taking place, the language of the AVP is one of inclusivity, tolerance and egalitarianism. 'Let's do it with joy', Krotov says at one point in *A practical guidebook for free travellers*, 'it is an op-portunity to find, feel, and share the feeling of brotherhood of all humanity!'[19]

Reading Anton's informative pocketbook guide, it is hard not to notice the sense of paternalism and prescriptive tone of how free travel and the HFA ought to be done – as he is caught between being an initiator of a project in public view and responding to those who take part but may have different ideas about it. The literature and rules for the AVP and HFA make it clear that these are not democracies, yet decentralised decision-making cultures do not evolve overnight; it may confirm Dennis Zuev's point that the long legacy of top-down sports and adventure clubs in Russia will inevitably continue to have an impact.[20] If they are struggling to reconcile their different notions of liberty – free from the tourist industry and State structures, but not choosing more participatory processes themselves – they wouldn't be the first to founder. The influential feminist hitchhiker Tatyana Kozyreva, whose travels and publications (700,000 kilometres and nine books) match those of her friend Anton, has been particularly vocal about the sexism inherent within the Russian hitchhiking scene specifically, and it is likely that many issues remain unresolved in the clubs described here, which language barriers prevent me from commenting upon.[21]

Heading westward from Moscow, it's clear that, in contrast to the AVP and HFA, the European Hitchhiker Gatherings (EHGs) are grounded in more anarchistic organisational principles, in keeping with the generation of 'Occupy', with an expectation that each person will have a voice in how events are run. However, when Jona Redslob and his friends set about their own outreach work during the organisation of the 2011 EHG, they probably wished that it had been as simple as one person supplying a grid reference, a picture of the Bulgarian beach at Kara Dere and a 'see you there with a tent' posting somewhere in cyberspace!

The selection of venues for the EHGs occurs through a voting process on www.Hitchwiki.org, which comes with its own challenges if proposed campsites have not been reconnoitred and the desire to have a scenic rather than accessible location triumphs. Jona's team who assembled in Magdeburg six months in advance had some thinking to do: the beach location was 200 metres away from the nearest water source, the shops considerably further, and there was some uncertainty as to whether enough shade was available if the event coincided with a very hot spell of weather. The organisers would have to arrive (by thumb) in good enough time to organise the different communal requirements of fire sites, latrines and wind breaks, and to haul large sacks of rice to the site, well in advance of the anticipated 150 hitchhikers. Then there were negotiations to be had with the 'locals', a problem which Anton's HFA did not usually have, as the participants were not wild camping.

The Bulgaria decision was part of a deliberate strategy of broadening the international hitching network. It also made a lot of sense: here was a country with a strong domestic hitching tradition and a good reputation for welcoming travellers. Just as Poland and Czechoslovakia had seen a blossoming of new youth culture movements and musical experimentation in the late 1960s, so Bulgaria had forged its own alternative lifestyles, into which hitchhiking fitted.[22] Coincidentally, Bulgarian hitchhiking was achieving a minor moment of art-house cinema fame, through the international distribution of Konstantin Bojanov's 2011 film *Avé*, which featured a road trip by two characters, each at a turning point in life, and whose journey together contains many authentic kinds of travel situations (uplifting, awkward and banal).

For all of these organisational differences, the EHG and the AVP events are similar in content: these are opportunities to exchange experiences and knowledge about life on the road and the issues which they and wider political forces bring to it. There will be everything one might have at a small music festival – performers, discussions, films, quiet spaces, health-and-safety information, communal eating and dancing. For a few days, these gatherings of hitchhikers become small alternative societies – 'temporary autonomous zones', to coin Hakim Bey's famous phrase – embodying the principles of *Dama* – everyone looking after one another.

Hitchhikers have banded together *as hitchhikers* on many occasions, as we have seen throughout the book, but the digital age adds the extra dimension of knowledge of other hitchhiking traditions and their current concerns. This information often comes through Hitchwiki.org news bursts – a new book, a transport conference, a postgraduate student's survey to fill in – or the announcement of a new development in the hitchhiker racing season. Then there are the really unusual moments when it seems as if all the hitchhikers across the globe are united by one single piece of inspirational theatre.

Alexej Vorov unites the world

In October 2014 I logged onto Hitchwiki.org to be greeted with the alarming news that the finals of the Transglobe Autostop Competition had been cancelled due to the political and military instability in Ukraine. Alexej Vorov – the initiator of the event in 1992 – had spent years organising the logistics, including the preliminary rounds, such as the one which Jona Redslob had taken part in as part of the Deutsche Trampsport Gemeinschaft (DTSG) team.

It must have been an easy but terrible decision to make. Everyone was wondering if Ukraine would turn into a bloodbath, open up a new Cold War frontline over the matter of whether its wobbly democratic government would opt for closer ties with the European Union or with Moscow. No doubt, Alexej's compatriot Anton Krotov was also watching, as he had announced over a year before that the HFA in July and August 2014 would take part in Ukraine (in Lvov, which is in the west). I like to imagine that there was a phone call between them – there is a mutual respect I believe, despite different club approaches. After all, each was individually finding a way to formulate a similar question: something along the lines of 'how can I positively respond to this?'

There's a reason why these men are revered, and it's not just that they are amongst the 'best' hitchhikers the world has ever seen, or that they initiate inspirational projects. It's their commitment to a vision of a common humanity, and the importance of demystifying power, artifice and misinformation in order to connect with real people. To those who know Anton and Alexej, how they chose to respond was probably no surprise at all. Anton decided to situate his HFA in the area of Ukraine that was most contested at the time – Sevastopol in Crimea – effectively annexed by Russia in those months. To my knowledge, plenty of people came and the event passed off without incident.

Alexej opted to try to prove that the people of the world were better at helping each other and living in cooperative harmony than spreading hatred and intolerance. His aim was to circumnavigate the northern hemisphere in 500 hours (or twenty-one days). The quicker the time, he said, the more friendly the world would have shown itself to be:

> Bearing the world's longest record in hitchhiking (close to 1.2 million miles) and having travelled the roads of many countries, I know quite well that our world is mostly inhabited by nice and friendly people. I feel it vile and stupid to hate those with whom you shared long hours on the road, those whom you assisted to change the wheel, those who offered you their hospitality. Smile at the world, and it will smile back.
>
> But what to do about those who can only see the world in distorting mirror of the TV screen? I have no humanity-saving recipes to offer. Yet, there is something that one man can do. So....[23]

Wow, I thought. For all of the races and epic journeys I had been writing about, this seemed in a different league altogether. It was exactly what Pippa Bacca and Silvia Moro had been trying to do with their 'Brides for Peace' performance, except they had not put a time limit on it. What would happen if something also went horribly wrong with Alexej's journey, given all he'd said? What if he took much longer than planned? Competing against the clock often goes against the temporal 'grain' of hitchhiking: it just doesn't feel right. But what did I know? I'd never tested the clock over such an enormous distance.

Alexej had already set off before I started to follow his journey, but it wasn't difficult. He'd got his virtual support team and his GPS avatar was heading east – three days in – across the vastness of Russia towards Vladivostok. From what I could glean, the autumnal conditions on the kerbsides looked more akin to a hard winter in the West. But this was another day at the office for Alexej and he was pretty visible in his yellow and red 'professional hitchhiking suit', whatever the conditions threw at him. For all of this, he was still staying true to his promises of posting a daily snapshot of at least one of his drivers, with a summary of their time together and any views shared about his epic journey.

The days slipped by. My son would come home from school and ask 'how far has that guy got now?' It all felt a bit unreal. How was Alexej feeling, given that he was having only two rest days whilst on planes across the Pacific and Atlantic Oceans? He was trying to make do with minimal sleep on land, which was just as well in some places – nodding off by the side of the road in subzero temperatures is life-threatening. Maybe he was motivated by those he knew were watching him in St Petersburg and beyond. I kept checking social media: no English-language tweets, but some international chatter on the Yahoo hitcher's group: Robert Prins helpfully forwarded a message from Ralf Platschowski (one of the founders of DTSG in 2012 – the team that Jona raced for – and a close friend of Alexej's) with the strapline 'let nobody say you are too old to hitchhike!' Well, he should know, as this was exactly the kind of crazy thing Robert would do, as a breaker of plenty of hitching records himself.

Meanwhile, after landing in Seattle and getting through the Rocky Mountains, Alexej had slowed down and then ground to a halt. Oh no, the US Mid-West – farm country stereotypes, maybe they thought it was a Greenpeace stunt what with the fluorescent gear! It didn't help that the news was full of suffering in Syria, Iraq (and Ukraine), everyone seemed on terror alert and closer to home the xenophobic UK Independence Party was gaining far too much publicity. Would the beacon of hope that was Alexej Vorov prove the world wrong?

Finally, he got to the east coast of the USA, but plane delays and complications meant he lost a day and had to start in Europe from Madrid, not Lisbon. My son started doing some calculations on the route-finder to estimate the time back to St Petersburg: 4,500 kilometres of driving time, or four and a half days. But Alexej had only four days and he was in Spain, one of the slower countries. I didn't dare look for a couple of days. It just seemed so overwhelming an idea, what he was doing; that he might actually make it still felt unreal. He's in Switzerland now, has negotiated the urban sprawl of Zurich, but it's dark and there's a long way to go still.

Then suddenly, incredibly, his web tracker avatar was positioned over Vilnius, with just twenty-four hours to go! Yes! I nearly burst into tears. If there is anywhere you want to be in the world with a hitchhiking deadline, it's Vilnius! It's only the distance from London to Edinburgh I reasoned – even I could do that, aged forty-nine; right now, he's the best hitcher in the world (and getting some well deserved sleep at the home of some members of the Vilnius Hitchhiking Club).

In the early hours of the morning of 22 October 2014, with eighteen hours to spare, Alexej arrived back home, having covered nearly 19,000 kilometres! Whilst no doubt Robert Prins was calculating that journey's place in road history statistics, I was thinking of it in terms of utopian plans, of alliances and networking. How could we turn this into something big, make this a bigger example of international unity? What did he say to the press in St Petersburg? Now I really did wish I could speak Russian! Later I checked in again with Jona, who had also been watching. He'd had no doubts at all: 'I knew he'd make it'.

Alexej is not the first adventurer to respond to the politics of their time with such a personal statement, nor will be the last hitchhiker to head out in search of the cooperation which they know is out there in the world, as an antidote to negativity. If a story such as Alexej's can capture the imagination of my son's generation, then the mutual-aid baton has been successfully passed on. What our trawl through the contemporary hitchhiking scene in former communist nations and their impact on the twenty-somethings of the West (the cohort of Jona Redslob) has told us is that there is a sense of unity through diversity which brings hope; that in the strange worlds of hitchhiking competitions or 'free traveller' expeditions to 'open a country', there are still common principles of association, and that whole societies are capable of turning their economies and social structures to align themselves with more cooperative transport methods given the commitment to it. We may not all be able to get to EHGs or learn Russian to feel comfortable at one of Anton's HFA events, but we can be aware of and take inspiration from them and the long-standing traditions upon which they are founded.

Narratives of hope boost us psychologically as well as providing templates for what is possible. As mental health becomes more critical as the climate crisis deepens, it is vital that we build up collective resilience through better tales and more empathetic listening to one another. So, although we know that it makes pragmatic sense to organise our societies more cooperatively in so many areas, the psychological and mental health benefits of trying to turn each of our journeys into an occasion for building community also need attending to. How we feel about ourselves as citizens on a planet in crisis is itself part of the politics of the freedom to go.

A prescription for hitchhiking? Travel and talk in the age of pandemics and extinction

Vagabond counselling

I knew something was wrong within seconds of getting into Peter's car. It was early evening, already dark and I'd just started a fairly straightforward hitchhike from Bradford to my old university town of Lancaster in north-west England, where my girlfriend of the time was still studying. Friday traffic was very reliable and I expected the 100-mile journey to take between two and three hours, which it did. Peter's was perhaps the fourth vehicle to pass me on the motorway slip road.

If the car that stops for you has no passengers, the driver directs you into the seat beside them, so communication is easier. Up to that point, nobody had ever asked me to get into the back of a car, so my alarm bells were jingling a little as I absorbed Peter's tale of a stressful afternoon earlier on, when he had been driving a sixteen-wheeler truck. Watching my reactions in the rear-view mirror, Peter offered to take me all the way to Lancaster if I didn't mind us detouring into Manchester for him to 'check on something'. I couldn't see a problem; this was the serendipity of the road: both of us should get something out of the arrangement.

We passed the miles amicably enough. Although he was clearly on edge about something connected to one of the deliveries, we still chatted good naturedly about our favourite pubs and late-night curry houses in Bradford and what hitchhiking was like 'these days'. I gradually relaxed and became more bemused than fearful, even as the roads turned from motorway to dual carriageway to the Manchester backstreets and deserted factory complexes with minimal street lighting.

'It's just down here', I heard him say, as we swung on to an unlit bumpy cinder track that seemed to lead nowhere. My heart rate increased notice-ably and I found myself flicking though the geographical options if this turned ugly. For the first and only time in my hitchhiking career, I fleetingly wondered whether this was really going to be 'it', and I would be the subject of the next day's headlines, but it still didn't make sense (why would he give me the option of hitting him over the head by putting me on the back seat?). We came to a halt with the car headlights focused on an unremarkable brick wall next to some wrought-iron gates.

'There', he said, pointing to the edge of the brickwork, 'that's where I thought I clipped the wall with my trailer. Can you see anything?'

Peering hard, I found myself almost laughing with relief: 'No it looks all right to me'. We hadn't even got out of the car. Peter sat for a moment thinking, reversed, and we drove north in near silence for half an hour, whereupon I opted out of the ride early to save him the extra miles. Just as I was about to scramble out, he turned and fixed me a slightly pitiful stare: 'So, you've only just met me, but do you think I am all right?'

The novice counsellor in me took over and for the best part of an hour we sat in a deserted lay-by and talked about his problems, which involved marital strain and the fear of losing his job. Peter worried about 'thinking too much' and whether or not to tell his wife about 'this evening' (which should have been spent down the pub). It was quite intense.

At the time I felt quite proud of myself, having dealt sensitively with another unusual situation which the road had thrown up. What I didn't think about for quite a number of years was how much of an admission Peter's would have been in other contexts. Masculine vulnerability was not something I associated with long-distance lorry drivers; however lonely and monotonous the job could be, there was a lot of pride in being able to put in those miles and hours, in being in command of their mobile homes. In the late 1980s, mental health issues were marginalised and stigmatised in public life, with few spaces for conversation and little in the way of infrastructure which could be confidentially accessed by employees. Even with a trade union to support them, a lorry driver would feel very isolated broaching issues of depression and anxiety.

At that point in my life I interpreted my very regular rides in truckers' cabs as being a combination of my astute tactical positioning and some half-baked idea about roadside solidarity. That I might be needed to provide some kind of psychological reassurance, and in Peter's case confirmation that he had probably imagined causing minor damage to a wall, just wouldn't have occurred to me.

In ordinary circumstances, most people give lifts for two reasons: to repay past hitchhiking debts and because they want company. There's some limited evidence to back this up, but surveys rarely ask drivers; they tend to infer this from the hitchhikers themselves, which does not provide much insight into the personal specifics of why a driver wants to talk to a stranger, beyond simply lessening the loneliness of the journey. Throughout the book we've touched on the social, economic and educational benefits of hitchhiking; now, as I write the final pages, the mutual mental health benefits of hitchhiking and sharing the road have been given added weight by the psychological impact of the COVID-19 pandemic, as it has transformed everything about our lives, most obviously our abilities to converse in person.

How are we going to travel together in the future? Will we want to go as far, meet new people, learn about them in the same way? What have we gained in the hiatus in terms of self-awareness about our emotional needs and how this corresponds to the stark realities of economic and ecological crisis which the pandemic has bequeathed us?

Some have already begun to answer these questions: the European Hitchhiker Gathering of 2021 at the time of writing was being planned online and the location selected, lockdowns permitting; many of its potential participants have thumbed lifts with masks on during the pandemic across Germany, Scandinavia and Hungary – reporting equal levels of incredulity, admiration and (understandably) suspicion. All of the participatory issues discussed in the previous chapter are back, including the conundrum of whether or not to select a 'host' country on the basis of criteria regarding regressive political stances taken over the pandemic – especially on LGBTQ and race issues. Most of those on the online hitchhiking lists are half my age and sharing all kinds of personal information about their mental health, which is a good thing in terms of emotional literacy, but it is a reminder that this is a generation facing up to global economic recession and the prospects of civilisational breakdown even if all fossil-fuel emissions stopped tomorrow.

There is a lot to talk about whether one should be masked up on a local car-share scheme, 'slugging' into San Francisco or assessing the wildfire risk of a long hitch across Siberia. Before the pandemic, it was rare to hear transport policy discussions even touch upon the topic of the social (and thereby economic) value of conversation, yet somehow I think the new world we are adapting to will frame these things differently. For this final exploration of the historical importance of hitchhiking, I want to try to play vagabond psychologist rather than sociologist and look at the wider health benefits which travelling together can bring to an understanding of ourselves (vaccines, masks and 'health passports' notwithstanding).

When I first started hitchhiking in 1982, few people talked about 'eco-psychology' or the relationship between person and planet. In those early days on the road, one or two books which described the world in this way may have graced my backpack, but I had not really connected that amazing feeling of cooperative possibility which hitchhiking gave me with the idea of healing or trauma. Yet, how I came to write this book is very much a story of extrapolating from the personal to the political. Twenty years after Peter's confessions to me in a lay-by near Preston, it was my turn to be undone by the pressures of work, and to be looking for some kind of epiphany to help re-energise me.

Lonely in nature

It had arrived on the morning of 7 January 2007, in a cottage on the North York Moors of England, where I was taking some much-needed recuperation from my academic job. My body had folded in on me as I'd been about to get on a train at the start of another prospective fifty- or sixty-hour week. Staff cuts, caring for my parents with Parkinson's disease and helping to bring up my young son had all conspired to send me a very clear signal that it was time to stop. Now here I was, lying in bed, signed off sick and reading a book, as the rain squalls pattered onto the Velux windows above.

The book was *Swimming to Antarctica* by the American long-distance swimmer Lynne Cox. Early on she shatters the record for swimming the English Channel, at only sixteen years of age. Two years later, in 1975, she is fighting the currents of Cook Strait, willed on by the New Zealand media, its prime minister and a flotilla of small boats. Suddenly, it starts to go wrong and she's going backwards, as the currents change and even her incredible strength begins to ebb. Out of nowhere a pod of dolphins glide up to her, clicking and chattering to each other, and form a protective corridor around her as she battles the swells in a notorious shark section of the swim. Rejuvenated, Lynne ploughs on, the dolphins staying with her until she's through the worst, before vanishing into the depths as swiftly as they appeared. She makes the shore of South Island.

Anyone who spends time in the natural world knows how interdependent it is, how traits such as cooperation and empathy are not just confined to the higher mammals and primates. Now, almost too late, there are signs that we have realised how important this is for our own survival as a species, as every week brings another example of an ecosystem threatened by the imbalances of the Anthropocene. The utilitarian aspects of our thinking about nature were exactly the kinds of thing which I tried to include in my lectures on the media, although sometimes having a professional hat on inured me to a more empathetic reaction to ecocide. Yet, on that bleak winter morning, Lynne Cox's account utterly overwhelmed me: interspecies communication and mutual aid, the uniting of people and planet. Beauty and hope flowed back into my world. I felt empowered by the sense of possibility and new direction. Lacing up my boots, I set off into the watery gales to mull over my epiphany.

It was a classic Romantic reaction to the world, as strong as that moment outside of Grasmere in 1982 on my first day's hitchhike, as I got out of my fifth and last car, and gazed around, stunned by what I had done. This time, it was less a case of discovering an 'amazing truth' about the world, more discovering that we needed to act on that truth, and perhaps I now had the social vocabulary to help facilitate this process. I knew that I wanted to focus those feelings of empathy and cooperation, stirred by Cox's cross-species encounter, into a sociological lens for how we live and travel, to increase connectivity in the world and live fuller and more equal lives as a result. Up to that date, much of my writing had been about environmental protest and marginal or oppositional lifestyles, trying to understand them utilising concepts drawn from the anarchist tradition: self-organisation, mutual aid, cooperation, anti-authoritarian and local.

Hitchhiking seemed to be the perfect continuation of this, being both of the margins and yet central to thinking about where we are going as a society (and a species). It took me quite a few hours of blustery ruminations and a lot of coffee to begin to conceive of a plan. But maybe I should have been reading the roadside runes a little differently: the previous day's huge heathery hike had taken me through the remote village where I had recently hitched with my partner and infant son; back at the cottage I had put my sore feet up to watch 'Sissy Hankshaw actress' Uma Thurman wielding large swords instead of thumbs; and only a week previously I'd had the pleasure of hearing my friend James Bar Bowen perform his beautiful new Kiwi hitchhiking song 'She is' (see Chapter 3). Cult American hitchhiker Irv Thomas (discoverer of Charles Brown Jr – see Chapter 1) would have seen these synchronicities as indicative of my destiny, whereas for me it was all about how I was seeing the world now that I had got off the bureaucratic competitive treadmill.

Being in a vulnerable position makes you look at the world differently; it is a 'liminal' state between the comfortable familiar and the terrors of sliding into the unknown. Romanticism comes out of such moments – where an emotional reaction to the ills of the world fosters a desire to connect with something greater than ourselves. The wounded individual aligns with the suffering of others and sees new forms of freedom and justice, but not bound by the limitations of a theological framework. Our Alaskan Highway hitchers (Chapter 6) were channelling this legacy of the Enlightenment, and in their driven personalities I suggested that they may even be regarded as 'outriders' of an empathic evolution yet to be realised, one where our species is more at ease with itself and the ecosystem.

To say that this can be hard conceptual work is an understatement. In her philosophical memoir *Thumbing it: a hitchhiker's ride to wisdom*, Dutch anthropologist Barbara Noske writes about how being by the roadside connects her to a more 'animal' side of herself, where self-care when travelling highlights the vulnerabilities we face once the layers of technology are stripped away. For her, the road has provided nearly forty years of insight on the relationship between human and animal cultures (her academic specialism) as well as some stark and troubling ruminations on the loneliness of being an independent-minded female traveller (Chapter 9).[1] In contrast, male writers sometimes talk about isolation as an existential form of vulnerability, as young Russian author Igor Savelyev puts it in his autobiographical novella *The pale city*: 'You suddenly realise that you're alone on that bleak and endless highway. The realisation is always so sudden and strong enough to take your breath away. The sense of solitude is striking, almost palpable, and infinitely more intense than the loneliness you feel in a city.'[2]

I've never been anywhere like the highways of Siberia, or found myself hitching beneath signs indicating that the distance to the next habitation is a three-digit number; nor have I ever felt any more alarmed whilst with a stranger (bad driving aside) than in my encounter with Peter from Bradford. However, I do understand that in the Anthropocene, the loneliness described by Noske and Savelyev may be a healthy, even respectful reminder of our place in the ecosystem. It is the kind of argument used by eco-psychologists and neo-Luddites such as Chellis Glendinning (Chapter 6), who see in our technological systems evidence of the trauma that is at the heart of our separation from nature and each other: we no longer behave as a functioning species able to contain, sustain and communicate with itself. For anarchist anthropologists such as Noske, we will struggle to re-heal or re-enchant ourselves back into those relationships, because the very structures and inequalities of our societies are more likely to exacerbate problems of mental health and loneliness (and consumer culture will encourage individual rather than collective solutions).

A gene for hitchhiking

Why we are lonely – in institutions, in cities, in traffic, in political systems, in relationships, on social media – is all too often a matter of how we misperceive and channel our relationship to 'power'. In Chapter 4, we looked at this in terms of the concept of ambivalence and how we dehumanise others through the creation of social as well as geographical distance; how communication and thereby empathy is easily inhibited. Terrifying though this can be, we also found that in the most dire conflict and trauma, people are capable of helping one another on the road or sheltering those at risk of persecution. Recently, whilst ploughing through the deluge of current literature on levels of social isolation and geographical loneliness, I came across a lovely argument from 'evolutionary biology' that tries to explain how we cope with these contradictions as set against the time it took 'us' to foster cooperative group strategies.

Next time you are in a relatively quiet part of town, or on a path somewhere in the countryside, think how hard it is to ignore a person coming the other way. You want to greet them or at least make eye contact, even when it's a cool teenager draped in wires and devices. This is because we are biologically hardwired to acknowledge others, which means that when we are in a city we're 'acting' until an incident makes us snap out of role and we help a passer-by who has fallen over or needs assistance to cross the road. It's why the eccentric stranger who says 'hello' to us in a bustling street has not got it wrong; their body 'thinks' it should be behaving more sociably, and is fighting the cultural anomie that a few centuries of concentrated living have imposed on it (they may also be feeling lonely).

The COVID-19 social-distancing measures and isolated living have taught us many things about our natures, reminding us of those moments deep in our genetic history when we realised that the social costs of not being cooperative were too prohibitive to ignore. We are at precisely that moment again, hundreds of thousands of years later, our mutual survival dependent on acting collectively for the good of the tribe, however unequal its structure. One of the few benefits to have come out of the pandemic has been the resurgence of mutual-aid groups in many countries, expressions perhaps of an underlying genetic truth that cooperative genes really can dominate when there is a collective crisis in any ecosystem![3] Staying local has made us concentrate more on what that means, in terms of the relative strength of our immediate geographical ties, all of which can have demonstratable health benefits, triggered by regular use of the problem-solving and reward centres of the brain. This is what the evolutionary psychologist Susan Pinker calls 'the village effect'.[4] Feeling connected to our community as a result of the pandemic and working from home alters our view of travel – it may make us feel happier and less alienated now that we may not need to do the routine packed Tube trains or gridlocked roads quite so often. Travel as a form of community in some parts of the world may alter irreversibly; in others, where not everyone uses or wants to use Zoom, life may look similar to how it was three or four years ago. What we don't know yet is whether our renewed desire for company will offset the concerns of communication analysts such as Sherry Turkle that the use of social media does not reward us as much as real conversation.[5]

But let's uncurl a bit from our foetal position in front of a screen meeting and think about how hitchhiking has and might continue to 're-enchant' the experience of being on the road through conversation, right from that first 'automobile panhandle' by Charles Brown Jr in October 1916, where we began our journey.

A talking cure

Several things happened outside Fort Wayne, Indiana, that day. We saw the imagining of a new mode of transport, when the good doctor stopped at Charles's hail and, in that same moment, the emergence of something else: a mobile 'confessional space'. This was somewhat different from that offered by a horse-drawn carriage or railway compartment; as an exclusively private environment, it freed both parties up for conversations that could exist outside of their usual life worlds. As such, the potential for all kinds of cross-cultural understanding became possible, to form what in other contexts I have called 'discursive bridges', these being free associational connections between groups who usually live quite 'ambivalent' lives from each other, on account of the divisions created by economics, religion, politics and geography.[6]

These informal contingencies of history matter. Put in terms of their potential social value, the impact of millions of unknown interactions over the last century are difficult to calculate, being precisely the aspects of human behaviour, under the economic radar, which are essential to the 'well-being' of a society, yet which do not fit into conventional frameworks of productivity. This is why economists have become more interested in 'happiness indicators' (Chapter 7), as there is a realisation that people are not just economic automatons performing to assumed rational patterns of behaviour. Depression and loneliness impact heavily on an economy, we know, yet few talk about it in terms of commuting, as the 'motor frontier' ideal of everyone as an individual car-owner benefiting from the freedom to go is now so obviously stalled in gridlock and frustration.

So, if we can't immediately change the infrastructure of jammed roads, perhaps we can introduce some new frameworks for thinking about what we could bring to the more 'lonely' spaces of mobility. There is plenty of precedent in other walks of life: the social care sector, for instance, in England, has begun to provide listeners and companions for folks of my late parents' generation who were isolated in their own homes with mental or physical health issues. No longer able to socialise in public, conversation had to come to them.

This is a demographic who have seen most of the motor age, witnessed the growth of post-war car-oriented culture, suburbanisation, the decline of public services during the neo-liberal era and the fragmenting of the extended family and yet whose talk of community is often misplaced for nostalgia. However we read these events, their pace is undeniable, which is why, when we talk of travel as a potential form of community, at some level this has to be an educational as well as practical issue. The 'smart thinking' required to help alleviate the isolation and 'dead time' of driving is exactly the same as with those who are lonely at home: mental health, the economy and the art of conversation are inextricably linked. Careless (lack of) talk costs lives!

You can't really plan one's communication needs, and a short-distance casual carpool ride into a city centre may not provide the time or anonymity of my ride with Peter, but it still may oil the cogs of community when one just wants a burst of serotonin rather than a major heart-to-heart. I've always thought the idea of a 'friendship bench' at primary schools – like the one in Yorkshire where my son went – was a really bold idea: that we might signal our need for a bit of company. Perhaps we need a 'conversation corner' at a motorway service station; better still, why aren't mental health charities like the Samaritans staking out such places and offering their help?

Societies have always had to find a space to cater for their citizens' mental well-being in some way. Religious confession fulfilled this purpose for an aeon (however reprehensible the idea of 'sin' may be) but in the age of modernity the psychoanalyst's couch, the newspaper problem pages, help lines, anonymous user groups such as Alcoholics Anonymous and, more recently, the online chat room: all have served as places for catharsis and facilitating self-knowledge.

'Vagabond counselling' may not cut it yet as a professional service, but it is anonymous and stands outside of formal power structures, which may have some advantage if one is in a country which persecutes particular lifestyles or attitudes. If Peter had turned to me and said 'I'm gay, but my wife doesn't know', I probably wouldn't have reacted any differently from how I did, but a priest or a therapist in some parts of the world might have regarded this confession very differently. Hitchhiking books are full of anecdotes where 'I've never told anyone this before' is as ubiquitous as 'I picked you up because there are a lot of crazy people out there'. These are 'establishing' moments between strangers, a confessional intimacy made possible by anonymity, which signals one's integrity. Few guidebooks or travellers' websites pay attention to the art of listening, but everyone realises pretty quickly that for all of their own 'scripted' questions and raising of unthreatening topics (like at the hairdressers), they may be required to take on the role of 'road analyst'.

My conversation with Peter only underscored what I already knew about the lonely, repetitive life of a driver: it was being a nomad without any of its benefits, owing to the monotonous journeys linking unremarkable and indistinguishable depots, ports and lorry parks. The pressures of deadlines and ever-busy roads, added to the sense of isolation, reinforce the politics of divide and rule, a fact well known to those using solitary confinement as a punishment in military or penal contexts.

Podcasts and internet access may have taken the edge off some of the long-distance loneliness, just as citizens' band (CB) radio served to build solidarity amongst hauliers in the 1970s and 1980s. Those venturing into mainland Europe may have benefited from listening to Radio Luxembourg, which used to run an impressive ride-share show called 'Je route pour vous' ('I drive for you'). For some years in the 1970s, the station arranged link-ups between cross-continental truckers (in particular) and hitchhikers, who would ring into the station to announce their intended routes and times. These would be coordinated in a similar manner to how we now match up the various requirements online, the difference being that these were two specific travelling demographics who were being encouraged to spend time together.

It is rare for mainstream radio stations to mention hitchhiking unless there is a petrol shortage or bad weather, or a local charity event is passing through a particular area. Given the obsession of these programmes with traffic flows, accidents and the sheer waste of time that constitutes sitting on a jammed motorway, maybe they could do a little more to promote a new social initiative to reduce the stresses of road users, by keeping a look-out for the Conversation Corps (coming to a reality near you).

Hitchhiking apprenticeships

I like to imagine members of this imaginary Conversation Corps as being a mixture of 'gap year' student and Peace Corps volunteer. They will be nominally supported or sponsored by a range of philanthropic organisations that work to alleviate mental health problems and that use counter-intuitive techniques to bring people together. The Conversation Corps will be part of their outreach programmes: designed to directly impact on the loneliness of drivers and, through public visibility, encourage greater empathy between road users. Hitchhikers signing up to the programme will 'follow the road' for six months – without returning home – and keep actual and virtual diaries of where they have been and who put them up for the night, in order to earn a special 'ambassador of humanity' diploma. As an uplifting example of reality television, a batch of travellers dipping their thumbs into the hidden gift economies which all societies possess seems as good a way of bringing people together as any other. If it worked for *Peking express* on Dutch television or the BBC's *Race across the world*, I am sure that this exercise in quirky philanthropy would find a home with audiences.

There is an inspiring precedent here. It is called the Confederation of European Journeymen: a guild of trades folk, who for over a century have been conducting a form of road-based apprenticeships – once on foot or horse and cart, now by hitchhiking – as the final part of learning a craft in order to be considered a fully rounded individual. Based largely in Germany, France and Switzerland, it is a test of the apprentices' skills at self-reliance; they are asked to stay on the road for up to three years, relying on the generosity of others – exchanging work for lodgings – and going no nearer than fifty kilometres to their place of origin. This is 'slow travel' or 'hitching time' at its best (Chapter 2) – exploring place and people with little mediation – and as skilled blacksmiths, carpenters, bakers, roofers, they are expected to move on regularly, to keep learning about new situations, not spending more than three months in any one place.[7]

If that sounds impressive – check out their fantastic attire! The Journeymen (and women) wear corduroy bell-bottom trousers, waistcoats and bowler hats, walk with a sturdy wooden staff and bear their very limited belongings in a colourful fabric wrap. A fair few of them carry musical instruments. Their look gives them a respectability and badge of honour amongst the public, of the sort reserved for pilgrims or monks; indeed, many assume that they have a medieval legacy, on account of their appearance and the longevity of the guild system itself.

With numbers estimated at around 7,000, the Confederation apprentices are sufficiently thin on the ground as to be a novelty over a large geographical area – a useful yardstick perhaps for our Corps. This matters in terms of public relations: for all of the moments in this book where hitchhiking received a boost due to official approval, there's always a moral panic around the corner, or instances where people have felt that their generosity has been tested. Even the traveller-friendly policies of prime minister Pierre Trudeau, who opened up a string of youth hostels in 1970 along the new Trans-Canada highway, to cater for the thousands of young hitchers he was encouraging to get out and see their country came in for criticism.[8] To avoid such repetitions, we require both sensitive media coverage as to the purpose of our Corps, and codes of conversational conduct to ensure a reliability of service, as well as a few forms to keep the insurance people happy.

We'll need them to look presentable, so for any launch event we'll have to enlist the support of some of our Lithuanian and Russian contacts to advise on exactly what the Corps uniform is going to look like so that it doesn't duplicate Alexej Vorov's definitive 'professional hitchhiking suit' that sports hitchers use. Something in orange perhaps – the colour of the emotions and enthusiasm and also very much associated with Kinga Freespirit, who was a great ambassador for hitchhiking. It would be apposite to have a Polish connection, given that it has produced the finest organised hitchhiking system anywhere (and still in need of repeating).

Hearing the heart of the nation

So, who is going to be the public face of all of this? Hitchhiking may be a grassroots self-organising form of mobility, but the hitchhiker could be useful as an identifiable figure to relate to: a kind of 'commissioner for conversation', with a bit of road history in their thumbs – somebody like the inspirational humanitarian Ruairí McKiernan, whose work with the youth organisation SpunOut earned him a place as a 'well-being' advisor to the Council of State of Ireland in 2012. Other relevant details on his philosophical CV included bringing the Dalai Lama to Dublin and having thumbed on three continents in his twenties! Asked to prepare a series of public lectures at McGill University Summer School linked to his community work, Ruairí decided to get out on the road again, and record people's views of the state of the Irish nation.

As he was at the time weighed down by his own problems of burnout, this self-styled 'Listening Tour' (or 'Hitchhiking for Hope') became something of a personal and political rebirth, as he reached out to understand others from a position of vulnerability. There was a lot to hear during the month he spent on the road – from the 'cattle mart in Connemara; with the resilient islanders of Inishbofin; with pilgrims on Croagh Patrick; with Orangemen in Derry; office workers in Dublin; monks in Glenstal; community workers in Moyross and tourists on the Hill of Tara'. The message he was getting, as though on a 'lift loop', was that his country had become a land of two tiers, where ordinary people were paying a high psychological price for political and economic mismanagement, as the austerity measures in the fallout from the international financial crisis of 2008 continued to devastate public services and reinforce division. Yet what reinvigorated Ruairí was not just the amazing support he received – accommodation, online funding of his journey, social media getting behind him, quick lifts (longest wait, forty minutes) – but the resilience of people's capacity to seek out each other and reinforce ideas of locality, community and nature as part of 're-imagining the country from the ground up'.[9]

It is an old story, one which we intuitively know, yet journeys such as Ruairí's, or Jacob Holdt's (Chapter 2) or Alexej Vorov's '500 hours around the world' statement against war (Chapter 10) serve to remind us – through their mad flights of fantasy – that hitchhiking provides an empathic litmus test of the cooperative reality of a region, a country, a globe. Perhaps it was instructive that one of the books in Ruairí's backpack was *Man's search for meaning*, by Holocaust survivor Viktor Frankl, whose belief in the power of recovery through trying to make sense of even the direst of human circumstances has nurtured many back from despair.

It would not be a bad book to be reading now, in a pandemic and climate crisis, a reminder perhaps that a Conversation Corps apprentice would have to be prepared to soak up a lot of pain. Even if we envisage our mobile counsellors more as guardian angels than as researchers, they might find that the road can reveal deeper truths about a society than might be gleaned from focus groups or selective opinion polls, hence the value of personal video diaries as snapshots from the road, as though they were a twenty-first-century equivalent of the Mass Observation records kept by ordinary people in England during the Second World War and its aftermath.

I think what Ruairí is getting at in his work and what the idea of a Conversation Corps might contribute to is how to use our sense of well-being – as with those alternative economic indices based around happiness – to facilitate greater participation and accountability in our societies, to help prevent us sliding into terrain where our worst sides prevail. Society-wide epiphanies are, of course, only a few political 'nudges' away, as we've seen throughout the book; one hopes that a more personal dimension to the climate crisis might encourage the urgent redressing of the need to restructure mobility accordingly.

Sometimes having a place adaptable and imaginative enough to nurture progressive shifts is all that is needed.

A Totnes tonic

In the August of 2012, whilst Ruairí McKiernan was pondering ideas which would eventually motivate his Listening Tour, my family was in need of our own revitalisation, following a series of bullying incidents – at school, at work, whilst campaigning and by reactionary neighbours – which had left us shaken. We headed off, by public transport, in search of a collective pick-me-up, to one of the few places likely to be able to provide this – the well kept bustling market town of Totnes, in south-west England. For those on the green-left of the political spectrum, it has long enjoyed a reputation as a progressive oasis amidst a wilderness of affluent landowners and parochial attitudes. To the ordinary tourist exploring Devon, Totnes is an appealing, pedestrian-friendly stopping-off point between the heathery horizons of Dartmoor and the commercial overload of the beach resorts of Paignton and Torquay.

Strolling around its narrow streets, one gradually begins to see evidence of a place that knows its own mind. Sure, there's the usual high street fare, but more striking is the rich diversity of independent retailers and a sense that this is an environment where pie-in-the-sky projects actually work. Some of this may have been enabled by the presence of the progressive educational facilities, Schumacher College and the Sands School, which have ensured a throughput of ideas, people and cultural momentum. It's probably why the Transition Town[10] movement began here, with its own parallel currency (the 'Totnes pound'), an advocacy for local food production through the Incredible Edibles network and a good record on car clubs and car-free days. Small enough to make people connected to something, large enough to wander without feeling cramped by obligations: it is one of the most interesting illustrations of what social ecologist Murray Bookchin described as 'urbanisation without cities' (premised on the idea of people freely associating and debating in new forms of the Athenian ideal of the polis, where face-to-face communication – rather than Facebook –is essential).

Just hearing about some of these ventures was inspiring, as we enjoyed a convivial shared lunch, on the banks of the River Dart, with the local Quakers, each of whom seemed to have an armful of ongoing family hitch-hiking stories or thoughts upon the viability of any new car-sharing initiatives. One of these was eighty-three-year-old Julian Brotherton, whose hitchhiking dated back into the late 1940s, when, after National Service, he had found himself odd-jobbing amongst a world of travelling salesmen and itinerant workers, hitching to save money and utilising what was a network of so-called 'commercial hotels'. Often below the official radar, these cheap lodging houses were known to many in poorer parts of the north-east of England: places where one could arrive in town and knock on any door and enquire 'Who puts people up around here?' and be directed to an address. As we talked, it seemed that Julian was describing to me another network of solidarity, of the kind which so many of our travellers throughout the book have accessed. This was how communities got by and supported one another when work or money was uncertain. Such things stay long in the memory, and it didn't surprise me that Julian and his wife Raku were members of the international hospitality network Servas, or even that they had thumbed lifts together only a few years before (he had a leg in plaster, to complete the picture of two septuagenarians by the roadside).

There was no sense of nostalgia or evocations of a golden age of hitch-hiking in Julian's answers to my questions; he didn't believe that people's capacity for empathy had altered in the slightest. In his sweep of hitchhiking across six decades, mutual aid was a constant; what he was concerned about was that the cultural memory of forms of cooperation might be lost. Hitchhiking might come and go, he thought, but there needed to be a constant reminder that people's ability to share and self-organise was central to lived experience, not some quirky life choice.

Re-energised, I set off walking back to the campsite at Stoke Gabriel, but found my thoughts slipping from the obvious progressive transport initiatives which I could see fitting into their Transition Town status, to Julian's reference to the idea of a 'well rounded' citizen. It is an Aristotelian notion, originally used to describe somebody who is civic-minded, trustworthy, good at negotiating and sharing, but which could equally apply to the skills needed to build an ecological society: to experience the gift economy, practise mutual aid, learn consensus decision-making, be happier with less, reach out to the stranger, see yourself as an animal in nature. This seemed to be what the members of Confederation of European Journeymen were doing in their capacity as just-qualified tradesfolk – getting out on the road for the real training. Generations of hitchhikers have (maybe less prescriptively) accumulated these life skills, contributing to the community of the road – and this has made them better debaters, listeners, social navigators. Our imagined Conversation Corps must be more than just a replacement for those roles, but touchstones for a 'vagabond psychology/sociology', where mobility facilitates a better understanding of how our well-being is best served by commonality, not structured opposition to others.

The walk away from Totnes was full of reminders of the strange disparities of the motor age: getting inadvertently involved in the plight of a stranded delivery truck misdirected by sat-nav on to impassable muddy tracks, and the police struggling to locate the driver and haul the thing out; then a series of narrow lanes with high hedges which were not built for the people-carriers or other metal behemoths to pass each other, leading to confusion every few hundred metres and barely faster progress than my own. And yet, around the next corner there was a string of houses, all with roadside stalls outside, each with unattended honesty boxes placed next to vegetable produce, jams, cordials and eggs. There was no one to talk to, but as I paused with a warm glow in my heart at this most trusting of transactions, reading the hand-crafted labels and notes, I felt I could almost have a conversation with the past.

Like beekeeper Tickner Edwardes, setting out a century ago just a few miles along the coast, trying his 'lift luck' with the occasional parson's dray or lumbering hay wagon, searching for peace of mind on the cusp of a new era of mobility, I was in no particular hurry.

Afterword:
the bookcase at the end of the road

When the motor age is at an end, what artefacts will remain to mark the passing of its culture? Will the monuments, archives and visual records pondered over by generations of future schoolchildren tell of how the automobile typified the selfishness of the primitive forms of economics practised until the mid-twenty-first century, when the human race brought itself back from looming extinction? Perhaps these healthier, much longer-lived versions of ourselves, residing on a recovered, less-populated biosphere will chuckle at the idea of expressing one's identity through a mobile device which looked like all of the other ones. Maybe some 'motor age' museum tours will include a macabre 'dungeon of death', which details all of the ways humanity conceived to kill one another; maybe Heathcote Williams's book *Autogeddon* will be revered as a canonical text of prophecy. I'm imagining the hushed silences and puzzled faces, before someone (as happens on every tour) blurts out the obvious question, which always draws groans for their knowing peers: 'Why didn't people share their transport in those times?'

One of the strongest images in my son's current favourite film, *Interstellar*, is a bookcase in a child's bedroom which becomes the communication device to send a message 'through' time to allow those in the present to save the starving mismanaged world from itself. The books themselves convey the message by literally leaping off their shelves in patterns which inspire leaps of imagination in the child and, later, her middle-aged self. I like this image. In the years I have been writing this book and the evidence on climate breakdown has grown more worrying, it has been so easy to feel that our task is insurmountable, that nothing we do will be fast enough. Whenever this happens, I look at my little library of around sixty hitchhiking books – perhaps Bernd Wechner has more but I haven't had the gall to ask him – and think of it as my own world-saving 'message'. It's all there, everything we need, blinking away in my peripheral vision, a 'prophecy of a human memory yet to be socially and politically achieved' in the lovely words of John Berger.[1] So, I like to think, can these books be part of that transformation.

Think about it. What other single-topic collection of books could better represent the evidence of human potentiality, *the best in and best of us*: the incredible generosity and spirit, the innovations in cooperative transport and gift economies, those empathic folks ahead of their time and their alternative visions to the one that has brought our world to a tipping point?

It took Anna Mills, a ninety-seven-year-old resident of Kew, west London, on a wet summer afternoon in 2009 to make me realise that all of the hitchhiking memoirs I was assembling, the online archives I'd trawled, my own limited travelling might be worth something. As I'd listened to her still-vivid experiences of hitchhiking in late-1930s Switzerland as part of the Wandervögel youth movement, I was feeling somewhat flattered by her remark that she had 'always wanted to contribute to something important', but I hadn't grasped the truth of the situation. These were stories she had not even told her own daughter about until relatively recently, a part of history which she could see herself as belonging to. It was the same kind of wisdom which Julian Brotherton had shown (Chapter 11), carefully detailing his perceptions about the role of cultural memory, in the knowledge that there are projects that need to be seen through, tales that are easily lost which reveal far greater things about societies and cultures than many official histories do.

So, here it is, nearly finished, a contribution to that bookcase: a commentary on a hidden history and a sociological observation about our own potential, as realised through a century of hitchhiking. It has been quite a journey, so let's just remind ourselves a little of where we've come from – how we've learned to think like a hitchhiker through the eyes of those roadside ambassadors.

Chronologically first on my bookshelf, *Lift-luck on southern roads* (Tickner Edwardes) sits next to the prickly dreamer Stephen Graham, whose *The gentle art of tramping* evoked dusty tracks and images of Edwardian gentlemen brewing coffee under hedgerows in the 1920s, in an age when purist trampers (such as his friend Vachel Lindsey) didn't really approve of sticking one's thumb or arm out. Laurie Lee did, and his *As I walked out one midsummer morning* is a poignant combination of a young man's adventuring and travel at a time when sections of Europe were gearing up for war. Lee, more than most, set up the art of the accessible literary travel book with a message, and as with Patrick Leigh Fermor, that other prodigious traveller and discoverer of the gifts which fellow humanity can provide, did much to shape the Romantic ideal of the (male) vagabond.

Much of this project has been a study of the gendered nature of the road, with men almost always having a head start on and in the culture of the highway. The worst of the propaganda has been aimed at deterring women or constructing sexist, vulnerable or criminal representations of female hitch-hikers. From the enterprising middle-class 'New York girls' (Chapter 1) to the ordinary working-class women of Moscow in the early twenty-first century, hitchhiking home with the family shopping, the history of hitchhiking is also that of feminism, marking many of the issues and struggles of the times: the different ways that women were treated on the road, how they seized cultural opportunities to construct the idea of women as independent travellers in their own right. It is a shift beautifully captured by Sharon Stine in *Gypsy boots* in 1959, comfortably rolling a cigarette for a lorry driver after spending the previous days on a hitched boat trip down the coast of Norway, realising that her world really has changed.

We see it too in the earlier *Trio's-trek*, whose adventurers, Mary Jaques-Aldridge, Joy Daneman and Nancy Blessley embody that strong-minded female spirit hitchhiking through northern and eastern Africa, challenging themselves and the cultural values underpinning the racism of empire. Then there's *Seven league boots* and remarkable, brave, eternally optimistic globe-trotting Wendy Myers beaming out of the front cover cradling her haversack (as they were called in the 1950s and 1960s), happy in the knowledge that she made it back with only a few scratches. In these two books, we see authors beginning to wrestle with wider questions of justice, as travellers are presented with the ethical dilemmas about the extent to which one should intervene, as Wendy does, taking a baby deserted by a system that wants a male heir to a police station.

Forty years later and on a different continent, Kinga Freespirit also assists a child outcast, this time a victim of slavery, and it is in her writings (and later those of Alyssa Hoseman) that we begin to see the issues of responsible tourism from the roadside manifested. It is always about *ways of seeing*, to use another John Berger term, and this in turn needs to inform how we conduct business and politics with other parts of our planet – cooperatively, with justice, with minimal ecological impact and with empathy.[2]

Most of my little library raises questions about boundaries and the consequences of mobility because of structured inequalities. Those euphoric realisations of Ian Rodger in *A hitch in time* – 'suddenly you could go anywhere' – were ideally suited to the immediate post-war optimism. His implied vision of a future of international cooperation, flags fluttering expectantly as the hitchers gathered at the Fountainbleau Obelisk outside Paris, seem terribly ragged and fragile seventy years later. And yet, even in these most xenophobic of times, Ida and Maurice Piller's advocacy of the possible – 'maybe we will meet a nice person' – haunts anyone who doubts our capacity to bounce back from the brink. Pick up a book about hitchhiking in the former communist world, or listen to interviews with the likes of Alexej Vorov or Anton Krotov, and it is impossible not to feel optimistic about the potential for transport innovations that can serve the common social and ecological good, if only we could encourage policy-makers to employ their hitchhiking genes a bit more regularly.

Glancing at my shelf, I know that some of these empathic 'messages' for our possible future still sell hundreds of copies per year, whereas most are lucky if they are borrowed from a library or found in the most distant corner of a second-hand bookshop. Some are just computer files now, and even unlikely to be available on Kindle, only on 'fast print' to order by oddballs like myself; others are only referenced in books like this one. Curiously, the more that I have become embroiled in the autobiographies of those for whom hitchhiking was one of the high points of their life, the more that I have seen myself as one of those 'characters' from Ray Bradbury's *Fahrenheit 451*, endlessly repeating the rich and secret lives of people whose books have been forgotten (rather than burnt by the authorities) as I pace in deciduous woodland somewhere outside of civilisation, until my dying day.

What set me on this journey may have been an empathic epiphany generated by the experience of an extreme swimmer, but such books inevit-ably offer alternative social topographies and histories. This, I hope, has been a new addition to these literatures and a paean to the art of hitchhiking in all of its beautiful realisations and potentialities. It has been an honour to help tell long-forgotten or little-known tales again, perhaps with a little bit of historical hindsight, artistic licence and smattering of theoretical speculation for good measure. Reading these long-forgotten books is to drink in, again and again, the glimpse of an ideal not yet reached by humanity, where one balances freedom and responsibility in harmony with one's environment. For many of the authors, this is their 'eureka' moment, a series of events that they just had to write about, so impacting were they on an existential level: the glimpse of a different social universe by the kerbside. All of it possible … if only.

It is an infectious thought and one which has sustained my own journey, as different combinations of those stories have leaped off my shelf and re-arranged themselves to help tell this unusual history and remind me of my responsibilities.

Sometimes it feels as though part of me is outside Fort Wayne in 1916, bearing witness to the moment when Charles Brown Jr makes his move into the road, and wanting to believe that those 800 miles were the first of many more, and that maybe they led to a whole history which I have not even touched in my research. Of Woody Guthrie: his journeys so inspiring to make me learn (and perform) a couple of his songs, take out a detailed map of the

USA and plot in felt-tip pen the journeys which he and other contemporaries such as the author of *A land so fair and bright*, Russ Hofvendahl, made during those difficult Depression-era times; to wonder about places such as Barstow, California (the muse of Harry Partch), the humility brought by having to beg from houses, and the joy of those transcendent moments of love with no strings attached.

That day I spent noodling about with films of the Alaska Highway as it is today, from the point of view of an RV driver accompanied by cheesy country-and-western soundtracks and unremarkable commentaries: how it made me think about Lorna Whishaw, alone on a snowy road in 1955, having got out of a vehicle dozens of miles from anywhere at night, to bed down under the trees and be wakened by a porcupine and a brown bear in the morning, as the weather worsened. I thought about the self-belief that had been boosted by friendships up and down the road and her standing amidst the snowy pines and calmly conjuring a potentially lifesaving pair of head-lights out of the horizontal sleet. How I wanted to talk to Lorna (who died in 1999), Ida (2011) to Sharon (?): all those pioneers, who, because of their hitchhiking in the mid-twentieth century, I have always been chasing for an interview or a connection whilst it is still possible. Irv Thomas seemed almost aware of his role as a hitchhiking cult figure and kept updating his 'I am still alive' blog – with the same unbearable 'waits' that no news can invoke (he died in 2013, at eighty-four, only a couple of years after his last hitch). Some of you folks mentioned in this book are very definitely alive – if you are reading this and I have not talked to you already – get in touch, today!

The joy of hitchhiking is of course always tinged with some sadness and there are many who, in the midst of trying to convey their rich individual in-terpretation of that idea, have fallen by the wayside: Kinga (our ambassador), Morgan (our communicator), Pippa (our artist), Chris (our dreamer), Benoît (our voyager), and of course those who have tragically lost their lives either doing what they dreamed of doing, or just trying to get home, because they were in the wrong place at the wrong time.

Yet, as we enter the second century of hitchhiking, those devoted to documenting and articulating it seem even more aware of the importance and responsibilities of that project. Bernd Wechner's question about why few people research hitchhiking seems now to be becoming answered in abundance, as new audiences and fresh minds emerge. It is the generation of Jona Redslob who hold the electronic baton now, coincidently proofreading one of my historical chapters whilst spending time with the administrator of Hitchwiki.org, Mikael Kopel, who rebooted the site in 2015 to include the kind of interactive gizmos that leave me breathless. There are academic departments now, such as the Centre for Mobility Research at the University of Lancaster, that have scratched together the resources to enquire about 'autonomobilities' and held conferences attended by a new generation of researchers into 'slugging', 'train hopping' and, of course, hitchhiking.

In telling my vagabond sociology of the motor age, I have missed out an awful lot of important hitchhikers, especially in countries where English is not the first language, but hopefully the character and purpose of their journeys are captured somewhere in these pages. Nowhere are these more apparent than in what the digital age has offered: countless roadside blogs, YouTube postings, anthropological vignettes and round-table discussions of the state of hitchhiking past and present, as well as an awful lot of roadside silliness for the camera.

It is clear that the spirit of the heyday of hitchhiking is unlikely to return – in that form at least – but as long as there are young folks who, with *Led by destiny* or *A practical guidebook for free travellers* in their rucksacks or with Hitchwiki as a 'favourite' on their handheld telecommunications device of choice, then we have a chance of invigorating the economies of the world into new forms of transport action.

Maybe they – or should we say *you* – will just settle for carpooling to work, or choose to take an ocean freighter rather than a plane, or be brave enough to strike out across country, phone free, not really knowing where you are headed that night. But perhaps, if the sun is shining and the world has done a few good turns for you that morning, some of you may stretch your arm out into the road and bravely meet the eyes of the next automobile driver, ready to pass on your gifts of communication and contribute to a new world of the possible.

Acknowledgements:
a hitchhiker's guide to the journey

This project has spanned many years and circumstances and involved so many people that this is a long list. In the great gift economy, reciprocity is everything, so if I have left you out by accident then I am truly sorry.

Impossible to forget have been the constant belief and dedicated empathy of two unique individuals. My fellow author, musician, sportsman and friend James Bar Bowen has shared this project with a fascination equal to my own over many years and read, edited and contributed ideas to every draft chapter. This has been his book as much as mine and his dedication to it has been unswerving, entertaining and relentlessly pedantic. My debt to long-time colleague Dr Nicole Matthews is similarly profound, for her continuous intellectual enthusiasm and personal encouragement (whether on a Scottish mountain or across twelve time zones). This book is yours too. Thank you.

I wish to thank all of the staff at Manchester University Press who have worked on this book and believed in its vision (including three anonymous reviewers). A personal thank you to Thomas Dark for being a supportive and insightful editor when it came to making tough decisions that retained the view from the passenger's seat. I am grateful for the help of Dr Lucy Burns on visual editing and to Chris Hart and Rebecca Mortimer for marketing the book to the wider world. My diligent copy-editor Ralph Footring deserves a lot of credit for helping to 'beautify' the prose on the final edit and in wise and instructive ways.

This project began gestating around 1993, after half a dozen people met up with the intention of forming a hitchhiking research collective called the Yorkshire Hitching Project. They managed a couple of workshops, compiled a newsletter (*The Frozen Thumb!*) and encouraged a number of dangerous eco-activists to keep hitchhiking diaries. Those people still remain committed to what appears here, and I thank Fiona Weir, Helen Kenwright and Clive Fudge for that enriching springboard; I also thank the diarists for their enthusiasm – Spencer Coake, Chris Swinburne, Claire Manners, Alex Begg, Roxanne Smith, Steve Rumbol, Cathy Ashley, Krayg from Lostwiththiel, James from Faslane Peace Camp – and others who took an interest at that time. Thanks to my Anarchist Research Group colleagues of those days for comment on my work, especially Tom Cahill, Sharif Gemie and Paul Rosen. An important voice throughout this project has been Ste Kenwright, whose interest and songs about life's roads play on in these pages.

To my favourite teacher and Romantic poet, Alan Newton, MA (of Hull), who taught me exceptional life lessons, including hitchhiking and fell walking at night: 'The pastoral mountains front you: face to face'.

To those who saw the long-time nature of the project and understood how to support it with wisdom and compassion: Olive Bowers, Stuart and Louise Ethelston-Clarke, Sebastian and Beatrice Brooke, and all of my wider transatlantic family of Purkises, Sorics, Landors and Katzes.

Nearer to home I have been graced with a fine set of regular well-wishers and news-watchers: Jacqueline Gaile, Matthew Bake, Mark Whyatt, Jamie M. Cooper, Karl Hornsby, Gillian, Hugh, Petronella and the rest of Clan MacNaghten, Nigel Sprigings, Alistair MacDonald, Tony Bowers, Alison Lock, Ian Prady, Dave Rigby, M. Valerio, Roger Cummings, Camilla and Tristram Kennedy-Harper, Jean Margetts, Sohail Khan, Tim 'Otter' Richmond, David North, Robin Stephenson, Lynne Russell, Barth Landor and the late Steve Perkins. Regular members of the Marsden-based Friday night footballers and the Sleepers Cricket Club have been personally supportive on a weekly basis for many years, whilst showing that travel as community is still possible!

In June 2009 I wrote a letter to the *Guardian* newspaper which yielded considerable response. Chapter 5 would be so much the poorer without the interest of Derek Foxman, whose insights and wonderful diaries I have attempted to dramatise! A special mention too for Cora Brockwell for the most beautiful anecdote of this project and the late Alison Prince for a writer's view of these issues. In addition, for all of their inspiring recollections of mid-twentieth-century hitchhiking I would like to thank: Lesley Morrison, Harriet Wordsworth, Deirdre Toomey, Donald Cole, David Lane, Martin Evans, David Watts, Geoff and Shirley Clayton, D. W. Findley, Jeffrey Portch, Alan Weir, John Black, A. F. Bennett, Dr C. Durie, Peter Rybolowitz, John Kennedy, Antonia Lister-Kaye, Barbara Noble, Dick Bentley, Sandy Gordon, Alan Weir, Jean Spinner, Simon Barnes, Diana Brown, Peter Stott, Bernard Lloyd, Celia Deerhart, David Gilbert, Leslie Caplin, Caroline Scott, Rob Tressidor, Philip Ashbourne, Alexander Barr and Valerie Lynch. To Alexander Ferguson (and his mate Tom) for discussion of the Croatia Link

Development Charity hitch on the Dover to Calais ferry and over email in 2013, and to Mathilde Ippolito for her interest in my work.

Hitchhiking serendipity lies behind my debt to Jona Redslob, who supplied me with invaluable information on the politics of hitchhiking competitions, which would not have happened if my friend Jacqueline Gaile had not stopped for Jona's friend Hannes Kühn hitching near Manchester. I am deeply indebted to Dana M. Williams for uplifting discussions on the intersections between hitchhiking, sociology and anarchism and to Professor Ruth Kinna for comments on 'The hitchhiker as a theorist' for her collection *The Bloomsbury companion to anarchism*. Discussions with the playwright Kieran Hurley about his 2010 play *Hitch* were really important to how I wrote Chapter 2. Thanks to the Huddersfield media group of researchers – Sean Leonard, Caroline Pringle and Clare Jenkins – for trying to get hitchhiking 'out there' in the ether.

The enthusiasm and experience of the following have spurred me on to think about hitchhiking in invigorating ways: Christopher Whitely, Sheri Lowther, Paul Kennedy, Deirdre Bergson, Philippe Denzinger, Anna Mills, Alex Jolly, Julian Brotherton, Christopher Sleight and Avantika Taneja. Some of the early research for this book was undertaken whilst working at Liverpool John Moores University between 1998 and 2006 and I am grateful for research leave in spring 2004. Thanks to my former colleagues for their interest, especially Professors Joe Moran and Gerry Smythe (and his list of hitching songs). I also raise a thumb to Graeme Chesters and David Smith for engaging with hitchhiking in thoughtful ways, and to Bernd Wechner and Mario Rinvolucri for some truly pioneering research. All UK hitchhikers owe a considerable debt to Simon Calder, who continues to wave his hitching sign in every professional context possible.

During the final stages of this project it was a privilege to be able to connect with some of the people whose lives and work have touched me over many years and I am grateful for the kind words of support from: Alyssa Hoseman, Miran Ipavec, Ana Bakran, Macdonald Stainsby, Anton Krotov, Bernd Wechner, Robert Prins, Shelley Segal, Mirek Wojcik from the band Czerwono-Czarni and Jon Szanto from the Harry Partch Estate.

From the outskirts of Carlisle (England) in 1982 to a lonely road on South Uist (Scotland) in 2009, I have received lifts from 1,309 drivers and their companions or families. I salute all of you for your faith in people.

Sections of this book have been written during tough periods in my personal life and I thank Chris Cameron, Carolyn Garland, Russ Elias, Martin Loughna, Diane Dequeno, Bryan Bayley, Sammi Burrows, Anna Thomas, Venessa and Uriel Ama-Hart for their friendships, and kind words of advice and professional support. Thanks to Huddersfield Quakers and Green Building Store for providing somewhere to work when needed and to Martyn Cowell for six months of inspiring writing accommodation in Staithes, North Yorkshire. Much of the book's second draft was worked on in Gatehouse of Fleet, Dumfries and Galloway, Scotland. The importance of this cannot be overstated. I am grateful to Jean and David Burchell for the regular use of their flat at Tannery Brae, and to those friendly folk in the town who helped me do that in their many (mostly unknown) ways.

Deepest gratitude to my dedicated readers: my oldest friend, Catherine Harvey, who enthusiastically commented on every second-draft chapter and held my hand through many long dark teatimes of the soul (as Douglas Adams might have said); the talented Huddersfield writer Georgina Hutchison, for her specialist psychology advice and the inspired times and words we shared on the 'Alaska Highway'; and to the playwright Vashti MacLachlan for walking the final lines of the project with me across many an anxious mile.

Most of all, my fellow life travellers and support team – Chayley Collis, long-time sufferer of my creative indulgences, and Murray Purkis, a hitch-hiker at eighteen months old and whose drawings, ideas and website designs constantly gave me hope throughout this long journey: 'It's not possible!'; 'No. It's necessary.'

Notes

Notes to Prologue

1 An American hitchhiker, Ben Bachelder, claims to have been the first person to hitch in Antarctica, in December 2005, according to his posting 'Hitchhiking in Antarctica' on 14 December 2005 to the now defunkt digihitch.com. See web.archive. org/web/20080611193855/http://www.digihitch.com/article840.html (accessed 8 July 2021).

2 The oft-quoted aphorism 'a good traveller has no fixed plans and has no intention of arriving', from chapter 27 of Lao Tzu's *Tao te ching* (see thetaoteching.com; accessed 4 July 2021), becomes 'good walkers leave no track' in Ursula Le Guin's translation (Boulder, CO: Shambhala, 1997), p. 50. The ideas in the *Tao te ching* (or 'the way') date from pre-Han China, probably the sixth century BCE, although this is much debated, as is the content.

3 Wes Enzinna, 'King of the ride', *New York Times*, 22 March 2018. www.nytimes.com/interactive/2018/03/22/magazine/voyages-worlds-greatest-hitchhiker.html (accessed 1 May 2018).

4 Heathcote Williams, *Autogeddon* (London: Jonathan Cape, 1991), p. 4.

5 John Adams has written widely on these subjects. A useful overview is 'Cross-thinking about sustainability. Hypermobility: a challenge to governance'. Public lecture, Amsterdam, 11 May 2006. See www.john-adams.co.uk/wp-content/uploads/2006/Amsterdam%20hypermobility4.pdf (accessed 5 July 2021).

6 The Drifter, 'In the driftway', *The Nation*, 19 September 1923. Stored at http://bernd.wechner.info/Hitchhiking (accessed 12 February 2016).

7 Sharon Stine, *Gypsy boots* (Bloomington, IN: Authorhouse, 2008), p. 25.

8 Jacob Holdt, 'Afterword' to the 2011 edition at www.american-pictures.com/english/book/American-Pictures-2011.pdf, p. 135 (accessed 20 June 2021).

9 Academy of Free Travel at http://avp.travel.ru/AFT.htm (accessed 29 September 2011).

10 Marcel Mauss, *The gift: forms and functions of exchange in archaic societies*, trans. Ian Gunnison (New York: Norton, 1967).

11 Mark Keck-Szajbel, 'A cheap imitation or tourist innovation? Polish tourism during state socialism through Eastern and Western eyes', *Polish-Anglo-Saxon Studies* 14–15 (2011): 138.

Notes to Chapter 1: The intention of a tradition

1 Irv Thomas, *Derelict days: sixty years on the roadside path to enlightenment* (Bloomington, IN: Author House, 2004), p. 220.

2 Thomas, *Derelict days*, p. 223.

3 Bernd Wechner notes how there might be another claim for a hitchhiker in the Bible, in the figure of the Apostle Philip, who gets a ride on a chariot whilst out walking between Jerusalem and Gaza (and later vanishes into thin air – similar to the later urban legend!). See www.bernd.wechner.info/Hitchhiking/bible.html (accessed 7 July 2021).

4 Thomas, *Derelict days*, p. 214.

5 John Schlebecker, 'An informal history of hitchhiking', *Historian* 20 (1958), p. 317.

6 'Hitch-hike in eighteen days, Arkansas to Yale', *New York Times*, 23 September 1923. https://timesmachine.nytimes.com/timesmachine/1923/09/23/issue.html (accessed 10 March 2016).

7 *New York Times*, 'Hitch-hikes 10 hours from capital here', 13 October 1926. https://timesmachine.nytimes.com/timesmachine/1926/10/13/issue.html (accessed 10 March 2016).

8 Schlebecker, 'An informal history of hitchhiking', p. 309.

9 David Kyvig, *Daily life in the United States, 1920–1939: decades of promise and pain* (Westport, CT: Greenwood Publishing, 2001), pp. 23–6.

10 Thomas, *Derelict days*, p. 215.

11 *New York Times*, 'Auto-hiking: a pastime for youth', 29 July 1923. https://timesmachine.nytimes.com/timesmachine/1923/07/9.htm (accessed 10 March 2016). At this point, the world of 'hobo's and that of the 'auto-hikers' was clearly differentiated, something which altered during the Great Depression.

12 A. Hiker, 'The truth about hiking is hitching', *New York Times*, 23 July 1922. https://timesmachine.nytimes.com/timesmachine/1922/07/239.htm (accessed 10 March 2016).

13 Schlebecker, 'An informal history of hitchhiking', p. 309. In 1926 the question of girls hitchhiking was first publicly raised by the New York Girls Service League.

14 See Bernd Wechner's overview 'Charles Elmer Fox – an ardent thumber who loves the rails', 1 July 2000, at www.wechnerinfo/fo/Hitchhiking/Suite101/?51 (accessed 4 July 2021).

15 Some dictionaries state that 'hotch' (Scottish) has associations with 'wiggle or small movements'. See www.merriam-webster.com/dictionary/hotch#h1 (accessed 28 July 2019).

16 Vachel Lindsay, quoted in Thomas, p. 216. See also the discussion of Lindsay in Elijah Wald, *Riding with strangers* (Chicago, IL: Chicago Review Press, 2006) p. 131.

17 Thomas, *Derelict days*, p. 217.

18 Tickner Edwardes, *Lift-luck on southern roads*, 1910 (London: Methuen, 1931), p. vii.

19 Edwardes, *Lift-luck on southern roads*, p. 10.

20 Edwardes, *Lift-luck on southern roads*, pp. 16–19.

21 Interestingly, in Stephen Graham's *The gentle art of tramping* (London: Ernest Benn, 1929), p. 17, there is reference to the practice in the mid-1920s of 'stepping' automobiles with a wave of the hand.

22 Schlebecker, 'An informal history of hitchhiking', p. 316. The article notes the pressure public transportation companies put on government to legislate against hitchhiking due to lost revenues. One electric rail firm claimed to have lost $50,000 a year because of hitchhiking (probably in 1930). It wasn't too hard to use crime statistics against those on the road, through selective reporting of arrests made, so that 40 per cent of hitchhikers might be claimed to have a criminal record.

23 *It happened one night*, directed by Frank Capra (USA: Columbia Pictures, 1934).

24 For a useful breakdown of the variety of ride share schemes see M. Furuhata M. Dessouky, F. Ordóñez, M.-E. Brunet, X. Wang and S. Koeniga, 'Ride sharing: the state of the art and future directions', *Transportation Research: Part B* 57 (2013): 28–46.

25 Bernd Wechner, 'Secure hitchhiking (in a new age)', 1 January 1999. http://bernd. wechner.info/Hitchhiking/Suite101/?33 (accessed 4 March 2007).

26 Thomas, *Derelict days*, pp. 223–4.

Notes to Chapter 2: How to think like a hitchhiker

1 Jacob Holdt, *American pictures* (Copenhagen: American Pictures Foundation, 1985), p. 126.

2 First published in 1890, Jacob Riis's book *How the other half lives: studies among the tenements of New York* was an early example of how photography could influence attitudes towards the poor and alter government policy.

3 Anton Krotov, *A practical guidebook for free travellers*, trans. Peter Lagutkin (Moscow: Self-published, 2014), p. 36.

4 The poem is included in Gary Snyder, *Mountains and rivers without end* (Berkeley, CA: Counterpoint, 1996), pp. 11–24.

5 Some of Snyder's poems focus on working in wilderness areas ('Crater mountain', 1952; 'Hitching south ca. 21 Sept, 1957'); others on long-distance relationships and the consequences of always being on the road ('Robin', 1954; 'Logging', 1960).

6 Mark Silverstein's research is available online at www.hitchinscriptions.com (accessed 24 May 2015).

7 Susan Sontag, *On photography* (Harmondsworth: Penguin, 1982), p. 18.

8 See Tim Edensor, 'M6-junction 19–16: defamiliarizing the mundane landscape', *Space and Culture* 6 no. 2 (2003), p. 168.

9 See Bernd Wechner, 'A North American hitch-hiker gathering', 1 December 2002. bernd.wechner.info/Hitchhiking/Suite101/?80 (accessed 4 July 2021).

10 Graeme Chesters and David Smith, 'The neglected art of hitch-hiking: risk, trust and sustainability', *Sociological Research Online* 6 no. 3 (2001). www.socresonline.org.uk/6/3/chesters.html (accessed 4 March 2007).

11 Morgan Strub, 'The story behind my first hitchhike', posted 8 July 2001, originally on digihitch.com, but that website collapsed in 2012; a version is now stored at web.archive.org/web/20110809121424/http://www.digihitch.com/article72.htm (accessed 21 February 2021).

12 Irv Thomas died in July 2013, aged eighty-four. One obituary mentioned the fact that he had done some short-distance hitchhiking two years before, which makes him the oldest hitchhiker on record.

13 Morgan Strub, 'Foreword' to Thomas, *Derelict days*, pp. xi–xiii.

14 Born in 1943, Dwurnik began his artistic career sketching roadside scenes whilst hitchhiking around Poland in the late 1960s. These evolved into intensely detailed and colourful interpretations, which conformed neither to logical visual perspective nor even a particular historical moment; indeed, they looked more akin to lopsided medieval 'bird's eye' views than Modernism. When he began to populate his cities with military figures in the early 1980s, indicative of the crackdown on the emerging Solidarity movement in Poland and other voices for democracy, the authorities came knocking and some of his pictures were removed from galleries.

Notes to Chapter 3: In search of Woody Guthrie

1 Partch's compositions included forty-three as opposed to twelve tones per octave, which required the construction of new instruments or the remodelling of existing ones, a feat in itself! The same method was utilised in his freight-train-riding 'US highball: a musical account of a transcontinental hobo trip' (1943).
2 Thanks to Jon Szanto at the Harry Partch Estate for clarifying this, 30 June 2021.
3 Written in 1940, the song had many lyrical permutations and first appeared on *Woody Guthrie: this land is your land – the Asch recordings volume 1* (1944).
4 Alex Stein, 'Memphis Minnie, genocide, and identity politics: a conversation with Lorna Dee Cervantes', *Michigan Quarterly Review* 42 no. 4 (2003). http://hdl.handle. net/2027/spo.act2080.0042.406 (accessed 28 June 2016).
5 Paul Garon and Beth Garon, *Woman with guitar: Memphis Minnie's blues* (San Francisco, CA: City Light Books, 2014), p. 271.
6 An equally shocking abduction and murder of a black hitchhiker occurred in Jasper, Texas, on 7 June 1998. A popular local man, James Byrd Jr, was picked up by three white supremacists, who beat him up and dragged him behind their pickup truck. The murder resulted in the Hate Crimes Act – legislation opposed at first by the then Governor, George W. Bush, and passed during the first term of President Obama in 2009. Musical references to Byrd's killing include Will Smith's 2005 song 'Tell me why', which places it alongside many lynchings and political assassinations.
7 Vanessa Veselka, 'The green screen: the lack of female road narratives and why it matters', *American Reader* 4 no. 1 (2012). http://theamericanreader.com/green-screen-the-lack-of-female-road-narratives-and-why-it-matters (accessed 3 August 2019).'

Notes to Chapter 4: 'Maybe we will meet a nice person'

1 Ida Piller-Greenspan, with Susan M. Branting, *When the world closed its doors* (Boulder, CO: Paradigm, 2006), p. 80.
2 Piller-Greenspan, *When the world closed its doors*, p. 127.
3 This much debated quote is at the end of 'An essay on cultural criticism and society' in Adorno's book *Prisms* (London: MIT Press, 1967), p. 34.
4 See Christopher Hill, *Puritanism and revolution* (London: Panther, 1968), pp. 270–88.
5 Both of these phrases appear throughout Colin Ward's work, in particular *Anarchy in action* (London: Freedom Press, 1973); and Colin Ward and David Goodway, *Talking anarchy* (Nottingham: Five Leaves, 2003).
6 'Has Holocaust history just been rewritten? Astonishing new research shows Nazi camp network targeting Jews was "twice as big as previously thought"', *Independent*, 3 March 2013. www.independent.co.uk/news/world/europe/has-holocaust-history-just-been-rewritten-astonishing-new-research-shows-nazi-camp-network-targeting-jews-was-twice-as-big-as-previously-thought-8518407.html (accessed 15 October 2015).
7 Max Weber, 'Science as vocation', in H. Gerth and C.W. Mills (eds), *Essays in sociology* (New York: Oxford University Press, 1946), pp. 129–56.
8 Zygmunt Bauman, *Modernity and the Holocaust* (Cambridge: Polity, 2008), pp. 118–50. The self-justifications and rationalisations described in that chapter – 'Soliciting the cooperation of the victims' – are utterly chilling.
9 The most famous of these was Philip Zimbardo's 1971'Stanford prison experiments', where students role-playing 'guards' did so with alarming brutality to the 'inmates'. See Philip Zimbardo, *The Lucifer effect: understanding how good people turn evil* (New York: Random House, 2007).

10 Dwight Macdonald quoted in Bauman, *Modernity and the holocaust*, p. 151.

11 Winfried Wolf, *Car mania: a critical history of transport* (London: Pluto Press, 1996), p. 204. The book includes some stark observations about the American military's reluctance to bomb oil and gas companies in Nazi Germany, including one of the suppliers of Auschwitz, because of the pre-Second World War business connections with the US oil barons (pp. 86–7).

12 Zimbardo, *The Lucifer effect*, pp. 444–90. See also www.lucifereffect.com/heroism.htm (accessed 20 August 2019). On the personal costs of whistleblowing in large organisations see: Alan Smith, 'When good deeds turn bad', *Guardian*, 22 November 2014, pp. 32–40.

13 Peter Singer, *The expanding circle: ethics and sociobiology* (Oxford: Oxford University Press, 1981).

14 Interestingly, in a model of gene evolution and its application to social structure, Herbert Gintis suggests that in relatively small groups, 'altruistic internal norms will tend to drive out norms that are both socially harmful and individually fitness reducing'. This takes place through norms 'hitchhiking' on 'personally fitness-enhancing norms', although it is not determined. Sometimes non-cooperative 'defectors' can be turned due to pressure of the cooperators, but this becomes problematic in a large political structure. See Herbert Gintis, 'The hitchhiker's guide to altruism: gene–culture co-evolution, and the internalization of norms', *Journal of Theoretical Biology* 220 (2003): 407–18.

15 A summary of the wider evidence can be found in Christopher Boehm, 'Egalitarian behaviour and reverse dominance hierarchy', *Current Anthropology* 34, no. 3 (1993): 227–54. An earlier exploration of how tribes deal with the problem of authority is provided by French anthropologist Pierre Clastres, *Society against the State: essays in political anthropology* (New York: Zone, 1987).

16 In response to the oft-held idea that non-cooperative processes are too powerful a genetic force for cooperation to take hold effectively, researchers have recently observed what they have lovingly called the 'Hankshaw effect' (after Tom Robbins's big-thumbed hitchhiking heroine Sissy, discussed in Chapter 5). In the modelling of the transmission of cooperative 'indicators', there is evidence that these are more active and prevalent than their more selfish 'defector' counterparts. See Sarah Hammarlund, Brian D. Connelly, Katherine J. Dickinson and Benjamin Kerr, 'The evolution of cooperation by the Hankshaw effect', posted 1 April 2015 on www.biorxiv.org/content/10.1101/016667v1 (accessed 14 August 2019).

17 Patricia Purkis, 'Childhood memories of the war', family letters, Hull, n.d. (probably mid-1990s).

18 Martin Pugh, *State and society: a social and political history of Britain 1870–1997* (London: Arnold, 2002), pp. 253–63.

19 'A college of thumbers' (editorial), *Times*, 23 February 1940, p. 9.

20 Mario Rinvolucri, *Hitchhiking* (Liverpool: Self-published, 1974). Available at https://prino.neocities.org/mario_rinvolucri/chapter9.html (accessed 11 November 2015).

21 Rinvolucri, *Hitchhiking*, https://prino.neocities.org/mario_rin_volucri/chapter10.html (accessed 11 November 2015). He notes the contrast between the negative tones emerging in 1942 issues of *Autocar* with those from 1929 which had carried letters outlining the social benefits of helping the poor to travel and, in doing so, reducing class hatred and resentment.

22 Alan Dein's work is part of a post-war tradition in education of documenting marginalised or unheard narratives of everyday life. His programme *Memory Wars* aired on the BBC's World Service during October 2010 and is available at www.bbc.co.uk/programmes/p009xbbr (accessed 29 October 2010). In it, Dein notes the perennial

reliability problems with such data, of memory and political bias. Many of the *People's War* memoirs are nostalgic and prone to repeating the aforementioned myths of unity, as these become the frames for re-articulating personal experiences.

23 Heather Simpson, BBC *People's War* archive at www.bbc.co.uk/history/ww2 peopleswar.htm (accessed August 2008).

24 Dorothy Barnes, BBC *People's War* archive (accessed August 2008).

25 Betty Bowen, BBC *People's War* archive (accessed August 2008). Knowing that at some point one's road luck would run out meant that alternatives had to be found. Also contributing to the BBC *People's War* archive was former RAF wireless operator Claude Osborne, who recalled a time when the lifts were slow: 'On one such occasion I had taken a friend home with me and we were rather late getting back. Normally this would have presented no problem as we would just climb over the barbed wire fence and go to our barrack room. However, on this particular night, or early morning, we saw a light in our barracks and shortly afterwards an RAF policeman rode away on his bicycle. We therefore decided to enter by the main gate and report ourselves late (we later discovered that the policeman was merely providing an early call for someone who was leaving that morning). As a punishment we were given three days "jankers" during which we had to help in the kitchen with cleaning of pots and pans.' Claude Osborne, BBC *People's War* archive.

26 Simpson, BBC *People's War* archive.

27 Pugh, *State and society*, p. 258.

28 Rinvolucri, *Hitchhiking*, https://prino.neocities.org/mario_rinvolucri/chapter10.html (accessed 11 November 2015).

29 Roman Krznaric, *Empathy: a handbook for revolution* (London: Rider Books, 2012), p. 173.

30 Harriet Wordsworth (Bristol), personal letters and telephone conversation, June and July 2009.

31 As recorded in the Afterword to *When the world closed its doors* (where the spelling of Maurice shifts to Morris), amidst the horrors of imminent detection and deportation, several members of her family manage to save others. Bronia, Morris's sister (who survived the war), stalled searches of the orphanage where she worked and hid the children, adopting one herself. Cylia, Morris's other sister and part of the Belgian resistance, was followed by German officers when she was walking home but she chose to walk on past the house, allowing those at home to escape her own fate in Auschwitz.

32 Merle Exit, 'Briarwood artist's life celebrated', *TimesLedger* (Queens, NY), 30 April 2016, at https://qns.com/story/2016/04/30/briarwood-artists-life-celebrated.htm (accessed 15 November 2016).

33 There are a number of specific studies in this field, published in journals such as *Biological Psychiatry* and the *American Journal of Psychiatry*. One media assessment of this sometimes controversial area of genetics is Helen Thomson, 'Study of Holocaust survivors shows trauma passed onto children's genes', *Guardian*, 21 August 2015. www.theguardian.com/science/2015/aug/21/study-of-holocaust-survivors-finds-trauma-passed-on-to-childrens-genes (accessed 14 August 2019).

34 The multi-agency international outcry against the Hungarian government included a Human Rights Watch report from July 2016, on its breach of basic rights of asylum seekers and refugees: 'Hungary: migrants abused at the border', www.hrw.org/news/2016/07/13/hungary-migrants-abused-border (accessed 15 November 2016).

35 The Turkey–European Union deal in March 2016 which 'swapped' those arriving in Greece from Turkey with others in Turkish refugee camps was decried by several charities and other non-governmental organisations, including Save the Children and Doctors Without Borders, on many grounds, not least the impact on children's mental health. See Human Rights Watch, 'Q&A: Why the EU–Turkey migration deal is no

blueprint', 14 November 2016, www.hrw.org/news/2016/11/14/qa-why-eu-turkey-migration-deal-no-blueprint (accessed 15 November 2016).

36 Jessica Reinisch, 'History matters, but which one?', History and Policy website, September 2015, www.historyandpolicy.org/policy-papers/category/reinisch-jessica (accessed 7 January 2020).

37 Lauren McCauley, 'Across Europe, tens of thousands rally to welcome refugees', 12 September 2015, www.commondreams.org/news/2015/09/12/across-europe-tens-thousands-rally-welcome-refugees (accessed 15 November 2016).

38 Helping refugees in contravention of European law is carried out via contact websites such as www.fluchthelfter.in. The intellectual justification – 'A manifesto for no borders' – can be found at http://noborders.org.uk/node/47 (accessed 10 November 2016). Material on the 'underground railway' can be found in Howard Zinn's *A people's history of the United States* (New York: Harper Perennial, 2003).

39 Lisabeth Zornig, 'Danish government persecutes people helping refugees', Dear Kitty blog, 11 March 2016, http://dearkitty1.wordpress.com (accessed 10 November 2016). Incidentally, 'Dear Kitty' is how Anne Frank started each of her diary entries prior to her arrest by the Nazis. Jacob Holdt's website includes many updates on Danish attitudes towards immigration; see www.american-pictures.com/english/racism/kkk-us-7.htm (accessed 21 January 2021).

40 One declaration, dated 23 September 2015, on the 'Transeuropa festival 2015: hitchhiking challenge' Facebook page stated: 'For most people, movement and migration are limited or even criminalised. For others, travelling and living abroad is encouraged and turned into a status symbol, a consumer good…. Let's reflect on movement and what it can be: crossing borders – visible and invisible – meeting different people, engaging in transcultural relationships, building new friendships and redrawing solidarity networks.' See www.facebook.com/events/942950219084865/?active_tab=discussion (accessed 10 November 2016).

41 Serbia Travel Club, www.thetravelclub.org (accessed 10 November 2016).

Notes to Chapter 5: The great European adventure trail

1 Alison Prince, personal emails, June 2009.

2 Prince, personal emails.

3 Ian Rodger, *A hitch in time: recollection of a journey* (London: Hutchinson, 1966), pp. 11–15.

4 David Lane seemed to epitomise this: 'I was at a boarding school (Kingswood School) in Bath from 1954–61…. After morning assembly we filled in forms to say how we intended to spend the day and where we intended to go, and then we cleared off for the day with a packet of sandwiches. On such occasions, I usually hitch-hiked (generally with a friend). The furthest I got was to London and back. I suffered no problem with stranger danger, though we were once stopped by a village policeman who presumably wondered if we were absconding from an approved school. After questioning us a little, he let us carry on, commenting that it was all right as "Your grammar's good".' Personal email, 3 June 2009.

5 Barbara Noble, personal email, 5 June 2009.

6 Martin Evans, personal email, 11 June 2009.

7 Derek Foxman (London, England), personal diary from summer 1957, shared with the author during July 2009.

8 Rodger, *A hitch in time*, p. 102.

9 Rodger, *A hitch in time*, pp. 22–36. Hitchhiking literature and oral history suggest that the lack of public places where socialising between homosexual men might take place

did overlap with the solicitation of lifts during the mid-twentieth century. Rodger's book also includes one troubling passage (pp. 170–3) where he has literally to fight off one deluded lorry driver who thought all English hitchhikers were 'players'.

10 Rodger, *A hitch in time*, pp. 42, 48.
11 Rodger, *A hitch in time*, pp. 50–1.
12 Rodger, *A hitch in time*, p. 94.
13 Rodger, *A hitch in time*, p. 50; pp. 175–83.
14 Foxman, personal diary.
15 Isaiah Berlin, 'Two concepts of liberty', in *Four essays on liberty* (Oxford: Oxford University Press, 1969), p. 120. Originally delivered as an inaugural lecture at Oxford University, 31 October 1958.
16 An example of humanistic psychology, Maslow's much-quoted 'hierarchy of needs' concept was a positive contrast to more neurosis-driven models and expressed in the book *Towards a psychology of being* (Princeton, MA: Van Nostrand Reinhold, 1962).
17 Stine, *Gypsy boots*, p. 70.
18 Antonia Lister-Kaye, personal emails, June 2009.
19 Stine, *Gypsy boots*, pp. 291–6.
20 Rolf Potts, 'We don't (really) know Jack', 5 September 2007, www.worldhum.com/features/travel-books/we_dont_really_know_jack_20070905 (accessed 1 November 2011).
21 Jeremy Packer, *Mobility without mayhem: safety, cars and citizenship* (Durham, NC: Duke University Press, 2008), p. 29.
22 Stine, *Gypsy boots*, p. 120.
23 Stine, *Gypsy boots*, p. 185.
24 Rodger, *A hitch in time*, pp. 183–5.
25 Stine, *Gypsy boots*, p. 254.
26 Rodger, *A hitch in time*, p. 191.
27 *The Asiatics* is thought to be based on an early twentieth-century world traveller of the likes of an Arthur Crone or an Otto Preussler. The narrator of Prokosch's tale of derring-do journeys from Turkey to China, and encounters all kinds of oddballs and escapees from the drawing rooms of the West amidst wars, coups and natural disasters.
28 Boasting was common amongst young hitchhikers in the late 1970s according to Chandra Mukerji, 'Bullshitting: road lore among hitchhikers', *Social Problems* 25 no. 3 (1978), p. 242. Farcical male prowess runs through David Childress's *A hitchhiker's guide to Africa and Arabia* (Chicago, IL: Chicago Review Press, 1977), although erotic prose writer Fiona Pitt-Kethley cheekily exploits these clichés in *The Pan principle* (London: Sinclair Stevenson, 1994), hitchhiking and seducing with great gusto in Greece.
29 The dance artist Sarah Morrison has performed *A tribute to Sissy Hankshaw*, complete with readings and soundtrack. See www.youtube.com/watch?v=QoDRi55jWF4 (accessed 16 September 2008). The 1994 film of Tom Robbins's book (directed by Gus Van Sant) was weak and confusing, with only a K. D. Laing soundtrack to really recommend.
30 Erik Cohen, 'Nomads from affluence: notes on the phenomenon of drifter-tourism', *International Journal of Comparative Sociology* 14 no. 1–2 (1973): 89–103. Many travellers did the Trail 'the other way', via Thailand and India from Australia, some of which is detailed in *Playpower*, Ricard Neville's idiosyncratic and irreverent guide to alternative living (Aylesbury: Jonathan Cape, 1970).
31 Theodore Roszak, *The making of a counter culture* (New York: Anchor, 1969), pp. 124–54.
32 See Louis Turner and John Ash, 'The last Romantics', in *The golden hordes* (London: Constable, 1975), pp. 255–79.

33 Neville, *Playpower*, p. 172.

34 James Bar Bowen, 'The irony monger' [song]. From *The lie of the land*. UK: self-produced, 2019.

35 Michael Hall, *Remembering the Hippie Trail* (Newtonabbey: Island Publications, 2007), p. 12.

36 Hall, *Remembering the Hippie Trail*, p. 145.

37 Hall, *Remembering the Hippie Trail*, p. 30.

38 Rinvolucri, *Hitchhiking*, https://prino.neocities.org/mario_rinvolucri/chapter2.html (accessed 11 November 2015).

39 Hall, *Remembering the Hippie Trail*, p. 215.

40 There are many books on the route. David Tomory's *A season in heaven* (London: Thorsons, 1996) is a collection of thirty-seven personal accounts. Sharif Gemie and Brian Ireland consider themes of sex and love, drugs and attitudes towards other cultures in *The Hippie Trail: a history* (Manchester: Manchester University Press, 2017).

41 One book which informed the 1960s radicalism was Norman Cohn's *In pursuit of the millennium*, with its depiction of fourteenth-century radical religious communities such as the Anabaptists and the Brethren of the Free Spirit – whose egalitarian visions were pioneering and murderous in equal measures (New York: Oxford University Press, 1970).

42 These associations are not without controversy; a key concern is 'the naturalistic fallacy' (applying ecological laws to human decisions). See Andrew Light (ed.), *Social ecology after Bookchin* (New York: Guildford Press, 1998), especially Glenn Albrecht's chapter, 'Ethics and directionality in nature', pp. 92–112. However, contemporary ecological theories of complexity may well render this 'fallacy' itself as part of the dualistic universe.

43 Remarkably, the Kurdish independence movements have picked up the work of Murray Bookchin and used it to organise their own egalitarian enclaves in places such as Rojava, a district of northern Syria, even as civil war rages all around them. The position of women in these communities is more liberated than in many parts of the Western world, let alone the countries around them. See Wes Enzinna, 'A dream of secular utopia', *New York Times*, 29 November 2015. www.nytimes.com/2015/11/29/magazine/a-dream-of-utopia-in-hell.html?emc=edit_tnt_20151124&nlid=56257975&tntemailo=y. See www.biehlonbookchin.com for more comprehensive resources (both accessed 26 April 2020).

44 Antonia Lister-Kaye, personal email, 5 June 2009.

45 Lesley Morrison, personal email, 2 June 2009.

46 Ian Martin, 'Sixty things I've learned at sixty', *Guardian*, 30 April 2013, G2, p. 6.

Notes to Chapter 6: The Alaska Highway hitchhiker visitors' book

1 Stephen Franzoi, 'The personality of the cross country hitchhiker', *Adolescence* 20 no. 79 (1985), p. 655.

2 Schlebecker, 'An informal history of hitchhiking', p. 308.

3 James P. Greenley and David G. Rice, 'Female hitchhiking: strain, control and sub-cultural approaches', *Sociological Focus* 7 no. 1 (1973): 87–100. See also T. Myers and J. Sangster, 'Retorts, runaways and riots: patterns of resistance in Canadian reform schools for girls 1930–60', *Journal of Social History* 34 no. 3 (2001): 669–97.

4 R. W. Johnson and J. H. Johnson, 'A cross-validation on the Sn scale on the Psychological Screening Inventory with female hitchhikers', *Journal of Clinical Psychology* 34 no. 2 (1978): 366–7.

5 Rinvolucri, *Hitchhiking*, ch. 1, https://prino.neocities.org/www/mario_rinvolucri/chapter1.html (accessed 10 November 2015).

6 Franzoi, 'The personality characteristics of the cross country hitchhiker', p. 666.

7 Krznaric, *Empathy*, p. 200.

8 Gertrude Baskine, *Hitch-hiking the Alaska Highway* (Toronto: Macmillan, 1944), pp. 2–6.

9 Baskine, *Hitch-hiking the Alaska Highway*, pp. 172–5.

10 Lorna Whishaw, *As far as you'll take me* (London: Hammond, Hammond and Co., 1958), pp. 125–6.

11 Linda Mahood, 'Hitchin' a ride', interview on www.tvo.org 3 July 2015. This covered some of the ideas in her article 'Hitchin' a ride in the 1970s: Canadian youth culture and the Romance with mobility', *Histoire sociale/Social History* 47 no. 93 (2014): 207–27.

12 Matthew Jackson, *The Canada chronicles* (Calgary: Summit, 2004), p. 386.

13 Benoît Grieu, 'Globe trotter' [interview]. http://beni.eurower.net/index.php/2006/08/22/1 (accessed 21 October 2014).

14 See Benoît Grieu, 'Never again: when a dream turns to nightmare', *Kalasha Times*, 26 August 2011. www.thekalashatimes.wordpress.com/2011/08 (accessed 21/10/2014).

15 The initial theory (of Krakauer's) that McCandless had starved to death due to toxins from wild potato seeds preventing the body from absorbing proteins was later disproved. Much clearer, however, was the fact that he did not have a map, and so did not know there was a wire pulley and cart system which would have allowed him to cross the swollen Teklanika River at a nearby hydrology station on his attempt to return to civilisation.

16 See Matthew Power, 'The cult of Chris McCandless', *Men's Journal*, 15 October 2012. www.mensjournal.com/features/the-cult-of-chris-mccandless-20121015 (accessed 26 November 2016).

17 Jon Krakauer, *Into the wild* (New York: Anchor Books, 1999), p. 188.

18 Baskine, *Hitch-hiking the Alaska Highway*, pp. 315–16.

19 See Macdonald Stainsby, 'We can't walk on water but we can hitchhike on it', 30 January 2008. www.macdonaldstainsby.com (accessed 14 June 2021). This was originally a www.digihitch.com posting from 2008.

20 Macdonald Stainsby and Dru Oja Jay, 'Offsetting resistance: the effects of foundation funding and corporate fronts from the Great Bear Rainforest to the Athabasca River', 2009. www.offsettingresistance.ca (accessed 26 November 2016).

21 Assessing the political significance of the Standing Rock action, activist-writer Rebecca Solnit noted that it was 'the first time all seven bands of the Lakota had come together since they defeated Custer at Little Bighorn in 1876' and they were supported by US army veterans who 'came to defend the encampment and help prevent the pipeline. In one momentous ceremony, many of the former soldiers knelt down to apologise and ask forgiveness for the US army's long role in oppressing Native Americans.' Rebecca Solnit, 'Protest and persist', *Guardian*, 17 March, 2017. https://www.theguardian.com/world/2017/mar/13/protest-persist-hope-trump-activism-anti-nuclear-movement (accessed 1 April 2017).

22 Kaufman estimated that he thumbed 110,400 kilometres in 1973, although I have never seen him in the record books. To date, the only hitchhiker to exceed 100,000 kilometres in a year is Benoît Grieu (he managed this four times).

23 This is an abridged version of the conversation that takes place on pages 98–101 of Kenn Kaufman, *Kingbird highway: the biggest year in the life of an extreme birder* (Boston, MA: Houghton Miflin, 2006).

24 Kaufman, *Kingbird highway*, p. 92.

Notes to Chapter 7: The power of the gift without return

1 Princess Kasune Zulu, with Belinda Collins, *Warrior princess: fighting for life with courage and hope* (Downer's Grove, IL: IVP Books, 2009), pp. 19–20. More recent publications and media profile identify her simply as Princess Kasune.

2 David Graeber, *Fragments of an anarchist anthropology* (Chicago, IL: Prickly Paradigm, 2004), p. 17.

3 Beverly Bell, 'Mali's gift economy', *Yes Magazine*, 22 July 2009. www.dailygood.org/more.php?n=3893 (accessed 3 November 2017).

4 Other measurements of a healthy economy include: the Happy Planet Index, devised in 2006 by the London-based New Economics Foundation, which multiplies 'life satisfaction' and 'life expectancy' and then divides it by estimated 'ecological footprint'; the World Giving Index, which measures generosity; and the World Peace Index, which looks at how violence affects quality of life.

5 Jean Baudrillard, *Symbolic exchange and death* (London: Sage/TCS, 1993).

6 Nigeria and South Africa in particular have strong film industries, although distribution to the wider world can be limited. *Life, above all* (2011) deals with many of the same HIV/AIDS social issues which Princess Kasune Zulu charts in her work. From a hitchhiking point of view, a British-made road-trip film, *Africa united* (2010), featured a trio of Rwandan teenagers thumbing their way through many classic 'African problems' to the football World Cup in South Africa.

7 Sociological studies of media coverage of African problems (and more recently refugees and 'the border crisis') at www.glasgowmediagroup.org suggest that they are invariably seen as tragic and disconnected from viable solutions or policy changes in or by the West. See Liza Beattie, David Miller, Emma Miller and Greg Philo, 'The media and Africa: images of disaster and rebellion', in Greg Philo (ed.), *Message received* (Harlow: Longman, 1999), pp. 231–67.

8 See James C. Scott, *Seeing like a state* (New Haven, CT: Yale University Press, 1998), pp. 223–61.

9 China's role in Zambia is controversial. The mining practices have been condemned by Human Rights Watch on the grounds of safety and the intimidation of workers and those engaged in union activity. See 'Zambian president urged to protect workers at Chinese-owned mines', *Guardian*, 3 November 2011. https://www.theguardian.com/world/2011/nov/03/zambian-president-workers-chinese-mines (accessed 21 July 2017). In other cases, development has involved Chinese rather than Zambian labour. Further, the success of some sixty agricultural projects may have been exaggerated. See R. Ntomba, 'Zambia-China – all weather friends?', *New African Magazine*, 13 March 2015. https://newafricanmagazine.com/10213/ (accessed 18 August 2019); and (Professor) John Stremlau, Interview on Al Jazeera UK, news feature, 4 December 2015, 1 p.m.

10 Christopher A. Williams, Niall P. Hanan, Jason C. Neff, et al. 'Africa and the global carbon cycle', *Carbon Balance and Management*, 7 March 2007. https://cbmjournal.biomedcentral.com/articles/10.1186/1750-0680-2-3 (accessed 10 November 2015). The contribution of local seed and soil knowledge to preserving ecosystems has been recognised at an international climate-mitigation policy level: see Sylvia Mweetwa, 'Zambia: traditional knowledge can help farmers adapt to climate change', 10 November 2011. https://allafrica.com/stories/201111100896.html (accessed 1 December 2015).

11 See in particular P. Develtere, 'Cooperative development in Africa up to the 1990s', in P. Develtere, I. Pollet and F. Wanyama (eds), *Cooperating out of poverty* (ILO/World Bank Institute, Geneva/Washington, DC, 2008), pp. 1–37. This identifies the problems

which 'structural adjustment policies' imposed by the International Monetary Fund have had, principally in terms of undermining local markets when cheaper goods are allowed to flow into the country.

12 Bus boycotts began at the same time as those connected with the civil rights movement in the USA. In Soweto, inflated bus prices impacted on those travelling from Alexandra to Johannesburg – which was seen as a race issue – leading to huge protests (many walked or hitched the twenty-two miles). Despite government intervention and reduced fares, the events had a wider – resistance-building – significance. See Isaac Mangena, 'Bus boycott which forced apartheid U-turn', 29 September 2012. http://news.iafrica.com/features/666218.htm (accessed 8 August 2018).

13 M. Sicwetsha, 'Hitch-hiking research report, reasons behind hitch-hiking in the Eastern Cape', 2009. www.ectransport.gov.za/uploads/Reports/reasons-behind-hitch-hiking-in-the-eastern-cape1.pdf (accessed 27 October 2017). The author notes in the conclusion (p. 26) that 'The interest of government, commuters and the industry should not be on banning or eradicating hitch-hiking but on providing a solution to benefit all interested parties, especially the vulnerable commuters'.

14 Quotes taken from Somik Vinay Lall, J. Vernon Henderson and Anthony J. Venables, *Africa's cities: opening doors to the world* (Washington, DC: World Bank, 2017).

15 Sean O' Toole, 'Rush Hour Rest Stop', posted 20 August 2014 www.urbanafrica.net/urban-voices/rush-hour-rest-stop/ (accessed 27 October 2017).

16 Mary Jaques-Aldridge, *Trio's trek* (London: W. H. Allen, 1955), p. 11.

17 Jaques-Aldridge, *Trio's trek*, p. 25.

18 Jaques-Aldridge, *Trio's trek*, p. 94. Perhaps Ali's song lasted even longer. Mary Jaques-Aldridge came back some years later and wrote several books about African animals and a children's story about the history of coffee, published in the 1960s.

19 Jaques-Aldridge, *Trio's trek*, p. 243.

20 Wendy Myers, *Seven league boots* (London: Hodder and Stoughton, 1969), p. 173.

21 See Alyssa Hoseman personal website, www.opendestination.ca/about-faq.html (accessed 17 October 2017). Kinga's original 'My Africa' blog has been retained at www.eioba.com/a/1iq7/my-africa-kinga-freespirit-part-i (accessed 17 October 2017).

22 https://web.archive.org/web/20080430152139/www.digihitch.com/tribute/kinga (accessed 17 October 2017). Some tributes included commitments to repeat her last journey, and it was fitting that some of the people, of many nationalities, at her funeral in Gdansk arrived by thumb.

23 www.eioba.com/a/1iqc/my-africa-kinga-freespirit-part-ii (accessed 17 October 2017).

24 See for example Robert Levine's work involved cross cultural comparisons using several variables for gauging 'helpfulness' across twenty-six major world cities. Robert V. Levine, 'Measuring helping behaviour across cultures', Online Readings in Psychology and Culture, Unit 5, 2003. Retrieved from http://scholarworks.gvsu.edu/orpc/vol5/iss3/2 (accessed 17 October 2017).

25 www.travelblog.org/Africa/Senegal/Tambacounda-Region/Tambacounda/blog-496704.html (accessed 27 October 2017).

26 See www.afdb.org/en/news-and-events/african-economic-conference-2018-focusses-on-africa-visa-openness-and-integration-18768 (accessed 14 August 2019).

27 www.travelblog.org/Africa/Guinea/Lab-/blog-507622.html (accessed 27 October 2017).

28 www.travelblog.org/Africa/Congo-Democratic-Republic/blog-583886.html (accessed 27 October 2017).

29 www.travelblog.org/Africa/Congo-Democratic-Republic/blog-583886.html.

30 See Frank Jacobs, 'Thumbs up? This map shows the best places to hitchhike in Europe', 14 June 2019. www.weforum.org/agenda/2019/06/thumbs-up-map-shows-europe-s-hitchhiking-landscape (accessed 20 January 2021).

31 The chocolate industry now identifies brands which are guaranteed not to use child labour. This is one part of the global fight against trafficking in many areas of work and exploitation. See the websites of the umbrella non-governmental organisation Stop the Traffik (www.stopthetraffik.org) and of Human Rights Watch (www.hrw.org) (accessed 17 August 2017).

32 www.opendestination.ca/southern-africas-deserts.html (accessed 27 October 2017).

Notes to Chapter 8: The myth of the great decline

1 Michael D. Reid, 'Salt Spring Islanders rally in drive to save hitchhiking tradition', *Times Colonist*, 6 June 2017.

2 The Bowen Island scheme was part financed by Environment Canada's EcoAction Community Funding Program. See Tristin Hopper, 'LIFT program aims to make hitchhiking the "friendly dependable" choice for residents of B.C. island', *National Post*, 4 March 2013. https://nationalpost.com/news/canada/lift-program-bowen-island-hitchhiking (accessed 19 February 2014).

3 Rosini Nair, 'Salt Spring residents defend island's hitchhiking culture', 6 June 2017. www.cbc.ca/news/canada/british-columbia/salt-spring-residents-defend-island-s-hitch hiking-culture-1.4147981 (accessed 22 January 2020).

4 Frans de Waal, 'The evolution of empathy', 1 September 2005. www.greatergood. berkeley.edu/article/item/the_evolution_of_empathy (accessed 9 February 2015).

5 Matthew Arnold, *Culture and anarchy* (London: Cambridge University Press, 1932), pp. 68–71.

6 Karen S. Cook, 'The significance of trust', in Karen S. Cook, Margaret Levi and Russell Hardin, *Cooperation without trust?* New York: Russell Sage Foundation, 2007, pp. 13–14.

7 Cook, 'The significance of trust', *passim*.

8 The status of women is relatively high for a Latin American country, especially in terms of access to higher education, health and political representation. During the so-called 'Special Period', after 1990, women came to play a wider role in public life, although they are still largely responsible for domestic and childcare arrangements. There are also relatively low rates of violent crime against women. See United Nations figures at https://evaw-global-database.unwomen.org/en/countries/americas/cuba? typeofmeasure=3ebd6d85ae4d4dfcab5553635944cfc9 (accessed 12 May 2020).

9 See Packer, *Mobility without mayhem*, p. 107.

10 K. E. Dallmeyer, 'Hitchhiking – a viable addition to a multimodal transportation system', Centre for Urban Transportation Studies, University of Colarado/National Science Foundation, 1975. https://trid.trb.org/Results?q=&datein=all&index=%22H itchhiking%22#/View/28681 (accessed 28 January 2020).

11 Dina Pinner, 'Thoughts on hitchhiking', *Jerusalem Post*, 23 June 2014. www.jpost. com/Opinion/Op-Ed-Contributors/Thoughts-on-hitchhiking-360314 (accessed 14 February 2015).

12 Smith and Chesters, 'The neglected art of hitch-hiking: risk, trust and sustainability'.

13 The 'trade plating' community is slightly different from the haulage industry, and is made up of professional car deliverers who drive a brand-new vehicle to a destination, hitch back with spare plates and claim the train fare off their employers. By contrast, the 'tacograph' is a circular piece of paper which records the duration of a lorry's journey and was a legal requirement in some countries to prevent drivers overwork-ing. Hitchhiking with one meant that you either drove a truck or another driver had decided that 'this person is trustworthy' and can be given a lift.

14 Joyce Dargay, Dermot Gately and Martin Sommer, 'Vehicle ownership and income growth, worldwide: 1960–2030', *Energy* 28 no. 4 (2007): 143–70.

15 *Social Trends* data quoted in Smith and Chesters, 'The neglected art of hitch-hiking'.

16 Dargay et al., 'Vehicle ownership and income growth', pp. 149ff.

17 Simon Calder and Rachel Palmer, 'The traveller: the complete guide to Inter-railing', *Independent*, 9 June 2001, pp. 2–3. Calder is Britain's best-known hitchhiker, with forty years of experience, and continues to advocate for it even in his role as travel editor of this publication and as a BBC correspondent.

18 AA/Populus, 'Hitchhikers swap their thumb on the road for a mouse on the super highway', 17 June 2009. www.prweb.com/releases/2009/06/prweb2541704.htm (accessed 20 May 2020).

19 Sixty-eight mostly UK-based hitchhikers responded to the online version of Joe Moran's 'A guide to hitchhiking's decline' article in the *Guardian*, 5 June 2009. www.theguardian.com/commentisfree/2009/jun/05/hitchhiking-decline-britain (accessed 9 June 2009). Whilst most chose to share stories, the numbers of those who offered explanations were as follows: 'fear', 14; the 'Thatcher factor', 4; the release of mental health patients into the community, 3; the haulage industry choosing not to pick up any more, 2; and motorway design as a disincentive to trying to hitch, 1.

20 AA/Populus, 'Hitchhikers swap their thumb for a mouse'.

21 Packer, *Mobility without mayhem*, p. 109.

22 As reported in 'Scrub glamour out of this hitchhike zest', *Daily Mirror*, 22 August 1950, p. 6.

23 The *Times* editorials and letters on the matter begin on 18 August 1955 (respectively on p. 5 and p. 10 of that issue).

24 For discussion of the Dangerous Drugs Act 1967 see https://prino.neocitie.org/mario_rinvolucri/chapter3.html (accessed 11 November 2015); for media responses to a proposal ban on hitchhiking see https://prino.neocitie.org/mario_rinvolucri/chapter4.html (accessed 11 November 2015).

25 A detailed discussion of these campaigns can be found in Rinvolucri, *Hitchhiking*. https://prino.neocities.org/mario_rinvolucri/chapter8.html (accessed 11 November 2015).

26 The 'white bicycle' scheme was devised in March 1966 by a group of Dutch anarchists – The Provos – who painted a few dozen cycles and distributed them around Amsterdam with the intention that people would use them as needed rather than sit unused in a hallway or garage. Although this was not a success, with many being stolen, something similar is now evident in commercial form in a number of cities across the world.

27 In 2015 the German city of Kiel officially unveiled a new 'hitching point', followed by one at the Dutch town of Oldemarkt, on 21 June 2016. See https://steenwijkercourant.nl/artikel/441966/feestelijke-onthulling-van-liftpaal-met-muziek-en-paal-dans-act.html (accessed 11 March 2020). The Netherlands has a number of *liftshalte* (in Amsterdam, Zoetemeer, Gronigon and Utrecht) as well as some where the signage has been withdrawn but the points are still used. See https://hitchwiki.org/en/Liftershalte (accessed 11 March 2020).

28 Don Wharton, 'Thumbs down on hitchhikers', *Reader's Digest*, April 1950, n.p.

29 John P. Davis, 'Stranger in the car', *Reader's Digest*, August 1959, p. 55.

30 Mark Osteen, 'Noir's cars: automobility and amoral space in American film noir', *Journal of Popular Film and Television* 35 no. 4 (2008), p. 188.

31 Packer, *Mobility without mayhem*, p. 85.

32 Packer, *Mobility without mayhem*, pp. 99–100.

33 Harry Priestley, 'Travelling man: interview with Tony Wheeler', *Citylife: Chiangmai*

17 no. 7 (2008). https://web.archive.org/web/20090215042500/www.chiangmainews. com/ecmn/viewfa.php?id=2228 (accessed 10 June 2020).

34 British backpackers Caroline Clarke and Joanne Walters, who were killed in 1992, and Germans Anja Habschied and Gabor Neugebauer, in 1991, were last seen near a youth hostel in Kings Cross, Sydney. Another German, Simone Schmidl, disappeared whilst hitchhiking in 1991, and James Gibson and Deborah Everist were also assumed to have been picked up by Milat, in 1989. One potential victim who escaped whilst hitchhiking – British man Paul Onions – gave evidence at Milat's trial in 1996.

35 Jennifer Cox, quoted in the *Big Issue*, 6 August 1995, p. 20. These remarks were part of a press release from October and November 1993 giving advice to would-be backpackers, noting that 'we always counsel against women hitch-hiking anywhere … even two women together are seldom entirely safe'. See *Daily Mail*, 30 October 1993, p. 56.

36 The Suzy Lamplugh Trust, which produces advice for travellers and was often in the newspapers in the 1990s and early 2000, is here quoted from Martin Symington, 'The hitchhiker's guide to nowhere', *Times*, 17 July 1999, p. 7.

37 Harriet Wordsworth (Bristol), personal letters and telephone calls, June 2009.

38 Naomi Klein, *The shock doctrine* (London: Penguin, 2008). Test run in 1973 in the US-backed overthrow of the democratic elected government of Chile, these policies are designed to undermine publicly accountable and democratic institutions in favour of deregulation and privatisation. To varying degrees their advocates favour socially conservative and punitive legislation which seeks to divide populations and weaken their opportunities for mobilising.

39 For evidence of grass-roots activism in these areas see Jean Stead, *Never the same again: women and the miners' strike* (London: Women's Press, 1987); Harriet Sherwood, 'The women of the miners' strike: "We caused a lot of havoc"' *Guardian*, 7 April 2014. www. theguardian.com/lifeandstyle/2014/apr/07/women-miners-strike-1984-wives-picket-lines (accessed 20 March 2021).

40 Ginger Strand, 'Hitchhiking's time has come again', *New York Times*, 10 November 2012. www.nytimes.com/2012/11/11/opinion/sunday/hitchhikings-time-has-come-again.html (accessed 23 January 2018).

41 See Jeremy Rifkin, with Ted Howard, *Entropy: a new world view* (London: Paladin, 1985). Much of the application of the principle of entropy into environmental and political realms comes from the economic work by Nicholas Georgescu-Roegen.

42 Link Community Development (www.lcdinternational.org) built schools in a number of East African countries. It used hitchhiking as a means both of fundraising and of educating the participants in adaptability, generosity and mutual aid on the road, with those less fortunate than themselves in mind. The last fundraising hitch was to Prague in 2016. See https://en.wikipedia.org/wiki/Link_Community_Development (accessed 17 August 2019).

43 Paul Smith, *Twitchhiker: how one man travelled the world by Twitter* (Chichester: Summersdale, 2010).

Notes to Chapter 9: Climatic dangers

1 Ahu Antman, 'Performing and dying in the name of world peace', *Rupkatha Journal on Interdisciplinary Studies in Humanities* 2 no.1 (2010). http://rupkatha.com/performing-dying-world-peace-metaphor-real-life-feminist-performance (accessed 25 March 2018).

2 Press release for the film *My Letter to Pippa*. www.asminfilm.com/press (accessed 25 March 2018).

3 John Adams, 'Risk and culture', in Adam Burgess, Alberto Alemanno and Jens Zinn (eds), *Routledge handbook of risk studies* (London: Routledge, 2016), p. 86.

4 Sharon Beder, *Global spin: the corporate assault on environmentalism* (Totnes: Green Books, 2002).

5 John Adams, 'Risk compensation in cities at risk', in Helene Joffe, Tiziana Rossetto and John Adams (eds), *Cities at risk: living with perils in the 21st century* (Dordrecht: Springer, 2013): 25–44.

6 Wes Enzinna, 'King of the ride', *New York Times*, 22 March 2018. www.nytimes.com/ interactive/2018/03/22/magazine/voyages-worlds-greatest-hitchhiker.html (accessed 1 May 2018).

7 Enzinna, 'King of the ride'.

8 Bernd Wechner, 'Hitchhiking: a course in personal development?', 1 February 1998. http://bernd.wechner.info/Hitchhiking/Suite101/? 22 (accessed 4 March 2007).

9 Ana Bakran, *What's wrong with you?* Self-published, 2019.

10 Rosita Boland, *Sea legs: hitch-hiking the coast of Ireland alone* (Dublin: New Island Books, 1992), p. 150.

11 Nina Nooit, 'Why I continue to hitchhike', 2014. http://youarealltourists.blogspot. com/#!/2014/10/why-i-will-continue-to-hitchhike.html (accessed 28 October 2015).

12 Ana Bakran, '40 tips: what does it take to be a single woman hitchhiker?', n.d. www. anabakran.com/traveling/lady-hitchhiker (accessed 31 October 2019).

13 World Health Organization, *Global status report on road safety 2018* (Geneva: WHO, 2018), p. 6.

14 Oliver Milman, 'Invisible killer: fossil fuels caused 8.7m deaths globally in 2018, research finds', *Guardian*, 9 February 2021. www.theguardian.com/environment/2021/ feb/09/fossil-fuels-pollution-deaths-research (accessed 15 February 2021).

15 See W. Pudinski, *California crimes and accidents associated with hitchhiking* (Sacramento, CA: Department of the California Highway Patrol, Operational Analysis Section, 1974).

16 Larry Evans and Don Evans report that, based on 1,000 surveys distributed around US colleges, 91 per cent of men and 92 per cent of women stated that all of their journeys had been undertaken without physical assault of any nature (this appears to include verbal aggression). Don Evans and Larry Evans, *Hey now hitchhikers!* (St Louis, MO: Peace Institute Publishing, 1982), pp. 291–4.

17 Research cited by Joni E. Johnston, 'Serial killers in 2016: an overview', 12 September 2017. https://www.psychologytoday.com/gb/blog/the-human-equation/201701/ serial-killers-in-2016 (accessed 5 December 2019).

18 Seven unsolved murders on or around Highway 101 near Santa Rosa, California, occurred between 1971 and 1973. They all involved girls or young women, whom it was presumed had been killed whilst hitchhiking – Maureen Sterling and Yvonne Weber (who disappeared together), Kim Allen, Lori Lee Kursa, Carolyn Davis, Theresa Walsh and the unidentified remains of one other.

19 The Céline Figard story prompted renewed press interest in the more recent disappearance of eighteen-year-old Dinah McNicol, who had been hitchhiking with a friend after a music festival in 1991 but had vacated their lift first. Peter Tobin, who had also murdered other teenagers in different contexts, was eventually convicted of her murder in 2009.

20 Kevin Drum, 'Lead: America's real criminal element', *Mother Jones*, April/May 2013. www.motherjones.com/mag/2013/01/toc (accessed 24 January 2021).

21 Michelle Block, Alison Elder, Richard L. Auten, et al. 'The outdoor air pollution and brain health workshop'. *NeuroToxicology* 33 no. 5 (2012): 972–84. www.sciencedirect. com/science/article/abs/pii/S0161813X12002100?via%3Dihub (accessed 20 January 2021).

22 Damian Carrington, 'Exposure to air pollution may increase risk of Covid death, major study says', *Guardian*, 13 August 2020. www.theguardian.com/world/2020/aug/13/study-of-covid-deaths-in-england-is-latest-to-find-air-pollution-link (accessed 20 January 2021).

23 Kurt Moser, 'The dark side of "automobilism", 1900–30: violence, war and the motor car', *Journal of Transport History* 24 no. 2 (2003): 238–58.

24 Ginger Strand, *Killer on the road: violence and the American Interstate* (Austin, TX: University of Texas Press, 2012).

25 Maggie O'Kane, 'Search for Céline reveals the end of the road for hitchhiking', *Guardian*, 30 December 1995, p. 2. The exact wording of questions (or methodology) was never divulged, something a number of letter writers (including myself) pointed out. See 'Letters to the editor', *Guardian*, 3 January 1996, p. 12.

26 Quoted by Shaun Usher, 'Mass murder movies moving into overkill', *Daily Mail*, 29 January 1993, p. 39.

27 Nooit, 'Why I continue to hitchhike'.

28 Bakran, '40 tips'.

29 Barbara Noske, *Thumbing it: a hitchhiker's ride to wisdom* (Sydney: Gleebooks, 2018). The book was originally published as *Al lifter* in Dutch in 2000.

30 This was under the auspices of the UN Committee on the Elimination of Discrimination Against Women (article 8 of the UN Charter). See Feminist Alliance for International Action, 'The CEDAW Inquiry', 2014. www.fafia-afai.org (accessed 30 June 2021).

31 Tomos Lewis, 'RCMP discriminates against and abuses First Nation women', BBC News, 13 February 2013. https://www.bbc.co.uk/news/world-us-canada-21447735 (accessed 17 October 2014).

32 Cited in Tanya Kappo, 'Stephen Harper's comments on missing murdered indigenous women show "lack of respect"', 19 December 2014. www.cbc.ca/news/indigenous/stephen-harper-s-comments-on-missing-murdered-aboriginal-women-show-lack-of-respect-1.2879154 (accessed 6 November 2015).

33 *Highway of Tears symposium recommendation report*, 2006. www.highwayoftears.org/resources (accessed 3 August 2019).

34 See for example N'we Jinan Artists, *The highway*, Kitsumkalum First Nation, 2017. www.youtube.com/watch?v=hG_9d26oYeI (accessed 3 August 2019).

35 Jacqueline Holler started doing research with the communities along Highway 16 in 2012, working with police and transport operators to count the number of hitchhikers and to interview those who used the route, to ascertain their circumstances and motivations. See CBC News, 'BC Highway of Tears study polls hitchhikers habits', 25 May 2014. www.cbc.ca/news/canada/british-columbia/b-c-highway-of-tears-study-polls-hitchhikers-habits-1.2653808 (accessed 27 October 2015). This work has been extended to look at other parts of British Columbia and Alberta.

36 'A new option for Highway 16 travel?', *North Coast Review*, 12 February 2013. www.northcoastreview.blogspot.com (accessed 29 March 2018).

37 James Keller, 'Highway of Tears plans unclear, BC government silent, say local leaders', 5 November 2014. www.huffingtonpost.ca/2014/05/11/highway-of-tears_n_5304023.html (accessed 27 October 2015).

38 Objections to the hitchhiking posts at Hutt were voiced in the local news in the light of the 2011 murder of Dagmar Pytlickova, a Czech hitchhiker. See Paul Easton, 'Hitch-hiking pickup signs condemned', 14 September 2012. www.stuff.co.nz/dominion-post/news/7678995/Hitch-hiking-pickup-signs-condemned (accessed 4 March 2020).

39 John Cousins, 'Hitch-hiking to work could free up Tauranga's roads', *New Zealand Herald*, 22 March 2018. www.nzherald.nz/nz/news/article.cfm?c_id=1&objectid=12016556

(accessed 4 March 2020); Hamish McNeilly, 'A hitchhiker's guide to local government', 22 January 2019. www.stuff.co.nz/national/110060988/the-hitchhikers-guide-to-local-government.html (accessed 4 March 2020).

40 Compared with other member States of the Organisation for Economic Co-operation and Development (OECD), New Zealand has a very high rate of violence towards women, with one in three having experienced some form of abuse. See Amy Nelmes Bissett, 'Grace Millane is not alone', *Independent*, 21 December 2018. www.independent.co.uk/news/world/australasia/grace-millane-murder-new-zealand-domestic-violence-women-auckland-christchurch-a8687421.html (accessed 4 March 2020).

41 Antman, 'Performing and dying in the name of world peace'.

42 Rob Cope, 'Men wanted for hazardous journey', TEDxWanaka, 14 July 2014. www.youtube.com/watch?v=OmRDLoiUZ20 (accessed 20 January 2021).

Notes to Chapter 10: Good news from Vilnius

1 Jona Redslob, personal email, 21 November 2014.

2 Michael O' Regan, 'Alternative mobility cultures and the resurgence of hitchhiking', in Simone Fullagar, Erica Wilson and Kevin Markwell (eds), *Slow tourism: experiences and mobilities* (Bristol: Channel View Publications, 2012), pp. 182–42.

3 DeVon Smith was a famous hitchhiking face in the 1950s and 1960s, and was as known for his robot-making as for his self-declared 'professional hitchhiker' status. The first to receive a Guinness world record award, for 200,000 hitched miles, he also set a record for hitchhiking to all of the mainland states of the USA, something he accomplished in thirty-three days (a feat that stood until 1984).

4 This text from 2007 reproduces the feel of older competitions and has only recently been replaced on the Vilnius Hitchhiking Club website www.autostop.lt for the ongoing 'Baltics' race. The original document remains at the Internet archive pages of the VHHC, archive.org (both accessed 21 February 2021).

5 Anne E. Gorsuch, '"There's no place like home": Soviet tourism in late Stalinism', *Slavic Review* 62 no. 4 (2003), p. 760. She argues that the politicians were planning this even whilst laying siege to Berlin in 1945 and it took only a couple of years for coverage of overseas destinations to begin vanishing from travel magazines such as the ironically titled *Dookola Swiata* ('Around the world').

6 Mark Keck-Szajbel, 'Hitchhiker's paradise: the intersection of mass mobility, consumer demands and ideology in the People's Republic of Poland', in Cathleen M. Giustino, Catherine J. Plum and Alexander Vari (eds), *Socialist escapes: breaking away from ideology and everyday routine in Eastern Europe, 1945–1989* (New York: Berghahn Books, 2013), p. 167.

7 See Simon Calder, *Europe: a manual for hitch-hikers* (Oxford: Vacation Work Publications, 1985), pp. 178–82.

8 Mark Keck-Szajbel, 'A cheap imitation or tourist innovation? Polish tourism during State socialism through Eastern and Western eyes', *Polish-Anglo-Saxon Studies* 14–15 (2011), p. 138.

9 Calder, *Europe*, p. 180.

10 Franziska Augetein, 'Who is Angela Merkel?', *London Review of Books*, 14 July 2011, p. 7.

11 Diane P. Koenker, *Club red: vacation travel and the Soviet dream* (Ithaca, NY: Cornell University Press, 2013), p. 238.

12 Here I am thinking of the anthropological work of Terje Toomistu, curator of the multimedia, multidisciplinary exhibition 'Soviet hippies: the psychedelic underground of 1970s Soviet Estonia' which opened in Tartu at the Estonian National Museum in

August 2013 and subsequently moved many other international venues. This evolved into a 2017 documentary film *Soviet hippies*, which enjoyed international distribution.

13 Johannes Voswinkel, 'For Alexej Vorov, hitchhiking is a sport', *Die Zeit*, 18 November, www.zeit.de/online/2010/47/interview-vorov (accessed 21 September 2011).

14 Dennis Zuev, 'The practice of free-traveling: young people coping with access in post-Soviet Russia', *Young* 16 no. 5 (2008): 22. http://you.sagepub.com/cgi/content/abstract/16/1/5 (accessed 29 October 2008).

15 See https://hitchwiki.org/en/Academy_of_Free_Travel (accessed 29 October 2008).

16 Gorsuch, '"There's no place like home"', p. 761.

17 Gorsuch, '"There's no place like home"', p. 785.

18 Gorsuch, '"There's no place like home"', p. 770.

19 Krotov, *A practical guidebook for free travellers*, p. 46.

20 Zuev, 'The practice of free-traveling', p. 23. This sage/acolyte model clearly does not dominate all hitchhiking scenes. Igor Savelyev's novella *The pale city* and Irina Bogatyreva's *Off the beaten track*, portray a much more self-managed and organic ethos in the hitchhiking communities than one gleans through the eyes of the more famous Russian clubs and their leaders.

21 Sadly, Tatyana Kozyreva died in a scuba-diving accident on 3 April 2016 in Bandar Aceh, Indonesia, aged forty-three years. See Nina Nooit's obituary at https://you arealltourists.blogspot.com/2016/04/an-obituary.html (accessed 22 April 2016).

22 Karin Taylor's work identifies a long history of youth resistance through music to the controlling vision of the Sofia elite. See 'Socialist Orchestration of Youth: the 1968 Sofia Youth Festival and Encounters on the Fringe', *Ethnologia Balkanica* 7 (2003): 43–61.

23 Alexej Vorov, '500 hours'. http://transglobal-race.org/index.php?option=com_conte nt&view=article&id=40&Itemid=35&lang=en (accessed 20 October 2014).

Notes to Chapter 11: A prescription for hitchhiking?

1 'Thumbing it in translation', University of Sydney press release, www.sydney.edu.au/ news/84.html?newsstoryid=648 (accessed 3 April 2007).

2 Igor Savelyev, *The pale city*, in Igor Savelyev, Irina Bogatyreva and Tatiana Mazepina, *Off the beaten track: stories by Russian hitchhikers* (Moscow: GLAS, 2012), p. 78.

3 See the wonderfully titled 'The hitchhiker's guide to altruism: gene–culture co-evolution, and the internalization of norms', by Herbert Gintis (cited in Chapter 4).

4 Susan Pinker, *The village effect* (Toronto: Vintage, 2015).

5 Sherry Turkle, 'Connected but alone?', TED talk, February 2012 (exact date unknown). www.ted.com/talks/sherry_turkle_connected_but_alone (accessed 23 October 2015).

6 See Jonathan Purkis and James Bowen, 'How anarchism still matters', in Jonathan Purkis and James Bowen (eds), *Changing anarchism: anarchist theory and practice in a global age* (Manchester: Manchester University Press, 2004): 213–29.

7 Bernd Wechner, 'Thumbers from another century: the C.C.E.G.', 1 December 1998. http://bernd.wechner.info/Hitchhiking/Suite101/?32 (accessed 15 October 2014). See also: Melissa Eddy, 'Cleaving to the medieval, journeymen ply their trade in Europe', *New York Times*, 7 August 2017. www.nytimes.com/2017/08/07/world/europe/europe-journeymen.html (accessed 20 August 2018).

8 Feminist historian Linda Mahood notes that between 1970 and 1975 there were an esti-mated 50,000–100,000 hitchhikers passing through Winnipeg on the Trans-Canada Highway. Some of the official youth hostels could not cope and ex-military bases were employed to prevent people sleeping in public parks (with bus services sometimes laid

on by local authorities). There were occasional standoffs in more conservative places, where locals were concerned about drug use and deviance. See Mahood, 'Hitchin' a ride in the 1970s'.

9 Ruairí McKiernan, 'Amidst this pain and hurt, Ireland is reconnecting with its core values', *Irish Independent*, 27 July 2013. www.ruairimckiernan.com/articles1/amidst-this-pain-and-hurt-ireland-is-reconnecting-with-its-core-values (accessed 24 August 2018).

10 Formalised by Totnes resident Rob Hopkins, the Transition Towns movement encourages community participation in low-carbon lifestyles which are economically beneficial to all. In 2010, some 500 Totnes households took part in a 'Transition Streets' project, funded by the Department of Energy and Climate Change, and kept diaries of their energy conservation. See Helen Beetham, 'Social impacts of transition together (SITT)', 27 September 2011. www.transitionstreets.org.uk/wp-content/uploads/2012/07/SocialimpactsofTransitionStreets-finalreport.pdf (accessed 24 August 2018).

Notes to Afterword

1 John Berger, *About looking* (London: Writers and Readers Publishing Coop, 1984), p. 57.

2 In his most famous book, *Ways of seeing* (London: Penguin, 1984), John Berger outlines how art and visual culture normalises a view of (particularly male) power as natural, thereby simplifying our understanding of history and who is represented in it.

Bibliography

'A. Hiker', 'The truth about hiking is hitching'. *New York Times*, 23 July 1922. https://timesmachine.nytimes.com/timesmachine/1922/07/29.htm (accessed 10 March 2016).

AA/Populus. 'Hitchhikers swap their thumb on the road for a mouse on the super highway', 17 June 2009. www.prweb.com/releases/2009/06/prweb2541704.htm (accessed 20 May 2020).

Adams, Douglas. *The hitchhiker's guide to the galaxy*. London: Pan, 1979.

Adams, John. 'Cross-thinking about sustainability. Hypermobility: a challenge to governance'. Public lecture. Amsterdam, 11 May 2006. www.john-adams.co.uk/wp-content/uploads/2006/Amsterdam%20hypermobility4.pdf (accessed 5 July 2021).

Adams, John. 'Risk and culture'. In *Routledge handbook of risk studies*, edited by Adam Burgess, Alberto Alemanno and Jens Zinn, pp. 83–94. London: Routledge, 2016.

Adams, John. 'Risk compensation in cities at risk'. In *Cities at risk: living with perils in the 21st century*, edited by Helene Joffe, Tiziana Rossetto, and John Adams, pp. 25–44. Dordrecht: Springer, 2013.

Adorno, Theodore. *Prisms*. London: MIT Press, 1967.

Albrecht, Glenn. 'Ethics and directionality in nature'. In *Social ecology after Bookchin*, edited by Andrew Light, pp. 92–112. New York: Guildford Press, 1998.

Amato, Joseph A. *On foot: a history of walking*. New York: New York University Press, 2004.

Amnesty International. *Stolen sisters: discrimination and violence against indigenous women in Canada*, October 2004. www.amnesty.org/en/documents/amr20/001/2004/en/ (accessed 11 April 2019).

Anderson, Nels. *The hobo: the sociology of the homeless man*. Chicago, IL: University of Chicago Press, 1923.

Antman, Ahu. 'Performing and dying in the name of world peace'. *Rupkatha Journal on Interdisciplinary Studies in Humanities* 2 no. 1 (2010). http://rupkatha.com/performing-dying-world-peace-metaphor-real-life-feminist-performance (accessed 25 March 2018).

Arnold, Matthew. *Culture and Anarchy*. London: Cambridge University Press, 1932.

Augetein, Franziska. 'Who is Angela Merkel?' *London Review of Books*, 14 July 2011, p. 7.

Bachelder, Ben. 'Hitchhiking in Antarctica'. 14 December 2005. web.archive.org/web/20080611193855/http://www.digihitch.com/article840.html (accessed 8 July 2021).

Baker, Sharlene. *Finding signs*. New York: Alfred A. Knopf, 1990.

Bakran, Ana. '40 tips: what does it take to be a single woman hitchhiker?' n.d. www.anabakran.com/traveling/lady-hitchhiker (accessed 31 October 2019).

Bakran, Ana. *What's wrong with you?* Self-published, 2019.

Baskine, Gertrude. *Hitch-hiking the Alaska Highway*. Toronto: Macmillan, 1944.

Baudrillard, Jean. *Symbolic exchange and death*. London: Sage/TCS, 1993.

Bauman, Zygmunt. *Modernity and ambivalence*. Cambridge: Polity, 1991.

Bauman, Zygmunt. *Modernity and the Holocaust*. 1989. Reprinted with new afterword, Cambridge: Polity, 2008.

Beattie, Liza, David Miller, Emma Miller and Greg Philo. 'The media and Africa: images of disaster and rebellion'. In *Message received*, edited by Greg Philo, pp. 231–67. Harlow: Longman, 1999.

Beck, Ulrich. *Risk society: towards a new modernity*. London: Sage, 1992.

Becker, Howard. 'Whose side are we on?' *Social Problems* 14 (1967): 239–47.

Beder, Sharon. *Global spin: the corporate assault on environmentalism*. Totnes: Green Books, 2002.

Beetham, Helen. 'Social impacts of transition together (SITT)', 27 September 2011. www.transitionstreets.org.uk/wp-content/uploads/2012/07/SocialimpactsofTransitionStreets-finalreport.pdf 24 (accessed August 2018).

Bell, Beverly. 'Mali's gift economy'. *Yes Magazine*, 22 July 2009. www.dailygood.org/more.php?n=3893 (accessed 3 November 2017).

Bennet, Joe. *A land of two halves*. London: Simon and Schuster, 2004.

Bennett, Alison Muir. *Hitchhiker's guide to the ocean*. London: Adlard Coles, 2005.

Berger, John. *About looking*. London: Writers and Readers Publishing Cooperative, 1984.

Berger, John. *Ways of seeing*. London: Penguin, 1984.

Berlin, Isaiah. 'Two concepts of liberty'. In *Four essays on liberty*. Oxford: Oxford University Press, 1969.

Berman, Marshall. *All that is solid melts into air: the experience of modernity*. London: Penguin, 1982.

Bey, Hakim. *T.A.Z.: The temporary autonomous zone, ontological anarchy, poetic terrorism*. London: Autonomedia, 1991.

Bissett, Amy Nelmes. 'Grace Millane is not alone'. *Independent*, 21 December 2018. www.independent.co.uk/news/world/australasia/grace-millane-murder-new-zealand-domestic-violence-women-auckland-christchurch-a8687421.html (accessed 4 March 2020).

Block, Michelle, Alison Elder, Richard L. Auten, et al. 'The outdoor air pollution and brain health workshop'. *NeuroToxicology* 33 no. 5 (2012): 972–84. www.sciencedirect.com/science/article/abs/pii/S0161813X12002100?via%3Dihub (accessed 20 January 2021).

Boehm, Christopher. 'Egalitarian behaviour and reverse dominance hierarchy'. *Current Anthropology* 34 no. 3 (1993): 227–54.

Boehm, Christopher. *Hierarchy in the forest: the evolution of egalitarian behaviour*. Cambridge, MA: Harvard University Press, 1999.

Boehm, Christopher. *Moral origins*. New York: Basic Books, 2012.

Bogatyreva, Irina. *Off the beaten track*. In Igor Savelyev, Irina Bogatyreva and Tatiana Mazepina. *Off the beaten track: stories by Russian hitchhikers*. Moscow: GLAS, 2012, pp. 79–225.

Boland, Rosita. *Sea legs: hitch-hiking the coast of Ireland alone*. Dublin: New Island Books, 1992.

Bookchin, Murray. *The ecology of freedom*. Palo Alto, CA: Cheshire Books, 1982.

Boyes, Nicola. 'Agencies declare hitchhiking safe'. *New Zealand Herald*, 23 September 2005. www.nzherald.co.nz/z//news/article.cfm?c_id=1&objectid=10346920 (accessed 13 April 2007).

Bradbury, Ray. *Fahrenheit 451*. New York: Ballantine, 1953.

Brookes, Tim. *A hell of a place to lose a cow*. Washington, DC: National Geographic, 2000.

Brugiroux, André. *One people, one planet: the adventures of a world citizen*. Oxford: Oneworld, 1991.

Brunvand, Jan Harold. *The vanishing hitchhiker: American urban legends and their meanings*. New York: W. W. Norton, 2003.

Buryn, Ed. *Vagabonding in Europe and North Africa*. New York: Random House, 1971.

Calder, Simon. *Britain: a manual for hitchhikers*. Oxford: Vacation Work Publications, 1985.

Calder, Simon. *Europe: a manual for hitchhikers*. Oxford: Vacation Work Publications, 1985.

Calder, Simon and Rachel Palmer. 'The traveller: the complete guide to inter-railing'. *Independent*, 9 June 2001, pp. 2–3.

Carcelle, Xavier. *Hitch-hikers*. Brussels: Husson Editeur, 2007.

Carrington, Damian. 'Exposure to air pollution may increase risk of Covid death, major study says'. *Guardian*, 13 August 2020. www.theguardian.com/world/2020/aug/13/study-of-covid-deaths-in-england-is-latest-to-find-air-pollution-link (accessed 20 January 2021).

CBC News. 'BC Highway of Tears study polls hitchhiker habits', 25 May 2014. www.cbc.ca/news/canada/british-columbia/b-c-highway-of-tears-study-polls-hitchhikers-habits-1.2653808 (accessed 27 October 2015).

Chatwin, Bruce. *The songlines*. London: Picador, 1988.

Chesters, Graeme and David Smith. 'The neglected art of hitch-hiking: risk, trust and sustainability'. *Sociological Research Online* 6 no. 3 (2001). www.socresonline.org.uk/6/3/chesters.html (accessed 4 March 2007).

Childress, David. *A hitchhiker's guide to Africa and Arabia*. Chicago, IL: Chicago Review Press, 1977.

Choszcz, Kinga 'Freespirit'. *Led by destiny*. Pelplin: Bernardinum, 2004.

Choszcz, Kinga 'Freespirit'. 'My Africa' blog, April 2006. Retained at www.eioba.com/a/1iq7/my-africa-kinga-freespirit-part-i (accessed 17 October 2017).

Clastres, Pierre. *Society against the State: essays in political anthropology*. New York: Zone, 1987.

Coekin, Chris. *The hitcher*. London: Walkout Books, 2007.

Cohen, Erik. 'Nomads from affluence: notes on the phenomenon of drifter-tourism'. *International Journal of Comparative Sociology* 14 no. 1–2 (1973): 89–133.

Cohn, Norman. *In pursuit of the millennium*. New York: Oxford University Press, 1970.

Compagni Portis, J. A. 'Thumbs down: America and the decline of hitchhiking'. BA dissertation, Wesleyan University, 2015.

Cook, Karen S., Margaret Levi and Russell Hardin. *Cooperation without trust?* New York: Russell Sage Foundation, 2007.

Cope, Rob. *Men wanted for hazardous journey*. Wellington: National Library of New Zealand, 2016.

Cope, Rob. 'Men wanted for hazardous journey'. TEDxWanaka, 14 July 2014. www.youtube.com/watch?v=OmRDLoiUZ20 (accessed 20 January 2021).

Cousins, John. 'Hitch-hiking to work could free up Tauranga's roads'. *New Zealand Herald*, 22 March 2018. www.nzherald.co.nz/nz/news/article.cfm?c_id=1&objectid=12016556 (accessed 4 March 2020).

Cox, Lynne. *Swimming to Antarctica*. New York: Alfred A. Knopf, 2004.

Crassweller, Peter, Mary Alice Gordon and W. Tedford. 'An experimental investigation of hitchhiking'. *Journal of Psychology* 82 (1972): 43–7.

Cresswell, Tim. *The tramp in America*. London: Reaktion, 2001.

Czuprynski, Jakub, ed. *Rideshare Poland: communism and modernity*. Kraków: Korporacja Ha!art, 2005.

Daily Mail. 'Phone home – it's on the road to safer backpacking'. 30 October 1993, p. 56.

Daily Mirror. 'Scrub glamour out of this hitchhike zest'. 22 August 1950, p. 6.

Dallmeyer, K. E. 'Hitchhiking – a viable addition to a multimodal transportation system'. Centre for Urban Transportation Studies, University of Colarado/National Science

Foundation, 1975. https://trid.trb.org/Results?q=&datein=all&index=%22Hitchhik
ing%22#/View/286681 (accessed 28 January 2021).

Dargay, Joyce, Dermot Gately and Martin Sommer. 'Vehicle ownership and income
growth, worldwide: 1960–2030'. *Energy* 28 no. 4 (2007): 143–70.

Davies, Miranda and Natasha Jansz, eds. *Women travel.* London: Rough Guides, 1990.

Davis, Fred. *Yearning for yesterday: a sociology of nostalgia.* New York: Free Press, 1979.

Davis, J. R. and A. Locke. *Out of site, out of mind: new age travellers and the Criminal Justice and
Public Order Bill.* London: Children's Society, 1994.

Davis, John P. 'Stranger in the car'. *Reader's Digest*, August 1959, p. 55.

Davis, Stacy C., Susan W. Diegal and Robert G. Boundy. *Transportation energy data book*
(edition 30). Washington, DC: US Department of Energy, 2011.

de Waal, Frans. 'The evolution of empathy', 1 September 2005. www.greatergood.berkeley.
edu/article/item/the_evolution_of_empathy (accessed 9 February 2015).

Dein, Alan. 'Memory wars: the ghosts of Europe'. BBC World Service, 3 October 2010.
www.bbc.co.uk/programmes/p009xbbr (accessed 29 October 2010).

Develtere, P. 'Cooperative development in Africa up to the 1990s'. In *Cooperating out
of poverty*, edited by P. Develtere, I. Pollet and F. Wanyama, pp. 1–37. Geneva/
Washington, DC: International Labour Organization/World Bank Institute, 2008.

DiMaggio, Paul. *A hitchhiker's field manual.* New York: Macmillan, 1973.

DiMaggio, Paul. 'The sociology of the hitchhiker'. BA dissertation, Swarthmore College,
1971.

Dinets, Vladimir. 'Hitchhiking to Oimyakon and beyond'. http://dinets.travel.ru/kolyma.
htm (accessed 18 October 2014).

Drifter, The. 'In the driftway'. *The Nation*, 19 September 1923. http://bernd.wechner.info/
Hitchhiking/nation.html (accessed 12 February 2016).

Drum, Kevin. 'Lead: America's real criminal element'. *Mother Jones*, April/May 2013.
https://www.motherjones.com/mag/2013/01/toc (accessed 24 January, 2021).

Easton, Paul. 'Hitch-hiking pickup signs condemned', 14 September 2012. www.stuff.
co.nz/dominion-post/news/7678995/Hitch-hiking-pickup-signs-condemned (accessed
4 March 2020).

Eddy, Melissa. 'Cleaving to the medieval, journeymen ply their trade in Europe'. *New
York Times*, 7 August 2017. www.nytimes.com/2017/08/07/world/europe/europe-
journeymen.html (accessed 20 August 2018).

Edensor, Tim. 'M6-Junction 19–16: de familiarizing the mundane landscape'. *Space and
Culture* 6 no. 2 (2003): 151–68.

Edwardes, Tickner. *Lift-luck on southern roads.* 1910. London: Methuen, 1931.

Eighner, Lars. *Travels with Lizabet.* New York: Ballantine Books, 1994.

Ende Michael. *Momo.* London: Puffin, 1985.

Enzinna, Wes. 'A dream of secular utopia'. *New York Times*, 29 November 2015. www.
nytimes.com/2015/11/29/magazine/a-dream-of-utopia-in-hell.html (accessed 26 April
2020).

Enzinna, Wes. 'King of the ride'. *New York Times*, 22 March 2018. www.nytimes.com/
interactive/2018/03/22/magazine/voyages-worlds-greatest-hitchhiker.html (accessed
1 May 2018).

Evans, Don and Larry Evans. *Hey now hitchhikers!* St Louis, MO: Peace Institute Publishing,
1982.

Exit, Merle. 'Briarwood artist's life celebrated'. *TimesLedger* (Queens, NY), 30 April 2016.
https://qns.com/story/2016/04/30/briarwood-artists-life-celebrated.htm (accessed 15
November 2016).

Feminist Alliance for International Action. *The CEDAW Inquiry.* 2014. www.fafia-afai.org
(accessed 30 June 2021).

Fiedler, Joachim, Rolf Hoppe and Peter Berninghaus. *Anhalterwesen und Anhaltergefahren: unter besonderer Berücksichtigung des 'Kurztrampens'* [Hitchhikers and hitchhiking from the specific perspective of shorter journeys]. Wiesbaden: BKA Bundeskriminalamt, 1988. www.hitchwiki.org/en/media (accessed 7 April 2018).

Fox, Charles Elmer. *Tales of an American hobo*. Chicago, IL: University of Iowa Press, 1989.

Francis, John. *Planet walker*. Washington, DC: National Geographic, 2008.

Frankl, Viktor. *Man's search for meaning*. Boston: Beacon Press, 1959.

Franzoi, Stephen. 'The personality characteristics of the cross country hitchhiker'. *Adolescence* 20 no. 79 (1985): 655–68.

Fried, Frederick. No pie in the sky: the hobo as American cultural hero in the works of Jack London (1876–1916), John Dos Passos (1896–1970), and Jack Kerouac (1922–1969). New York: Citadel Press, 1964.

Frisby, Terence. *Kisses on a postcard*. London: Bloomsbury, 2009.

Furedi, Frank. *Culture of fear: risk taking and the morality of low expectation*. London: Continuum, 1997.

Furedi, Frank. *Therapy culture: cultivating vulnerability in an uncertain age*. London: Routledge, 2003.

Furuhata, M., M. Dessouky, F. Ordóñez, M. E. Brunet, X. Wang and S. Koeniga. 'Ride sharing: the state of the art and future directions'. *Transportation Research: Part B* 57 (2013): 28–46.

Ganser, Alexandra. 'On the asphalt frontier: American women's road narratives, spatiality, and transgression'. *Journal of International Women's Studies* 7 no. 4 (2006): 153–67.

Ganzel, Bill. 'Hitchhiking', n.d. 2003. https://livinghistoryfarm.org/farminginthe30s/water_08.html (accessed 31 July 2019).

Garner, Alice. 'Time and the hitchhiker'. Borders and crossings/Seuils et traverses conference. Melbourne University, Australia, 2008. www.raspunicum.de/misc/Garner_Time_Hitchhike.pdf (accessed 9 March 2016).

Garon, Paul and Beth Garon. *Woman with Guitar: Memphis Minnie's Blues*. San Francisco, CA: City Light Books, 2014.

Gemie, Sharif and Brian Ireland. *The Hippie Trail: a history*. Manchester: Manchester University Press, 2017.

Gintis, Herbert. 'The hitchhiker's guide to altruism: gene–culture co-evolution, and the internalization of norms'. *Journal of Theoretical Biology* 220 (2003): 407–18.

Gladding, Effie. *Across the continent by the Lincoln Highway*. New York: Brentanos, 1915.

Glendinning, Chellis. *My name is Chellis and I am in recovery from Western civilisation*. Gabriola Island: New Society Publishers, 2007.

Glendinning, Chellis. *When technology wounds*. New York: Morrow, 1990.

Glendinning, Chellis, Kirkpatrick Sale and Stephanie Mills. 'Three luddites talking', 2009. www.chellisglendinning.org/society.html (accessed 26 November 2016).

Gorsuch, Anne E. '"There's no place like home": Soviet tourism in late Stalinism'. *Slavic Review* 62 no. 4 (2003): 760–85.

Graeber, David. *Fragments of an anarchist anthropology*. Chicago, IL: Prickly Paradigm, 2004.

Graeber, David. *Towards an anthropological theory of value*. New York: Palgrave, 2001.

Graham, Stephen. *The gentle art of tramping*. London: Ernest Benn, 1929.

Grant, Richard. *Ghost riders: travels with American nomads*. London: Abacus, 2003.

Greenley, James P. and David G. Rice. 'Female hitchhiking: strain, control and subcultural approaches'. *Sociological Focus* 7 no. 1 (1973): 87–100.

Grieu, Benoît. 'Globe trotter' [interview]. http://beni.eurower.net/index.php/2006/08/22/1 (accessed 21 October 2014).

Grieu, Benoît. 'Never again: when a dream turns to nightmare'. *Kalasha Times*, 26 August 2011. www.thekalashatimes.wordpress.com/2011/08 (accessed 21 October 2014).

Grundstad, Robert. *Anti-hitchhiking laws*. Salem, OR: Legislative Administration Committee, 1982.

Guardian. 'Letters to the editor'. 3 January, 1996, p. 12.

Guardian. 'Zambian president urged to protect workers at Chinese-owned mines', 3 November 2011. www.theguardian.com/world/2011/nov/03/zambian-president-workers-chinese-mines (accessed 21 July 2017).

Guéguen, Nicholas. 'Bust size and hitchhiking: a field study'. *Perceptual and Motor Skills* 105 (2007): 1294–8.

Guéguen, Nicholas. 'Effect of humour on hitchhiking: a field experiment'. *North American Journal of Psychology* 3 no. 2 (2001): 369–76.

Guéguen, Nicholas and L. Lubomir. 'Hitchhiking women's hair colour'. *Perceptual and Motor Skills* 109 (2009): 941–8.

Guthrie, Woody. 1943. *Bound for glory*. London: Penguin, 2004.

Hall, Michael. *Remembering the Hippie Trail*. Newtonabbey: Island Publications, 2007.

Hammarlund, Sarah, Brian D. Connelly, Katherine J. Dickinson and Benjamin Kerr. 'The evolution of cooperation by the Hankshaw effect', 1 April 2015. www.biorxiv.org/content/10.1101/016667v1 (accessed 14 August 2019).

Hardy, Dennis. *Alternative communities in nineteenth century England*. Harlow: Longman, 1979.

Hardyman, Hugh. 'The art of hitchhiking'. *New Republic*, 29 July 1931, pp. 283–4. www.hitchwiki.org/en/Media (accessed 25 October 2018).

Hawks, Tony. *Round Ireland with a fridge*. London: Ebury Press, 1998.

Hayes, Donald. 'Review of Walter F. Weiss: *America's wandering youth*'. *Contemporary Sociology* 4 no. 4 (1975): 455.

Heckert, Jamie. 'Anarchist roots and routes'. *European Journal of Ecopsychology* 1 (2010): 19–36.

Highway of Tears symposium recommendation report, 2006. www.highwayoftears.org/resources (accessed 3 August 2019).

Hill, Christopher. *Puritanism and revolution*. London: Panther, 1968.

Hobbes, Thomas. *Leviathan*. 1651. London: Penguin, 1981.

Hofvendahl, Russ. *A land so fair and bright*. Dobbs Ferry, NY: Sheridan, 1991.

Holdt, Jacob. *American pictures*. Copenhagen: American Pictures Foundation, 1985.

Holdt Jacob. *American pictures* (2011 edition). www.american-pictures.com/english/book/American-Pictures-2011.pdf (accessed 21 June 2021).

Hopper, Tristin. 'LIFT program aims to make hitchhiking the "friendly dependable" choice for residents of B. C. island'. *National Post*, 4 March 2013. https://nationalpost.com/news/canada/lift-program-bowen-island-hitchhiking (accessed 19 February 2014).

Howard, J. A. 'The "normal" victim: the effects of gender stereotypes on reactions to victims'. *Social Psychology Quarterly* 47 no. 3 (1984): 270–9.

Human Rights Watch. 'Hungary: migrants abused at the border', 13 July 2016. www.hrw.org/news/2016/07/13/hungary-migrants-abused-border (accessed 15 November 2016).

Human Rights Watch. 'Q&A: Why the EU–Turkey migration deal is no blueprint', 14 November 2016, www.hrw.org/news/2016/11/14/qa-why-eu-turkey-migration-deal-no-blueprint (accessed 15 November 2016).

Hurley, Kieran. *Hitch* [play]. Leeds: Carriageworks, 2010.

Hutchinson, Brian. 'With one murder solved, difficult "Highway of Tears" investigations go on', 26 September 2012. https://nationalpost.com/news/canada/with-one-murder-solved-difficult-highway-of-tears-investigations-go-on (accessed 4 March 2020).

Iaquinto, Benjamin Lucca. 'Fear of a Lonely Planet: author anxieties and the main streaming of a guidebook'. *Current Issues in Tourism* 14 no. 8 (2011): 705–23. doi.org/10.1080/13683500.2011.555527.

Illich, Ivan. *Energy and equity*. London: Marion Boyars, 1974.

Independent. 'Has Holocaust history just been rewritten? Astonishing new research shows Nazi camp network targeting Jews was "twice as big as previously thought"', 3 March 2013. www.independent.co.uk/news/world/europe/has-holocaust-history-just-been-rewritten-astonishing-new-research-shows-nazi-camp-network-targeting-jews-was-twice-as-big-as-previously-thought-8518407.html (accessed 15 October 2015).

Ipavec, Miran. *Hitchhiking tales from European roads*. Self-published, 2014. www.autostop.si/hitchhiking-tales-from-european-roads (accessed 10 November 2016).

Jackson, Matthew. *The Canada chronicles*. Calgary: Summit Studios, 2004.

Jacobs, Frank. 'Thumbs up? This map shows the best places to hitchhike in Europe', 14 June 2019. www.weforum.org/agenda/2019/06/thumbs-up-map-shows-europe-s-hitchhiking-landscape (accessed 20 January 2021).

Jacobs, Jane. *The death and life of great American cities*. New York: Random House, 1961.

Jaques-Aldridge, Mary. *Trio's trek*. London: W. H. Allen, 1955.

Johnson, R. W. and J. H. Johnson. 'A cross-validation on the Sn scale on the Psychological Screening Inventory with female hitchhikers'. *Journal of Clinical Psychology* 34 no. 2 (1978): 366–7.

Johnston, Joni E. 'Serial killers in 2016: an overview', 12 September 2017. https://www.psychologytoday.com/gb/blog/the-human-equation/201701/serial-killers-in-2016 (accessed 5 September 2019).

K, R. *Travels with a road dog: hitchhiking along the roads of the Americas*. Self-published, 2012.

Kappo, Tanya. 'Stephen Harper's comments on missing murdered indigenous women show "lack of respect"', 19 December 2014. www.cbc.ca/news/indigenous/stephen-harper-s-comments-on-missing-murdered-aboriginal-women-show-lack-of-respect-1.2879154 (accessed 6 November 2015).

Kaufman, Kenn. *Kingbird highway: the biggest year in the life of an extreme birder*. Boston, MA: Houghton Miflin, 2006.

Keck-Szajbel, Mark. 'A cheap imitation or tourist innovation? Polish tourism during State socialism through Eastern and Western eyes'. *Polish-Anglo-Saxon Studies* 14–15 (2011): 131–46.

Keck-Szajbel, Mark. 'Hitchhiker's paradise: the intersection of mass mobility, consumer demands and ideology in the People's Republic of Poland'. In *Socialist escapes: breaking away from ideology and everyday routine in Eastern Europe, 1945–1989*, edited by Cathleen M. Giustino, Catherine J. Plum and Alexander Vari, pp. 167–86. New York: Berghahn Books, 2013.

Keller, James. 'Highway of Tears plans unclear, BC government silent, say local leaders', 5 November 2014. www.huffingtonpost.ca/2014/05/11/highway-of-tears_n_5304023.html (accessed 27 October 2015).

Kempton, Richard. *Provo: Amsterdam's anarchist revolt*. New York: Autonomedia, 2007.

Kerouac, Jack. *On the road*. 1957. London: Penguin, 1984.

Klein, Naomi. *The shock doctrine*. London: Penguin, 2008.

Koenker, Diane P. *Club red: vacation travel and the Soviet dream*. Ithaca, NY: Cornell University Press, 2013.

Krakauer, Jon. *Into the wild*. New York: Anchor Books, 1999.

Krotov, Anton. *A practical guidebook for free travellers*. Translated by Peter Lagutkin. Moscow: Self-published, 2014.

Krznaric, Roman. *Empathy: a handbook for revolution*. London: Rider Books, 2012.

Kumar, Ajay and Fanny Barrett. *Stuck in traffic: Africa's urban transport*. Washington, DC: World Bank, 2008.

Kyvig, David. *Daily life in the United States, 1920–1939: decades of promise and pain*. Westport, CT: Greenwood Publishing, 2001.

Lall, Somik Vinay, J. Vernon Henderson and Anthony J. Venables. *Africa's cities: opening doors to the world*. Washington, DC: World Bank, 2017.

Laviolette, Patrick. 'Why did the anthropologist cross the road? Hitch-hiking as a stochastic modality of travel'. *Ethnos: Journal of Anthropology* 81 (2016): 379–401.

Lee, Laurie. *As I walked out one midsummer morning*. 1969. London: Penguin, 1971.

Levine, Robert V. 'Measuring helping behaviour across cultures'. Online readings in Psychology and Culture, Unit 5, 2003. http://scholarworks.gvsu.edu/orpc/vol5/iss3/2 (accessed 17 October 2017).

Levy, Andrew. 'Convicted killer Peter Tobin, murdered two teenage girls and buried them in his back garden', 24 June 2009. www.dailymail.co.uk/news/article-1194995/Convicted-killer-Peter-Tobin-accused-1991-murder-A-level-student-Dinah-McNicol.html (accessed 26 June 2020).

Lewis, Tomos. 'RCMP discriminates against and abuses First Nation women'. BBC News, 13 February 2013. www.bbc.co.uk/news/world-us-canada-21447735 (accessed 17 October 2014).

Light, Andrew, ed. *Social ecology after Bookchin*. New York: Guildford Press, 1998.

London, Jack. *The road*. London: Macmillan, 1907.

Luhmann, Niklas. *Observations on modernity*. Stanford, CA: Stanford University Press, 1998.

Mackinnon, Audrey. 'Greyhound makes final passenger trip on BC's Highway of Tears'. CBC News, 23 June 2018. https://newsinteractives.cbc.ca/longform/last-greyhound (accessed 4 March 2020).

MacMahon, K. 'The invisible women of the Great Depression'. www.peakoilblues.org/blog/2009/01/14/the-invisible-women-of-the-great-depression/&gt (accessed 28 June 2016).

Mahood, Linda. 'Canada's thumb wars: hitchhiking, youth rituals and risk in the 20th century'. *Journal of Social History* 49 (2016): 647–70.

Mahood, Linda. 'Hitchin' a ride in the 1970s: Canadian youth culture and the Romance with mobility'. *Histoire sociale/Social History* 47 no. 93 (2014): 207–27.

Mahood, Linda. *Thumbing a ride: hitchhiking, hostels and counterculture in Canada*. Victoria: University of British Columbia Press, 2019.

Maitland, Sara. *A book of silence*. London: Granta, 2009.

Malinowski, Bronislaw. *Argonauts of the western Pacific*. London: Dutton, 1961.

Manaev, Georgy. 'A hitchhiker's guide to the Russian galaxy'. *Russia Beyond the Headlines*, 14 August 2013. www.rbth.com/arts/2013/08/14/a_hitchhikers_guide_to_the_russian_galaxy_28895.html (accessed 25 June 2014).

Mangena, Isaac. 'Bus boycott which forced apartheid u-turn', 29 September 2012. http://news.iafrica.com/features/666218.htm (accessed 8 August 2018).

Marcus, Greil. *Lipstick traces: a secret history of the twentieth century*. London: Seeker and Warburg, 1990.

Martin, Ian. 'Sixty things I've learned at sixty'. Guardian, 30 April 2013, G2, p. 6.

Maslow, Abraham. *Towards a psychology of being*. Princeton, MA: Van Nostrand Reinhold, 1962.

Mauss, Marcel. 1923. *The gift: forms and functions of exchange in archaic societies*. Translated by Ian Gunnison. New York: Norton, 1967.

McAdam, Doug. *Freedom summer*. New York: Oxford University Press, 1988.

McCandless, Carine. *The wild truth*. San Francisco, CA: Harper One, 2014.

McCauley, Lauren. 'Across Europe, tens of thousands rally to welcome refugees', 12 September 2015. www.commondreams.org/news/2015/09/12/across-europe-tens-thousands-rally-welcome-refugees (accessed 15 November 2016).

McKiernan, Ruairí. 'Amidst this pain and hurt, Ireland is reconnecting with its core values'. *Irish Independent*, 27 July 2013. www.ruairimckiernan.com/articles1/

amidst-this-pain-and-hurt-ireland-is-reconnecting-with-its-core-values (accessed 24 August 2018).

McNeilly, Hamish. 'A hitchhiker's guide to local government', 22 January 2019. www.stuff. co.nz/national/110060988/the-hitchhikers-guide-to-local-government.html (accessed 4 March 2020).

Mickens, Julie. 'Robot man and world record hitchhiker: DeVon Smith 1926–2003'. *Pittsburg City Paper*, 12 June 2003. www.pghcitypaper.com/pittsburgh/robot-man-and-world-record-hitchhiker/Content?oid=1335168 (accessed 17 May 2020).

Milman, Oliver. 'Invisible killer: fossil fuels caused 8.7m deaths globally in 2018, research finds'. *Guardian*, 9 February 2021. www.theguardian.com/environment/2021/feb/09/fossil-fuels-pollution-deaths-research (accessed 15 February 2021).

Mitchell, Don. *Thumb tripping*. London: Jonathan Cape, 1971.

Moran, Joe. 'A guide to hitchhiking's decline'. *Guardian*, 5 June 2009. www.theguardian.com/commentisfree/2009/jun/05/hitchhiking-decline-britain (accessed 9 June 2009).

Morgan, C. J., J. S. Lockard, C. E. Fahrenbruch and J. L. Smith. 'Hitchhiking: social signals at a distance'. Bulletin of the Psychonomic Society 5 (1975): 459–61.

Moser, Kurt. 'The dark side of "automobilism", 1900–30: violence, war and the motor car'. *Journal of Transport History* 24 no. 2 (2003): 238–58.

Mukerji, Chandra. 'Bullshitting: road lore among hitchhikers'. Social Problems 25 no. 3 (1978): 242–3.

Mweetwa, Sylvia. 'Zambia: traditional knowledge can help farmers adapt to climate change', 10 November 2011. https://allafrica.com/stories/201111100896.html (accessed 1 December 2015).

Myers, Tamara and Joan Sangster. 'Retorts, runaways and riots: patterns of resistance in Canadian reform schools for girls 1930–60'. *Journal of Social History*, 34 no. 3 (2001): 669–97.

Myers, Wendy. *Seven league boots*. London: Hodder and Stoughton, 1969.

Nair, Rosini. 'Salt Spring residents defend island's hitchhiking culture', 6 June 2017. www.cbc.ca/news/canada/british-columbia/salt-spring-residents-defend-island-s-hitchhiking-culture-1.4147981 (accessed 22 January 2020).

Neville, Richard. *Playpower*. Aylesbury: Jonathan Cape, 1970.

New York Times. 'Auto-hiking: a pastime for youth', 29 July 1923.

New York Times. 'Hitch-hike in eighteen days, Arkansas to Yale', 23 September 1923. https://timesmachine.nytimes.com/timesmachine/1923/09/23/issue.html (accessed 10 March 2016).

New York Times. 'Hitch-hikes 10 hours from capital here', 13 October 1926. https://timesmachine.nytimes.com/timesmachine/1926/10/13/issue.html (accessed 10 March 2016).

Nooit, Nina. 'Why I continue to hitchhike', 2014. http://youarealltourists.blogspot.com/#!/2014/10/why-i-will-continue-to-hitchhike.html (accessed 28 October 2015).

Noske, Barbara. *Thumbing it: a hitchhiker's ride to wisdom*. Sydney: Gleebooks, 2018.

Notes from Nowhere. *We are everywhere: the irresistible rise of global anti-capitalism*. London: Verso, 2003.

Ntomba, R. 'Zambia–China: all-weather friends?', *New African*, 13 March 2015. https://newafricanmagazine.com/10213/ (accessed 18 August 2019).

O'Kane, Maggie. 'Search for Celine reveals the end of the road for hitchhiking'. *Guardian*, 30 December 1995, p. 2.

O'Regan, Michael. 'Alternative mobility cultures and the resurgence of hitchhiking'. In *Slow tourism: experiences and mobilities*, edited by Simone Fullagar, Erica Wilson and Kevin Markwell, pp. 182–42. Bristol: Channel View Publications, 2012.

Osteen, Mark. 'Noir's cars: automobility and amoral space in American film noir'. *Journal of Popular Film and Television* 35 no. 4 (2008), 183–92.

O'Toole, Sean. 'Rush hour rest stop', 20 August 2014. www.urbanafrica.net/urban-voices/rush-hour-rest-stop (accessed 27 October 2017).

Packer, Jeremy. *Mobility without mayhem: safety, cars and citizenship*. Durham, NC: Duke University Press, 2008.

Pekárková, Iva. Truck stop rainbows. Translated by David Powelstock. New York: Vintage International, 1992.

Piller-Greenspan, Ida, with Susan M. Branting. *When the world closed its doors*. Boulder, CO: Paradigm, 2006.

Pinker, Susan. *The village effect*. Toronto: Vintage, 2015.

Pinner, Dina. 'Thoughts on hitchhiking'. *Jerusalem Post*, 23 June 2014. www.jpost.com/Opinion/Op-Ed-Contributors/Thoughts-on-hitchhiking-360314 (accessed 14 February 2015).

Pitt-Kethley, Fiona. *The pan principle*. London: Sinclair Stevenson, 1994.

Post, Emily. *By motor to the Golden Gate*. 1916. Annotated by Jane Lancaster. Jefferson, NC: McFarland, 2004.

Potts, Rolf. 'We don't (really) know Jack', 5 September 2007. www.worldhum.com/features/travel-books/we_dont_really_know_jack_20070905 (accessed 1 November 2011).

Power, Matthew. 'The cult of Chris McCandless'. *Men's Journal*, 15 October 2012. www.mensjournal.com/features/the-cult-of-chris-mccandless-20121015 (accessed 26 November 2016).

Priestley, Harry. 'Travelling man: interview with Tony Wheeler'. *Citylife: Chiangmai* 17 no. 7 (2008). https://web.archive.org/web/20090215042500/www.chiangmainews.com/ecmn/viewfa.php?id=2228 (accessed 10 June 2020).

Prokosch, Frederic. 1935. *The Asiatics*. London: Robin Clark, 1991.

Pudinski, W. *California crimes and accidents associated with hitchhiking*. Sacramento, CA: Department of the California Highway Patrol, Operational Analysis Section, 1974.

Pugh, Martin. *State and society: a social and political history of Britain 1870–1997*. London: Arnold, 2002.

Purkis, Jonathan. 'A sociology of environmental protest: Earth First! and the theory and practice of anarchism'. PhD thesis, Manchester Metropolitan University, 2001.

Purkis, Jonathan. 'The hitchhiker as a theorist'. In *The Bloomsbury companion to anarchism*, edited by Ruth Kinna, pp. 140–61. London: Bloomsbury, 2014.

Purkis, Jonathan and James Bowen. 'How anarchism still matters'. In *Changing anarchism: anarchist theory and practice in a global age*, edited by Jonathan Purkis and James Bowen, pp. 213–29. Manchester: Manchester University Press, 2004.

Purkis, Patricia. 'Childhood memories of the War'. Family letters, Hull, n.d.

Putnam, Robert D. *Bowling alone: the collapse and revival of American community*. New York: Simon and Schuster, 2000.

Reid, John. 'The acceptance of hitchhiking in American culture, 1929–1988'. BA dissertation, Southern Illinois University, 2010.

Reid, Michael D. 'Salt Spring Islanders rally in drive to save hitchhiking tradition'. *Times Colonist*, 6 June 2017.

Reinisch, Jessica. 'History matters, but which one?', History and Policy website, September 2015. www.historyandpolicy.org/policy-papers/category/reinisch-jessica (accessed 7 January 2020).

Reitman, Ben. *Sister of the road: the autobiography of Box-car Bertha*. New York: Harper and Row, 1937.

Rifkin, Jeremy, with Ted Howard. *Entropy: a new world view*. London: Paladin, 1985.

Riis, Jacob. 1890. *How the other half lives: studies among the tenements of New York*. Whitefish, MT: Kessinger Publishing, 2004.

Rinvolucri, Mario. *Hitchhiking*. Self-published, 1974. https://prino.neocities.org/mario_rinvolucri (accessed 10 November 2015).

Robbins, Tom. *Even cowgirls get the blues*. New York: Bantam, 1976.

Rodger, Ian. *A hitch in time: recollection of a journey*. London: Hutchinson, 1966.

Roszak, Theodore. *The making of a counter culture*. New York: Anchor, 1969.

Saggin, Giuilo. *So I did*. Self-published, 1999. http://soididbook.blogspot.com (accessed 28 July 2019).

Said, Edward. *Culture and imperialism*. London: Chatto and Windus, 1993.

Savelyev, Igor. *The pale city*. In *Off the beaten track: stories by Russian hitchhikers*, edited by Igor Savelyev, Irina Bogatyreva and Tatiana Mazepina, pp. 7–78. Moscow: GLAS, 2012.

Schlebecker, John. 'An informal history of hitchhiking'. *Historian* 20 (1958): 314–16.

Scott, James C. *Seeing like a state*. New Haven, CT: Yale University Press, 1998.

Scott, James C. *The art of not being governed*. New Haven, CT: Yale University Press, 2009.

Seldon, Anthony. *Trust: how we lost it and how to get it back again*. London: Biteback, 2010.

Shanin, Valery. 'From Moscow to Sicily and back', 22 June 2005. www.digihitch.com (accessed 23 June 2014).

Sheller, Mimi. 'Automotive emotions: feeling the car'. *Theory, Culture and Society* 21 no. 4–5 (2004): 221–42.

Sherwood, Harriet. 'The women of the miners' strike: "We caused a lot of havoc"'. *Guardian*, 7 April 2014. www.theguardian.com/lifeandstyle/2014/apr/07/women-miners-strike-1984-wives-picket-lines (accessed 20 March 2021).

Sicwetsha. M. 'Hitch-hiking research report, reasons behind hitch-hiking in the Eastern Cape', 2009. www.ectransport.gov.za/uploads/reports/reasons-behind-hitch-hiking-in-the-eastern-cape1.pdf (accessed 27 October 2017).

Singer, Peter. *The expanding circle: ethics and sociobiology*. Oxford: Oxford University Press, 1981.

Smith, Alan. 'When good deeds turn bad'. *Guardian*, 22 November 2014, pp. 32–40.

Smith, Paul. *Twitchhiker: how one man travelled the world by Twitter*. Chichester: Summersdale, 2010.

Snyder, Gary. *Back country*. New York: New Directions, 1968.

Snyder, Gary. *Mountains and rivers without end*. Berkeley, CA: Counterpoint, 1996.

Snyder, Gary. *Myths and texts*. New York: New Directions, 1978.

Snyder, M., J. Grether and K. Keller. 'Staring and compliance: a field experiment on hitchhiking'. *Journal of Applied Social Psychology* 4 (1974): 165–70.

Solnit, Rebecca. 'Protest and persist'. *Guardian*, 17 March 2017. https://www.theguardian.com/world/2017/mar/13/protest-persist-hope-trump-activism-anti-nuclear-movement (accessed 1 April 2017).

Solnit, Rebecca. *Wanderlust: a history of walking*. London: Verso, 2002.

Sontag, Susan. *On photography*. Harmondsworth: Penguin, 1982.

Stainsby, Macdonald. 'We can't walk on water but we can hitchhike on it', 30 January 2008. www.macdonaldstainsby.com (accessed 14 June 2021).

Stainsby, Macdonald and Dru Oja Jay. 'Offsetting resistance: the effects of foundation funding and corporate fronts from the Great Bear Rainforest to the Athabasca River', 2009. www.offsettingresistance.ca (accessed 26 November 2016).

Stead, Jean. *Never the same again: women and the miners' strike*. London: Women's Press, 1987.

Stein, Alex. 'Memphis Minnie, genocide, and identity politics: a conversation with Lorna Dee Cervantes'. *Michigan Quarterly Review* 42 no. 4 (2003). http://hdl.handle.net/2027/spo.act2080.0042.406 (accessed 28 June 2016).

Steinbeck, John. *The grapes of wrath.* 1939. London: Pan, 1982.

Steinbeck, John. *Travels with Charley: in search of America.* 1962. London: Pan, 1976.

Steves, Rick. *Travel as a political act.* New York: Nation Books, 2009.

Stine, Sharon. *Gypsy boots.* Bloomington, IN: Author House, 2008.

Stoakes. David. 'Vital clue holds key to double murder riddle'. *South Wales Evening Post,* 3 November 2000, p. 15.

Strand, Ginger. 'Hitchhiking's time has come again'. *New York Times,* 10 November 2012. www.nytimes.com/2012/11/11/opinion/sunday/hitchhikings-time-has-come-again.html (accessed 23 January 2018).

Strand, Ginger. *Killer on the road: violence and the American Interstate.* Austin, TX: University of Texas Press, 2012.

Strub, Morgan. 'Foreword' to Irv Thomas, *Derelict days,* pp. xi–xiv. Bloomington, IN: Author House, 2004.

Strub, Morgan. 'The story behind my first hitchhike', 8 July 2001, web.archive.org/ web/20110809121424/http://www.digihitch.com/article72.htm (accessed 21 February 2021).

Sykes, Simon and Tom Sykes, eds. *No such thing as a free ride.* Fredericton: Goose Lane, 2008.

Symington, Martin. 'The hitchhiker's guide to nowhere'. *Times,* 17 July 1999, p. 7.

Taylor, Karin. 'Socialist orchestration of youth: the 1968 Sofia youth festival and encounters on the fringe'. *Ethnologia Balkanica* 7 (2003): 43–61.

Theroux, Paul. *The tao of travel.* New York: Houghton Harcourt, 2011.

Thomas, Irv. *Derelict days: sixty years on the roadside path to enlightenment.* Bloomington, IN: Author House, 2004.

Thomson, Helen. 'Study of Holocaust survivors shows trauma passed onto children's genes'. *Guardian,* 21 August 2015. www.theguardian.com/science/2015/aug/21/study-of-holocaust-survivors-finds-trauma-passed-on-to-childrens-genes.htm (accessed 14 August 2019).

Times. 'A college of thumbers' (editorial). 23 February, 1940, p. 9.

Tomory, David. *A season in heaven.* London: Thorsons, 1996.

Transeuropa Festival. 'Hitchhiking challenge', 23 September 2015. www.facebook.com/ events/942950219084865/?active_tab=discussion (accessed 10 November 2016).

Turkle, Sherry. 'Connected but alone?', TED talk February 2012 (exact date unknown). www.ted.com/talks/sherry_turkle_connected_but_alone (accessed 23 October 2015).

Turner, Louis and John Ash. *The golden hordes.* London: Constable, 1975.

Turner, R. 'Gypsies and British parliamentary language: an analysis'. *Romani Studies* 12 no. 1 (2002): 1–34.

Tzu, Lao. *Tao te ching.* Translated by Ursula Le Guin. Boulder, CO: Shambhala, 1997.

University of Sydney. 'Thumbing it in translation' [press release]. www.sydney.edu.au/ news/84.html?newsstoryid=648 (accessed 3 April 2007).

Usher, Shaun. 'Mass murder movies moving into overkill'. *Daily Mail,* 29 January 1993, p. 3.

Vaughan, Genevieve, ed. *Women and the gift economy: a radically different worldview is possible.* Toronto: Ianna Publications, 2007.

Veselka, Vanessa. 'The green screen: the lack of female road narratives and why it matters'. *American Reader* 4 no. 1 (2012). http://theamericanreader.com/green-screen-the-lack-of-female-road-narratives-and-why-it-matters (accessed 3 August 2019).

Viard, Sylvian. 'Auto-stop: Approche géographique'. MA thesis, Université de Paris, 1999.

Villarino, Juan. *Hitchhiking in the axis of evil.* Buenos Aires: Südpol, 2013 (first published 2011).

Vorov, Alexej. '500 hours'. http://transglobal-race.org/index.php?option=com_content& view=article&id=40&Itemid=35&lang=en (accessed 20 October 2014).

Voswinkel, Johannes. 'For Alexey Vorov, hitchhiking is a sport'. *Die Zeit*, 18 November 2010. www.zeit.de/online/2010/47/interview-vorov (accessed 21 September 2011).

Wald, Elijah. *Riding with strangers*. Chicago, IL: Chicago Review Press, 2005.

Ward, Colin. *Anarchy in action*. London: Freedom Press, 1973.

Ward, Colin and David Goodway. *Talking anarchy*. Nottingham: Five Leaves, 2003.

Weaver, C. Kay. 'Crimewatch UK: keeping women off the streets'. In *News, gender and power*, edited by Cynthia Carter, pp. 262–75. London: Routledge, 1998.

Weber, Max. 'Science as vocation'. In *Essays in Sociology*, edited by H. Gerth and C.W. Mills. 129–156. New York: Oxford University Press, 1946.

Weber, Max. *The protestant ethic and the spirit of capitalism*. 1930. London: Allen and Unwin, 1976 (reprinted with new introduction).

Wechner, Bernd. 'A North American Hitchhiker gathering', 1 December 2002. http:// bernd.wechner.info/Hitchhiking/Suite101/?80 (accessed 4 July 2021).

Wechner, Bernd. *Anywhere but here: memoirs of a hitchhiker, 1997–2004*. http://bernd.wechner. info/Hitchhiking/Memories (accessed 28 July 2019).

Wechner, Bernd. 'Charles Elmer Fox – an ardent thumber who loves the rails', 1 July 2000. http://bernd.wechner.info/Hitchhiking/Suite101/?51 (accessed 4 July 2021).

Wechner, Bernd. 'Hitchhiking: a course in personal development?', 1 February 1998. http://bernd.wechner.info/Hitchhiking/Suite101/? 22 (accessed 4 March 2007).

Wechner, Bernd. 'Hitch-hiking in the Bible', n.d. http://bernd.wechner.info/Hitchhiking/ bible.html (accessed 7 July 2021).

Wechner, Bernd. 'Professional hitchhikers: Britain's trade platers', 1 May 2001. http:// bernd.wechner.info/Hitchhiking/Suite101/?61 (accessed 28 July 2019).

Wechner, Bernd. 'Secure hitchhiking (in a new age)', 1 January 1999. http://bernd. wechner.info/Hitchhiking/Suite101/?33 (accessed 4 March 2007).

Wechner, Bernd. 'Thumbers from another century: the C.C.E.G.', 1 December 1998. http://bernd.wechner.info/Hitchhiking/Suite101/?32 (accessed 15 October 2014).

Weiss, Walter F. *America's wandering youth: a sociological study of young hitchhikers in the United States*. New York: Exposition Press, 1974.

Welsh, Ken and Katie Wood. *Hitch-hiker's guide to Europe*. London: HarperCollins, 1994.

Wernig, Phil. *The hitchhikers*. Milbrae, CA: Celestial Arts, 1972.

Wharton, Don. 'Thumbs down on hitchhikers'. *Reader's Digest* (April 1950), n.p.

Wheeler, Tony. *Across Asia on the cheap*. London: Lonely Planet Publications, 1975.

Whishaw, Lorna. *As far as you'll take me*. London: Hammond, Hammond and Co., 1958.

Wilkinson, Richard and Kate Pickett. *The spirit level: why more equal societies almost always do better*. London: Penguin, 2010.

Williams, Christopher A., Niall P. Hanan, Jason C. Neff, et al. 'Africa and the global carbon cycle'. *Carbon Balance and Management*, 7 March 2007. https://cbmjournal. biomedcentral.com/articles/10.1186/1750-0680-2-3 (accessed 10 November 2015).

Williams, Heathcote. *Autogeddon*. London: Jonathan Cape, 1991.

Wittimack, Edgar Franklin. 'The hitchhiking hobo' [cover illustration]. *Saturday Evening Post*, 24 October 1925.

Wolf, Winfried. *Car mania: a critical history of transport*. London: Pluto Press, 1996.

Wordsworth, William and Samuel Taylor Coleridge,. 1798. *Lyrical ballads: with pastoral and other poems. In two volumes*. https://archive.org/details/lyricalballadswiooword/page/6/ mode/2up (accessed 20 March 2021).

World Health Organization. *Global status report on road safety 2018*. Geneva: WHO, 2018.

Yining, Peng. 'Thumbing a ride to grab an adventure across the nation'. *China Daily* (Beijing, English language version), 5 April 2013, p. 9.

Zimbardo, Philip. *The Lucifer effect: understanding how good people turn evil*. New York: Random House, 2007.

Zinn, Howard. *A people's history of the United States*. New York: Harper Perennial, 2003.

Zornig, Lisabeth. 'Danish government persecutes people helping refugees'. Dear Kitty blog, 11 March 2016. http://dearkitty1.wordpress.com (accessed 10 November 2016).

Zuev, Dennis. 'The practice of free-traveling: young people coping with access in post-Soviet Russia'. *Young* 16 no. 5 (2008): 22. http://you.sagepub.com/cgi/content/abstract/16/1/5 (accessed 29 October 2008).

Zulu, Princess Kasune, with Belinda Collins. *Warrior princess: fighting for life with courage and hope*. Downers Grove, IL: IVP Books, 2009.

Art productions

A tribute to Sissy Hankshaw [dance]. Choreographed by Sarah Morrison, 2001. www.morrisondance.com/sissy (accessed 16 September 2008).

Long, Richard. *Ben Nevis hitchhike* [artwork], 1967. Tate London. www.tate.org.uk/art/artworks/long-untitled-t02065 (accessed 10 June 2020).

'Soviet hippies: the psychedelic underground of 1970s Soviet Estonia' [exhibition]. Curated by Terje Toomistu. Tartu, Estonia: National Museum, August 2013.

Filmography

Africa united. Directed by Deborah Gardner-Paterson. UK: Pathé, 2010.

Amélie. Directed by Jean-Pierre Jeunet. France: Canal+ et al. 2001.

Avé. Directed by Konstantin Bojanov. Bulgaria: Element Films, 2011.

Chastity. Directed by Alessio de Paulo. USA: American International Pictures, 1969.

Detour. Directed by Edgar G. Ulmer. USA: PRC Pictures, 1945.

Even cowgirls get the blues. Directed by Gus van Sant. USA: Fourth Vision, 1993.

Finding dawn. Directed by Christine Welsh. Canada: National Film Board, 2006.

Henry: a portrait of a serial killer. Directed by John McNaughton. USA: Greycat Films, 1986.

Interstellar. Directed by Christopher Nolan. USA: Paramount Pictures et al. 2014.

Into the wild. Directed by Sean Penn. USA: Paramount Vantage, 2007.

It happened one night. Directed by Frank Capra. USA: Columbia Pictures, 1934.

Life, above all. Directed by Oliver Schmitz. USA: Sony Pictures, 2011.

Mississippi burning. Directed by Alan Parker. USA: MGM, 1988.

My Letter to Pippa. Dir. Bingöl Elmas. www.asminfilm.com, 2010.

On the road. Directed by Walter Salles. USA: American Zoetrope et al, 2012.

Pay it forward. Directed by Mimi Leder. USA: Warner Bros, 2001.

Peking express [television series]. Netherlands: Net 5, 2004.

Race across the world [television series]. UK: BBC, 2019.

Rebel without a cause. Directed by Nicholas Ray. USA: Warner Bros, 1955.

Soviet hippies. Directed by Terje Toomistu. Estonia: Kultusfilms, 2017.

Stremlau, John [television interview]. Al Jazeera UK news feature 1 p.m., 4 December 2015.

Taken for a ride. Directed by Jim Klein and Martha Olsen. USA: New Day Films/ITS, 1996.

The Bride. Directed by Joël Curtz. France: Le Fresnoy, 2012.

The devil thumbs a ride. Directed by Felix E. Feist. USA: RKO, 1947.

The lord of the rings/The hobbit (trilogies). Directed by Peter Jackson. NZ: Wingnut et al, 2001–5; 2012–14.

The march. Directed by David Wheatley. UK: BBC, 1990.

The postman always rings twice. Directed by Tay Garnett. USA: MGM, 1946.

The Romantics [television series]. Presented by Peter Ackroyd. UK: BBC, 2006.

The hitcher. Directed by Robert Harmon. USA: HBO, 1986.

The hitch-hiker. Directed by Ida Lupino. USA: RKO,1953.

Vagabond. Directed by Agnes Vardes. France: Ciné Tamaris, 1985.

Wolf creek. Directed by Greg McLean. Australia: Film Finance Corporation, 2005.

Songs and musical compositions

Atlanta Rhythm Section. 'Hitch-hikers' hero'. From *A rock and roll alternative.* USA: Polydor, 1976.

Attila the Stockbroker. 'Contributory negligence'. From *Cocktails.* UK: Cherry Red, 1982.

Baez, Joan. 'The hitchhiker's song'. From *Blessed are.* USA: Vanguard Records, 1971.

Bowen, James Bar. 'She is', 2007. www.youtube.com/watch?v=MTcE7vDeZTM (accessed 27 August 2016).

Bowen, James Bar. 'The irony monger'. From *The lie of the land.* UK: self-produced, 2019.

Cole, Nat King. 'Nature boy'. USA: Capital, 1948.

Cooper, Jamie M. 'Bundanoon Town', 2015. www.youtube.com/watch?v=a7OOzRcKVIw (accessed 27 August 2016).

Creedence Clearwater Revival. 'Sweet hitchhiker'. From *Mardi gras.* USA: Fantasy,1972.

Crow, Sheryl. 'Every day is a winding road'. USA: A&M, 1996.

Czerwono-Czarni. 'Jedziemy autostopem' ['Let's go hitchhiking']. Poland: Muza, 1964.

Denver, John. 'Hitchhiker'. From *Spirit.* USA: RCA Records, 1976.

DiFranco, Ani. 'Every state line'. USA: Righteous babe, 1992.

Dylan, Bob. 'Tangled up in blue'. From *Blood on the tracks.* USA: Columbia, 1975.

Dylan Bob. 'The lonesome death of Hattie Carrol'. From *The times they are a-changing*, USA: Columbia, 1964.

Eagles, The. 'Take it easy'. From *Eagles.* USA: Asylum Records, 1972.

Guthrie, Woody. 'Deportee: plane wreck at Los Gatos'. From *Hard Travelling.* USA: Rising Son Records, 2000 (performed by Hoyt Axton and Arlo Guthrie – no original recordings available; lyrics written 1949, set to music and copyright 1961).

Guthrie, Woody. 'This land is your land'. USA: Folkways Records, 1997.

Guthrie, Woody. 'Tom Joad', 'Pretty boy Floyd', 'Do re mi'. All from *Dust bowl ballads.* USA: Folkways Records, 1964.

Heart. 'All I want to do is make love to you'. From *Brigade.* USA: Capital, 1992.

Holliday, Billie. 'Strange fruit'. USA: Commodore, 1939.

Johns, Sammy. 'Chevy van'. USA: GRC, 1973.

Johnson, Robert. 'Cross road blues'. USA: Vocalion, 1936.

Joplin, Janis. 'Me and Bobby McGee'. From *Pearl.* USA: Columbia, 1971.

Levellers, The. 'Battle of the beanfield'. From *Levelling the land.* UK: China Records, 1991.

Memphis Minnie. 'Going to 'Frisco town'. USA: Columbia, 1929.

Memphis Minnie. 'In my girlish days'. USA: Okeh, 1941.

Memphis Minnie. 'Nothing in rambling'. USA: Okeh, 1941.

Mitchell, Joni. 'Coyote'. From *Hejira.* USA: Asylum, 1976.

N'we Jinan Artists. *The highway.* Kitsumkalum First Nation, 2017. www.youtube.com/watch?v=hG_9d26oYeI (accessed 3 August 2019).

Ochs, Phil. 'Freedom riders'. From *Best of broadside.* USA: Smithsonian Folkways Records, 1989.

Old Crow Medicine Show. 'Wagon wheel'. From *O.C.M.S.* USA: Nettwerk, 2003.

Palacio, Andy. *Watina*. Belize: Cumbancha Records, 2007.

Partch, Harry. 'Eight hitchhiker inscriptions on a guardrail at Barstow, California'. 1941 From *The world of Harry Partch*. USA: Columbia Records, 1969.

Paul, Ellis. 'The ballad of Chris McCandless'. From *The speed of trees*. USA: Philo records, 2002.

Paxton, Tom. 'Goodman, Chaney and Schwerner'. From *Ain't that news*. USA: Elektra, 1965.

Runrig. *The cutter and the clan*. UK: Chrysalis, 1987.

Segal, Shelley. 'Hitchhiking song'. From *An easy escape*. Australia: True Music, 2014.

Simon & Garfunkel. 'America'. From *Bookends*. USA: Columbia, 1968.

Simon & Garfunkel. 'He was my brother'. From *Wednesday morning, 3am*. USA: Columbia, 1964.

Simone, Nina. 'Mississippi goddam'. From *Nina Simone live in concert*. USA: Philips Records, 1964.

Smith, Kate. 'God bless America'. USA: Irving Berlin inc, 1939.

Smith, Will, feat. Mary J. Blige. 'Tell me why'. From *Lost and found*. USA: Interscope, 2005.

Springsteen, Bruce. *The ghost of Tom Joad*. USA: Columbia, 1995.

Vedder, Eddie. *Into the wild* (official soundtrack). USA: J, 2007.

Waters, Roger. *The pros and cons of hitchhiking*. Harvest Records: UK, 1984.

Witts, Jenna. *Hitchhiker*. UK: Jenna Records, 2013.

Young, Neil. 'Southern man'. From *After the gold rush*. USA: Reprise, 1970.

Young, Neil. 'Bound for glory'. From *Old ways*. USA: Geffen, 1985.

Please note: these are not all hitchhiking songs. A comprehensive list of hitchhiking-related music is available at wikipedia.org/hitchhiking, on hitchwiki.org/en/media as well as on the author's site, www.jonathanpurkis.co.uk.

Internet sources

Academy of Free Travel. http://avp.travel.ru/AFT.htm (accessed 29 September 2011).

Alyssa Hoseman (personal website): www.opendestination.ca (accessed 27 October 2017).

BBC News: http://news.bbc.co.uk (accessed 7 June 2010).

BBC *People's War* archive: www.bbc.co.uk/history/ww2peopleswar.htm (accessed August 2008).

Guide to Hitchhiking the World!: https://hitchwiki.org (accessed 29 October 2008).

Hitchhiker Graffiti: www.hitchinscriptions.com (accessed 24 May 2015).

Human Rights Watch: www.hrw.org (accessed 17 August 2017).

Merriam Webster Dictionary: www.merriam-webster.com/dictionary (accessed 28 July 2019).

Stop the Traffik: www.stopthetraffik.org (accessed 17 August 2017).

TravelBlog: www.travelblog.org (accessed 27 October 2017).

Travel Club: www.thetravelclub.org (accessed 10 November 2016).

Index